Epic Series Vol.3

2023 & BEYOND

Return of
THE TWINS
make love not war, literally!

In Memoriam
Jordon Maxwell 28.12.1940 - 23.03.2022
Grandfather of the modern truth movement

Willow Willis

Copyright © 2022 Willow Willis

All rights reserved.

Willow Willis asserts the moral right to be identified as the author of this work.

willowwillis.com
Fb/2020&beyond

No part of this book may be reproduced or transmitted in any form or by any means without permission from the author. This book contains mature content and some course language, however, this book is for everyone. Fair use is implied throughout this work for educational purposes.

Cover art: Arise Chickens

ISBN: 978-0-9953951-4-5

RETURN OF THE TWINS

For all the lovers out there

RETURN OF THE TWINS

	Forward	
1	Loud as Truth	1
2	Mama's Coming Home	16
3	The Power Couple Returns	35
4	Time is a Lie	51
5	Mum & Dad, Husband & Wife, Goddess & God	72
6	Replication Vs. Duplication	103
7	Everything is a Ritual	142
8	'Jesus' & 'Mary' – The Christ & The Magdalene	162
9	The Norman Bates Club	175
10	Alien Psychology	185
11	But Why…?	197
12	Toy Kings	215
13	Nazis & the Fake Alien Invasion	240
14	Children of Destiny	260
	ABOUT THE AUTHOR	282

DEDICATION

One day in the future, our forebears
will look back with reverence, appreciation
and awe at what we have achieved in these final hours.
They will know all the wastage of human life in our long past
was honoured with the highest calling and that, in the end,
we did not ignore our obligations to them who went
before us nor did we shirk our duties
to those who come after us.

We are them,
They are us.
We are you,
You are us.
Wherever or *whenever* you are,
Whoever you are…

This one's for you

FORWARD

Through the ever-narrowing perspective of 'modern' science, all things mainstream and 'accepted' history considered, the human race has become obligated to participate in a reality that is clinical, superficial, hard, and false. Human beings are naturally caring and loving. They have also had their naivete˜ sadly taken advantage of as their collective psyches are used to manifest a world without magic or wonder and for the few beings who are actually capable of magic and wonder, this is a sentence worse than death. Systems of economy, structured religion, and the legal system have been placed in front of us like an iron fist clutching the earth in an unhealthy grip. When mainstream religions like Christianity tell you we are headed for doom as punishment for simply being alive, understand that is not a 'prophecy'. This is the execution of a *plan* long in the tooth incorporating parallel warfare at its most diabolical and includes the smothering social blankets of economics, politics, media, and 'medicine' working hand in glove with a combat war machine so powerful and all-consuming, we accept it as 'normal' because we don't know any different.

There is, however, real prophecies by seemingly magically foresighted people, the indigenous-native people, the pure of heart - the truly righteous – and this is why there has been an all-out attempt to systematically obliterate them all around the world. The *true* fate of the human race is *true* freedom, not *some* freedoms granted to your divine manifest form, your human body, by a select few self-proclaimed 'elite' alien interlopers whose very existence has been an offence to our forebears since time immemorial. The overwhelming numbers of indigenous prophecies say we will 'dance' into our future and that there will be global, even universal, celebration as we finally come together at the end of a long and torturous cycle to end the violence and ascend to spiritual bliss or 'heaven'.

There seems to be a version of the much-prophesised outcome, underpinned by numerous religions, who propagate a so-called 'doomsday culture' in the near future leading us to a sense of driving at high speed toward a brick wall. This is the usual fear tactics used by a pseudo culture nurturing money, inequality, class distinctions and a wholly sick and dangerous society headed up by psychopaths that are not even fully human. By 'indigenous' I refer to the people who have populated areas of the planet for such a long time they have learned to live in harmony with nature and coexist in a balanced state in contrast to the use and abuse mentality of false ego driven invaders who then subsequently call the land their own and commenced the destruction that now threatens everyone, everywhere on our planet. I believe that there are two distinct species of

RETURN OF THE TWINS

'human' on this planet, most probably from different planets or even from different constellations. One is passive the other is ruthlessly violent. We now have an opportunity and indeed are obligated to identify who is who and do what is necessary for the ongoing safety of this world. I think it's easy to identify who is who here and I will spend my days doing what I have to and acting accordingly as a free thinking free acting conscious being of the universe.

There is no need to be afraid, especially of the filth - the dregs of the universe known as the global 'elites' - and their bodyguards, their politicians, and armies that they use, *and have always used*, to enforce their devilish ways over us. Their trickery and treachery is nearing its end and know that at the end of it all, they are afraid of *you*. We will show them the mercy they never showed us. Why? Because we are better than them and it is our *destiny* to take back what was stolen from us, the Earth itself, and care for her and each other the way all our human ancestors from all races of humanity did in a time before they made us fight each other just to stay alive. It's a cruel game and yet we will forever, and with dignity, hold our heads high and do *what must be done* like the true nobility of this planet that Human race really is.

Excerpt from my first draft of, The Teenage Human Race - May 2012, that would go on to become my first book, 2020 & Beyond – This is Not a Drill.

Onwards and upwards.

Willow Willis

RETURN OF THE TWINS

Questions From A Worker Who Reads

Who built Thebes of the seven gates?
In the books you will find the names of kings.
Did the kings haul up the lumps of rock?
And Babylon, many times demolished
Who raised it up so many times? In what houses
of gold-glittering Lima did the builders live?
Where, the evening that the Wall of China was finished,
Did the masons go? Great Rome
Is full of triumphal arches. Who erected them? Over whom
Did the Caesars triumph? Had Byzantium, much praised in song
Only palaces for its inhabitants? Even in fabled Atlantis
The night the ocean engulfed it
The drowning still bawled for their slaves.

The young Alexander conquered India.
Was he alone?
Caesar beat the Gaul's.
Did he not have even a cook with him?

Philip of Spain wept when his armada
Went down. Was he the only one to weep?
Frederick the Second won the Seven Year's War. Who
Else won it?

Every page a victory.
Who cooked the feast for the victors?
Every ten years a great man?
Who paid the bill?

So many reports.
So many questions.

Bertolt Brecht 1935

RETURN OF THE TWINS

PART ONE

Don't pour from your cup
Give from your overflow

"My cup runneth over"
Psalms 23

Chapter One

LOUD AS TRUTH

The path of the righteous is beset on all sides by the inequities of the selfish and the tyranny of evil men. Ezekiel 25:17

There is nothing more unnecessary than the darkness of ignorance. We were never supposed to deplete Earth's resources. We were only ever to utilise them (even the morbid ones like whale oil) until evolution took us to the next rung on the ladder of ascension in a brief, if painful, period of acceleration until we rapidly arrived at free energy available all around us in the very air we breathe. Mother Nature does not mind sharing...within reason, of course. We were not to wallow in the gluttonous waste of Mother Nature's beautiful bounty spinning the wheels in the quagmire of evolution until we consumed even ourselves. No. We were *supposed* to have arrived at our destination of peace and freedom by now via the *correct management* of this planet *many* eons ago. Yet some horrifying hidden force keeps us from our rightful place even on our own world. It is some sort of invisible monster that has lurked at the periphery of our vision, cast the dark shadows in every stinking alleyway, has squelched on every mud-soaked high street torn by the wagon wheels of ancient carts, has seared every rope burn and badly tended injury aboard every creaking sea fairing vessel that men have sailed and died on and women have wept over for millennia and beyond! We have lived under the skies of a brutal intruder who hides in every blind spot, takes breath from every lie, and has shattered every childhood dream since time immemorial. This intruder, a savvy leech, awaits us now upon our last path to our final destination in Earth's last trudging mile.

The brutal truth is... *the thing* has finally arrived.

The thing. The thing that has always been there. The thing I wrote about in my first book. The thing of horror. The thing that wakes you up in the middle of the night and suddenly gasp 'Oh my god! They just injected half the world's population with an unknown virus!' It's done. And all the warnings and all the power of the information age didn't stop half the *Western* world's people, the chief target of this military operation perpetrated by a beast of unparalleled proportions, from lining up *en masse* like lab rats for the greatest medical experiment the world has ever seen! Even Christians among many other religious people worldwide rolled up their sleeves, despites the warnings of *their very own scriptures* telling them this would happen and, like cowards or traitors, turned their backs even on the warnings of their own god. Believers? Hardly. *The very beast* who poses as their heavenly father has most cunningly bought them to the very end it warned them of. Nazi Germany would be proud. Funny that, *three's a charm*. The whole world has become a laboratory now and the fall out from this will not be fully known in its entirety for a number of years, even decades, yet. Oh, there's more. Oh joy. Humans are so gullible. Which is why the elite, the establishment scientists behind all this *hate* you *so much*. Only we're not all the same. We cannot, and many of us *will not*, be lumped in together with all the dullards willing, even still, to trust the *most obvious* and incredible evil enemy standing right there before you in all its audacious pomposity *daring you* to try and stand up to it. Preening itself. Purring in self-righteous idolatry. The monstrous thing. The unbelievable thing. *It*. Has arrived and the brutal truth of it is, we *still* don't know how to deal with it, in fact, we are more vulnerable now than ever before! Incredible.

So much has occurred not only in my own personal life since I first wrote, *2020 & Beyond – This is Not a Drill*, in 2015. To watch events unfold in real time just as I said it would happen *when* I said it would happen, word for word, literally, has not left me awestruck or amazed, granted, somewhat weirded out, but alas, I feel nothing except occasional anger, a deep frustration and a contempt that was not hardened before the way it is now. Like many others in the world who have finally woken up to the brutality of the aristocratic overlords who run every aspect of our lives, I think I've finally fallen over the line into the *inhumanity* of adulthood. I never wanted to be an 'adult' in the societal sense of the word and have held it off for as long as possible. I've always believed a sense of innocence, curiosity and hope keeps you young even if only at heart. Now I feel like I'm being restrained in one of those comical situations where a large bully is holding the little guy at arm's length and no matter how hard the little guy swings, he cannot reach his opponent. And everybody laughs. The laugh riot is in full chorus now. It's kind of horrible to watch as you realise the next generation of complete and utter idiots, the last hope for Humanity, will eventually be in charge and that spells the end for Mother Earth and any hope we had of achieving our 'happily ever after' as prophesised for thousands of years.

RETURN OF THE TWINS

It's a bitter end.

It wasn't meant to be like this. It really wasn't. There was *supposed* to be another route, another path, that was *supposed* to unfold just as the dark road at night leads you home with only a few meters of light before you, and yet you find your way *because the road is already there. The path is already laid out before you* and you know this *for sure* because, somehow, we have been here before. *We know this road!* But this road chops and changes. It becomes, as I said in my first book, mercurial. It anticipates us. It waits. It watches. And it alters its route until the place you were supposed to be is somewhere else when you thought the road, however tough, was solid, was reliable. Nothing is reliable now. Nothing is solid. We enter a dreamscape as we pass through the belt of hell that keeps us from the light housed at the core of the galaxy not only in space and time, but *inside ourselves* as well! Nothing was *or is* solid now and all the innocence of hope that we were, the surety, even cockiness, is coming to realise the brutal truth. And that truth is - despite the tears, anger, rage, love, music and all the usual things humans do to bolster themselves up and reinforce their confidence in times of turmoil and terror, to remind ourselves regardless of how stupid most people are, *we will prevail no matter what*, and yet, to date, we are losing this battle. What battle of light and dark? When was this battle? *Where is it?* It's business-a-usual for them. The dark just rolled over the light quite easily. There was no battle. We are missing something, something crucial, something the opposition has at its beck and call. Something that *once belonged to us.*

Something that was stolen.

So much has happened since I wrote my first book in 2015, tapping away in my tiny little Chiswick studio in London, endlessly writing. Working overtime (just like now, nothing's changed, they keep me hidden). D*esperate* to share what I saw before me. What I knew in my heart was coming. And it came. And I got held off and am still being held prisoner as they pull every dirty trick in the book to keep me from my birthright, *my* platform, to prevent the world form knowing my story and the level of treachery and betrayal they are willing to engage in to fulfill their sick demonic plans and they are, by and large, demons - not angels - and certainly *not* guardian angels. I have to laugh when I hear people talking about 'peace, love and light'. What a croc of shit. Two thousand years ago there were people pulling out the 'blessings' and 'peace, love and light' clap trap and, as with today, it was just another stalling program to get them to drop their guard and let someone else take control. To get them to believe that there is some force on our side, something, or *someone,* or, as most of the world's religious people would love to believe, *some bloke!* who will save us and that everything is going to be okay. God is coming. Jesus, Maitreya, Allah, Buddha, Krishna – they're all coming to save us. The Heavenly Father has a plan. And he works in 'mysterious' ways. So, just hang in there, kids! It's gonna happen. Just around the corner! Anytime soon, dad! Kinda out on a limb here! Holding my breath. Waiting. Anticipating. About now would be great…still waiting. *[Checks watch tapping foot nervously]*

This is *exactly* what the evil overlords want you to do. It's like taking candy from a baby, literally, and although it may sound a little cliché and a little fantastical to call them 'evil overlords', that is and always has been *exactly* what they are. Around the world there are endless protests at what has happened since the inception of the fakedemic in 2020, just a coincidence mind that this world altering event should occur in 2020 symbolic of *20/20 vision* when we were *supposed* finally 'see straight'. And because they have a sense of humour, they are damaging people's vision and hearing with the 5G rollout, the thinnest, highest wavelength millimeter frequency that literally shatters DNA. So, I now wear glasses from writing my last book, *2022 & Beyond – Rosestorm, Return of the Feminine*, and that's funny to them. Hilarious. They find it endlessly amusing that just when we're *supposed* to come together, we're 'socially distancing'. Just when we are *supposed* unveil ourselves, we're wearing masks. Just when we're *supposed* to 'come out' we're locked inside under 'house arrest' like criminals. Why not wear a balaclava in court when they fine you for not suffocating yourself with medical masks especially in the tropics where I live and it's *98% humidity* and 35C. The kids working at the fish n chip shop where it must be 50C inside are wearing *masks* while working over the vats of hot fat and hot plates. Staff shortages? People simply give in and give up. You can't ask people to work under those conditions it's cruel and unusual punishment. People are dropping like flies and its effecting people even on the *simplest levels*. It *should* be a health and safety concern to have people wearing masks under certain conditions. But no. Even the complete idiots are yelping *"I can't do this!"* But the upper-class engineers never let up. Once you give a bully power, they will mercilessly run you into the ground no matter how 'compliant' you are. If anything, this entire charade has only served to snap the secret conspiracy nuts out of their apathy and into action to see, just as I said, the *mask* as it falls from the monster's face.

But the monster isn't just out in the open. The monster is attacking the best ones among you, alone in their houses, using secret weapons custom designed for the secret Targeted Individuals who are *growing in numbers* by the day. This *remote technological harassment* comes in quite handy for the ones they are most afraid of, the ones they *most* want to hide from the public eye and the world stage at this time. Where are we? And yet if you watch the emerging alternative mainstream journalists, some quite good, you will think an intensifying conversation is happening about sudden radical social changes that endanger children and the future of humanity. Yet Operation Mockingbird is a CIA program designed to use the mainstream media and 'rogue' journalists as a diversionary propaganda tactic to make people think we are 'fighting back' and more people are 'waking up'. But they *aint* talking about the *really rotten* shit hiding just beneath and beyond all this 'woke' ideology. We are supposed to be awakening instead we get this 'woke' shit. So many amazing researchers who have been working their arses off for decades are nowhere to be seen. Yet they are known to the machine who target them with anything from paranormal activity to demons, to electromagnetic direct energy torture right in their own homes where they cannot hide in a crowd or call for backup. And hardly anyone believes them. You haven't heard from the most compelling and shocking conspiracy researchers yet but it's coming! Batten down the hatches! Here comes the next wave of warriors! Here's a question, if they can use direct energy weapons to 'microwave' people protesting the COVID madness, then...um...why aren't they using microwave weapons to disperse hooligan mobs tearing up America? Question mark. Question mark.

    I'll dive right in here. To recap, in case you haven't read my first two books, *Rosestorm* in particular, I recall a program in which I was 'beamed' into my body at the age of about 3 and a half years old. I recall a scientific facility and being shown my family (the family that had been chosen for my assignment) on a trapezoidal shaped computer screen. Based on this information I agreed to 'come in' and as I was walking up a corridor the guy escorting me said 'oh, by the way, don't bother trying to remember, nobody remembers!' I knew I would remember as I trusted my intuitive and psychic skills to the point where I was not like other people however talented and skilled *they were*. I was better. We were told we were volunteering to help the world at this crucial time in history and that we would be undercover agents that would be called upon a the right time to do our work as leaders, speakers, musicians, artists etc. I was promised a music career as compensation for hiding me in a very tough childhood that nobody would suspect an operative to hide. I was led to believe that it had to be done like this so that nobody would find me, and my memory was wiped so I couldn't blow my cover. Nobody was to know who I was or know that I was a part of a space program designed to take down these motherfuckers from *inside* the game. Like Neo in the Matrix. They put all this information in movies so that if you try to expose them, they just say you're a delusional 'fan' and are subsequently disregarded. They do really crazy things so if you try to expose them you just wind up looking really crazy. Evil genius. And you guys are way out of your depth, by the way.

We were assigned to be sleeper agents, lifelong undercover special operatives, who would emerge at the right time to really shake things up! I say 'we' because I am assuming, logically, that there must have been others and I may have even met one although she didn't remember yet bears an *exact same mark* on her wrist as I do on mine (although mine is on the other wrist). The moment I met this lady she announced, 'have you seen the mark on my wrist?' She showed me and I said, 'I have the same mark on my wrist!' and showed her mine. She said quite innocently, 'I talk to them' and I said, 'So do I!' Yes, 'them' the ones who are watching us all the time, the analysts, who monitor us constantly using an array of remote technologies to manipulate our lives to a certain end however it suits them. Honestly, why anyone would trust these people at this time is beyond me, but then they were more innocent days back then in the 1970's and 1980's. I don't think the full import of the reality of how big this really is was made fully aware to me or just how treacherous our 'own people' are who think *nothing* of betraying their own people and destroying lives of whole families because they have the 'right' to do so. Because they're the 'upper classes'. All beneath them are simply toys to be played with until broken then simply discarded and get another toy, only in this case, their 'toys' that they play with are human beings. They've always done this and think nothing of wrecking people for shits and giggles as they are not human and see humans as insignificant pets. They are unscrupulous and beyond cruel and you have only just witnessed the beginnings of the horrors yet to be shown by them.

What I am about to tell you will leave a lot of people reeling in horror that these things *could* happen let alone *are* happening. What I agreed to and what I later discovered they had *deliberately* planned for me was *two very different things*. But hey, who cares, right? They just lie and cheat and stitch people up even though we were supposed to be on a team. But there is no team. There is no 'us'. You need to remember that now more than ever. There is only YOU, their 'enemy', to be waylaid in any way they desire. This club of misfits and psycho fuck ups get a thrill out of the power they have and no control over where it is ultimately leading because, at the end of the day, it's run by demons and 'aliens' beyond the veil who want to destroy the human race and eventually, planet Earth. Use and abuse. There is no 'team'. There is no 'us' not even for them who are higher up or deeper into the ranks of 'the team'. There's no fucking team, okay? Just an evil plan by non-humans to USE ALL THESE DICKHEADS, IN THE END, FOR WHATEVER WEIRD PURPOSES IT DESIRES. All are expendable. There is no 'family'. Everyone is a target. Everyone who approaches you on the team are a potential smiling assassin. Let me repeat, EVERYONE IS EXPENDABLE. And why these a-list agent celebrities laughing their heads off while fucking around playing the field and pretending they were gods, turns out they were just being drawn deeper and deeper into a trap in which there is no way out but to waylay anyone and everyone, *even family*, in their attempts to save their own selfish skins. There's no loyalty. There's no plan. Even those who truly believe there is a 'plan' for the future, the laughable masonic 'great work', must surely be realising by now that these demonic aliens from under the Earth (not from space although they came from deep space at some time in the past), these creatures have ANOTHER plan...and it involves consuming all of them.

So, as it turns out they have all been betrayed in the end because now that the opportunity has come to take this planet and destroy humanity, any and all are expendable and there is no fucking plan, okay? Not for us and not for celebrity agents who come from elite families who have secured their wealth and fame before they even got started, who buy their position, buy their awards and buy their place in history. We have entered the danger zone and the 2020's will be a decade of court cases and public scandals the likes of which have never *nor will ever* be seen again! Rather fitting though to kick off our ascension. It's the line in the sand, the 'before' and 'after', and we are on that line *now* in limbo awaiting our opportunity to do what must be done. There is a time and a place for everything, and that time is *now*. There is nothing that can prepare you for those moments when the mortifyingly impossible is, at last, possible!

It's sad when you see people's lives *wrecked* by the *complete lack of care* for the subjects, the pawns, being used in these programs who were either roped in against their will or, like myself, *tricked* into getting involved in something that no *justice* can account for. It seems the program I remember was intrinsic to the ultimate 'purpose' of a *ridiculous* off-the-wall plan to birth the fucking anti-Christ if you can believe it! They were 'beaming' people into other people's bodies to ultimately manifest the 'prophecies' of the Bible insofar as, out of this super-secret plan they were trying to invent the one world leader personified in the flesh! *The Devil Incarnate.* Rosemary's

RETURN OF THE TWINS

Baby! All cleverly concealed under *layers* of conspiracy and amnesia that could *never* be discovered! Only problem was, I remembered enough of what happened and stuck to my duties, my pledge, so-much-so that there seems to be an unknown and inclement amount of shit about to hit the proverbial fan. Bring it. I *should* have recalled my own memories of all this by now as the Earth lines us up with the galactic central hub, *the core*, where all information is housed triggering our deepest memories no matter how fancy the technology is to conceal them. This is all cleverly dressed up as 'fiction' by Hollywood in movies like *Avatar* as the 'tree' that holds all the memories and souls of their loved ones can be tapped into with the power of their nervous system found in their *hair!* All of this is in folklore and fairy tales and boy are *you* in for a wild ride! We too *should* be able to access all information stored at the galactic center, a massive black hole sun and cosmic 'brain'. All of us, me, you, everyone *should* have experienced 'total recall' by now which I wrote about in my first book. In the lead up to the solar eclipse on 14th November 2012 I was living at the zero-point location. During this time, I saw an image of Europe swirling down into black vortex. For many months before and after the solar eclipse, I received I number of very concise messages including the following:

- Once the eclipse is done the house of cards will fall rapidly. New leaders will emerge from the ranks of ordinary people. They will be dragged into the new roles-jobs kicking and screaming.

- The darkness has elevated itself to a godlike status and threatens the entire universe.

- The human race is walking into a huge trap.

- You will experience what is called 'total recall'. For those who have suffered under mind control the walls between their personalities will literally crumble.

RETURN OF THE TWINS

- They are planning to do something so terrible the whole world will, quote, 'never forget'.

- We are objects existing in space in the eternal now.

- Inorganic things have no power over organic things.

All this was *supposed* to have happened between 2018 and 2020 and indeed many people said at the time they were experiencing incredible 'lucid' dreams and 'clarity'. But their full memories never returned as the 5G rollout occurred *at the same time*. Just coincidental mind. Our heart has its own powerful energetic sources that activate our primary intuitive energy and all the alignments in the galaxy are *supposed* to jolt our memory not just of past lives but of the powerful life you were *supposed* to live in THIS life. When you remember how your life was supposed to play out and realise that you were DELIBERAETLY steered away from your destiny, conned out of everything worth living for by poisons, remote technology, the use of demonology and negative energy attachments and attacks as well as *constant mind control* and psychological warfare preventing your greatness from ever coming into being - that they laughingly refer to as 'persistent random misfortune' – you will get angry, really angry. There is a biofeedback between our human bodies and the Earth and universe beyond all of it supposed to work in a harmonious opus of coherence and awareness only we are being held back, disconnected from the natural flow by distortions and powerful energy attacks both on and off world but it is getting harder for them to be able to continue to hold up the charade. As such they intend to do the most drastic things available to them in their attempts to keep us as unwilling pets in their weird galactic zoo false 'gods' that they are, aliens, reptiles and demons that they are who have dogged us since the *legends of old* that spoke of them.

Even Harry Potter who is 'the one' and 'saviour', another 'Jesus' character, finds his *original* name in the 1986 move Troll whose writers tried to sue the modern Harry Potter production for intellectual property theft. They are *telling* you something quite plainly. Harry is the prime Hindu god Hari, as in Hari Krishna, and 'troll' is code for reptilian-demon. As a side, Krishna is Christ. So, they are saying this 'god' is a reptilian half-breed and as it turns out, the Vatican seem to feel the same way. In fact, there is a secret story being told via movies as they cleverly reveal their ancient script that stretches long before Hollywood came along. It was all in place the whole time simply awaiting the right moment to carry it out. They are agents of a dark order that stretches into antiquity and expose their plan subtly by linking up actors in movies to previous productions, some quite obscure, from 30 or 40 years ago with the same or similar names and plot twists to current movies. On further inspection, they can be traced back to productions from the dawn of Hollywood. These 'people' are a troupe from generations of specific family lineages assigned roles to unfurl the big legend before our eyes. It's quite something. It's not for our entertainment, it's definitely for theirs!

This is why most if not all A-listers are 'related' to royalty. They are royalty and they know it too. This intrigue unveils who they really are and what they are really doing via 'embedded confessions' across many decades of film characters and plotlines. For example, Quaidermass and the Pit is an original production from the 1950's. While tunnelling the London Underground at 'Old Hobbs Lane', they discover a spaceship buried under ground. Old Hob is a colloquial name for the Devil. Via psychic transference one character sees a 'mantis' or 'grasshopper' type *military* species on Mars before they blew it up. Mars is the god of war. Remember, this is a 1950's production long before the reptilian-mantis-grey thing became a thing. Then we find Dr Quaidermass in *Gremlins 2* played by Christopher Lee who is conducting experiments on how to manifest the demonic 'gremlins' plane into the material 3D plane. It's an unusual name and I immediately remembered the 1950's production. If you want an unfolding narrative look at Christopher Lee's films, he will only associate himself with productions that are symbolic of what is really happening, like Dracula and Lord of the Rings, and an admitted practitioner of the dark arts.

What they are saying is the 'devil' is some type of alien-demon, it is psychic, it has advance science and technology. It is destructive, militant and some type of bloodthirsty creature that looks human but can shift into a demonic form. It is an aristocrat. It came from Mars and is now on Earth. In the original poster of *Invasion of the Body Snatchers*, right, it clearly depicts an alien taking over the heart chakra turning the human body into a pod. Leonard Nimoy played the main antagonist secretly helping the alien takeover and also played Mr. Spock, a Vulcan. Vulcan was a god of fire and another version of the devil. The 'devil' is the dragon or snake, the reptilian component on Earth, also called the 'green man' and the 'beast'. They are *telling us the real story* through associating certain actors with plotlines that evolve through an unfolding series of movies. He's all logic. No emotions. Pure intellect. Aren't they *just* like that for real? The 'Pod People from Mars' is a poster in the movie *Troll* and mentions a 'Channel 11 Star Trek marathon' because, ultimately, this is all about the looming space age and the separation of them from us as they move on to create a new human race and new age. And the number 11 is all about enlightenment which is not some airy-fairy crap, its simply IQ, intelligence, however clinical. The Body Snatchers had pods sucking the life out of humans while they 'slept' (or unawakened?). The 'hair' like tendrils that would make a 'copy' of a real person bear a creepy resemblance to the weird 'spaghetti' organisms now being pulled from the dead bodies of people who died after receiving COVID shots and claimed they could 'feel insects under their skin and crawling around in their brain'. Scientists are saying that 'insect' bio-organisms and 'self-aware', 'self-assembling', replicating nano creatures that can grow *massive* in a short space of time. That keeping the vials at sub-zero temperatures, in a cryogenic state, is because at room temperature, the living material start to 'move', assemble and grow. Doctors are saying that what is contained in these weird vials is beyond their training and have never seen anything like it before. Here's a tip, its alien, *that's* what they've been working on in those underground bases for 60 years. Like the rest of us, these brave doctors are teaching themselves. Welcome, is all I can say. It fucken twisted to be sure. But it's all linked in a continuous thread of movie themes via certain characters. The Navaho have legends of the 'ant' people who live under the ground bearing a striking description to that of the 'grey' aliens. It's all there. We *ARE* being told we just need to listen.

They are evil twisted low lifeforms from an 'anti' life dimension, a war dimension deep in space, who travelled here long ago to enslave the light found in the human body via the chakra system and make us their slaves under horrendous humiliating and degrading circumstances in worship of their ego as 'kings' and 'gods'. They call themselves 'gods' because they could never just admit they are lowly evil scum who steal other people's planets. But *we* are the kings and queens here, humans are the true 'gods'. This is why the aristocratic reptiles, false kings and queens, love to hunt and shoot the most exotic game because these animals are 'majestic' and represent the 'royal goddess' found in the majesty of Mother Nature or simply Life itself. It is also why they kill foxes as an effigy of the Devil and smear its blood on their faces, blooded, as F.O.X numerologically is F=6th letter of the alphabet O=15th letter of the alphabet reducing to 6 and X=24th letter of the alphabet reducing to 6 or 666. It's a 'fun game' to 'kill' an effigy of the 'devil' found in the poor little fox that is often red, the colour of Satan. It's like 'pin the tail on the donkey' for psycho aristocrats from a bygone era.

What they are *really* doing is killing the 'goddess' as 6 inverted is 9, the number of the goddess, as found in femi-*nine* and 'enlightenment' which is the only word that spells the number eighteen (18) in consecutive letters which reduces to 9. They are killing the goddess. 9 represents the end of a massive cycle and the prophecy about the end of them so, they are killing Mother Nature, LIFE, and laughing about it too. They are death. They are jealous of life. The Goddess give life. The Devil takes it. Even the simplest of pleasures we take for granted is beyond their scope of comprehension and they need a human body to experience the wonders of the physical which, of course, they turn into depravity. You need to understand that what we think of as mundane is EVERYTHING to them. Even the simple act of riding a bicycle or enjoying a meal is something they can only watch on in hatred and seething envious rage as human beings enjoy such simple things that are so full of life these creatures must surely feel less than zero when compared to magnificence of the light being we are and boundless pleasure and joy we are capable of. That's why they take such glee in morbid 'pleasure' like lust and wrath and drugs and alcohol because it is just another way to mock the 'god', the human body, and the simple joy of what it means to be a human being in full command of our senses. And that's not even beginning to touch on our extra-sensory abilities, our psychic and intuitive abilities, along with our potential IQ etc. In that regard, *they* are out of their depths if WE ever consciously comprehend the full enormity of the power we possess in the celestial wonder of our human bodies. We're going to be talking about how to unlock these powers in this book so, hang in there!

The mass global memory recall that was supposed to happen was the result of incredible cosmic alignments that occurred in lead up to and during 2020 that connected us like cosmic wi-fi system to the central transmission of the galaxy - the black hole sun at the galactic core. It was during this time that an intolerable blanket of a demonic attack was slapped on me by these black magicians in their hope of holding me off smothering *my* signal and preventing me from *receiving* or *sending* further information shutting down my chakras and concealing the full memories of the program I recall in part. Yet still I managed to receive tiny memory fragments of being transported to a facility seemingly out in the desert. I recall being referred to as 'Brenda'. I have since found out that 'Brenda' is a code word used by A-list celebrities as an inside joke on the trickery perpetrated against women, the universal feminine, and is a reference to one of the rare occasions in *ancient* history where a woman was deemed less intelligent than a man or specifically, reptilian men, behind all this. Brenda is actually *Brendan* from an ancient mythological tale and one of the few times a male was ranked higher than a female in *ancient* times. Celebrities throw around mythological buzz phrases in their films and interviews to prove to their secret masters they've done their research and are 'worthy' of their positions in this *alien* empire about to snatch Mother Earth right out from underneath us! They're all jockeying for position. It's close now. Citing the term 'Brenda' is a warning to others in their class not to mess with them because they 'know their stuff' in that they are competent at *Black Magic*. It's the name of the A-list game and a language all of its own to hide these things in plain sight. Hollywood and specifically celebrity is the heights of the Nazi secret war machine in plain sight. The *One World* plan and their looming satanic leader will emerge from celebrity audaciously posing as your leader, your saviour, but then celebrities are known for their BLIND ego and make such easy fodder for the demonic super plan to destroy us all. All the big ones are doing it. I am realising now that many a-list celebrities were once highly ranking Nazi aristocratic scientists appointing themselves THE BEST POSITIONS in the upcoming culture of celebrity fame and fortune. They had themselves 'beamed' into the best opportunities all of it hidden under layers of exotic technology to conceal their workings so deeply that it was unlikely anyone would ever be able to find out.

    No one knows about this but me and now you're gonna know.

    They gave the best lives to themselves and gave the shittiest lives to the women they *tricked* into being 'beamed' in, like myself, mocking the female candidates they had lined up to be their 'goddess' wife characters – the Bride of Christ and/or the Devil - in a *predetermined script* where she is *doomed to die* tragically like Monroe, like Diana! Entrapment! Ultimate betrayal! Ruthless doesn't quite cover it! Those women were set up in advance by their own families and friends, all of them men, who see it as an honour to kill the 'goddess' in their fiendish fake boy's club all the while slapping each other on the back and laughing it up but not so loud as to drop their guard when it comes to *each other*. They must have eyes in the back of their heads. As said, there is no club, just a gaggle of psychopaths looking to one-up each other and stab each other in the back in the quest for ultimate power. But when you're dealing with aliens and demons beyond all this, then I don't fancy your chances at that! As the technology improves it's getting harder and harder to expose what they are doing. If they could do this back in the 1960's, 70's and 80's imagine what they are doing now?

RETURN OF THE TWINS

They are streaking ahead of us. That's because 'there can be only one' and it is an *all-in-one* combined male-female-animal-mutant-alien god – the Baphomet - The Beast! It's sickening. It's pathetic. And if you knew who and what these people really were you'd never watch another movie again. Disgusting filth!

Planet Earth is one big ritual. They are obsessed with the details of myth and legend and keep replaying ancient history over and over hoping to convince the universe that *their* signal is just the way things are here on planet Earth. These cunts are trying to override the new codes being broadcast by the Universe's and so they are rebroadcasting the old codes, old storylines, which are all about male dominance, hierarchy and emotional superficiality. This is why in the year 2022 they are releasing the movie 'Elvis' and he was 'the king' while Kim Kardashian wore Marilyn Monroe's dress she wore at the birthday of JFK. They even dyed her hair blond. Ridiculous! They even released the film Marilyn movie 'Blonde' because this year, 2022, is the year of the 'king and queen' or the 'god and goddess' as '2' signifies the pair or 11. Monroe was the 'goddess' and 'Elvis' was the king and ancient legend of the 'king marrying the goddess' or the reptilian marrying the human woman who represent Osiris and Isis of ancient Egyptian legend, the original king and goddess, that started all this. They are *so detailed* in recreating the past in ways you do not recognize. Hollywood is ingeniously dressing up these ancient codes, this duplication, to make us go around again and why so many if not all Hollywood actors and support staff are *Satanists*. This is their cult. This is their religion. It is one that is rooted in lies and deception to con the human race into a megalithic trap with all the 'bright lights' taking us there! They know they are doing this. They are complicit. This is why the old saying goes 'the devil is in the details', but they can only feed you the lies *you* have eat it up and do the job for them.

There is supposed to be 'free will' although they are blatantly breaking the rules as the end looms and this massive program goes into overdrive. They believe they are unstoppable and as such they are covertly feeding you poisons in the food and water supplies to muddle your ability to determine free will. THIS IS BLATANTLY AGAINST ANY RULES OF THE UNIVERSE AS YOU ARE SUPPOSED TO HAVE A CHOICE. THE FACT THAT THEY LAUGH IN THE FACE OF THE UNIVERSAL PROCESSES WILL SPELL THEIR DOOM. They will punish you as much as possible for *their failures* to coerce you. It is what it is. They are what they are. They are *so fixated* with the minutia that one can only say that these details are not born from the minds of ordinary people therefore, our world must be run by demons orchestrating all this via the inbreeding of the *aristocracy* whose scrambled genetics increasing suffer a royal *OCD as their DNA breaks down at this time in cosmic history!*

It's true, you know, the people of the past were warning us of this very moment to the point of carving it in stone, hiding this knowledge in terracotta pots in caves, literally building geoglyphs into mountains and the open plains, *see*, the massive Nazca lines. They went to *such lengths*, such efforts, to warn us of a time that would come again, a time way off in the future, *thousands of years ahead of them*, simply because it was *so important* to keep the human race alive and Mother Earth intact! I will not fail those people who fought so hard for us. Will you? I will not give up on the people of the future. *Will you?* These ancient people need our fullest respect and acknowledgement for their hard work to keep the information alive for the next and the next generation until we reached the last Age in which the Dark Order would rise in its fullest and most final capacity and perpetrate, *again*, the foulest betrayal as was perpetrated against them of old. They were our ancestors, *they are us*, as history repeats and we run out of time *for the last time*, we find we are connected to them of old in ways this fake 'modern' society has spat on and taken for granted. Those people of the ancient world, our people, knew us long before we knew them. They knew that in many ways we are them just a those who come after us *are us.* It all goes round and round again, and in this book, I will reveal the horror of the long-lasting entrapment we have endured as a sentient species like no other author has ever relayed to you before. Everything you think you know about yourself is, by and large, *bullshit* and it's about time you faced the enormity of who you really are, what you are really involved in and how the great spirits of the past have foretold that despite the seeming impossibility of freedom, *liberation* from this demonic empire is *assured!* This time, the last time, we will complete a job that is *supposed to be impossible.* It *must* happen or the whole galaxy and maybe even the universe beyond is lost and that cannot be allowed. Take heart, my friends! The time is now! It is a promise and a legacy!

I hope you're ready.

CHAPTER TWO

MAMA'S COMING HOME

"What we call reality is, in fact, nothing more than a culturally sanctioned and linguistically reinforced hallucination". Terence McKenna

I'm not going to beat around the bush here, if you want a more detailed and more involved telling of this following story refer to my previous book, *Rosestorm - Return of the Feminine*. The fact of the matter is, humans are, as is all life, electrical beings. *We are electricity.* It runs through our bodies it powers the rotation of our planet and lights the Milky Way Galaxy found in the twinkling of the stars. Electricity is the rocket fuel and the turbine of the Universe. It is the very air we breathe. If you rub your eyes, the bio luminous image you see is the electricity in your blood. If you crunch a hard candy in the dark, you will see blue electricity being released from the micro explosion of the lolly particles. The fact that this most simple *fact* has been deliberately kept from us by a series of civilisations, and in recent history, institutions masquerading as our leaders and 'guiding lights' (what a joke!), is a major *historical* and *current* betrayal the world at large is yet to face. They lied. You see, the energy to gift ourselves every day with the most abundant lives of happiness and grateful reverence for the wonder of living inside *actual life* on a *living planet* in a *living Universe* lighted by the eternal electricity of life itself, is freely available to us *inside our own bodies.* When the world finally accesses the electricity, the POWER, within our own bodies the whole world will look upon institutions, for example, like the Catholic Church and most mainstream universities, with utter hatred as is they rightfully deserve.

But let's not stop with them.

All the organised major Abrahamic religions as well as intermediate and minor religions *worldwide* are complicit in a *megalithic* lie to funnel the Human Race, who they rely on for their riches and positions of power,

RETURN OF THE TWINS

toward our most terrible and dastardly end - mass death and further, for those left alive, the impossibility of evolving *ever again*. I was shown a vision of the human race being herded into a funnel and out the other end black sludge was dripping out into a black pit, *right*. They intend to do this to ride on the waves of energy released by the mass murder of *billions* of human light beings as energy doesn't die, it simply changes form. There has to be a sacrifice in order for them to get their looming new space age and that sacrifice is mass numbers of human death. We were going to be a mass offering to their alien-demonic masters  to ensure they were elevated to the 'next level' of their sort of 'evolution' if you can call it that. They were and still are planning to do this via mass depopulation programs chiefly connected to illness and cancers injected into people via mass inoculation programs that have chiefly targeted *first world countries*, specifically, America, Canada, the United Kingdom, Europe, Australia & New Zealand for a 'flu' with a 97-99% survival rate! The hysteria whipped up by the mainstream media that caused so many to wig out and run to the nearest injecting station, is nothing short of a military manoeuvre to strategically implement the most successful example of *mass psychological warfare* the planet has ever seen. They have *specifically* targeted Western Nations because we are the *most* modern, the *most* progressive, the *most* educated, the *most* stable, the most advanced, and therefore, the *most* dangerous threat to outdated and obsolete *control systems* relied on by the *redundant elite* and therefore, we are the *most likely* to succeed in finally freeing Planet Earth from their sex and death cult who have ensnared Humanity in endless traps for thousands of years. They spin us in confusion making us chase our tales in an ultimately self-defeating drudgery, pitiful shame and personal loss until death is preferable to life. Until now. Reviewing the writings of Friedrich Engels in his work titled The State and Revolution written shortly before the Bolshevik Revolution, Vladimir Lenin concluded that state power, "consists of special bodies of armed men having prisons, etc., at their command". The elite utilise many repressive manoeuvres to protect the aristocratic state against a rebellion from the working classes. This oppression uses the judiciary, the police, intelligence and military devices to identify and eliminate potential threats against their plan from all levels of society foreign and domestic. Everything else is just for show until they get what they want.

RETURN OF THE TWINS

I'll break this down into really simple to understand snapshots to help you comprehend where all this came from and how long it's been going on. Hopefully, like most people, you won't simply switch off and start snoring at the first mention of the Knights Templar. In ancient times the Habiru were a renegade eclectic band of criminals, desert people, who received information about the power of the chakras and how to activate them releasing the 'coiled snake', the kundalini, at the base of the spine to 'raise the waters' of the powerful feminine electricity found there. Upon discovering this 'treasure of the world', they left the desert and built the first temple in Jerusalem on Temple Mount and proceeded to take over the known world. The 'temple' is a geographical structure, literally a building, that represents the human body. The human body is *literally* the 'temple' and the 'temple' is the Church that they recreated *in effigy* as *Mary-Isis-Shakti* found in the various holy sites of religions. It is 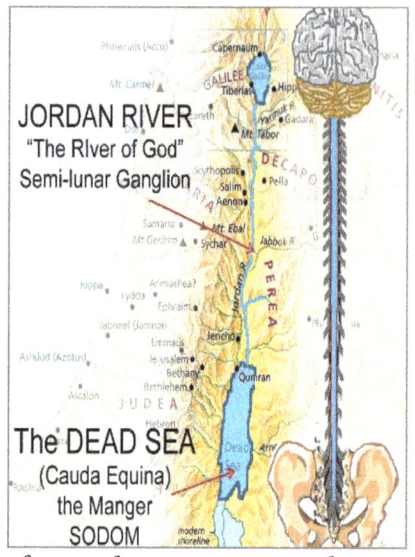 the same as the 'Tower of Babel', a 'place of sacred marriage', a gathering place, representing the chakra tower of the human body also found in fables like Rapunzel and her 'tower' accessed by the 'hair'. It's all symbolic of hidden *godlike* physiological processes found in the human body, the church/temple or 'my body is my temple' (literally) dressed up as external monuments to have us looking outside ourselves when the answers lie within, Luke 17:21 "Behold! The kingdom of God is *within* you!"

Temple Mount was the original Temple of Solomon and means 'Sol' as in sun and 'Mon' as in moon. It is the sun and moon temple as it is the human body also the 'sun and moon temple' as it contains the electrical aspects of the sun and moon, or electro-magnetism found in the male and female *electrical* polar opposites or 'AC' (female Alternating Current) and DC (male Direct Current). These electrical poles were referred to by the ancients as the 'waters' (feminine) and the 'fire' or 'spark' (masculine). These counter poles keep repeating over and over again throughout the body and in the world and space beyond. They are *binary* as in 'two' poles so, when new-agers demand they are 'non-binary' they are basically saying they have no electricity in their bodies and, if true, they would be dead. No remnants of the Temple of Solomon have ever been found although it is referenced in the Bible as being destroyed in 586BC. In 1099AD crusaders from Europe drove out the Muslims and reclaimed the area as Christian lands. These Crusaders called themselves the Poor Knights of Christ & the Temple of Solomon or simply the *Knights Templar* for short. They promised to live a life of poverty, chastity and obedience seeing themselves as the 'spirit' of Christianity seeking to find the 'treasure of Solomon'. Paris was the headquarters of the Knights Templar and 'Paris' is the Latin term 'Par-Isis' or 'near the temple of Isis' shortened to Paris, the city of Love!

Solomons Temple had two spires representing the male and female towers and he 'commanded many demons' as it was believed that in the 'presence of Christ', demons will bow down and submit to the Christ light produced by the sun and the moon. These are the electrical polar opposites unlocked in men and women via 'sacred sex' or what we know today as tantric sex hence, 'holy matrimony' or 'sacred marriage' as it was known in ancient times. The word 'holy' is derived from the word 'holly' as druids made their wands from the wood of the holly tree. Therefore, the term 'holy matrimony' literally means *'holy'* as in magical, 'matri' as in mother and 'mon' as in moon and translates quite literally as a 'magical mother moon ceremony'. Any men of 'god' who are not inclusive of the feminine energy is worshipping Satan using demons to do their bidding and because the female energy is 50% of the Christ light, then feminine energy is *essential* to force the demonic realm to fully submit. These men are thus set up in advance to lose this battle of light and dark to lead us to *exactly* the position we find ourselves in today.

King Solomon was a black magician and exorcist which is not necessarily a bad thing for the purposes of understanding the depths of despair that these alien-demons come from. *Someone* has to find out what it's all about and, if utilised in the execution of ultimate good, then their dark quest, although terrible, is a much-needed data mine of critical information required to best these evil creatures at their own game, take our planet back and move on fast before they catch us again! The biggest problem we face is that our world is controlled by unseen demonic forces that influence our lives down to the finest details in a stupendous feat of foresight as a result of operating outside our linear concept to time that they trapped our consciousness in eons ago. Humans once operated on multiple levels of awareness called 'dimensions' right up to and beyond the 11th dimension. Dimensions are simply the energetic levels of frequencies that the human heart, mind and body are capable of accessing and is precisely why we are so coveted by many alien and demonic species in their attempts to access our chakra system and our innate connection to the 'christ' light of the universe. The Christ light is also called Aether or Luminiferous Aether and is an atomic energy that appears not to have any substance or form and yet it exists. It is the Life Force or the native 'Great Spirit'. You will be more familiar with this force as Chi, Prana, Ki Life Energy and Qigong among other names applied to it from around the world. Many modalities attempt to harness this energy including Tai Chi and Reiki etc., with varying successes.

It seems that behind all the fire and brimstone of a male wrathful god who loves you, is a *feminine* force. God is actually the Goddess, and this is the key reason why our world has fallen into disrepair because the aristocratic males who have lied to you about *everything* also lied to you about 'god', of course! They're liars. They lie. They know the ultimate force is feminine and they are green with envy over it too. Once you know this you will see so many Hollywood movies and tv shows that depict the most gross and underhanded slander of the 'goddess' force and dress up her destruction and murder in ways that will shed light on just how fucked up and nasty these creeps really are. They are the lowest scum imaginable solely in it for whatever cheap thrill or money they can scratch out of their betrayal of an entire planet and human species upon it in their attempt to be a fabricated concept of god.

Solomon wrote the Testament of Solomon over two thousand years ago and is therefore older than the Book of Revelation. He built his temple using a 'magical ring engraved by god' and as we shall see the 'ring' being referred to here just as the same 'ring' of Richard Wagner's opera *Ring of the Nibelungen* from which the Lord of the Rings was based. Beyond the obfuscation, it is simply a wedding ring and the power of tantric sex enlightenment via holy matrimony/sacred marriage to unlock the seven chakras of the human body and give one access to the invisible supernatural psychic realms who are currently kicking our arses! In the book *The Power of Magic* by Derek and Julie Parker they described that, 'After much practice, the Tantric could bring into play the supreme energy of the kundalini, a sort of psychic snake inhabiting the lowest chakra in the body. This, while powerful enough to destroy the body, can rise throughout the passages of the spirit and bring about complete ecstasy, oneness with the universe – the state which the alchemist desired, of golden fusion with all things'. This meant that while one could attain a godlike omnipresence and a high IQ unlocking the dormant 'mega-mind' via the power of 'true love' or 'true love's first kiss' (sex) as found in fairy tales. By this practice one could attain the 'glowing coat' of awareness and become 'bathed in the light of the sun' found in the activated torus field and why humans were once called 'the golden race' as we literally glowed!

We can have this again, we just gotta learn how.

So, one thing you need to understand about the reptilian and demonic realms who covet this light found in humans, is that *they* do not reflect light as they do not house the light body or the chakra and torus field that humans have. This is why many eons ago they infiltrated our planet, divided the once androgynous human light-being into men and women, used men for labour and to facilitate their blood lust in wars while using beautiful talented women to breed their preferred genetic traits for their sons dressed up as princes and kings with increasingly more elaborate titles. Any women they didn't desire to breed with were potentially just prostitutes, maids or breeding stock with human men to create more people populate their empires. They breed us like cattle.

Sometime in what we would call prehistory between ten and thirty thousand years ago, Planet Earth, MOTHER EARTH, was a planet that existed in a state of perpetual 'Spring', a state of constant perfect balanced weather. Earth was an evergreen planet where there was no winter, no summer and certainly no autumn and if these other seasons occurred, they occurred in such a soft manner as to be barely discernible from the ongoing day to day Springtime that our species once enjoyed. The North and South Poles, if they had any ice at all, were only covered in very small areas of snow and ice – *maybe*. The race of Man, back then, was an androgynous feminine with internal masculine parts for self-procreation called Parthenogenesis: the spontaneous development of an embryo from an 'unfertilised' egg. 'Partheno' from the ancient Greek word for 'virgin' and 'Genesis' from ancient Greek 'to give birth' or simply 'Life' where the 'virgin' myth comes from so famous in ancient and modern religions chiefly as Mother Mary who apparently gave birth to Christ without the aid of a human man. One plain fact is, in those days, if a woman became pregnant outside of marriage she would be stoned to death or killed in any number of inventive macabre psychopathic ways from the same regions today, it seems, who *still* engage is such lovely practice so, nothing has changed there. In these same regions where these stories originate from - North Africa and the Middle East - the mother of life, the Goddess, is discarded and treated as an animal, less than a dog or a camel. I hate to point fingers, but some Arab men, *even still*, won't even shake hands with a woman because she is 'dirty' due to her menstrual cycle. This is, as usual, hypocritical and even hilarious coming from men who hold their dicks when they piss and *never* wash their hands. Just sayin'. That said, although they won't touch a woman because she's dirty, they don't mind her making them a sandwich when lunch rolls around because, well, evolution.

The rather incredible Parthenon, a temple, or for our purposes, *a church*, is named for this mythical 'virgin', Athena Parthenos, a warrior goddess who inspired and fought alongside heroes in battle. She represented the 'intellectual' and 'civilised' side of war insofar as she was no war monger unlike male 'gods' who love to kill and invade other people's lands for no real reason at all. No, she represented the *defensive* aspect of war insofar as she would inspire and fight *in defense* of herself, her lands and her people. She was not in the *offence*. She did not invade others. In ancient Egypt when the male pharaohs had screwed things up to such a degree that their civilisation was crumbling, when they had no friends left after conquering killing and insulting *everyone* in their geographic locale reachable by the long arm of their military, it was common to install a female Pharaoh, a Queen, as she was *known* for her diplomacy and crisis management skills. When everything had settled down and order (and the money supply) was restored, she was unceremoniously tossed out and the boys would continue their war mongering, looting and fucking around until the next time the shit had hit the gold leaf fans and then a woman was, once again, placed on the throne to sort their shit out for them and then it was back to business as usual. Reset. Press play *ad infinitum*.

This is the symbolic story of the sun god Ra who sent his wife Hathor (Sekhmet of the Sun) to punish men for not worshipping him because, obviously, when you are the almighty god of the universe, you send the little Mrs. to do your dirty work, literally, because he wouldn't or couldn't do it himself. She is the 'waters' of the famous flood although she is never recognised for 'cleaning' the world of the mess men created. She is Hindu Kali who kills men when imbalance prevails for too long. So, who is really the powerful one here? Did 'god' send his wife to punish men or did the Goddess simply get sick and tired of mens abusive behaviour - stealing, lying, cheating and insulting the Goddess, Planet Earth, - that she became an environmental catastrophe encapsulated by Mother Nature and 'cleaned' house by sending 'natural' disasters which they then predicably ascribed to their male god because they refused to admit mummy had whooped their ass? Even though the 'goddess', mother nature, figuratively punishes men, it is "god's wrath". This is the looming 'climate change' weather weapon extravaganza they've got lined up for you. She's coming around again, folks. Are you going to keep testing her patience or acknowledge the truth? That without masculine/feminine energy balance we're basically screwed, and the overlords know this and use it to their advantage.

The weather weapons being deployed, especially against the Southern states of America, is because the area of the gulf region and Mississippi is a mirror of the gulf region of the Nile and Cairo. The last pharaoh, Cleopatra, was trying to create a 'one world' with Egypt and Rome as the 'returning goddess' is a prophecy that heralds ascension and a unified planet. In this ritual the 'waters' of the feminine do no elevate, they destroy. So, in recreating the last era of Egypt in the southern states of America, they hope to destroy the myth of feminine ascension by destroying them with the biblical 'flood'. They rejig the myths here and there to suit their plans, but Ra and Hathor is the same story as the biblical 'flood'. Waters are associated with the feminine as her 'waters' break when she gives birth, and the world is 70% water while our bodies are also 70% water. The 'waters' of the tides are controlled by the moon – a feminine astral body - and the moon affects when a woman will get her menstrual cycle which then allows for the birth of the human race. I'm sure you can understand why they have placed her in such a low position compared to theirs in all this religious fakery and that is because the wonder of the feminine body was ever truly revered due to their fear of losing power. They downgraded the feminine so that men, specifically, male reptilians, would attain a renaissance of the soul not seen since legend and myth and as the overlords sure as hell don't want women calling them to higher order! They're rich kid party boys. Once again, we can see we are *intrinsically* connected to the cosmos astro-logically as even women's periods, endocrine system, are affected by the moon but all this astrological talk is apparently just rubbish, that's so *you* don't tap into the *power* they (the powerful satanists killing us) use to run this planet. Satanists 'worship' celestial process because the astral energies, the cosmos, really does affect us and if you can harness it, well, you too can run a world for ten thousand years and build a space empire! But wait, there's more! Queue: gimmicky sales pitch about the astral. As such, the 'flood' of the bible was another example of the feminine 'cleaning' earth of all the filth and debasement left in the wake of unenlightened men, dirty boys. This is why they depict women as 'cleaners' to this day. Christ am I sick of ads depicting women overjoyed about clean the shithouse. It was my calling, my destiny, to sweep shit. So, allowing a woman to take over until things have calmed down is a trick they are evoking even now as a female American president looms on the cards. It's only for *symbolic* purposes to fit the ancient script as the boy's club are *too scared* to try anything new lest their Karma, after eons of first-degree mass murder, finally bites them on the arse as rightly deserved. So, they just replay the old scripts, tried and tested, and *force* it to work with straight up thuggery and corruption.

Yet Athena Parthenos, 'warrior virgin', military strategist and brains behind the empire, is a symbolic reference that goes back *much further* than the ancient Greeks. We can thank the ancient Greeks, however, for keeping the original story of the Virgin Warrior Queen alive, a story that harkens back to an *androgynous* prehistoric original species, Man, *note*, not men, although men have taken full credit for the entire species and relegated the Goddess to the kitchen and the laundry. Awesome job, guys. Nice work there for the last, how long, 6,000 years? Excellent. Evolution. It's been a shit show, let's just say that. But if we are going to evolve and indeed save our own skins, then you can't turn down your free ticket out of hell just because you don't like the fact that your ticket has a vagina or is black or tall or skinny or short or *whatever* physical trait you personally don't like instead preferring to *die* rather than team-up with women to get the fuck out of this mess. Denying the feminine her rightful input, especially at this time, is morbid suicidal stupidity in action and can only lead to complete annihilation of everything we considered 'human' as a dark demonic-alien force rounds off against us in the 'final conflict'. The much prophesised 'battle of light and dark' that we appear to be experiencing at this time finds us losing despite hopeful rants from the stayers! I don't think many people are denying we're on the ropes here, indeed it *looks* as though these ancient fables are coming to pass in our lifetime and the bad guys are winning and easily so.

MELTED STAIRS AT THE TEMPLE OF HATHOR-ISIS

The warrior 'virgin' legend is a reference to a much earlier version of the Race of Man, an all-in-one powerful androgynous feminine, who was self-procreating in a garden of Eternal Spring in a time only ancient myths spoke of. This story was passed down from the last of an ancient empire long since lost the ocean floor. An empire that speaks only of *one* island, Atlantis, although the City of Atlantis that we are told of today is but one fragment of a *global* ancient empire every bit as advanced as our civilisation and even more so! In case you think I am blowing smoke up your arse, then read on because I can prove it. This ancient civilisation created feats of architectural genius we can barely comprehended today. These prehistoric marvels go back to the last great intellectual civilisation of which Atlantis is the most famous and yet there were many cities of equal beauty and importance. If the stories of the Titans and the Olympians are anything to go by, coupled with the ancient Vedic-Hindu stories of great nuclear battles and 'sky' chariots as well as Erick Von Daniken's *Chariots of the Gods* etc., then there was an *incredibly advanced global civilisation* the remnants of which can be found in the 'airports' of the Nazca Lines, Mt. Kailesh, The Princess of Hope, the melted stairs of the Temple of Isis, and the ruins of Puma Panku which many archaeologists observe to appear to have been 'obliterated' by incredible weapons with huge stones strewn in all directions like pebbles. It seems not only did this incredible empire actually exist, but it reached a point of such knowledge and power that they began breaking away from the so-called 'gods', just as we are doing now, and were destroyed by direct energy weapons that appeared to *dustify* and melt their huge cities in a very short period of time. The Vedas also speak of this in their texts. This *unbelievable* prehistoric 'myth' is apparently where the fictional 'Lord of the Rings' comes from and in Dr Judy Wood's book *'Where Did the Towers Go?'* She speaks of exotic weapons that 'dustified' the buildings before our eyes and that some sort of sky beam was used in a 'suite of forces' that melted the buildings from the inside! They have this technology again and it looks like this was the way they destroyed the ancient world and crashed us back to zero point forcing us repeatedly to climb out of the dust of prehistory only to shove us back down again resetting our evolution again and again, so we don't get away from them in a far-reaching space empire of alien 'gods'. Their success lies in mimicry in space stations that look like moons and aliens that look like humans. They are very careful not to show the true extent of their fabulous technology that makes everything appear 'natural' and 'normal' while totally *unnatural* 'inexplicable' things keep happening like global wars that nobody wants yet they *continue* to happen.

If true, it is dangerous times we face as they intend to do this again and why wouldn't they? They are the same ancient demonic aliens that have kept us prisoner for tens of thousands of years – the 'Archons', the 'Nephilim' the 'Anunnaki' – they have gone by many names throughout history. They are demons from the 4th dimension who can physically manifest as the 'reptilian' phenomenon, 'that old dragon', 'the serpent' - the Devil! - that has dogged our species since before living memory! In fact, the technology we widely use today is dribbled down to us from *them* but not enough that we actually compare with anything *they* have. We are outgunned. Once again, the self-hating dullards wade into the storm and insist these ancient structures were the product of 'ancient aliens', but no, it was us, Humans, who built those structures in a time when our pineal glands were open, a time of 'gods' – yes, we were the 'gods' then – a time of 'giants', great feats of strength and megalithic structures. It was a time of heroes, warlocks, and powerful warrior queens the last hints of which is found in fairy tales and the prophesised 'happily ever after' we were promised, and they have denied us. The real question is, can they keep denying us?

So, *the truth*, much to the chagrin of an ever-growing egomaniacal global faction of politically minded men who seem take propriety over women (even our bodies! Incredible!), is that the original species that inhabited this planet was a parthenogenetic female, a formidable androgynous 'dolphin' like species from where we get the French masculine title 'Dauphin'. A Dauphin is a prince, the eldest son of the king, receiving the title and the lands of his father as passed down to the next generation. Yet despite getting their precious sons from the female, stealing all the female symbols and phrases while looting this feminine planet, Mother Earth, even nicking off with her bounty found in Mother Nature (the real metaphor of the 'thief' archetype in fairy tales), females were not considered for the top job in France unless there were no brothers  available, even if she was the eldest by direct descent, it always went to a son or 'male default'. Notice, *right*, the sun symbol and crown on the thief poster in Rapunzel - more on that soon. Making the Goddess, females, take second place is unnatural as to maximise the output of an electrical circuit you need to have both poles operating in unison hence, the image of Jesus and Mary pointing at their hearts or 'true love'. It's unnatural, unless, of course, you're not human and then you wouldn't want the human feminine operating at optimum with the human masculine or you just might wind up losing your slaves and you wouldn't be top dog anymore in an alien syndicate harvesting planets just like Earth. Men…are you listening? Here comes the important stuff. Dolphin is also Delphi, yes, the famed Oracles of Delphi, the ancient Greek virgin priestesses who apparently worshipped Apollo who was the son of Zeus, an old name for the modern-day deity known as Satan, from a time when they apparently didn't question the demonic gods populating the Bible. But we are evolving now, and they need to rebrand if they are to continue to trick us so, you can expect some of the highest high-jinx in the near future as they pull of this rather curious show. Why would the Virgin Goddess wind up worshipping a Satanic deity? There are reasons for all this that I will get to.

RETURN OF THE TWINS

Dolphins are known for their problem-solving skills, complex communication and social structures as well as passing their knowledge onto others just like humans. In fact, dolphins are so similar to Humans not only intellectually but socially, that I suppose the whole female dolphin myth could simply be symbolic of the fact that ancient intelligent Humans were likened to the smart natures observed in dolphins and thus were subsequently symbolised as rather similar. But there is more to this *physiologically* than that. Dolphins have bigger brains than humans, have lungs like humans, give birth like humans. The word dolphin means 'a fish with a womb'. Therefore, it's interesting the 'Aquatic Ape' theory seems to be a laugh-a-minute ripping yarn that the scientific community pay no attention to in any serious measure. When there is such contempt among mainstream academia for a particular subject, especially when their contempt borders on outright insulting derogatory hit-and-runs and below the belt cheap shots, then you might want to take a closer look at that subject.

The Aquatic Ape Theory was considered more 'popular with the laypublic' than with scientists because, obviously, the general public are just plain *stupid* and *wouldn't understand* anyway even though education is an expense most people *can't* afford and therefore, academia is the realms of those who *can* afford it aka the upper classes (especially at the time this theory was postulated in 1960). This is why all your big academic names in history are ALL from the aristocracy with the exception of a (questionable) tiny few. Therefore, it's not 'intellect' that's prevents the 'laypublic' from understanding the big subjects, it's the 'economy'. 'Laypublic' - a person without professional or specialized knowledge in a particular subject, "the book seems well suited to the interested layman". How sweet, the 'kids' might like this fairy tale, but the academic adults know its bullshit. How much more condescending and privileged can you get? As Isaac Asimov said, 'Self-education is, I firmly believe, the only kind of education there is'. The money system creates a *gaping chasm* between the have's and the have not's as proven by the apparent 'learned' class (who have plenty of money) and the 'great unwashed' dickheads in the street (who don't have any money). But, that said, the internet is the great leveller, and we are coming along just fine thank you very much, uppers!

The Aquatic Ape theory was postulated initially by English marine biologist Sir Alistair Hardy who, on the advice of esteemed colleagues (academics all), waited for *thirty years* to garner enough academic and social status as a luminary in the field of marine biology, even being knighted for his contributions, before he seemingly *dared* to voice his opinions on evolution in the 'safe' space of the British-Sub-Aqua-Club in 1960. He described 'functional hairlessness' and 'bipedalism' as the result of competing for habitat and food causing ancient apes (a hundred million years ago) to forage at the seashore for crustaceans and other edibles. Geographer Carl Sauer stated that the role of the coastal regions in human evolution, "stimulated tremendous progress in the study of coastal and aquatic adaptations" inside marine archaeology. Separately, German pathologist, Max Westenhofer, proposed that hairlessness, subcutaneous fat, the regression of the olfactory organ, webbed fingers, direction of body hair etc., could have derived from an aquatic past during the cretaceous period 145 to 66 million years ago. So, there's a bit of wiggle room then? He did not believe humans were apes, as such, stating, "The postulation of an aquatic mode of life during an early stage of human evolution is a tenable hypothesis, for which further inquiry may produce additional supporting evidence'.

Touted at the time as 'pseudoscience', Hardy's brave pitch pointed to a stronger connection to *aquatic* possibilities in human evolution although was not taken seriously by a no doubt *very* serious academic fraternity (mostly, if not all, male). However, in the 21st century with sixty more years of archaeological data under our belts, it is admitted the Aquatic Ape Hypothesis (AAP) is a 'viable one'. Elaine Morgan picked up the ball and ran with it when she published her first book *The Descent of Woman* in 1972 which became an international bestseller translated into ten languages. Her book highlighted the apparent 'sexism' that was inherent in the savannah-based 'killer ape' theory postulated by Raymond Dart in the 1950's claiming that war and interpersonal aggression was the *driving force* behind human evolution. You know, if I didn't know better, I would think we were being persuaded to believe that we are *genetically* 'bad' and 'evil' or the famed 'sinners' of the Bible routine all, by and by, promoted by an *Establishment* boys club who appear to be quite violent and covetous. Maybe they're talking about themselves and *their* roots quite different from ours?

The establishment boys club, *the aristocracy*, behind the accepted if derogatory implications of the Darwinian theory of evolution insofar as claiming humans are basically monkey's, might also want to *address* that in times of crisis, humans are *known* for their philanthropic and charitable contributions to those less fortunate, known for their bravery in emergencies and their resilience in the face of destruction. The aristocracy, who actively *create* these malignant states of destruction especially in war, seem to largely avoid the fray only handing out a medal here and there to those who did the job for them. My point is, if the 'laypublic' are just fucken animals, then in times of crisis, we should be clawing each other's eyes out! But no! It doesn't quite fit the picture, does it? Charitable organisations, by the way, are largely owned and operated by the elite who LOVE to posture and pose when a good charity run garners enormous proceeds most of which *rarely* reach the intended recipients. This has been proven time and time again as the funds donated are *routinely* siphoned off as people naively presume the cause was managed ethically and thus don't follow up. Once the show has left town, like the famous "Live Aid" *celebrity* feel good fest back in the 1980's, the money seemingly disappears into thin air! You mean people have suffered and the donations were pilfered? Who could have done all this, I wonder...? And let's not mention the latest bushfire appeal here in Australia that generated *hundreds of millions of dollars* for those in need and yet several years later, the money *still* remains in the coffers of the biggest charities who claim they'll give out when the 'next' crisis happens. And when will that be? Since then, we've had further crisis involving floods where more money was raised, and that too seems to have not reached it's intended recipients. The point I'm making is that the Darwinian 'survival of the fittest', might is right, dog eat dog theory of evolution and Raymond Dart's 'killer ape' theory does not *adequately* explain the gaping *differences* in the behaviour of the so-called 'lay-public' and the average person's tendency to *give until it hurts* (even their own lives in defence of others whom they will never meet!) and a bunch of self-serving *greedy* posturing cunts called the *Aristocracy* who, like academia and Biblical lore, *insist* the Common person is a piece of shit, monkeys no less, while they kill and destroy and horde everything in sight! Where is the 'what the hell is wrong with the aristocracy and their innate differences to the common people' theory of evolution white-paper? I haven't seen *that* one yet. We have lots to discuss. You might want to put your feet up. This could take a while.

Elain Morgan drew attention to the sexism in these all-male-academic clubs and their learned establishments emanating out of the Universities and 'fellowships' of the best houses of Elite education. Seems to be a bit of bias going on and leads to a conflict of interest that inspired her wildly popular book *The Descent of Woman*. In this work she states the 'Tarzanist' gender stereotypes of evolution failed (once again) to adequately account for the *women's contribution* in Human evolution. Women who? She postulated that many characteristics of modern humans distinguish us from chimpanzees as a result of a period of close proximity to water giving rise to questions that no related theories can adequately explain including the much-touted chimpanzee myth. I don't suppose the movie franchise

Planet of the Apes helped given it was released around the same time that these aquatic theories were emerging in the 1960's. She claimed that female apes raised their young away from the male apes unless they were in their estrous cycles, on heat, and that semi-aquatic environments caused the female apes to evolve to accommodate front-to-front sexual intercourse rather than the 'rear entry position' or 'doggy style' as so eloquently put by the 'lay-public'. She wrote that female orgasm went from being a 'natural sexual response' to becoming 'very difficult'. She countered the theory that evolution occurred for the 'benefit of male hunters' which stated *nothing* about the protection of the children. Despite being lampooned as 'wishy washy' and 'bearing no resemblance to...scientific views' and a 'thoroughly unscientific romp riddled with errors and convenient conclusions', she was named as one of 'the 50 greatest Welsh men and women of all time'. Despite her detractors, she was nonetheless awarded an OBE, Order of the British Empire, and a fellowship from the Royal Society of Literature for her contributions to literature receiving her Honours from the Queen of England which she saw as an acknowledgement of her *Aquatic Ape Hypothesis* even though the subject was 'controversial'.

American cognitive scientist Daniel Clement Dennett whose research centres largely on philosophy of biology particularly in the area of evolutionary biology stated, "Many of the counterarguments *[to the aquatic ape theory]* seem awfully thin and ad hoc. During the last few years when I have found myself in the company of distinguished biologists, evolutionary theorists, paleo-anthropologists, and other experts, I have often asked them just to tell me, please, exactly why Morgan must be wrong about the aquatic ape theory. I haven't yet had a reply worth mentioning, aside from those who admit, with a twinkle in their eyes, that they have often wondered the same thing". Famous South African anthropologist Phillip V. Tobias stated in a BBC-Discovery Channel Documentary, "I see Elaine Morgan, through her series of superbly written books, presenting a challenge to the scientists to take an interest in this thing, to look at the evidence dispassionately. Not to avert your gaze as though it were something you that you hadn't ought to hear about or hadn't ought to see. And those that are honest with themselves are going to dispassionately examine the evidence. We've got to if we are going to be true to our calling as scientists". Or just true to the Human Race in general. Always last on the list.

The official historian for the Zulu nation, Sanusi, Credo Mutwa, was quoted in an interview with David Icke as saying that they have legends in their culture that reptiles came down from the sky in great ships and created two caves. At the time, humans were one, *an androgynous species*, male and female housed in one. The reptiles created two caves - one cave was red, and the other cave was green. The humans were herded into the caves and out the red cave came men and out the green cave came women. This story is telling us that the reptiles invaders 'split' the humans into two different polar opposite sexes and therefore, the 'caves' seem to have been possibly underground laboratories that interesting represent the colours of the red root chakra (sex) and the green heart chakra (the feminine). The wife of the leader of the reptiles saw that the humans were unhappy being split apart and put to work mining for metals and so she taught them to make love to become 'one' again. What does this mean? Firstly, that the reptiles knew that 'sex' and 'make you one'. This lizard race that so many victims of royal families and high-ranking politicians claim to have witnessed, is a covetous militant hypermasculine alien race who rule us to this day. Their souls come from the 4th dimension, a death dimension of darkness and chaos, it is a dimension that does not conduct light indeed, the reptilian's bodies do not conduct or reflect light. The inability to reflect light is where the vampire myth comes from as the they have 'no reflection' in a mirror because the universe is the colloquial 'the mirror' and if they want to access the higher dimensions, they have to splice their genetics with beings who can harness the light spectrum which in this case is humans as found in our chakras.

The light spectrum found in the human chakras generate the complex 'feelings' we experience as part of our emotional spectrum allowing the full magnitude of our multidimensional bodies. The reptiles came to Earth from deep space, even another universe, and travel around the Milky Way galaxy, and no doubt other galaxies, looking for environmentally abundant planets and species whose bodies contain the chakra system of universal light, a cosmic wi-fi system that connects us to the core of the galaxy and the highest vibration of all - love-light-life – at the 11th dimensional pitch where all information is housed sometimes referred to as the 'akashic records' or the 'akashic construct'. It was described as 'home tree' in the movie avatar that they connect to via their hair symbolic of the nervous system. The highest vibration of light is a place of bliss, calmness, tranquillity, and eternity. Therefore, the original androgynous 'aquatic' feminine species, that Human's once were, became targeted by a hypermasculine reptilian species. All these millennia later these reptiles are collectively referred to as 'the devil', Satan, who, by the way, is depicted as red, the 'red devil', and is all about sex or the red root chakra. *See right*, he's got the same grin as 'Flynn Rider' a reference to Errol Flynn or 'riding' sexually, cowboy style. The story Credo Mutwa tells is not unlike the story of the Bible and no doubt many other mythological stories concerning our beginnings and how it all happened. It's a history that they have desperately tried to delete. His story also involves humans being taught to 'make love' in order to become 'whole' again which is exactly where this needs to go in order to attain our unity consciousness and ascend as prophesised for thousands of years. In fact, the classical image of a 'heart' is actually two hearts fused together in 'true love'.

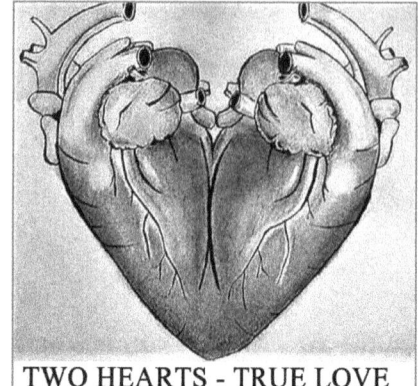
TWO HEARTS - TRUE LOVE

Credo's story describes that humans were telepathic but after the split they were taught language which was an insufficient method of communication and therefore, people were misunderstanding each other leading to conflict. His also says the newly formed women were shocked at the 'snake', the penis, between the men's legs which is interesting as the snake of the Bible, in opinion, is symbolic of the penis. The penis was also depicted as the long neck of a 'swan' hence, Zeus (a reptilian god) seduced the Spartan queen on her wedding night disguised a 'swan' as this is code for 'big dick'. Credo described how the 'chief' of the reptilian 'gods' was angry at his wife for teaching the people how to become whole again, and the solution was to make women have babies to try and stop them from having sex all the time as the men were covetous of other men's wives etc. In the Bible story god punished Adam and Eve by making women give birth in pain and suffering and men's punishment was to 'toil in misery', hard work, until the end of his days. The symbols are largely there , that working in the mines 'toil in misery', women having babies in pain. It's all very similar as are all creation 'myths' from around the world.

This story is like many others bear common themes and although a little muddled, it is telling us *symbolically* that reptilian scientists split humans from an androgynous being into men and women, a pair. Men were red. Women were green. This is because the red root chakra is the first chakra of the sexual organs and the 'spark' of life from the 'fires' of a man's loins, or *sex*, is associated more so with males aka testosterone. Green is the colour of the heart chakra as heart is an anagram of Earth associated with mother nature-mother earth as the heart associated with love associated with the mother, with females. This is why males were red-sex root chakra and females were green-love heart chakra. This story shows up in Greek myth as well when the reptilian god Zeus 'fearing their power split them in two to forever search for their other half'. The classic image of the heart shape we all know is not one heart but two hearts combined to give us the classic heart shape. This is why a 'treasure chest' houses gold because your physical chest house your gold, your light, and therefore 'treasure chest' isa actually you heart. And they will do everything they can to destroy it, to smash it to smithereens and break it irreparably because it is via your heart that you can transcend this shithole of a reality.

The chakra tower is activated by sex and through the practice of sacred sex known today as tantric sex. Therefore, we can become 'one' again or the famed 'twin flames' reunited. It is the happily ever after, it is Beauty and the Beast, it is Rapunzel and her 'tower' and 'hair' as found in all the famed 'children's' fables as they don't want you to realise, this is very much for the adults. The difference between 'god' and the 'devil' (who masquerades as 'god') is that the devil's chakra tower is activated by sex while lovemaking between a husband and wife as symbolised by Jesus and Mary Magdalene, activates the chakra tower via the meditation of 'love making'. This anchors the heart of the masculine to the Earth to 'ground' his electricity, his fire, so that he doesn't become too 'fiery' hence, the 'fire of his loins' and 'spark of life' are symbolic of the 'fires of hell' when a man is given to his internal 'devil inside'. If a man isn't anchored or grounded the 'fires of hell', testosterone, is unleashed and death and chaos abounds. This is indeed what has happened as mother earth is consumed by the fires of rampant hyper-masculinity and the whole world burns as a result. You don not fight fire with fire, you fight fire with water.

The unanchored male is exactly what the 'devil', hypermasculine reptilians, want as they covet Earth's resources and encourage human men to behave like them so that they do not seem so out of place in their rampant sexuality, violence, destruction – the god of war – of which human men take the blame but is actually engineered by an alien-demonic 'devil' element *masquerading* as human men. Straight up sex, if performed at the right times of the month, will initiate enlightenment of the chakras when they are switched on as epitomised by 'sleeping beauty' or the 'seven dwarves'. When unactivated, the chakras are dormant and diminished. When they are activated, they 'awaken' or the 'great awakening' when the 'dwarves' become 'giants.

There is a warning about achieving enlightenment the reptilian 'devils' way as wanton sex with anyone, anywhere may activate the chakras asap, it also leads to destruction and is the *foundation of Satanism* and where they are getting their power from and why they are running rings around us. Otherwise, lovemaking with your 'twin', your 'other half', who you were split from when all this chaos happened tens of thousands of years ago, allows the male ego to be anchored deeply into mother earth where he is strong and has power, has intellect and confidence to speak, to harvest the fruit from the Tree of knowledge and the Tree of Life found in the human body. The 'apple' among other things is the 'Adams Apple' when the boy becomes a man, when he becomes 'The Speaker' and 'The Voice' also known as the 'Messenger' as were all 'god' and 'goddess' characters throughout history known as 'the messenger'. Malachi 3:1 "Behold, I send my messenger, and he will prepare the way before me". Malachi means 'Messenger of God'. Christ is not a man or a god. Christ lives inside you, and you *will* do the job prophesised from the dawn of time.

How you like them apples?

CHAPTER THREE

THE POWER COUPLE RETURNS

The 'power couple' is every woman and every man with their chakras electrically activated reaching the heights of the 11th Dimension and beyond.

There was a civilisation who came before ours. It was a global civilisation overseen by the veneration of the Goddess who was the monotheistic deity at the time. The term 'goddess' is simply an old word to describe a replicating universal energy found largely in the collective feminine, ultimately housed in women, who produce babies, the precious next generation. It's not that men don't hold this energy, they do, but they hold a more direct 'masculine' electricity giving them their natural traits as a man. Both genders hold the two prime energies in different degrees and why it is so important to sit down together and unify these energies to make the most of the conduit of electricity. Electricity is power, that's why it's called a 'power' bill when you ludicrously pay for something that is inside your body.

At the time of this ancient society, the newly emerging human race was quite precarious, and any loss of a generation could spell the sudden end for humankind. Therefore, it was the 'portal' of the feminine bringing forth the light force of the universe in new life found in babies, a new hope, that was held above all and so, men used their robust direct energy in defense of the feminine to ensure their own future was secured. It is a natural trait to defend the one who will ensure your future and the unnatural spiritual crisis of men who kill women is in fact some sort of demonic possession of their bodies that seeks to destroy the feminine in order to destroy men and vice versa. They destroy themselves. The *natural* balanced people of the distant past worked in concert with the seasons of the Earth. They revered life. They acknowledged that the bounty of Mother Nature was their literal meal ticket to the next and next season and if they could survive long enough, they could attain stability and security, a most prized possession in the uncertainly of possible floods, droughts and famines that, if unprepared, could render them extinct within a short time. The threat of extinction was always front and center in the early days and our natural drive for survival even in the most harsh circumstance is a testament to a vision that lives in our hearts to attain super-consciousness when we don't have to worry any more. It's about going home after a LONG arduous journey.

Therefore, at the time it was simply about making through the next year, the next harvest, and this gave rise to the first well planned agricultural systems and the 'saving for a rainy day' mentality that we seem to have lost as we scab anything of value from this planet and quickly discard it without revering the hard work *and time* it takes for nature to create such bounty. The feminine was consider the highest form of the universal light as women, who carry a dignity, ease and lightness not easily taken on by men, and nor should it be, were likened to the 'flow' of the light of universal life force as were rivers and oceans as the 'flow' of the currents run a certain course. If the course is respected, it will lead you to golden shores in the bliss of heaven far above the material fears that dog those on the journey home. This effortless ease with which life showed up was called Grace and so were some of the first terms coined to 'name' the life force as 'Grace' or ease of flow, dignity and beauty, Dawn – a feminine name – as the sun rose over the lush garden of Mother Earth, Eve – the twilight before the 'moon', also feminine, shone a faint glow in the darkness by which to travel if one was caught out in the dreaded dark. She was considered as a 'protectress' in this way, a life bringer, and as the 'life' is spawned by electricity, the 'life' is the 'light' and the 'light' bought growth and bounty to allow the continued existence of her children under the care of her Love. Light, life and love are one and the same.

She trained her children by giving them the opportunity, if they studied the stars, the seasons, the tides etc., to create for themselves from her 'flow' or 'mothers milk', the possibility for unbelievable growth, comfort, acceleration and enjoyment of life. She was therefore considered a 'tutelary' goddess from old French tutor 'guardian, private teacher', from Latin 'tutorem' 'guardian, watcher' variant to 'watch over, look at'. It's a word from uncertain origin as it goes back beyond the boundaries of current civilized knowledge as did the veneration of the feminine. It suggests a connection to Sanskrit 'tavas' meaning 'strong powerful' and ancient Greek 'safe, safe and sound, healthy' from a root word 'to be strong' also, 'tutor' relating to 'tutoring'. 'To tutor' from Latin 'intuit' or to 'perceive directly without reasoning, to know by immediate perception' a back-formation from *'intuition'*. She has 'knowing' without the need for intellectual breakdown and 'mind'. She is heart and heart is an anagram for earth. Nature. Natural. She is a teacher who watches over her class of students protectively as do all teachers, or at least they should and did, until something evil happened, and a new teacher entered the arena of Mother Earth. This new 'teacher', a cruel hierarchical masculine god, punished his children, denied his students true knowledge and postured as a supreme being over celestial toddlers who in their truest and highest form would run such a creature off like sweeping cockroaches out the door.

These students under the Goddess reached such heights of power and knowledge that they were destroyed seemingly by weapons that were blasted onto them from above. It seems that the Space Ex roll out of the current global satellite program around earth is the same sort of control model used by them of old as they seemed to have been destroyed by megalithic weapons from an outside source, a source that couldn't be reached. They are doing it again. Some have referred to this ancient civilisation as Tataria and claimed that there was a 'mud flood' that destroyed them. Maybe there was a mud flood or maybe the chaos and upheaval was caused by weather weapons and exotic space technology like that used on 9/11 to literally 'dustify' the buildings before our eyes and leave only pyroclastic ash, like volcanoes produce, in the wake of where massive buildings once stood. Even the laymen at the time couldn't understand where 110 stories of rubble and debris could have 'disappeared' to? Shouldn't there have been 110 stories of broken metal, glass, and cement on the ground in a massive pile? No. But then the same cabal of demonically possessed half-bloods are running the world today setting up the technology required to do the same thing to us as was done to them ten thousand years ago.

If they can't bring their demonic god, the anti-Christ, into power, they intend to destroy us all as this time around, it is not supposed to be just one, either the god or the goddess, but both together, working in harmony. When the feminine and masculine are working in concert, they are unstoppable. In understanding just a little bit of the *monumental charade* we are involved in we need to look at the first cab off the rank; the very *language* we use. Whatever is behind our brutalisation as a sentient species is *not human* and the more one becomes aware of just *how big this is,* you cannot help but arrive at any other conclusion than the *historically recorded* 'demonic' element controlling us from the wings. It is global, interdimensional, and galactic *if not Universal.* It's big, folks. Our ancestors *weren't* lying when they *persisted* in their quest to impart this essential knowledge gathered, no doubt, from many millennia before them on their mission to save the future of planet Earth and the human race upon it in the much prophesised 'final conflict'. Even if we don't realise how important we are ourselves, *they knew* how important the human race and planet Earth *really is* and the battle to save our kind from an insidious alien takeover that sprang from the depths of some horrible omniversal hell hole, *literally*, a nightmare dimension of hopeless psychopathic drudgery that seeks to suck us unto the vortex with it.

As such, Priest Malachi Martin was Professor of Palaeography at the Vatican's Pontifical Biblical Institute and, along with other priests, claimed the Pope was a 'false prophet' and that the Vatican was a place of black magic and satanism where children and babies are abused and even sacrificed. He was a key figure and a fairly high-ranking priest, not some idiot fringe, a member of the *inner core* of the highest levels running the world today who worked with the controllers on a daily basis. He knew the bible like the back of his hand. You'd must be pretty damn confident in yourself if you are going up against people who are possessed by evil and who know the dirty tricks of the dark arts! As such, Malachi Martin was a man of *deep faith* in his knowledge of good and evil. There is some strange force that the ancients recorded in their symbols, however disconnected we are from their knowledge, that, worldwide, spoke of certain powers. Ironically, or not, strange symbolic communications keep showing up attempting to guide us on a certain path, not necessarily a biblical path in the mainstream sense, but a *deeply spiritual way* and those messages show up *repeatedly*. Historically, Malachi was the last of 12 books called the Prophecy of the Malachias from the 'Old Testament' of the Hebrew Bible in the Jewish 'canon' meaning 'law' or 'lore' i.e., history, *legend*. It is a tried and tested way of being, and a direction to judgement and thus *natural progression* to *ascension* by something much greater than our conscious comprehension and yet *found within us!* Malachi means *'my messenger'* and this 'messenger' will become increasingly more important as you read this book and not because of some 'returning' Jesus character that, sadly, so many people rely on to get them out of this crisis. The man, Jesus, aint coming, folks, sorry. The god, *Christ* within, yes, *that* is coming. It is you.

Malachi Martin blew the whistle on Vatican Satanic paedophilia claiming an "enthronement ceremony" was held there in 1963 by Satanic Cardinals and that there was an "irremovable presence of a malign strength" that "knowledgeable Churchmen called the 'superforce" tied to the installation of Pope Paul VI's reign in 1963. It was the same year President Kennedy, the King of America, was assassinated and this too shall become important as was the death of another King 2,000 years before who these evil people claim to represent! 369 is a frequency, it is also a reference to time as in the clock face at 3 o'clock, 6 o'clock & 9 o'clock which are symbolic references of *a journey to be completed* but we never quite reach the 12th gate or '12 o'clock' and 'get out'. The 12th gate is when we are supposed to be 'let out', ascend, as we enter the 12th house of 'Aquarius', the final portal of the zodiac gateways to release us through the 'gates' of heaven in the stars as time is literally up for all involved. Jesus had 12 disciples, Buddha had 12 followers, Quetzalcoatl had 12 followers, the 12 nights of the roundtable, Hercules and his 12 labours, the 12 tribes of Israel, the 12 great patriarchs, 12 Old Testament prophets, 12 jewels of the high priest. 12 signs of the zodiac, 12 months of the year, 12 hours of the day, 12 hours of the night, 12 inches in a foot, 12 days of Christmas, 12 grades in school, 12 step-programs, 12 jurors, 12 notes before the octave, 12 eggs in a dozen, 12 years of childhood before the teens. And it goes on and on. As such, we *must be let out* of this time warp, this zodiac trap, or all others will forever damn *themselves* and it seems they, the 'malign superforce' behind all this, prefer the latter. 369 is also an Egyptian legend associated with the family of life insofar as the sun father or 'god' holds up or 'carries' the 'sun' symbolised as the 'boat', the 'mother', who is the 'ship' carrying their babies and thus means *natural procreation* giving rise to the *generations* found in the symbolism of the scarab beetle that represents birth, life, death and resurrection – reincarnation – in the 'eternal cycle of life'. This life force was also represented by the *fleur di lis*, a prehistoric representation of the iris flower *Iris* being a 'goddess' and an earlier version of Isis who is the Goddess of Light who just like the scarab beetle means the *light bearer*, the *essential electricity born into human babies* carried by the (mother) 'ship', the mother who carries the *life-force* called by ancients the 'animating force', the aether, or the fifth element! The fifth element in modern science is 'electromagnetic' energy, an *electrical force* that, amplified, can be used for good or evil. Clearly, evil is having a field day with this *literal* power. They often tell you what's going on in movies dressed up as fiction and in the movie Gothic with Julian Sands he says, "Lightning is the fundamental force of the universe, the aether, the spirit!"

Without this universal light we are dead or worse than dead, a sort of 'living dead' also 'prophesised' to return as found in such movie titles as '*Return of the Living Dead*'. It's all around us once you know the signs. Malachi Martin stated, "Satan is having his last stand, this is his Waterloo, but he is going to destroy as much as he can before he is finally shoved out of the abyss again chained by Michael" describing demons as "sophisticated spirits who are there to harm us and they're real". This is true and they surrounds us in invisible hordes or 'legion'. In my first book, *2020 & Beyond – This is not a Drill*, I said that you would get your world, *Mother* Earth, back but it would be a 'fixer upper'. It's no coincidence then that everywhere you look these days all you see is the slander of the feminine, the abuse of the feminine and men claiming to be women in a Norman Bates extravaganza being 'celebrated' because we're 'progressive' and thus 'evolving'. It is to appease a tiny demographic that the term 'expectant mother' has been removed in favour of 'birthing person' because the 1% is calling the shots on the 99%...because.... evolution. Firstly, the Goddess of Light, the Mother also called the 'mother goddess', literally mothers, was the monotheistic deity way back before the rise of a hateful vengeful 'heavenly father' who became the big daddy of this world and seems to want his 'children' tortured to death. People thank 'god' for everything they are about to receive on their plates when everything on their plates and their backs come from the Goddess – Mother Nature. This evil and clever 'identity thief' of the Devil, distorted hyper-masculine alien-demons, poses in the place of the 'goddess' and is trying to delete her with *endless charades* blocking out the feminine presence at this time when incredible portals and alignments have prophesised her return. These unprecedented series of portals and cosmic alignments, as chiefly seen in the year 2020, make it easier for a spiritual connection to be made with the *cosmic brain* found at the centre of the galaxy - a black hole sun. This central core 'black sun' is the 'mirror' of what is contained in the human physics of the *nervous system*, a cosmic *replicated* electromagnetic circuit board that requires a return path in order for it to work effectively. That's where we come in. We broadcast our electromagnetic signal as an organic being to the moon which broadcasts it to the sun which broadcasts it to Sirius which broadcasts it to the centre of the galaxy. This communication is simply genius and a totally logical, indeed astro-logical, method of connecting us to the entire Universe and means that 'god' and 'goddess' shines out from within biological men and women of Earth. When there are *massive galactic alignments* of planets, moons and suns as occurred in the year 2020, it creates a *clearer signal* enabling huge cosmic leaps and bounds leading to a sudden spike in innovation, development, inventions, quality of life, personal communication between each other and a deeper reverence for the planet. Our DNA is being activated in ways never before seen and they are using every filthy trick; poisons, 'entertainment', politics, chemicals, wi-fi and everything else you can imagine, to keep us from accessing these higher codes because they can't go all the way, but we can. We are not separate from the Universe and are as much a part of the entire enormous Universe as the ignition in a car. It is one big working engine, and this incredible engine is fueled by the Fifth Element also called Luminiferous Aether, life force, the force, verve, chutzpah etc., but you would be more familiar with it as 'Chi', 'Prana', Qi Life Energy, Ki, Soul, and Great Spirit.

Every two thousand year these alignments occur in such a way as to herald a new zodiac sign or 'house' that we live under. This is what they really mean when they say, 'the house of the lord' as they boys club typically equate the galactic rings to a male force. The 'house' is the dome of the sky or 'heaven', it's literally the stars, and what particular alignment of the galaxy we are in at that time. This is what the entire story of Jesus and the Bible is built on and all the reference to 'fish' and 'loaves' and all that is an unfolding narrative of how celestial processes are repeated inside our body's ad infinitum. We are supposed to evolve, it is ordained by the Universe, literally, and yet, somehow, we can't. This book is dedicated to explaining how this 'malignant superforce' of evil keeps us locked inside a limited bandwidth called '3D-five sense' reality, a tiny range, making us slaves to an actual *physical* clock found in the planetary movements of our galaxy and galactic movements in the greater 'clock' of the Universe, complete with 'cogs' and moving parts, in the universes beyond *that*. This dark force removes us from our extradimensional abilities that would allow us to 'see' outside the 'timeline' into the spiritual realm which has NO TIME and NO SPACE insofar as NO CONSTRAINTS on our universal spiritual movements harnessed beyond our physical body and yet requiring a physical body to even exist in this reality. We are about to get our passport to the stars, folks, and when that happens the insidious force holding us prisoner will shrink away from the brilliance of our collective light, Earth will be healed, humans will be free and there will be no more evil, pain, fear or sufferance on this beautiful planet ever again. It's about time we joined the big kids out in the realms of Outer Space and beyond!

So, the *message* being sent at this time by these cosmic *criminal* elite alien *males* who run our planet emanating out of Hollywood, global religions, politics, education, the media and the military, is that women are the bad guy, men are women, women abuse men, expectant mother is now 'expectant person' or 'birthing person', and pharmaceutically castrated females and males are so poisoned they can't even think straight to *question what is being done to them* and honestly believe the 'wife' is the 'father' and the 'husband' is the 'mother'. They are so *spiritually neutered* let alone mentally and physically limited by 35 years of *increased* vaccine and pill related physiological injuries caused by a militarized juggernaut bent on destroying the human race, largely with lies, that they have you believing that the Great Goddess *is now a man* specifically, *a reptilian male*. Just a coincidence mind as we near the astro-zodiacal 'end date' of the Age of Pisces in 2033, the year 'Christ' 'died' on the 'cross' as we enter a NEW AGE supposed to bring social, political, personal, and ideological change and, quote, 'For those living in the United States, this might be connected to the upcoming transition of presidential power'.

The 'transition of presidential power' is not just another election and not just *another* stooge standing before you broadcasting a *river of lies* to wash you away. No, this means *a complete change in everything the Americans thought they knew* and a true renaissance of Independence that, like the values Christ preached 2000 years ago, *should* have been granted to them already. Instead, all we see is the *fleecing* of that great nation until they are on their knees as the international lynch mob jeers at the blinding of the bear, the nailing on the cross of a once great figure, calling the mother - *the wife* - a 'prostitute' slandering her and casting her out with only a few loyal companions to keep the dream of freedom alive. Stoked up into a hideous frenzy, the world looks upon America now, even *willing* their end, and yet, if America goes down the whole world goes down which is *precisely* what the 'malignant super force' wants and, for the most part, you are all pieces on a chessboard being moved around at their will. Oh, it's been done before - *many times! See right,* ancient Egyptian lightbulb. Ecclesiastes 1:9 "What has been will be again, what has been done will be done again; there is nothing new under the sun". So, they cut off the head of the king and hold it up for his dejected and crushed subjects to witness the horror and fall compliant under the wheels of indominable evil. It's close call and yes, it's big, folks, I don't mind telling you.

SNAKES ARE THE SYMBOL FOR ELECTRICITY ALSO USED IN THE CADUCEUS

As a result, these elite males who 'worship' (study) the stars and Earth changes as a cult have monitored these vibrational *effects on human psychology, mood and reactions,* and think it's *hilarious* to have you chasing your tales running in all directions like it's the end of the world - and it is - the end of the *old world* and *thus the end of them.* Yet they are *quite assured* they have got their success in the bag *already* and that this charade of crashing us back to zero point has been done to Earth and Humans *many times* before, for at least ten thousand years. Let's just say, they are quite convinced they have studied all that needs to be studied and laid every trap that needs to be laid and told every lie that needs to be told. Their 'god' is Hermes who carried the caduceus, *right*, a symbol of crown chakra activation and high IQ that carries electricity up the spine via tantric sex. It's how they get their power which I will describe in more details shortly. Yet it is also true that they nearly didn't make it through with their plans *many times*. They have nearly come to their end many times over the course of the last few thousand years. They must create a reign of terror and go underground, literally, to emerge at a later date to try *again* in another 2,000 years. They are not as powerful as they would have you believe or as Lao Tzu said, 'Appear weak when you are strong and strong when you are weak'. They must be worried because they sure are putting on a display! It's an old trick and it's worked quite well until now. As such, we are caught in a language trap that underpins a zodiac trap with many layers and seemingly complex nuances but once you learn the basic symbolism and history, you'll look at and speak about the world and yourselves *totally differently*.

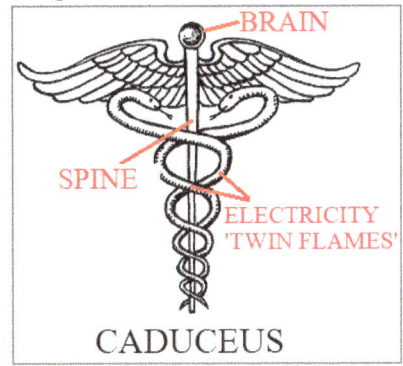

We've come full circle as we arrive back at the destination in that there was a civilisation(s) before ours every bit as advanced, maybe even more so, with staggering monuments and mind-blowing structures. Everyone knows about the legend of Atlantis, the 'lost city', *see*, the 2022 movie the *Lost City* as celebrities scramble to associate their icon with these ancient legends to position themselves in the 'new' zodiac cycle via the mass broadcast from unwitting human minds or the old adage, 'it's not *what* you are but what people THINK you are that matters'. In this ancient civilisation it was the Goddess, not god (small 'g'), who was the monotheistic deity worshipped by the people. At the very beginning of 'modern' civilisation found in ancient history, it was a goddess who gave these masculine civilisations the 'right' to exist *as required* in the founding lore of Rome, a lore that preceded them into the mystery of 'pre-history'. There is a lot of bullshit floating around about this ancient civilisation and most people, even researchers, choose to believe that our current society is the height of *millions of years* of human evolution. If that is true, then we are all done for because, quite frankly, our current state of being is rather pathetic! There's no evolution here just an endless duplication of old processes dressed up as 'new'. We are not living in a simulation although they have some pretty amazing 'virtual' methods to influence our reality. Our world does not exist somewhere else. If anything we have been severely limited in our ability to access our soul selves, our 'higher' self and vice versa that only shines through for *some* people when an *imminent* disaster is occurring. Our higher selves are screaming at us trying so desperately to get through, but we cannot hear us, we cannot see us. We are in lockdown in so many ways. It seems when humans reach a certain level of evolution some outside force, maybe from even outside our world, smashes us back to zero point to start over again. I have often mused that what if asteroids are the perfect weapon like a sort of cosmic gorilla warfare? A low-tech tactic to cause utter annihilation to entire world's without exposing the identities of hateful 'gods', off world advanced aliens, behind all this seeking to keep us prisoner on this island Earth. If this were true then it is genius. What if they are lobbing giant rocks at us from space to cause environmental destruction and mass extinction to force us to start again and again?

In the Balochistan province of Pakistan there are rock formations that have caused people from all over the world to pilgrimage to this region to see for themselves the incredible marvel of what has been termed (by Angelina Jolie of all people) *The Princess of Hope* as well as the nearby 'sphinx'. It bears a striking resemblance to the three pre-Islamic goddesses worshipped before the current male idols. The Princess of Hope and the Sphinx is located in the area of infamous Indus Valley Civilisation also called the Indus Civilisation lasting, they say, from 3,300 to 2,600BC and was the most widespread of three ancient civilisations including ancient Egypt. They spanned from Northeast Afghanistan and much of Pakistan to Western and Northwestern India

'PRINCESS OF HOPE' RESEMBLES PRE-ISLAMIC TRIPLE GODDESS & LION

BALOCHISTAN SPHINX

EGYPTIAN SPHINX

today. It's not hard to see that ancient borders of foundational civilisations have been eroded to create a sense of 'us and them' not only between the old people and current people, but across the perimeters of modern countries and cultures who have been made to slowly diverge as the human race evolves. It's just another way to keep us apart and keep us down. He Indus cities were known for sophisticated planning, housing, drainage and water supplies as well as industrial areas, handcrafts and metallurgy. These guys were seriously beautiful and evolved!

It's claimed, and I say claimed because there is always more to this, the Mehrgarh people were a farming people from 7000BC who took approximately two and half thousand years to become a 'ceramic' making society. Basically, they are saying they went from early food producing to the basic foundations of a society in 2,500 years. Bull. Shit. You can smell modern mainstream archeological obfuscation from miles away. Given the opportunity humans evolve in leaps and bounds and there appears to be an ardent attempt by the established forces of 'accepted' academic history to promulgate the idea that it takes eons for people to become even slightly civilized. Are we sick of this shit yet? The fact is, our DNA is *designed* to rapidly accelerate when cosmic alignments occur in conjunction with the galactic core where all information is housed. We're an antenna. It would be like if you didn't have the internet, then had the internet for a while, then didn't have the internet again. If you're smart, you'll learn while you've got it and put that knowledge to good use until the next time you get the internet.

Out of the Mehrgarh evolved the Harappan who created quite an impressive civilisation rivalling that of ancient Egypt. They flourished, all up, for over 6500 years until 600BC creating the Indus Valley Civilisation, a cultural and political state that flourished in the northern region of the Indian Subcontinent although little is known of their decline or why. So they say. There total population was thought to be around 5 million with cities of 50,000 people or more (more) and stretched from the banks of the Indus river in all outward directions their sites being located in Nepal, Afghanistan, and the coasts of India. It is thought that Northern Aryan people whose ethnicity is current day Iranian Persians, migrated south blending their cultures. A British soldier serving the East India Company, James Lewis, deserted with another soldier and in their travels, they discovered the site of Harrappa in 1829. James altered his name to Charles Masson and upon his return to England, he published a book called *Narrative of Various Journey's in Balochistan, Afghanistan and the Punjab* in 1842. When the British Raj took command in 1858, within three years they were excavating the site under the direction of British engineer Alexander Cunningham whose attention to this area was attracted by Masson's book nearly 20 years earlier.

RETURN OF THE TWINS

From 1904 the site was being fully excavated (Indiana Jones, hello?) and later surrounding sites revealed the Indus Valley Civilisation was part of three major ancient civilisations including Mesopotamia whose *earliest developments* occurred around 10,000BC in the Northern part of the Fertile Crescent - Sumer being their earliest known in 5,550BC. This whole region of civilisations and societies tracking alongside each other stretched from the Fertile Crescent in the West to the Caucasus mountains in the North to the Indus Valley in the East! It's interesting that this whole region was called Mesopotamia but as with Mesoamerica, the word 'meso' simply means 'middle' or 'intermediate period'. So, who came first given the accepted (even by their own narrow admission), officially recognized, civilised population of this region goes back to 10,000BC? It's because in the ten thousand years *prior* (up to 20,000BC) there was an even more ancient and likely MORE advanced civilisation the remnants of which can be found even today! You don't have to look far to see the legends spring to life especially when it comes to the relationship between men and women in Samina Quraeshi's book "Legends of the Indus Valley; Epic Tales of Love from the Indus Valley". This book is a compilation of poems and *oral histories* as told by native people passed down since time immemorial. The oral traditions of fables and story telling of historical accounts have been traced to prewritten languages up to 60,000 years old and beyond! We have a history that is being concealed from us and it is so rich and wonderful that we can hardly bear it! Even Nicola Tesla said his own father could recite the epic poems and entire books so that is the information was lost he could simply rewrite it word for word. The talent of memory has been lost to us.

The Vedas speak of ancient nuclear wars and technology that could melt or *dustify* anything it was beamed at, much like the exotic frequency weapons used on 9/11 as described by Dr. Jury Wood in her work "Where Did the Towers Go?" If you look at a really high-resolution image of the Princess of Hope it literally looks like it has been melted with clearly female attributes. In fact, the entire region looks like it has been melted from space with incredible cosmic weapons and is all that remains of a mind-boggling *prehistoric civilisation*, an intuitive fancy all but wiped from our collective memories and wiped off the face of the planet, only preserved in the most ancient of verbal myths. This civilisation occurred around 11,000 years ago or around 9,000BC. Then there is a great veil drawn across history as spoken of by many researchers throughout time including Manly P. Hall who said of the stupendous megalithic ancient stone monuments, "It is almost certain that the great ruins of Carnac in Brittany had some definite scientific or religious usage. These were built by persons *who already knew something*. They were not built by the Cro-Magnons but apparently, they were standing there *long before we come to this dark curtain that divides prehistory from history* as we know it now".

The ancient Greek poet Hesiod 750BC-650BC listed in his poem, Works and Days, a Golden Age that fell under the rule of Cronus who is today's Devil-Satan, an evil 'god' of 'time'. There are many legends worldwide that speak of a golden age that descended into a silver age then a bronze age until finally we reach the lowest age, *the Iron age*, that we *still* live under today in a 3rd Iron age that never seems to end having dragged it on far longer than necessary. we see the melted stone steps at the Temple of Hathor. The floor is not 'worn' down from thousands of years of human traffic, the stone is *clearly* melted into pools. What could do such a thing? Perhaps electromagnetic expert scientist John Hutchison could give us some ideas about *what* powerful electromagnetic forces might have melted stone as his laboratory experiments have created the *same effects* and seem to be the *same forces* utilised in the Nicola Tesla inspired Philadelphia Experiment that caused and entire naval ship to 'disappear' in 1943. What happened in ancient history that bears a striking resemblance to technology only just being rediscovered today and what threats does this present to us given what seems to have occurred last time this power was discovered? It appears an entire civilisation was melted from space and now we see Elon Musk's SpaceX program insisting on setting up 42,000 satellites orbiting Earth whose capabilities include *Direct Energy Weapons*. This is not my theory, this is an openly admitted fact on mainstream news channels and, as usual, it's the Russians and the Chinese, the usual suspects, causing the 'need' to have a rapidly accelerating 'star wars' program signed into law by Ronald Reagan in 1982 LONG BEFORE we could foresee the *purpose* of what they could be used for eliminating mass human life being *one* of those purposes! Werner Von Braun said the person to lead the Mars mission would be called 'Elon' this is because the ancient Satanic script calls for a lion king to lead the new space Age. Every age requires a sun king solar deity to kick it off and then it's business as usual. Elon is Hebrew for Leon and leon is lion. His mothers names is Maye Musk because the mother/wife effigy is Mary Magdalene and Mary was the mother of Jesus who was the Sun-Lion king of the last age. MM is simply Roman numerals for 2000, the year 2000 when the new space age was scripted to begin. Nest time you sing 'Noel, Noel, Noel, Noel born is the king of Israel' you are singing Leon, leon, leon or lion, lion, lion born is the sun-lion king of Israel as Leo the zodiac sign is a sun symbol his HAIR epitomizing the rays of the sun.

RETURN OF THE TWINS

But not only does there appear to have been a *massive attack* on the ancient world that plunged us back into a neanderthal like state, into a mysterious dark time that *no records* seem to adequately explain. It seems that similar if not *exactly the same* technology used to destroy the ancient world was also the same technology used by the ancient residents of those times to craft *incredible megalithic marvels* with such precision that engineers today openly admit we are yet to invent such wonders! Let's just say if you can carve the stone into beautiful artifices, then that same tech could easily be used to destroy it too. To the right we see Mount Kailesh in the remote southwest corner of Tibet in what appears to be the face of Shiva *quite clearly* depicted *somehow* in the face of the same mountain. Shiva means electricity. Or the *massive* OM symbol carved into the very mountain top only visible with snowfall. Perfection! How can we reconcile in our minds that this is even possible and yet *there it is before us*, undeniable! And yet they will deny it, *even still*, considering the information we have at hand about such things was handed to us by *none other* than scholars notorious for their affiliations with *secret societies* bent on hiding our historic greatness. So, why wouldn't the men in these secret clubs who have always harnessed the secret powers of

SHIVA FACE MT. KAILESH

Mt. KAILESH | OM SYMBOL

ROOT CHAKRA OM SYMBOL

the ancient world for themselves, who themselves are the SAME personality types who controlled the planet in vast empires throughout history, not *still* be accessing the same *secrets* today? These are the very secrets that warrant the title 'secret societies' successfully ruling over us *right now*. It is *absurd* to think they will tell you the truth if such truth exists. It is not in their benefit to empower you. They only seek to empower themselves. That is the way it has always been and that is the way it is today.

Why do people, even still, struggle with the idea that everything we have been told is a monumental lie given the current fallout of our world crumbling all around us for very flimsy reasons? Clearly, these men behind the scenes are not bothered by the failures of society and the planet in general or they would put a stop to it. When they want to act, they act fast and in surprisingly well coordinated structures, *see*, the Corona world shut down for your proof there. In fact, most if not all famous scholars of history are connected to the Masons and therefore, *by association* cannot be trusted to share the truth of our great past for fear of losing their footing of power over us in the future compulsive liars that they are. *See right*, the Naka Cave in Thailand that will make you wonder *just what* the hell the ancients were doing to create the anatomically perfect structure of an *enormous snake* carved in stone. It is so perfect some claim they are the *petrified remains* of giant people and creatures all since lost to folklore, myth and nonsensical legend. This 'prehistory' is retold in the epic trilogy *Lord of the Rings* spoon fed to us as 'fiction' once again steering us away from our greatness and what our ancestors were *really* doing. It is a secret so tremulous that our whole civilisation is built around *concealing it* and yet they can't keep it from us for much longer. So, *treacherous that they are!* They move on us like a thief in the night posing as our well-meaning *trustworthy* leaders *working hard* for your future in an increasingly difficult 'global village' mash up. Cowards!

NAKA CAVE MEGALITHIC SNAKE, THAILAND

Can we not look with our eyes at these structures and not bow to the 'ridiculous' notion that surely there *must have been* something in our history that was so marvelous and magical that those ancient people *deliberately* left tantilising evidence of the once great civilisation that went before us? Even today no scientist can tell you *how* or really *who* built the great pyramids of Giza with now the *totally absurd* notion that it couldn't have been humans, but increasingly 'academics' rather pass *our* achievements off to some ludicrous 'ancient alien' theory who they simultaneously claim don't exist. While beings from other places were most likely lurking around, as always, they were not then or now assisting us. It seems our self-esteem as a Human species has been so damaged and maligned that we could not imagine that *our ancestors* could do such incredible things given the *degraded state* we find ourselves in so many millennia later. The pyramids represent the male space program that came here and set up shop. It is a phallic symbol, a sword, and the pyramid aptly represents their 'fiery' nature as every planet they reach goes up in smoke. Where did evolution go? *See*, the Romanian 'Sphinx' whose proportions and directions are mathematically *practically impossible.* Why are people so disinterested in the power of our history? It's embarrassing that we have to put up with our own achievements being sideline in favour of some unknown 'other', an 'alien' 3rd party, 'ancient aliens', who repeatedly bashes us down and stands in our place. Could it be the same force destroying us today? See left, the sadly *devolving* state of a people's trying to recreate what their great ancestors were obviously capable of achieving and failing miserably. How sad. Or the Nazca lines, commonly referred to as 'airstrips' as some great ancient airport or space port *obviously* appears to show what was once a tarmac long since removed or eroded

ROMANIAN SPHINX

NAZCA LINES 'AIRPORT'

away. No one even really knows to this day what they are for, who built them, when they were built or by what means they were constructed with some mountains having their entire tops apparently sheared off only, there is *no rubble* in the valley below so where is it all? As with so much of the ancient world that could fill *many books* with the unknowns of a civilisation that seems to have predated ours by *at least* ten thousand years, it all just simply disappeared. It's unfathomable that we could be so blind to it all. It's as if they laugh at us by the magnitude of their absence. Who were they and as a result, who are we?

You may say I'm a dreamer, but I'm not the only one.

TIME IS A LIE

There is no such thing as eons and ages, only, one continuous calendar that spans ten to thirty thousand years.

We are living in times that require great maturity, responsibility and courage as the lies and the 'solid' ground of all we thought we knew drummed into our heads by an establishment reliant on our ignorance and weakness, falls apart *by the day*. Predictably the 'teachers pets', the average minded who blindly believe their Dr's advice, who queue in the rain to vote, who make sure they log their toilet breaks at work, who feel 'good' when they shop, who watch the six o'clock news for their information on reality, who diligently take their pills, get their 'shots' and 'abide' by an obviously Satanic society as they inch ever closer to a premature death, lampoon and laugh at the 'idiot fringe' for daring to suggest there is any *malice* or *design* in our apparent fate. We need strong people now, centered, fair, and not emotionally involved in the trickery and scandal. People who can separate from the psycho vortex and rationally deduce a safe path out of the nightmare house of mirrors we find ourselves in. Those who wish to be guided by these rare leaders will themselves find a way out while not bowing down to anyone when the information doesn't fit. There are not many of these truly special people around at this time while the chemically lobotimised abound in all directions and it's no coincidence.

Once again, I will keep this short and to-the-point and if you require a deeper perspective on these subjects, read my previous books *2020 & Beyond - This is Not a Drill* as well as *Rosestorm - Return of the Feminine* and you will find a *much deeper* insight into how all this works. I intend to keep this book short with easy-to-read large text as most of you have been poisoned to the hilt and are in a horrible brain fog induced by all the toxins you willingly let them inject into and prescribe for you as well as a whole range of hidden poisons in everything from water to food to air but then they are trying to stop the ascension. Sufficient to say, the Nazi war machine is in full swing as we speak. The reality of this is unfolding all around us to the point that it is being broadcast *on a daily basis* posing as the Hollywood magic machine along with all their mind-controlled dolls who project images of a historic and mythological story that their class have been worshipping and playing out *repeatedly* for thousands of years and it's reaching its peak *right now*. In fact, I am beginning to think that the entire calendar was altered to fit with the *never-before-seen cosmic alignments* happening *now!* There are some researchers who believe 300 years was added to the calendar to align us perfectly with the UNPRECENTED planetary and cosmic alignments that occurred in the year 2020.

In ancient times the god was always accompanied by the goddess regardless of which side of the ocean you were from. The deities often consisted of 6 males and 6 females and were depicted as husband and wife or 'brother and sister' as all humans are 'family'. As there were 12 major constellations, they were simply highlighting that the male and female are electrical forces with two polar opposites and each constellation has a 'mate', a companion, as do humans. The Roman Catholic Church were not the first to amalgamate the 'gods'. Egyptian pharaoh Akhenaten (his earlier name being Amenhotep) reigning from 1351BC-1334BC, attempted to amalgamate the gods into one god but his son, Tutankhamun revoked this decree restoring the former gods. Glad you could oblige, Tut, because...god/s....are all powerful and stuff. They're lucky to have you. Arguments aside of whether Constantine was a converted Christian or Baptised on his deathbed or even after death, he is credited with endorsing the ONE god model. The fact is he was the last Roman Emperor and the first Catholic Pope cited with having officially done away with the 'pagan' gods in favour of Jesus Christ being god born into a man and therefore one 'god'. Then or now, they couldn't say 'the Devil' is 'god' as human's, despite our stupidity, simply wouldn't have it certainly not out in the open like that. People would never admit to worshipping Satan because, again, despite our stupidity, we do not intrinsically identify with darkness because we KNOW we are from the light. So, they had to sell you the Devil as Jesus. It's no secret that the crimes carried out by the Catholic church are not representative of the teachings Jesus supported. So therefore, they sold you the Devil, told you it was Jesus, and they represent him as 'god' and the rest, as they say, is history.

Guys like Keanu Reeves associate their icon with this pope-king, priest-king, in their movies called 'Constantine' about demons etc., because that's what's behind all this. A-listers are 'light kings' who have opened their third eye chakra via tantric sex and, as did all kings who went before them, they 'fuse' their image with the 'sun' god as a declaration to the tantra club that they have attained enlightenment and are now a 'king' or even a 'god'. This process makes you into a virtual living god with incredible abilities to transcend the time-space matrix of 3D delusion and become 'omnipresent' or godlike, with incredible psychic abilities and what not. Whether we like it or not, Constantine was the first pope, and it was sometime in the 4th century approximately 350 years after Jesus was martyred-assassinated, that one god was declared and anyone who didn't worship the one god or continued to worship the old gods were tortured and killed. It was basically open season on anyone who wasn't onboard with the 'new age' program, *much like today*. Given the calendar is based on when Jesus was born and died, then the *current date* is based on these highly significant dates from 2,000 years ago. A zodiac Age last 2,150 years so, it looks like they ADDED three hundred years to fit the calendar with the current emerging Age of Aquarius, with the year 2020 and with the *2,000th anniversary* of Jesus's death in 2033. They did this to fit with galactic timeframes heralding the coming of a new age which really means a shitload of alignments during which, like antennas with a clear line of transmission to a satellite dish, our DNA antenna picks up on 'intuitive' knowledge broadcast from the universe and the true nature of our power and importance is 'remembered' because the galactic core is a big brain where all information is housed and no matter how much lies and evil is dumped on top of it, when the alignments occur *the truth manifests*. It's like watching a shitty tv channel of pop culture garbage and every now and then the BIG TV IN THE SKY manages to get a signal through and broadcast Truth TV for those who are willing to tune in. Sometimes the signals are so strong that all other channels get blocked out and only one broadcast is occurring no matter what channel you tune into or where you go as is happening now at the end of this massive cycle.

This is why covid deaths numbered '33' all over the world and people are saying 'why is 33 everywhere' well, this is to encode that the tantric spine of 33 vertebrae and the christ crown who died at '33' at the top of the spine, is symbolically destroyed in our hearts and unwitting minds to send the message to the galactic core that '33 is dead' here and there is no more 33 awakening for humans. Once the damage is done to people, you will find all the 'shiny happy people holding hands' and 'we're all in this together' woke psychological warfare goes out the fucken window and you're on your own. This is why throwing out old school practicality and pragmatic progress in favour of the 'new age' touchy-feely shit is really dangerous. The Devil was said to have people in their emotions in the end. There are a few things that has gotten the human race to this point; not trusting authorities being number one, family and community are really your only hope and lastly don't mess with the natural processes of your body and go to mother nature when there is illness or injury - she will see you right. Oh, and beware of strangers bearing gifts. The various pharmaceutical brands for the covid 'vaccines' are an experimental roll out to see which ones work the best and go undetected the longest as basically in the next few years we will be seeing the rise of the first morbidly mutated people that will make your blood run cold. Weird 'fungal spaghetti' and, *literally*, mushroom type organisms that grow on their own after being extracted are being pulled out of people's dead bodies just a year after being injected and these things are growing so fast that if they can do that in a year, wait for the next ten years to be truly horrified at the freakish mutations you will be soon witnessing.

Not everyone is getting the same stuff injected in these vials of Nazi psycho bio-warfare. Some vials will contain straight up poison, some will contain mutating alien viruses, some will contain the 'razor' graphene particles, some will simply be saline, some will be nutrients as some people report even feeling *better* after a vaccine, they just got a vitamin B shot, lucky them. This is, as is all their operations, multi-pronged with multiple objectives. Operation Warp Speed is obviously a reference to Star Trek as we are SUPPOSED to be stepping into a star trek type reality or at least have that technology *by now*. So, they are coding that our 'Star Trek' future is basically a horrible nightmare pandemic while they ramp up THEIR private *corporate* space program in the weird role out of Space Force and SpaceX Star Link at that same time. So, the elite get a space age, but the humans don't. It's the big separation as there can be only one so, they set up everyone else, kill them, and promote their own. This is happening *now* as we wake up by the dray loads and the controllers struggle to keep a lid on the truth shit-storm upon us as we speak. This knowledge is encoded in our DNA and activated when signals from the core switch on and start the reactor, Quaid! And yes, the figurative mining company of users and abusers will send their goons to head us off at every turn but the power waves of light just keep on coming as more people than ever before push knowledge out into the sludge swamp of falsity attempting to pass itself off as the real deal and becoming increasingly more desperate to shut it all down before they are washed away by waves, a tsunami, of truth, light and righteousness. But they *can't* shut it down and are starting to realise that no matter which way they turn there is another book, another documentary, another person who suddenly realises the big picture and kicks them is the spiritual balls for their lies and cruelty toward us. So, they either go down with a sinking ship or at least *pretend* to join the truth avalanche to save themselves long enough to find another way to get back into control again *down the track.*

Michael Tsarion, one of the most credible researchers in my top three of David Icke, Jordon Maxwell and Tsarion. He also agreed that it was at least possible that altering the calendar was true and who is going to tell otherwise? Who was there? Is anyone BUT THEM, the dark priesthood, keeping any records on the history of the world? Many ordinary people over the eons, just like today, have tried to expose the truth burying scrolls in terracotta jars in caves only to have them miraculously be found *just before* the new Zodiac age and coming 'new' christ. So, clearly, it mattered dearly to them to try and contribute to the overarching story instead of just having a bunch of demonically possessed priesthood misfits tell us how it goes. It does make a kind of sense as the Emerging new solar male-default civilisation is riding on the backs of the knowledge gained from ancient Egypt who were themselves riding on the backs of knowledge garnered from the destroyed Atlantis who some claim was a city but I believe was the advanced global civilisation *at the time* that reached a pinnacle of technological and spiritual power that rivalled 'the gods' who are an offworld alien empire managing planets like Earth in a far reaching syndicate harvesting worlds of their natural resources. The information was nearly lost in other words and threads and fragments of the knowledge of the internal 'Christ' functions of the human chakra body enlightenment capabilities survived just enough for them to create the rather amazing but somewhat less impressive multi eon society of Ancient Egypt and what a sight to behold it would have been! But although they may have kept the tantric sex chakra activation alive for themselves and shamed and sullied sex for everyone else in an audacious diabolical manoeuvre to psychologically control ordinary people preventing them from the wonders of what can be achieved via sex, they may not have retained enough information to understand he full breadth of the Zodiac implications that stretches over *tens of thousands of years*, hence when they realised they were not going to align themselves with the next age and all the obsessive compulsive fakery it potentially holds, they jumped the gun. They added three hundred years to the calendar to fit with the alignments to make sure that all the numerology was encoded at this time with simultaneous rituals and secret assassination happening BY THE DAY to feed the energetic links to the galactic core and install their new 'god' who is ABSOLUTELY the devil in disguise, the Anti-Christ, to control the new age! It's their wet dream in the flesh. Maybe they can all fuck each other in a big gay demonic orgy slathering up the physical pleasures in a fit of lust in a big celebration of an alien sexual extravaganza. Once again, they are not 'gay' the way ordinary people are gay. These creatures just want a body and can morph any human being into a twisted all-in-one ghoul from the depths of hell carrying out a weird parody human behaviour's just to experience the physical and spew their poison on anyone who will indulge them.

The current Age of Aquarius, the 12th gate in the *PRECESSION* (backwards) of the zodiac given every zodiac age lasts 2,150 years, indicates that this whole cycle is 26,000 years if we take the 12 zodiac signs into account. You might think this is not an exact figure but remember, the Age of Aquarius is only just *starting*. Therefore, there are 2,150 years in the coming age before the full process is finally complete when we will enter the Age of *Sagittarius*. So, what they do is tack on the extra 150 years because it takes about that long to *formally* cross over from the old age into the new age. Therefore, 12 x 150 years is 1800 years bringing us right smack bang on 26,000 years with a couple hundred years spare to snip here and there like the 300 years they added to the calendar 2,000 years ago. It's all in movies that, if you follow the broader narrative of major actors, is telling you a much bigger picture. There are movies within a 'big' movie that span many movies. It's about themes. As such, you've got to remember, zero isn't an actual number, it means nothing, which is why it takes a whole year before you get 'year one'. Year one didn't start on the first day of the year. Year ONE occurs when the first *whole year* is complete. The same goes for 100 and 1000 which is why even though, for example, the century of the 1900's is called the 20th century because there was one hundred years at the beginning of it all that occurred *in full* before you

could even count off 'one century'. Zero inflates numbers even though in and of itself it is technically nothing. So, even though it's 2000 years, it's the twenty FIRST century because one happened at the outset of the calendar to initiate the time frame in question. This is why this new age is particularly important as depicted by the Satanic 666 because 999 is actually the 'zero' point of the first millennium until it ticks over into 1000. This is why they consider that when 9 ticks over to 10, it's actually just going back to 1 again hence, the *repetitive* nature of their civilisations with males ruling, endless wars and destroying mother nature for fake money. It's *one* big fake civilisation and when we are supposed to reach the end of it and MOVE ON or EVOLVE, they simply switch us back to year one again and we go around and around and around ad infinitum. That's because the darkness doesn't evolve as it doesn't reflect light so it can only get so far before it has to go back to the beginning again whereas humans who do reflect light can evolve to the umpteenth most incredible levels of the cosmic-spiritual game FOREVER and they simply cannot keep up with that so crash us back down as happened to Atlantis, Egypt, Ancient Phoenicia, Ancient Greece, Ancient Rome (currently resetting that one for their next fake man 'Christ' character and new civilisation), the Aztecs, the Assyrians, the Acadians, Minoans and ALL THE SOCIETIES OF MYTH AND LEGEND that actually once existed GLOBALLY. Only, like what is happening to us now, they were smashed back to ZERO POINT, plunged into ignorance and darkness again and again and could never quite get over the line into the new cycle of LIGHT and EXPANSION. It's a program, a big alien satanic demonic space program, that has been playing out here on Earth for up to 30,000 years which actually isn't that long when you really consider it.

Every movie and major event are a *symbolic ritual* and shows they must be getting desperate as they code it by the day now in the hopes of holding of the inevitable. Like the queen 'dying' on 8/9 at 96 so, the 'queen' of Earth, the effigy 'goddess', 'died' at on the eve of 99 because we never make it over the line and start a new cycle. It's why Betty White (Snow White), her middle name 'Marion' for Maid Marian, died at 99 on New Year's Eve 2021 because the 'white' maiden of purity doesn't get over the line into 2022 the year of the big showdown between men, women and the demon male, the devil, this is another take on the 'trinity' and the light and dark side of all three, the '11'. It won't take much now to knock them off course and shows that however powerful they portray themselves to be they are indeed fragile to warrant such excess. Indeed, the motto of the Israeli secret service, the MOSSAD, is 'make war by deception'. War against who you might ask? War against *you* and the destiny you are promised from a galaxy far greater than any machine they can create.

Nazis are like herpes. Just when you thought you got rid of them, they spring up again. You might think the Nazis and Israel have nothing in common however, they are playing out a script that says the end times will occur when Jews return to Israel. Coincidentally, once they got done with the Nazi distraction of WWII, the winners carved up that region and gave it back to the Jews thus heralding the beginning of the biblical prophecies...but they're surely not complicit in a diabolical plan to create the 'anti-christ' or anything like that. The terrible plan for the human race incorporates all their favourite methods of hate which encompasses biological warfare or, sorry to say, the rising number of LGBT 'gender confused' people and in the near future, the new 'mutant' strains of people about to be introduced to the world as genetically modified 'vaccines' rewrite our DNA and Humanity are increasingly morphed into a new ugly species downgraded by these alien pathogens created by the Satanic establishment injected people under the guise of 'health'. Roll up! Roll up! Roll up your sleeve! One of the theories put forward to explain the inordinate and ever-growing number of 'gender confused' or 'nonbinary' phenomenon is that in one particular 'cell line' of vaccines, WI-38, contains female aborted fetal material used to cultivate pathogens (viruses) in vaccines. This female biological material already carries two X chromosomes and is being injected into male babies some of whom have XXY syndrome possessing two X chromosomes and a third *weak* Y chromosome. Males born with XXY syndrome can experience delayed puberty, smaller penis and testicles, infertility and other symptoms like a sort of naturally occurring biological eunuch. As such, an overload of X chromosome introduced via vaccines with certain 'cell lines' containing female biological material is said to explain some of the gender identity issues or males 'identifying' as females as they are receiving an extra Y chromosome when they *already* possess an existing weak Y chromosome. Similarly, MRC-5 is the code given to the 'cell lines' of viruses cultivated in male aborted fetal material in vaccines culminating in females identifying as males although this not as prevalent due to the already existing two X chromosomes. They are then getting an extra X and Y chromosome so the effect is not as all-consuming yet could explain the growing trend of 'bi' sexuality in women. The media, entertainment and political juggernauts then 'celebrate' and write into law that this biological *experiment*, a Nazi wet dream, is punishable as 'hate' crimes and 'discrimination' if one suggests that there might be something evil behind all this which means the people suffering from various 'identity' related gender crises are actually the victims of a mass medical *crime* deliberately perpetrated against them for social engineering purposes to bring about the biblical end times or the 'Apocalypse' in all its variant chaotic forms. Even still, people are like guinea pigs willingly waltzing off the spiritual cliff face like intellectual Disney lemmings. That is why the elite science masterminds hate you so much as most people let them experiment freely on their beautiful human bodies. Predictably, many young and middle-aged people alike are regretting their gender reassignment surgery and major damage caused to their bodies from botched operations and ongoing surgeries and courses of ongoing pharmaceuticals required to keep it all in place. Let's just say the difference between a biological man and woman and trans 'men' and 'women' is that externally introduced pharmaceuticals and medical procedures are not part of the natural processes of Mother Nature. Pill are not required to be *either* gender in the natural world and without these synthetics one's gender would simply be confirmed at birth whether they liked it or not. It is a matter of fact that 80% of children who identify as the opposite sex in childhood will identify with their birth gender by the time they reach adulthood. The gender crowd often speak of their 'traumas'. Fantasising about being another person is often a way of escaping brutality experienced as a child. By 'becoming' someone else, one can erase themselves and the pain associated with the 'other' person they once were who experienced such things. It's a form of dissociation. It's actually very sad. That said as ancient Greek 'fabulist' and storyteller Aesop philosophized "Those who cry the loudest are not always the ones who are most hurt".

It appears the majority of people waving around their university degrees make up the numbers of those most deeply in denial about our collective plight and let's not mention that Universities and schools are *lowering* their academic requirements as people are simply not able to pass exams as well as people did even twenty years ago. What's done is done. We can try to come back from it but for many, I'm sorry to say, I find it difficult to see this dumbing down being rectified as long as people *refuse* to understand that they are under a *coordinated* attack from a third party posing as your friends. I can assure you the establishment are not injecting *their* kids. Most people cannot compute this information because despite the very fancy pieces of paper they get from distinguished 'learned' institutions, they seem to have not read a single book on history or even watched a documentary on past events. Either that or they are simply *too naïve* and unworldly to see that the *same* people running the world today are the *same* people who were running the world 50, 100, 250 and 1,000 years ago. Otherwise, it seems their characters are just weak, and they will do what they are told like good little children of god. The modus operandi and the criminal profile of the ambitious elite remains the *same* today as repeated throughout history ad infinitum and could explain why some of us who have seen this before in many lives simply have a natural adverse reaction to their weird elite presence in our midst.

All the craziness is coming from the *same* mentality, the *same* psychological profile, the *same* personality types, *the same people, the same class* and the *only* constant in *every one* of these social upheavals throughout history and it is the bloody-minded aristocracy! Plainly put, they want this planet for themselves and the sooner you own up to that little fact the more likely it is you will survive, and even thrive, through this shit storm. Today's youth are in the cross hairs of this demonic plan to reroute the natural path of Human evolution and biological warfare is being injected into them via the convincing mode of 'inoculations' genetically rewriting and downgrading the future generations of the human race. It's the island of Dr. Moreau and in time we will learn just how they did it, how they contaminated the vaccines with all manner of elements and biological material from cats, rats, dogs, monkeys - aliens – no wonder people are identifying as 'trans' animals among other things. Chemical warfare is also being introduced via vaccines as well as prescription drugs for all manner of previously unseen 'behavioural' problems in children, the next generation, who are being chemically lobotimised at the *exact same time* an electromagnetic shift elevates our consciousness via frequencies being broadcast from the black hole sun at the centre of the galaxy. Psychological warfare is the 'vehicle' by which this lunacy is being introduced in the unending 'advertising' and 'marketing' campaigns promoting these 'health' methods as 'the answer'. You're a bad person, even dangerous, if you don't go along with it! In keeping with the looming dystopia the bad and increasingly criminal behaviour of children will lead to military style schools to control them and humanity will breath a sigh of relief as corporal punishment and 'boarding' schools are created to stem the tide of uncontrollable kids. Once again, they will get you to celebrate your enslavement as you encourage the harsh treatment of children as 'when I was a kid' dad would 'give us a hiding' if we did what these kids do. They set you up. They knock you down. You will want these prison schools and even applaud those who bring them in. The damage is done with poisons and pharmaceuticals and now the kids need to be controlled the hard way.

Police routinely fired on unarmed civilians worldwide in the wake of the uprisings against forced injections - mandatory vaccinations - despite these unprecedented medical mandates having *very little information* on the harmful effects they induce. The system even *breaks their own rules* and conventions on the 'safe' time frame to trial these drugs and dosage amounts before being used on humans. The reason they have been poisoning the water supply with fluoride for fifty years is because it makes you slow and foggy. When you are clear headed and energized you stand in your 'power' and have 'conviction'. Even unlawful or unfair sentences in court (*royal court*, you are present at the discretion of the king) are passed down without a second thought because they have the numbers, they have the power, they have the 'system' behind them and therefore, they have 'conviction' which is why they 'convict' you and a prisoner is called a 'convict'. It's their conviction not yours. When you take their drugs and injections without reading the insert, which is your lawful right to do, you are agreeing to trust the word of the salesperson, in this case the doctor, who, like a car salesperson, will sell you a lemon if you don't read the fine print or negotiate a different contract. This is why they have a clause in their 'terms and conditions' on their website or in the insert and it does not allow you to sue them for injury caused because you agreed to their contract by simply allowing yourself to be injected in the first place. When they decide to pay out a few cases, they do this at *their discretion* and only, really, to keep the falsehood of the system lie alive long enough to 'close the deal' on the whole world. Most people have no recourse and cannot sue. It is a corruption clause they place in every transaction you make with them and means that a contract can be 'wholly implied' simply because you went along with it and in many ways just by being 'present' at the injection station. *You* are the present, you give yourself freely.

When you are born you are 'berthed' and 'dock' at the 'port' in the 'canal' this is when your umbilical cord is 'docked' (cut) at the umbilical 'port' (belly button) from the 'birth canal' where the *cargo* 'berths'. Your berth certificate is simply a delivery docket, a notification of trade that a transaction has been made as you are on their turf, in their hospital, with their staff. This is why babies were born in the home and old people died in the home. Home is where the heart is. Home is mother, it is the church, Mary is the church, it is sanctuary and why they must go to all manner of lengths to get the proper paperwork and 'right' to enter, to cross the threshold of your property, to enter your territory without their own *passport*. A 'writ' or a 'court order' is a 'temporary visa' to cross your borders and it is under strict conditions to do so. These 'rights' to enter are being eroded by the day and now they just storm in without reason because people don't know the WHOLE SYSTEM is based on a facsimile of the REAL SYSTEM which is MOTHER EARTH and NATURAL LAW RIGHTS also called 'COMMON LAW' as it makes 'common sense' to 99% of the population called the 'common man'. You shouldn't need a university degree to understand the law. It's all fake. This is why 'births, deaths and marriages' are lumped in together because your 'birth' registers you as an up-and-coming trader, your death dissolves your entity as a business and your marriage is a *merger between two businesses*. Thanks to increasing prices of PRIVATE BUSINESS once owned by the government and thus the people, households are now *nothing but a business* and one must run it as a business or go broke. They are eroding your natural law position and replacing it with corporate terms and conditions. Once a generation or two is born into the 'new world' or corporate terms and conditions, you will not have natural common law rights to fall back on. This berth certificate, an inventory receipt, it is your 'ticket' into the false system that duplicates as the real system of mother earth - a *bountiful* world abundant with 'trade' products found in her minerals, land, trees, animals. It's all up for grabs. Only, who has the right to trade it? Who has the right to buy and sell it?

Oaky, so, this is how it works and how they get away with it.

'They' are an alien trade empire of merchants and your registration at berth is your inventory receipt, proof of purchase, as you are 'leased' to them for the duration of your childhood. It is proof you were delivered, you have arrived, and not in a good way. You are moveable trade, you are cargo, nothing but a passenger on a ship given a 'ticket to ride', to pass the port of the dock (they put prisoners in the 'dock') just like immigration processes people with a *passport* to navigate the 'port' of the berth canal where the 'ships' dock. The mother ship is your biological carrier, your *mother*, who has more power over this situation than anyone else and why they hate her so much. Ships are referred to as 'she' even today. This pass-port, berth certificate, allows you to enter the 'country' where you are born and trade in a *merchants market* called the 'system' in the 'world'. It is a big processing unit using phonetics to get you to agree to a *counterfeit* world, a facsimile of the real world, that only *they* know how to 'navigate'. But you are never taught how to trade and therefore are ripped off at every turn even selling your body, even worse than a prostitute, and giving away your health which is a gift from the universe. Your light is your currency and how much light you have will depend on the value they place on you.

You were first traded on the 'stock' market – stock is cattle – by your parents who agreed to enter you into their learning institutions, school (fish are a school), in the *current* sea or the 'current' trading system called 'currency'. They were supposed to teach you how to trade but they don't want you knowing how to trade! How ridiculous to teach you how to play their game?! It explains why the school system is a joke and people know nothing when they enter the trading world after twelve years of school. When you get a Tax File Number or Business Number you agree trade with the 'system' as an adult then. You're on your own. This is why PARENTS are the custodian, the OWNERS, the *charge*, in charge of their offspring because CHILDREN are not old enough to trade on their own and cannot be charged of their light on their own. But the *parents* have the right to allow their children to be charged, robbed of their light, and yet they can refuse the charge, *the price*, against their children's health via so many pills and vaccines. Children cannot barter with their life under these 'mandates' to 'trade' with the system and so their parents do it for them.

RETURN OF THE TWINS

This is why one is 'charged' when they are 'appear' in court like an apparition. They are 'appearing' because the real person is absent, they are an emanation, a trader, presenting on behalf of the earthly person who has the real value inside their body found in their light. When you trade with the system you are agreeing to do business with the 'world', a false economic system that sees YOU as the product who is given permission via various 'licenses' to trades inside its 'universe'. This is the construct, it is another form of the 'matrix', a series of numbers and transactions of products only. In leaving the mother ship and coming 'onboard' the big fake ship of the economy that is *patently* stealing from this planet, you are accepting their empire over you and become ANOTHER passenger onboard ANOTHER ship but it's not the natural ship, it's not your mother and it's not MOTHER Earth either. You become nothing more than an automaton, a robot, without natural law rights. Trade.

When you are clear of poisons and toxins that sap your energy, *your power, your light* - you are in a 'sovereign' state of mind. You become your own country. You are lawful land, territory – MADE OF CLAY – as the Bible puts it, made of EARTH, made of soil or matter as matter is *mater* Latin for *Mother*, and soul the ethereal – *AEHTER* – the fifth element, life force, light, chi, prana – the animating force that animates your 'vehicle' - your body in the 'matrix' which also means MOTHER, the universe!! The original word 'matrix' refers the *uterus* and refers to a situation or set of conditions in which something forms. When you are from your mother, you are whole and complete. They then commence to separate you from the mother in every way, we are not connected to the Earth. They siphon your light as this is all you have of value to them. If they invade your territory, your body, they have declared war against you plain and simple and war *requires the right* to defend your territory. But if you don't even know you have territory then they can walk all over it, all over you, and plunder it as they see fit. And they do. When I worked in corporate, we had commissionable targets and I saw people routinely doing reprehensible things like forging signatures on contracts, altering dates of contracts to be more recent or simply making up numbers to claim sales had been made that were not made in order to meet their targets and get their commission. I realised then that it was only a matter of time before the whole economic framework of the worlds' trading system would crash as people are being paid for jobs that have not been done with money that does not exist, credit. A bubble that was designed to burst. But when you have bills to pay, and you don't know how to trade properly, then you are reduced to lying and cheating which then further nullifies your sovereign position of power. You sell yourself out. You have no 'conviction' to 'stand' on - *no foundation*. People fighting for their 'rights' have simply misunderstood the contract. Which is why human rights are routinely trampled on. You don't have any. Any business claiming to be a charitable 'foundation' is posing as a *person* and it's all donations then! Untaxed! What a lark! The whole thing is lies. Maybe I should declare my body a charitable foundation and only accept donations? From cradle to grave the system you think you are engaging with and the world you think you are living in is a *phonetically induced* neuro-linguistic con job of 'permissions' cleverly acquired via trickery and a deep knowledge of natural law, universal law, and the rights of the individual - the *stand-alone* sovereign nation of you. It's all about sound which is why when something is good it is considered to be 'sound'. Even while trying to write this suddenly my word doc doesn't respond, suddenly I cannot save what I have written, low flying helicopters suddenly fly overhead – I mean it's a fucking shemozzle being a targeted individual due to all this but then they play dirty. But that doesn't mean they're *right* or have *rights* and it doesn't mean their day isn't coming. It is.

So, the thinking is to shoot people with bullets who refuse the 'shot' and 'get' shot anyway because it's about health. Sigh. You're gonna get shot either way, apparently. That's called *Satanic* thinking. It's a Satanic system. 'If you don't take my dubious injections that will hurt you, I'll shoot you and hurt you anyway...because it's about health'. They really put the 'Hell' in 'health'. Even the dumbest people are finding it difficult not to notice that something is up. As such, it's imploding all around us as the minds of strugglers, particularly law enforcement, sink into a confusion from which they may never arise. Often armed to the teeth, these idiots are unleashing weapons on the general public they swore to protect and in a few years' time they will apologise and say they thought they were 'helping' and were only 'doing our job'. But when it comes to their turn, the same establishment that told them it was okay to shoot people for not getting injected is now telling *them* they will be *fired* for not getting injected too! Suddenly, lo! A turnaround of sentiment as the police *themselves* refuse mandatory vaccinations they were shooting other people from *different industries* into taking! Hypocrites. They even put forward a very formal young police officer to say that he'd resigned over the harsh treatment of people and that he had told them of his disappointment...and they were sorry and willing to change. Nice try. They are only willing to change *after* they realise THEY ARE NOT GOING TO BE PROTECTED FROM THE SAME SYSTEM THAT IS DESTROYING EVERYONE ELSE. So, now we're friends again.

RETURN OF THE TWINS

Only *now* the Australian public eye the police forces with the lack of trust and betrayal they deserve. Safety in numbers, guys, you might want to remember that next time your senior managers tell you to *shoot people* at the Shrine of Remembrance. People can get a little toey when you piss on the graves of their war dead many still within *living* memory. You and your officers are just as expendable as everyone else. There is no team. The MACHINE is carrying out directives that will ensure a certain outcome and EVERYONE is mincemeat, *everyone* expendable. It's the Masonic 'great work' as the end looms into view. There's always an enemy whether black or non-conformists or women – there's always an enemy – and that 'enemy' will be allowed to join the club whenever they see fit to placate the masses that 'we're inclusive now', we're evolving. If you don't like it, *you* become the enemy no matter how loyal you have been to the cause and the club. The devil is a traitor, it makes no bones about that. Whatever it takes is what it takes. As a result, court cases abound, medical injuries abound and new strains of all sorts of illness are springing up in the most recent round of coercion. *Children* are being injected as previously unseen cases of Hepatitis appear in the kids who've received the 'vaccine'. Great. Everything is going as planned then? I must also mention the rather obvious 'spiritual warfare' leaving people conflicted about their beliefs, who they are, and what is happening here as more people return to conventional religions (rather outdated belief concepts) to find their 'faith'. Holy fuck. We're also engaged in a societal 'asymmetric warfare' or what is commonly termed 'gorilla' warfare or 'low tech' attacks in the guise of rage filled people from diametrically opposed cultures or just jacked up psychos as we see the first generation of all things vaccine related as well as pills, chiefly Ritalin, among other hard core pharmaceuticals that have been deployed on the most recent generation as psychopathic behaviour rises among the young who were the promise of so much. Talk about a 'new hope', the next generation are all but destroyed before our eyes. Sad.

So, there are two things happening now, there are 'random' attacks on shoppers and commuters in broad daylight with any weapon at hand, cars, axes, kitchen knives! The offenders are now being labelled as having a 'mental illness' because it's 'not' about religion or *assimilation* and/or appropriate levels of immigration and/or assistance programs to identify people who are a risk to themselves and others. You wouldn't ever put someone on a probationary basis until they are more comfortable with their new country and/or proved themselves, or even, shock horror, not allow *some* of them in *at all* based on the fact that they may be, for example, a war criminal as discovered in Torquay in Melbourne when an African

RETURN OF THE TWINS

war general responsible for genocide moved his family to one of the fanciest suburbs in the world no doubt on the funds pillaged from his many victims living it up by the seaside with all the Western trimmings. Checking their past would be 'racist' and a 'hate crime', and 'hate speech' to even discuss measures to prevent religious-cultural-social clash when the old world meets the new world. It's not even the 'old' world, just one intimidating group's distorted version most likely under Western satanic agency mind control to achieve all this.

It's not about race *at all* given many people from the same faith can easily and happily reside in the West without feeling the need to behead someone in public. I can see how the West could be quite confronting to some people given *some* of them have only seen a woman in large tent-like coverings so, unsurprisingly, sunbathing women in bikinis on the beach might be a little more than some dullards are able to cope with. Hilariously (not for the victims), a judge let off a pervert because he claimed he didn't know he wasn't allowed to sexually assault women in bikinis because in his country it would be allowed given their attire...and he was let off! You don't have to be a genius to see that *no other men* were sexually assaulting women on the beach that day so,

IRAN 1960'S

AFGHANISTAN 1960's-70's

why did this particular man think it was okay for him to do it? This tells me that the system *itself* is engaged in a covert attack against women and children using 'cultural sensitivity' and 'tolerance' as the excuse to allow criminals to get away with despicable crimes because, *that* is what Satanism is all about – unleashing chaos. It wasn't that long ago that the most stringent areas of the Middle East were just like the West with women wearing miniskirts, going to university and driving cars alongside a very *normal* emerging masculine community who were *not threatened* by this at all.... but the 'Taliban'...but 'ISIS'. You don't get to say 'religion' or 'culture' when you hurt someone, okay? The moment you let 'religion' or 'culture' pass your lips by way of a personal acquittal for injuring another person, you become a non-entity in the most lame sense. Attempting to enroll others in your *self*-worship and personal appointment as 'god' over another person unable to defend themselves against you, is equal in criminality to the actual crime. Ego is a lesson in how quickly we can devolve if we tolerate the intolerant.

The Western model for society is the most popular model so far in Earth's history and has spread so fast that underdeveloped regions who seek to have the security and cleanliness of the West along with all the creature comforts, conform their societies in with the most stringent administrations. And to keep up a semblance of normality, many harsh administrations have given in to public pressure to allow their society to more resemble the open markets of the West, particularly America. As such, the dark masters behind the scenes had to nip the Western model in the bud in order to keep a legion of nut cases on standby for future purpose if their plans didn't pan out as expected. Sure enough, they're using these mentally deficient turds to carry out 'hysteria' operations on decent people evolving into a balanced normal reality. They just can't let it go, they MUST perpetrate horrible acts hiding behind all sorts of organisations from religion to 'mental illness' serial killers, all orchestrated to cast us repeatedly into the darkness of uncertainly and fear. There is a percentage of human minds capable of *anything* even beating a person to death for the wrong clothes. The suppression of Middle Eastern women is all in lead up to 'releasing' the feminine in a ritual to send the message to the universe that women on Earth are 'free' when in fact it will be business as usual, boy's clubs and women picking up after them. Mummy! I hate you! I love you! I hate you! I love you! I hate you! Tantrums. They love you when dinners on the table. They hate you when it's decision time.

There's always an enemy and left to fester long enough, this has led to a situation where previously progressive *normal* countries have regressed and now embrace barbaric beliefs and behavour's because *they're afraid not to!* Convert or die. Gee whizz, I wonder which one I'll pick? I'm no bigot. The *bigots* are the ones orchestrating all this via covert global alphabet agencies who are given their orders by the aristocracy of England and Europe who worship Satan and the demonic realm who do their bidding. It's a reptilian thing to force people to act on their lowest survival instincts. It is they who are choreographing the 'end times' theatre production and all eventual 'changes' that will emerge out of it only to benefit them, of course. It's a tried and tested military tactic from ancient history perpetrated by a military species. Only problem is we're a little more evolved and informed now and it's not as easy as they thought it would be. We're not as stupid as they assumed we'd be. Moreover, we have men who believe they are women attacking women who are against their beliefs as 'TERF' or trans-exclusionary radical feminist. The most explicit violence is being encouraged toward women by the Norman Bates Club who now have a 'human rights' agenda to destroy anyone who doesn't agree with them. Just looks like men beating up women again...and again. Exacerbating the issue is the nutty 'random' attacks now as people are demonically possessed due to their aura's being worn down by poisons and injections. Just google 'random attacks' as weird crimes are perpetrated like someone just kills all their housemates with a kitchen knife or kills a bunch of people in their community with an axe. It's getting weird folks. It's what happens when the serpent spits its venom in all directions burning up anything it can find.

America, the 'Empire State', is a 'client state', *an* amalgamated *franchise* of 'old-world' European countries, including England, ultimately headed up *specifically* by the *Roman Catholic Church*. The Roman Catholic Church are simply ancient Rome *rebranded* emanating out of England and Europe who went on to become the various new world western 'empires' under Spain, England, Portugal, France, Germany, Holland – *all of them* – and their 'royal' households who have all been interbreeding with each other for centuries if not millennia as one big *family*. Borders are for underling dickheads. These guys *rule the world* and don't even have passports and if you think the Mexican border wall is to keep Mexicans out, you're beyond saving. That wall is to *keep Americans in* and the only reason why you get penned in is when there is a slaughter on the cards. It is they, 'royalty', who colonised the 'new world' of America, Australia, New Zealand, Canada and some pretty cool tropical island nations in the Pacific. They quashed the original inhabitants and their existing empires some of whom were quite advanced like the Aztecs etc. The Euro-British (Roman Catholic) Empires replaced the temples and sites of worship in the 'new world' with CHURCHES built on top of old temple sites regardless of which European-British country was conquering them. As such, Ancient Rome is hiding behind the Roman Catholic Church and all its 'denominations', offshoots, who hide behind the *countries* that adopt the 'religion' *Christianity*.

They all went on to conquer *other people's lands* in a massive PAINT BY NUMBERS military plan that has played out for thousands of years in their attempt to conquer the *whole world*. And they've nearly done it. Now the Roman Catholic Church hides behind politics and celebrity who openly worship Satanism and that is because the royal houses of Europe and England secretly worship Satan who hides behind the Roman Catholic Church who was previously the Roman Empire who hides behind all these countries who are hide behind politics and celebrity who turn out to be royalty after all so the circle is complete. It is *celebrity* who are selling you all this satanic shit distracting you with glitzy smiles, fabulous lifestyles, awesome block buster movies, fancy clothes, galas, events, awards ceremonies, fan clubs, awesome cars and all the pomp and pageantry Hollywood 'Royalty' enjoys because...they are the continuation of ancient Rome in plain sight, ancient 'royal' families, rebranded for the 21s century. They are reinstalling the ancient world model of social hierarchy as it has always been, Digital Rome, at a time when the world was prophesied to come together and ascend. And it is ascending, only, you're not invited. They can trace their genetics back to the ancient Egyptian Kingdom, just ask George Bush Jr. about that, and it is they who intend to emerge the ancient world in the *new*-new world of space travel and all things upper class along with all the trappings of the super elite. They are loving this! It's so close now! But it's *still* ancient Rome which, by the way, was chiefly the ongoing empire of ancient Egypt co-opted with ancient Greece to create an ancient super empire still operating today. It's pharaohs with flat screens. It's their awesome vision and it's nearly complete as we round off against the Age of Aquarius, the last age and a super age, to *replace humans* with their hybrid breed and *take the entire world* as they have always dreamt of! They have been patient and diligent you gotta hand it to them. They know their stuff.

Which brings us to New Atlantis, New Rome, New Egypt, *America*, the fall guy. These old-world aristocrats intend to destroy America to initiate the *New World Order, the 'Great Work'*, out of the ashes of the 'new' world stolen from the natives to emerge as victors of a *new* age and *new* planetary system although, behind the scenes, still worshipping the same old demon gods as they always have, is the aristocracy! It's a step-by-step, paint-by-numbers PLAN and yet it is not the average 'American' in the street who is doing this although they take the blame for it as did the German people with the Nazis. Via alphabet agencies headed up by 'secret' societies who are (at the top) *all royalty*, emerging out of the old world of England and Europe, it is a 'winner takes all' race to the finish line and yes, our planet Earth is the meat in the sandwich. Further to all this, we are confounded by 'non-linear warfare' a termed coined by politician, businessman and adviser to Vladimir Putin and Boris Yeltsin, Vladislav Surkov. Non-linear warfare is described as not knowing *who* your enemy is, *where* your enemy is, *why* they are attacking, *when* they are attacking, *who* they are attacking and *how* they are attacking. It's the old 'who, what, where, when, why, and how' trick and it manifests as the plethora of attacks society is under *across the board* from insurgents, terrorists, police brutality, political parties and all their different mandate as well as Dr's. sworn to do no harm and their pimps - pharmaceutical companies - aka Mengele Inc and all their nutty professors pimping out psycho pills and injections to all the lunatics and their 'random' attacks. This plan includes dumbing down the education system, identity politics, marginalised groups, 'woke' ideologies from 'progressives', 'critical race' theory, gender politics, 'conservatives', 'traditionalists' and technocrats as well as environmental fears, nuclear war and *global* EVERYTHING. I mean, Jaysus! Who isn't attacking us right now? The name of the game is fear, and it is rife at this point in history.

They key to understanding all this is the term 'at this point in history'. Why was it that the *first year* of the new millennium, 2001, that the greatest attack on civilians during peacetime occurred on 9/11? Why? We have not even dealt with *that* yet we are onto the next and the next major catastrophe until we are numb to the pain and consumed by battle fatigue. As the weary trundle on and on we hope that *somehow*, we will be spared the most dreaded conclusion - the end of our kind - and at this stage I think it's fairly obvious that there is definitely an 'us' and 'them' emerging here. The last words uttered by the victims of 911 who managed to get a message out as 911 *literally went down* was, 'I love you'. These were messages of hope, to never give up, to go on, to live a good life in spite of the horror, to love and be loved. Their lasts words were *selfless testimonies* about the truth of the human heart and that truth is, even in the face of our own destruction, we only think of others and love. Every father, every mother, every boyfriend and girlfriend, every son and daughter, brother and sister, all said the same thing, 'Live! Love! And be happy!" I go into more detail on the overarching and all-consuming RITUAL that 9/11 was and ultimately represents the death of the natural family, the Family of Life and the death of Humans. Lilith, Adam's first wife, became the monster. Hindu Kali becomes the monster, the man killer. Medusa was sweet but became the monster. The wrath of Egyptian Sekhmet was the monster. How can the mother and wife become a monster? Because she represents the *waters* and in her dark side as a force of nature The Flood is the monster. They flooded the world the last time, *this* time they are going to burn it with fire. It looks like at some point in the next decade or two there might be a nuclear war, a mass extinction event after decades of turmoil.

The history books will say we had it coming.

I can tell you *exactly* why we are under attack *at this time* and the truth is so far from what you expected it to be that NO ONE could see it for what it truly was. I only managed to decipher this information as a matter of *self-preservation* as my own life has been rigged up from the wings to make me the cherry on the Satanic cake, an offering to their demon god, to get them over the line and appease the dark forces whose agenda encompasses the

RETURN OF THE TWINS

Universe itself! Cowards! Motherfuckers! This *conspiracy* is all around us and once you are aware of it, you too will see the all-pervading RITUAL as the *unnatural duplication* of an A.I. demonic-alien *male* program tries to destroy the *natural replication* of Mother Nature. They are out in the open now. Get out your pitchforks, folks, we got a beast to take down. So, what's it all about?

Hang on to your wellies. Here we go, kids!

CHAPTER FIVE

MUM & DAD – HUSBAND & WIFE
GODDESS & GOD

The hand that rocks the cradle rules the world.

Inside the human brain is type of mesh called the 'claustrum'. Technically speaking 'Claustrum' is from the Latin word meaning 'claus' or 'close' and translates as the 'end' or 'close of a period' which is rather fitting for what we now face. It is a thin bilateral structure connecting the cortical and sub-cortical region of the Prefrontal cortex and Thalamus. It is located between the insula laterally and the putamen medially. The blood supply is via the middle cerebral artery and is considered to be the most densely connected structure in the brain. It allows for the integration of various cortical inputs of *sound, colour and touch combined into ONE experience rather than singular events.* Now that we have that out the way, what does this mean and what does it do?

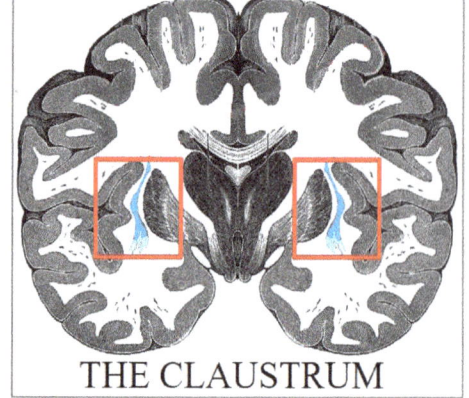

THE CLAUSTRUM

The Claustrum catches 'life force' energy, *aetheric light*, a fine soul energy, that runs through the chakras connecting them like a silver cable stringing together a necklace of pearls. This energy is so delicate that thoughts (static electricity) obliterate it so, a still mind is important to adequately harness its power and why monks seek to 'quiet the mind'. Once this fine soul-force energy is captured by the Claustrum, this 'universal energy' is transmuted, distilled like a fine liqueur or 'spirits', and released into the cerebrospinal fluid once a month when the moon is in your sun sign. This *hormone* released by the Pituitary and Pineal glands resembles a fine oil that the ancients called 'Christos' or simply *Christ* white and yellow in colour that literally means *'light'*. This fine oil, *the Christ hormone*, is released once a month when the moon is in your sun sign so its quite specific to each individual and says something for the reality of what 'astrological' really means and how connected we really are to the galaxy and universe beyond. We really are connected to the cosmos and why it's called astro-*logical* because it makes sense, *it's logical*, that our magnificent and incredible human electrochemical bodies are working in unison with an electromagnetic universe hence, astro-LOGICAL. The white and yellow oil was referred to by our ancestors as 'milk' and 'honey'. *This* is the 'land of milk and honey' and it is not a place, *it is function inside you!* Luke 20:17 "Behold! The kingdom of god is within you!" Utopia lies within! Read on. This milk and honey oil was called 'Christ seed oil' 'Christos oil' 'Chrism' 'The Sacred Secretion' 'The Sacred Seed' or quite simply, *Christ*. Christ is not 'male' and certainly not a man. Christ simply means 'light' and is another word for 'electricity' which is the animating force of the galaxy! The 'Christ seed oil' of inner 'light' was why 'Christ' was 'anointed' (anoint means oil) on the forehead of the third eye chakra pineal gland or the *All-Seeing Eye* because that is where this 'oil' comes from and once the circuit of the spine is complete, the 'lights' switch on hence, Christ! It also is the major site of the bodies melatonin that regulates sleep and thus your mood and energy levels. It's really important.

This spiritual energy distilled into an oily secretion from the brain is 'material energy', the non-physical become physical, *alchemy*, although you would be more familiar with it as Chi, Prana, The Force, The Source (sauce?), Qigong energy, Qi Life Energy, Qi or simply Ki (key?). It commences in your brain works its way down the spine and the back up again, *above*. The endocrine system is your glandular super-highway, a series of gateways, connecting a wonderful network of glandular secretions, HORMONES, to correctly allow your body to function on all levels. Once distilled by the Pituitary and Pineal glands this oil is released into the Cerebrospinal Fluid to commence its journey down the spinal column. Once a full circuit of the spine is complete, it was said one had reached the land of milk and honey and as such this discipline must have been chiefly practiced *inside the boundary of marriage* when we go on our 'honeymoon' (a goddess reference). This was why one was to abstain from sex before marriage and why it was bad luck for the groom to see the bride

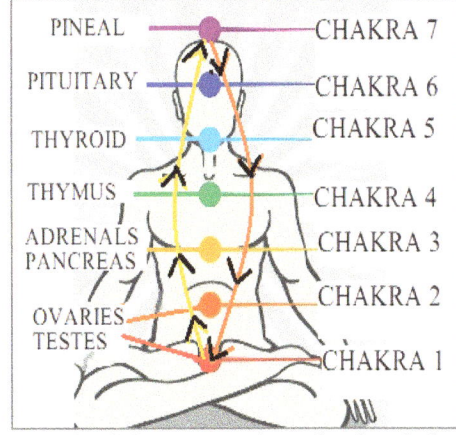

in her wedding dress before the ceremony. Holy Matrimony literally translates as 'Holy' from the wood of the Holly tree considered to have magical properties and why druids had their wands made from the wood of the holy tree hence, *Hollywood* is the 'magic machine' or 'where magic happens'. 'Matri' is Latin for Mother and 'mony' is Old English for 'moon' hence, 'holy matrimony' literally translates as 'Magical Mother Moon Ceremony'. The ceremony is chiefly considered a feminine contract to bind a man to a woman as women would activate his chakras and once activated, you don't want them running away with all your power. Further, the kundalini which resides at the base of the spine in both men and women, was considered a 'feminine' energy where it is believed to be a force or power associated with the divine feminine, the higher female electricity, considered a 'formless' aspect of the goddess. Recap: 'goddess' and 'god' are simply the old-world words for *AC* feminine electricity or Alternating Current and *DC* masculine electricity or Direct Current or the 'waters' as her 'waters' break when she gives birth and the 'fire' or 'spark of his loins' associated with the sexual organs and root chakra also called the 'throne' that one 'sits' on.

Once the Christ (oil) traverse the base of the spine it passes via the Sacral Plexus - the five fused vertebrae at the base of the spine at the lumbar spinal and coccyx region. At this lowest part of the spine or cauda equina meaning the 'horses tail', it is activated by a mild electrical charge or 'the fires' of 'hell' as the lower part of the body was considered the 'underworld' and the head was considered 'heaven', the upper and lower body. The thermodynamics created by the friction and heat of tantric sex 'boils' the 'waters' of the feminine 'kundalini' found at the base of the spine pushing the Christ hormone back up the 33 vertebrae of the spinal column (colloquially called 'the chimney') passing through the energetic chakras, the psychic centres, of the torso connected to clusters of major organs via nerve pathways. The natives say 'the end comes when the water boils'. This is the universal prophecy of the return of the fire-the light ghat sets us free. This is the fire of tantric sex boiling the water pushing the christ seed up the spine to enlightenment and THEN the madness ends as we'll be too smart to put up with it anymore. There are 11 major organ systems in the body and include the integumentary system, skeletal system, muscular system, lymphatic system, respiratory system, digestive system, nervous system, *endocrine system*, cardiovascular system, urinary system, and reproductive systems. These nerves, like tendrils, connecting to the organs is called the 'parasympathetic' nervous system, *a parallel supportive system* the core of which is the spinal column-spinal cord. The parasympathetic nervous system functions via the spine that is made up of the lowest part or the Sacral plexus followed by the Lumbar spinal region then the Thoracic then up to the Cervical spinal region and finally the Cranial region of the spine. It operates the constriction of the pupils, slows your heartbeat, constricts bronchial Tubules, stimulates bile release from the liver, constricts blood vessels, stimulates Digestive activity, relaxes the uterus, and increases Urinary system output. Then you've got the Sympathetic Nervous system that dilates pupils, increases Heartbeat, dilates Bronchial tubules, stimulates secretions of sweat glands, increases the rate of Glycogen to Glucose in the liver, decreases digestive activity, stimulates production of Adrenalin from the Adrenalin glands, vaginal contractions from the Uterus, and relaxes the bladder from the Urinary system when you hang a slash like a donkey. The *spinal cord* is called the 'central nervous system' proper and includes its CPU, *the brain. We're a spiritual machine* and why they say you are 'born' in 'sin' because 'flesh' or the 'material' physical body is the lowest expression of our highest spiritual selves. To ignore our spiritual being in favour of the physical IS THE ULTIMATE SIN as this wastes the 'gift from god' in the form of the Christ-light secretion hormone *essential* to activate our chakras, light body and spiritual *godlike* functions. We are far more than our bodies hence, 'born' *physically* into sin. It is a quest to elevate ourselves from this ignorance of flesh and the brutality that often goes along with it.

The *activated* electrochemical function of the inner Christ hormone circulating via the Cerebrospinal Fluid (CSF) 'switches on' these internal energy 'psychic' centres, the chakras, like mini nuclear reactors and you attain the 'armour of god' as said in the Bible, quite simply, your auric field! This is the knight in shining armour or the glowing coat of awareness – your light body – your electrical 'god' within! Indeed, this is the true meaning behind the lightning bolt symbology of all

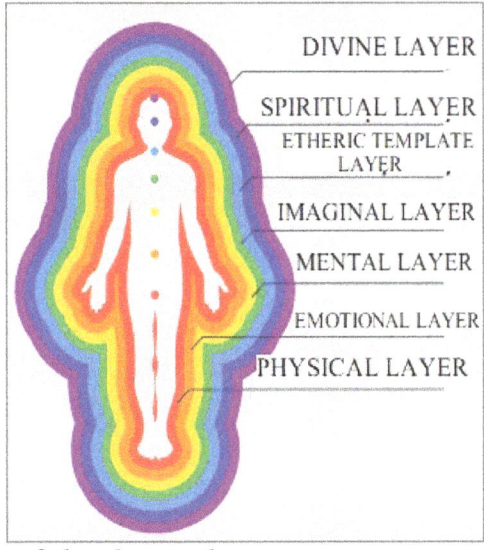

ancient 'thunder' gods, they are gods of the electrical nervous system. It is the true meaning behind the celebrity 'lightning' bolt symbology. Yes, they are all practicing and forget to include you in the loop...forgot. The right eye is the sun, and the left eye is the moon but more on that soon.

This process correctly applied allows for the *correct flow* and function of chi-prana, a universal flow, which in turn correctly allows the body to designate the perfect amounts of sugars, salts, chemicals, compounds, proteins and electrochemical signals, *energy*, allowing for the conglomerate of intestinal functions, the digestive system, the trunk, and crucially the endocrine (glandular) systems – THE ENGINE - to work in *orchestral perfection* with the operating system, the brain, like a magnificent metaphysical opus! That's when the man and woman become 'God' and 'Goddess' or 'crowned' king and queen, mum and dad, as the crown chakra lights up like a halo! Carl Jung stated about this process, *"When you succeed in awakening the kundalini, so that it starts to move out of its mere potentiality, you necessarily start a world which is totally different from our world. It is the world of eternity"*. Manley P. Hall described Christ enlightenment as

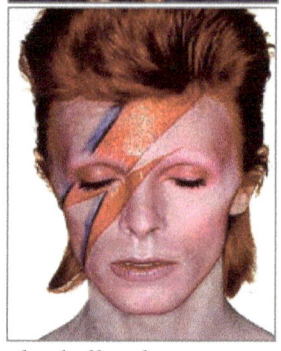

follows, *"This radiance is so great that it cannot be limited by the skull and it pours out from the head, especially from the back of the neck where the uppermost vertebra of the spine articulate with the condyles of the occipital bone. It is this light pouring out in a fan-shaped aura around the posterior part of the head that has given rise to the halos of saints and the nimbus so often used in religious art. This light signifies human regeneration, and it forms part of the auric bodies (protective torus field) of man"*. So, you have Harry Potter and his 'Nimbus 2000' (a witch's broom) as the female tantric sex priestesses were called prostitutes, witches and even 'nightmares' to frighten, in particular, women and anyone else away from practicing this incredible art form. The Nimbus or Halo forms as part of the process by which blood essence is etherized, an effervescence of sorts, by the heart once it has become attuned or activated by the Christ seed extract. It's all about the blood as they say 'the blood is the life', they were not lying. The Solar Christ seed essence from the heart flows upward to create the glowing crown when a man become 'king' and a woman become 'queen' hence, 'crowned' king-queen. Royalty is not some smarmy geezer perched of a fancy stool arrogantly flashing their stolen good. Harry is the prime Hindu god *'Hari'* whose 8th incarnation was *Hari Krishna* while Potter is the Egyptian god Khemu who made man of 'clay' (earth) on his 'potters wheel'. This is because the root chakra is the 'earthing' chakra that connects us like a lightning rod *deeply* to the planet energetically. The electricity is also 'earthed' via the feet and diffused into Mother Earth as we do not fry with the power of this and are then connected to *everything*. The 'nimbus' is the halo as found in images of 'Christ' and 'Mary' so 'nimbus 2000' is code for enlightenment 2,000 or Jesus Christ 2000 only they do not plan of bringing back this practice, no they plan on making an effigy of this practice with an actual man, *the anti-Christ!* They are getting their power by dressing up this process as clever phonetics, linguistics and double talk! CIA sex slave and mind control survivor Kathy O'Brien said that an operative pointed out a sign reading 'service entrance' although it was relayed to her as 'serve us in trance'.

Christ and Krishna *are the same thing* aka the release of glandular fluids into the brain to facilitate chakra-DNA activation and whole brain access. There is no 'junk' DNA, and we only use 5% percent of our brain not because we can't access the other 95%, but because it was shut down for the sole purpose of preventing our escape from the alien controllers using this method! While the elites use this method to activate *their* own super-intelligence, DNA, chakras and psychic abilities, they have kept us down for tens of thousands of years by suppressing this information! Without us they are nothing. The ancient Egyptians called the skull 'the vault of heaven' and this is why 'Satan' is cast out of 'heaven' meaning the un-activated 'Christ' goes down the spine and when it reaches the bottom, 'Christ' ascends. This is why Satan and Christ are 'spiritual brothers'. This is also why Santa and Satan are an anagram as Santa 'arrives down the chimney' on Christmas Eve and 'Christ' rises on Christmas day. Santa wear red for the root chakra. The highest form of spiritual achievement is attained via the heart chakra and crown chakra between the masculine

RETURN OF THE TWINS

and feminine. This is the story of Jesus Sun god and Mary Moon goddess as the polar electrical opposites, just like batteries, fire and water, activate the nervous system and the lights switch on all via tantric sex or what they called Holy Matrimony, sacred marriage or sacred sex. This is why they point at the heart or Love while Satan points as the root, sex. So, God and Goddess are simply the *unlocked secret functions* of our marvelous *godlike* human bodies. This is how you too can become every bit as smart, talented, savvy, RICH and POWERFUL as any celebrity or politician as *this is what they are doing to achieve their wealth and status.* You're welcome.

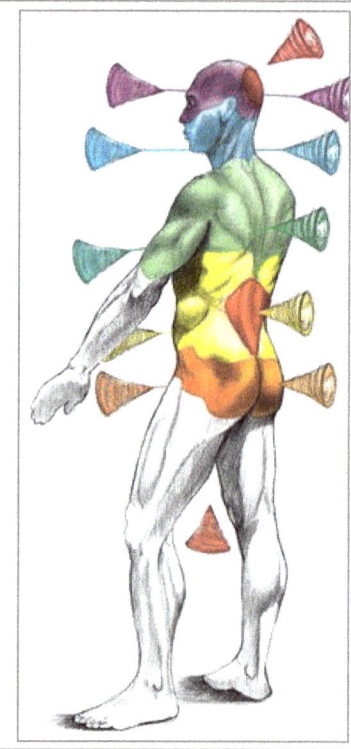

Once the Christ hormone descends the spinal column and rises again, it 'germinates' (activates) at the 'solar plexus', the visceral region of the stomach area - the diaphragm - where *billions* of nerve endings converge. It then continues up the spine to the base of the brain entering the core of the brain where it pauses at the Hypothalamus for three days. The newly activated Christ hormone then releases back into the brain igniting the 12 cranial nerves and further goes on to cross the Optic Nerve where it *massively increases in voltage* as the electrical circuit, now complete and activated, releases fresh blood generating new brain cells and the lights 'turn on' known in ancient times as 'enlightenment'. This is the true meaning of the biblical story of Jesus and Mary and ALL OTHER RELIGIONS WORLDWIDE. *This* is the true meaning of the 'halo' around the 'crown' when Jesus became 'King' and Mary...ah, Mary...she didn't fare so well in

CUPS, CHALICE, BOWLS, TRUMPETS, HORN, FLUTES, 'SOUND HOLES'

this story but more on that soon and yes, they hate women because it's women who will have the right and the power to return this knowledge to humankind as, karmically speaking, whether men want to admit this or not, women are owed *a massive spiritual debt* for risking their lives to bring babies, the human race, into this world and who know the true hardship of what life and death really means and why men, by and large throughout history, so casually take life because they haven't respected the miracle to produce it in the first place. Fear not, men, we are coming out of all that now. It will be difficult for men to explain their brutish behaviour throughout the eons and why the fuck you killed so many of your brothers and raped your sisters because some aristocratic cunt told you to. We have been under a spell, all of us, even I wonder how women have put up with this shit for so long but then, it's not because men are smarter than women, actually quite the opposite, it's just that they're bigger. Brawn over brains. It's beauty and the beast. That said, it's not a competition and there is a bigger game at stake here than pointing fingers at each other.

In short, women, the goddess, are the Angel of Light, the Life/Light Bringer/Bearer and why aristocratic men are the Devil, reptilians, who take life and get human men to do the same and act in their 'lower' vibration as a chip off the old reptilian block becoming mini-me devils themselves. That said, human males can become God again in his highest function when this knowledge is returned via the Love of women, their wives and mothers, the two Mary's, of the human race. This is why your spine is called the 'spinal cord' or *chord* is a musical note and your *organs*, like a piano are an 'organ', are references to *music* as this is all about energetic frequency's or 'musical notes' broadcast from your chakras resonating with the musical broadcasts from the entire Universe. This is why Pythagoras said, "There is geometry in the humming of the strings, there is music in the spacing of the spheres'. Which is why the chakras of internal balance and wellbeing have been depicted as 'cups' 'chalice' 'singing bowls' 'flutes' 'trumpet' or 'horn' 'sound horns' 'sound holes' as well as 'bells' and why *wedding bells* ring in the 'bell tower', the chakra tower, on the *wedding day* to celebrate what marriage is *really* about – ASCENSION – and what couples SHOULD be doing, practicing tantric sex with their true love, their 'twin flame', inside marriage like Jesus and Mary as well as Osiris and Isis and all the rest of the major 'god' and 'goddess' couples throughout history. These 'trumpets' are

often found on the Egyptian 'barks' or 'ship' still referred to today as 'she' because the human body is the 'ship', the 'vessel', while a dog 'barks' and Sirius, the goddess, is the 'dog' star and 'dog' is *god* spelled backwards. There seems to be a heavy influence of the feminine in all this. Bells are bowls and ring in the bell tower of the church to replicate the beautiful music of the feminine temple, the body, and the tower of the chakras as a symbolic effigy of the beautiful music of her chakras and the beautiful frequencies of the feminine body when they are singing and activated. This is why Mary is he 'church' as the spires and turrets doubles as an effigy of the mountains and valley of *Mother* Mature, the Goddess. The friction causes the chakras to vibrate and to produce the perfect pitch, frequencies, so you need the perfect bowl, a very special and unique woman indeed. I wonder who she might have been? This is why they have wedding bells when the bride and groom marry, again, to signify that tantric sex was to be practiced inside sacred marriage all of which is ritualised in these ceremonies, but you don't get the real thing cleverly hidden behind these layers of effigies. These sounds 'touch your soul' in a way that heightens the soul's ability to traverse really fine vibrations elevating your frequency, your pitch, to vibrate at much higher levels called 'dimensions' as you become 'enlightened', literally light. This is why when the Egyptian died they would 'weigh their heart against a feather' and those who were 'light of heart, could pass through death.

The chakras have been studied for thousands of years in the hope to perfect the abilities of our *godlike* potential. All great minds and famous people throughout history were practicing this method. So, when they talk about the 'tower of Babel' pronounced 'babble' the tones of the chakras in the chakra tower are 'out of tune' and are not 'singing' and thus 'babbling' incoherently. Not forgetting the waters and the 'babbling brook', incoherent females. All biblical and religious allegories are based on *phonetics* and double entendre's presented to us in a complex *indecipherable* hodgepodge of biblical, religious and spiritual *bibble babble* in an incredible lie, *double speak*, that the *aristocracy* and their institutions of power have used to control us for *thousands of years* keeping us away from our true power while putting it right in our face at the same time. Woody Harrelson correctly said, "I was getting into theology and studying the roots of the Bible, but then *I started to discover the man-made nature of it*. I started seeing things that made me ask, 'is God really speaking through this instrument?' My eyes opened to the reality of the bible being just a document for control". Even the word 'spiritual' is spi-ritual the Latin word 'spi' meaning breath, breathing, air, soul, life. Therefore, 'spiritual' is a repetitive ritual of life and soul intrinsically connected to air and breath or breathing. We are inherently connected on multiple levels to the aether which is air-breath-soul and light which seem to *all be one*. The truth is so simple!

We've been living under an *orchestrated* global religious con job. They are ALL in on it worldwide to hide the truth of who we are from ourselves! Yeh, these people are fucken arseholes. You'll kick yourself for not being able to see this sooner and be very grateful it was revealed to you hopefully in time to save the Human Race and Planet Earth *as prophesised!* You might get mad after reading this information and seeing how the power centres of earth; religion and politics, owned and operated by the aristocracy, have cleverly harnessed this power *for themselves*, a power they stole from you in the first place hence, the 'thief' theme in every fairytale throughout history. The devil is a thief and a liar, an imposter, because that is what the aristocracy are - a gaggle of extraterrestrial alien misfits the souls of which are demons from the 4th dimension. There it is. Now you know. Human souls are angels from the highest dimension, 11D and beyond, and it is because of our chakras abilities to reach the highest levels of light, the 'most high' and the 'highest of the high', that was the chief reason this alien interloper targeted us way back in prehistory and set out splicing their genetics with ours to use these power and emerge as our 'gods' and then later One God as 'royalty' and now 'celebrity' are practically gods on the Mount Olympus of Hollywood! And the circle is complete. Which brings us to the story of Jacobs Ladder which is only *one* example of COUNTLESS examples all around us past, present and future, making a mockery of Humans as they steal your birthright only to poison and humiliate you into the dust because ultimately, they are afraid of you if you ever find out... Afraid you will discover your true potential and how to harness it and kick these pieces of filth out of your world with the power of your combined light! As such, this information is found in the story of Jacobs Ladder and cross referenced in a pick n' mix of other biblical allegories and religious texts from around the world which only proves this *alien takeover* is global and long-lasting ensnaring every human being black, white, brown and pink in every country around the world. There you go, we really are equal after all. Equally shafted.

An 'allegory' is a story, poem, or

picture that can be interpreted to reveal a hidden meaning typically a moral or political one. It's *very* political but the moral here is that there *is* no morals (not among this horde of 'elite' trash who aren't even from this world anyway). The name Jacob in Hebrew means 'the supplanter' from the Old Testament interpreted as someone who 'seizes, circumvents, or usurps'. Yes, well, that is a very adequate interpretation of what is going on. The story goes, Jacob 'rested his head on a stone' and dreamed of a 'ladder' stretching from Earth to 'Heaven' with 'angels' ascending and descending the 'ladder'. In ancient times the spine column was referred to as the 'ladder' because it literally looks like a ladder. The ancients also referred to the Sacral Plexus as 'the stone' because it literally looks like a stone So, 'Jacob' resting his 'head' on the 'stone' means that the Christ seed oil emanating from *the head* circulates via the 'ladder', the spine, to the Sacral Plexus, the 'stone', then back up the 'ladder' of the spine to the Solar Plexus which they called 'the manger' where the Christ seed 'germinates' or activates hence, *Christ is 'born' in a manger*. 'Christ' 'Ascends' at '33' as the Christ hormone descends the spine, 'the ladder', traverses the sacral plexus, 'the stone', and ascends or 'climbs the ladder' to 33 as there are 33 vertebrae in the spine. 'Satan' being 'cast out of heaven' also means that is the un-activated (unenlightened or non-germinated) Christ seed hormone is basically useless without activation thus rendering one dumb, gullible, and susceptible to lies and lying or the 'devil inside' lost darkness in so many ways. Therefore, 'Satan' is the un-activated Christ seed and, as such, the unenlightened human.

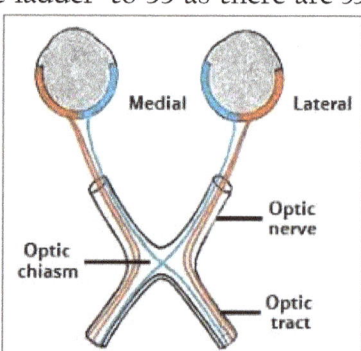

When the Christ seed hormone germinates-activates or is 'born' in the 'manger', the solar plexus, it continues up the spine aka the ladder to the top of the 33 vertebrae. At 33 Christ 'died' and rested in the 'tomb' for three days. The 'tomb' is what the ancients called the Hypothalamus as the Christ seed pauses in the Hypothalamus for three days before continuing on into the brain. Once released into the brain the activated Christ ignites the 12 cranial nerves or the '12 disciples'. It then continues into

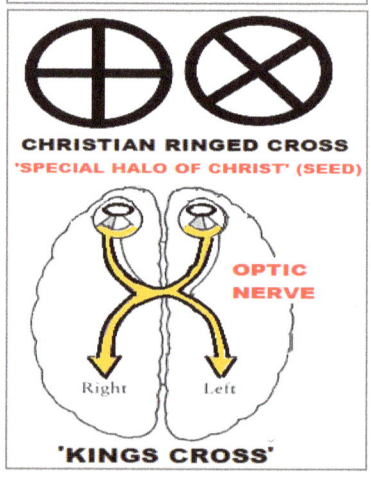

the brain where it crosses the optic nerve and as such, Christ is 'crucified' on the 'cross'. The circuit almost completed, the active Christ hormone unlocks the pineal gland also called 'the stairway to heaven' and is then 'raised to heaven' via the pineal gland symbolised as *the light* emanating from the stars in the 'heavens' completing the tower of the chakras and lighting up the 'christ mass tree' or the nervous system called the Tree of Life and Tree of Knowledge unleashing the 'crown' chakra or the mega-mind. This is why the Christmas Tree has baubles on it to signify apples and the 'apple' or the fruit from the tree of knowledge and life is found in the chakras and the torus field of the body that resembles and apple. This is Newton's Apple. It is Adams Apple – Adam from the Garden of Eden. When 'Christ' was 'crucified' it happened at Golgotha which literally translates as 'place of the skull' specifically, THE BRAIN! It's all about overlapping symbology to *phonetically describe* our spiritual connection to and relationship with the Universe dressed up as geography, plants, and anything that they could relate this practice to in the hopes to pass the information along to us to save ourselves! Thanks ancients! Nice work! Once the circuit is complete the 'binary' frequencies of the brain, the positive and negative AC/DC poles of electricity (just like a battery), become 'hemispherically balanced' and 'enlightenment' ensues as the DNA is activated, the IQ shoots up, motor functions increase, coordination, spatial awareness, confidence, intuition, *psychic abilities*, telepathy, omnipresence, foresight – the whole shebang! We therefore become God and Goddess. Superman and Wonder Woman. Christ. The 'Sun King' and 'Sun Queen'. Yes, we are! I was blind but now I see.

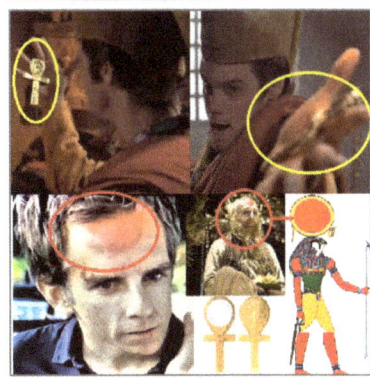

A-list celebrities are practicing this hence, their incredible lifestyles, wealth, and fame. *See right*, Ben Stiller in a scene where the little boy is being raised to be a genius and their name is the Focker's, or more precisely 'fuckers', because that's what it's all about. *Right*, the wife and mother, the Mary's, women, in this scene is the French word 'truth' because Mary ran away to France after the political assassination of Jesus. Jesus was likened to a donkey maybe because he was hung like a donkey. Or is an 'ass'? While

RETURN OF THE TWINS

Mary, The 'goddess', the feminine, means 'mare' as in 'female horse' because the 'Stone' of Jacobs ladder, the Sacral Plexus in Latin is called Cauda Equina, the 'horse's tail'. This is why there are ancient white chalk horses as chalk naturally conducts  electricity symbolised in the tantric electrical spine. The root word of 'mare' means female horse and why she has the 'bridal' gown on at her wedding as is the 'bridle' worn by the horse. The wedding symbolises the celebration of male-female tantric sex enlightenment with your partner as this power of the gods was supposed to be practiced inside the sanctity of marriage or 'mary-age', a feminine time. Tantric sexual electricity is the true ultimate force of the universe. These celebs, for whatever they are involved in, are TELLING you something VERY important. They are leaking information covertly via their films however that ultimately translates. Adam Sandler aptly put it in his movie *Murder Mystery* (note, MM is Mother Mary/Mary Magdalene, Magic Mirror is the universe, and MM is the Roman numeral for the year 2000) that his wife gets confused and calls him 'sometimes I'm the king sometimes I'm daddy'. Because Dad and Mum are God and Goddess, Lord and Lady, *is* King and Queen who become royalty when practicing crown chakra enlightenment via meditative love making or tantric sex. It is a type of yoga or 'sexual kung fu'. In *Ace Venture When Nature Calls* Jim Carry says, 'I'm yet to attain omnipresent super galactic oneness'. He then holds out the Egyptian Ankh the symbol of Isis, the goddess - the wife and mother - which is essentially a mirror, an infinity mirror, of the 'eternal' universal and the flame of Christ light consciousness in a continuous circuit between light beings, men and women, and the universe! The sun disc on the head of the pharaoh represents a mirror reflecting the sun or the 'light' of God *forever*. The light of the universal electricity is found in our *internal* Christ light creating the 'circuit' of the universe as represented symbolically by reflecting mirrors called 'infinity' also found in 'infinity pools' found at government monuments worldwide. Deemed 'there is no end' represented by the golden band of the wedding ring, a golden circle, the has no beginning and has no end to the golden flow of electricity - chi and prana. Icke calls it 'all that ever was, has been or will be'. Sol Invictus the 'undying sun'. These are the ancient phrases from all around the world to describe the 'sleeping beauty' of 'snow white', the purity within, or 'pure as the driven snow'.

RETURN OF THE TWINS

This power has always been called *'the eternal flame'* when the CIRCUIT is in place it is *forever!*

Now that you know all this, feast your eyes upon the image of this *naive young Russian soldier - Japanese, Australian, American, French - it's all the same - broken humans, broken men. Open your eyes to how unspeakably hideous and insidious the rule of 'aristocracy' and 'royalty' is, **aliens,** to use this universal power, *our own power*, against us and leave us bereft of any hope or joy in our own world of endless abundance (if managed properly) with this power while they regale themselves as 'gods' lauding it over us with all their pomp and pageantry, jewels and *luxury*. They *ritually* distract us from the true meaning of this knowledge to cryptically anchor us to physical objects, *effigies*. This is the reason IDOL WORSHIP is forbidden precisely BECAUSE God is, *in fact*, a process inside our bodies! Anything else is a Satanic distraction. This is the reality of what you are up against. I suggest you look hard at this picture. This poor guy, limbless and in every way *destroyed*, is bent over a fucking *symbolic effigy* of the 'eternal flame' when the *eternal flame of Christ light* IS INSIDE HIM AND EVERYONE ELSE and they damn well know it! If *he* only knew how SIMPLE it is to unlock this power, he would never be duped by lies to sacrifice his beautiful body of universal light to a soulless demonic hater in a system of *despicable deceit!* He WOULD BE A LIVING GOD just *as are YOU and* never would have wound up in this pitiful situation *deliberately dehumanised* and degraded in order for a bunch of demonic scum to *bring a God to his knees* by these fucking posturing fake cunts - aristocrats - who *hate* humans because they are not human and want *all the light for themselves*. But they can't have it. It's not there's to have. Thieves that they are.

We are destined to come into this knowledge, and they have tried to twist our destiny to keep it from us as they attempt stand in our place, blame all the problems of the world on 'humankind' when it is the aristocracy who are to blame for EVERYTHING. The intend to receive our golden chalice, our cup of christ, our CHAKRAS OF LIGHT, *of LIFE* and *cast us* into the abyss this time! As a zodiac sign, *Scorpio* rules over the *sexual organs* and thus tantric sex initiated from the erogenous zone. The 'serpents' are the kundalini serpents of the caduceus rising up the tantric spine. I hope you do what is right and never shy away from your opportunity *this one time* to do away with this madness and those who perpetrate it.

The electrical symbols for this power are mirrors, the sun, lightning, stars. Trees, hair, roots are the nervous system. The ram or sheep's 'fleece' is crown chakra enlightenment 'crowned' by 'golden hair' or the 'halo' as

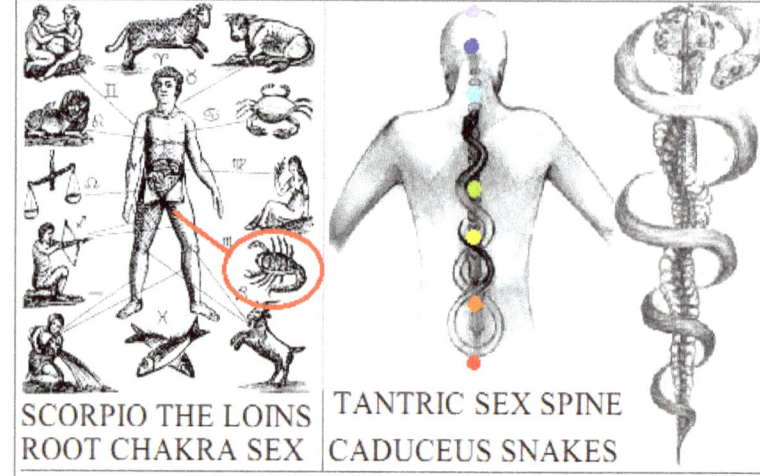

SCORPIO THE LOINS ROOT CHAKRA SEX | TANTRIC SEX SPINE CADUCEUS SNAKES

Luke 10:19, "Behold I give you the power to tread on serpents and scorpions and all the power of the enemy, and nothing by any means shall hurt you".

Can I have a 'thank you', Jesus?

Aries rules over the head in the zodiac. Snakes represent electricity. The cross is the neck and shoulders, optic nerve, the zodiac and clock or time and 'cycles'. The penis represents rods, wands, *canes* (Cain & Abel or is it just the 'able cane' or Biggus dickus?), staffs, sceptres, batons, bats, clubs, swords, knives, thorns or 'Thor', spears are also electricity as the penis is the DC Direct Current or 'lightning rod' which also represents the spine and pineal gland as this 'third eye' had 'rods' and 'cones' just like a normal eye or 'thy rod and thy staff comfort me'. Bulls 'taurus' and apples represent the torus fields. Apples also represent the 'fruit' or chakras from the 'tree' meaning the nervous system as well as the throat chakra or 'Adams apple' the voice box or 'speaker'. Lions represent the masculine as the sun another symbol of light-electricity. Waters, pearls represent the moon and scallop shells represent the feminine 'fire' or the sun in the feminine. Mountains represent the 'goddess' or the feminine body as 'mother earth' and the 'tower' of her chakras or 'mountain mama' to 'climb the mountain' of her chakra tower as the 'church' and 'temple' (also palace or castle) or 'my

RETURN OF THE TWINS

body is my temple'. Stringed instruments represent the zodiac or the 'guitar' of the natal chart. The rose and lambs represent the innocence and 'soft' nature of the feminine. Rocks represent the 'life' found in nature or 'rock god'. Wings, angel wings, birds including ravens, swans, hawks and eagles etc., birds in general, represent the pineal-pituitary gland and a 'birds eye view' when you reach crown enlightenment, and your psychic abilities increase or 'omnipresent' to 'see' things in advance as 'foresight'. Enlightenment is represented by crowns, rays of light, halos. Flowers, flutes, trumpets or 'horns' (hence, why a man's penis is called a horn) 'singing' bowls, cups, chalices, sex or flowers in general, snakes, the 'thorn' is 'thor' or the 'prick' of the pain of electricity as he was a 'thunder' and *lighting* god for tantric sex electrical activation, the hammer as he is a 'maker' or 'craftsman' or a 'blacksmith' often associated with the 'trades' as in masons, stonecutters, architect's, the set square and compass that designs the 'temple' as the temple *really is* your body and why 'Mary' is the 'Church', the temple or 'sanctuary' as her ability to recreate life is sacred. The church or temple is and effigy of the 'mountain', the cave is a vagina the hills and valleys are the 'breasts' of the goddess. As well as 'weaving', spiders, the spinning wheel, the ships wheel, the number 11 the 'two towers' of the chakras of men and women, it is the twins of the lovers of men and women and the brothers and sisters of humanity. It is also the light and dark side found within us all as well as the 'twin flames' of the 'snakes' of the caduceus rising up the spine. The twins are the moon and sun while the planets, stars and constellations are the 'kings' and 'queens', 'god' and 'goddess', 'saviour' and 'Samaritan' and 'saints' deified as people as the same light in the stars is *the same light in us*. Important numbers are 7 for the 7 chakras or 7/7 for the male female chakras side by side, 9 for the end cycle or 'feme-NINE' the goddess of completion and 11 is electricity or enlightenment. All are chakras found inside and outside our bodies.

The twins are the Twin Towers as 'T' is the 20th letter of the alphabet and becomes TT 22 or 11:11. The word 'Jenga' is a Swahili word meaning 'tower' so, we have the 'Jenga' tower game to see how many blocks can be removed before the 'tower falls'. So, what do you know, given the Twin Towers were a sacrifice to Satan and a massive sun ritual, Jeffrey Epstein had a painting of George Bush Jr. throwing paper planes at two collapsed Jenga towers while laughing symbolically suggesting he was involved or at least happy about the collapse of the 'twin towers'. Joaquin Phoenix was asked why he threw paper planes at the 'twin sisters' in the movie Joker. The Joker is the 'clown prince', the devil, always laughing, always mocking. That's because the 'gods', soon to be one god, laugh at our naivete. The movie Paul about a grey alien calls a victory 'Jenga'. Phoenix is the 'bird' of the feminine kundalini 'born from its own ashes' rising up the enlightened tantra spine. So, from this I deduce that the reptilian hierarchy are receiving their directives from the grey-alien demonic realm who use these effigies of the 'towers' to initiate a state of chaos in which ultimately, the 'twin towers' of the male female chakras towers will collapse and be destroyed. In particular they want to destroy the feminine 'twin towers' of the light and dark side of the feminine. 911 is code for 999 as 1 is I in Roman numerals and 'I' is the 9th letter of the alphabet. 999 is the feme-NINE, the end of a massive cycle of alien control and the return of the human feminine: mother nature, the wife and the mother. Only, they are trying to code this massive end cycle of mother nature as the end of the *feminine* completely! Behind all this is 'the joker' the IQ enhanced 'joker' *is the devil*. The 'Devil' is a singular noun for the reptilian collective aka the alien cabal. Right, Joaquin Phoenix in the movie *Joker* which means the 'clown' prince, the Jester, the Devil. The 'twin sisters' are the light and dark side of the balanced feminine, their worst nightmare. In freemasonry Jachin and Boaz r epresents the twin pillars of Solomons temple, the 'female' and 'male' pillar or the sun and moon pillars. Jachin is Joaquin in this little game, the Joker, the devil, who passes himself off a as male and female, the

When the teacher asks why I threw a paper airplane at the twin sisters

IG: CONNECTING CONSCIOUSNESS
Does anyone else think it's weird that Jeffrey Epstein had a painting of George Bush playing with paper airplanes, sitting in front of two collapsed Jenga towers?

JENGA TOWER CRASHES DOWN

Let's not forget about the first alien we rescued from Area 51

AND THAT'S JENGA

THE IQ CHAKRA GAME... AND THAT'S JENGA...

all-in-one Baphomet, the beast. 'Joachimthaler' is the original one dollar considering they were the trade centres and U.S. one-dollar bill is the 11:11. This ritual means the Joaquin-Jachin Phoenix rising from the ashes of the feminine trade towers have been summarily crashed in this 11 tantric sex ritual. And that's 'Jenga'.

These are all terms and symbols *among many* for the same thing, the ability of self-enlightenment via sacred lovemaking or 'tantric sex'. Now you know. All this was stolen from us by a hierarchical *alien* syndicate who call themselves 'royalty' yet they know damn well who the true royalty of this planet are, the humans, who they've slung beneath their feet in morbid self-idolatry with the need to be worshipped and loved as they are ego maniacs called 'the gods'. They use this power to enhance their black magic and energy manipulating abilities to control *your lives* and influence reality in ways that are 'godlike'. But we will best them yet as prophesised by our ancestors. They have twisted these terms to mean something else *outside us* so that we don't look *within* where the true god, Christ seed enlightenment, resides that literally turns us all into living gods. In the film Billy Madison, Adam Sandler is *telling you* straight-up all the subjects he has studied. The 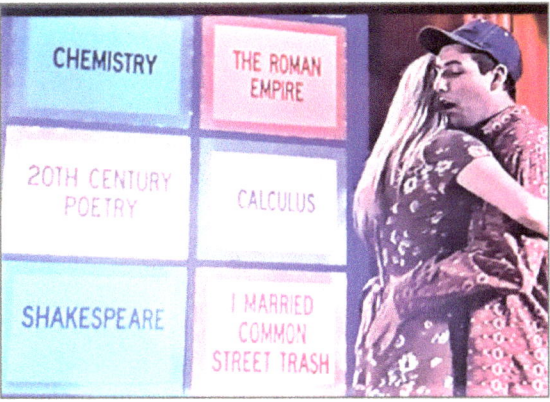 old royals from Europe aren't the only ones who've studied Latin and ancient Greek. These American guys know it's all bullshit as they have been afforded a reprieve by experiencing a reasonably NORMAL life outside the bunkers, battlements, and damp old castles of the shitty old world where one is magnificently constrained by pomp, precedence, dogma, and 'polite' society (when people are looking) and the strict hierarchy of an oppressive bunch of inbred filth. These old coots from the Old World are very much about the ANCIENT practice of this alchemical artform and due to their OCD and strict adherence to 'tradition', ritual, they've turned something beautiful into a cosmic crime. They can't evolve. Just because it's traditional, doesn't mean it's right. They haven't evolved this process unlike their American *cousins* who have had the last century of openly boozing, drug taking and fucking up in public LIKE EVERYONE ELSE in modern society and as a result, there is an underlying, *unspoken*, mutual comradery between new age a-list aristocrats even if behind the scenes at the top they must adhere to the old rules. If I could talk to anyone about what I have discovered, it would be Adam Sandler.

Russell Brand, tantric practitioner, even associates his image with Jesus, Gandhi, Che Guevara, Malcom X (and Hitler) as his poster says of his Messiah Complex tour of 2014 and the MC looks like a Charlie Manson swastika on his forehead. Notice, the 33 on the left wrist. This is the  tantric left-hand path – the dark side. His latest internet series has a farting raven because the raven represents the dark side of tantric sex or enlightenment or the 'birds eye view' and these modern 'gods' are educated enough to know, its' all bullshit. It's ancient reptilian-demonic mind 'ritual' paranoid obsessive-compulsive disorder of nutty aliens. But these modern guys are half-human and it's the HUMAN side of them that gives warnings as even did Queen Elizabeth II when she said there were 'dark forces' at work in Britain. They are torn to a degree but involved in something that hardens their heart in a way that only a blind eye can survive. As such, the Norse god Odin was the god of war, death, sky (aether), poetry, wisdom (he's the god of everything and another version of the Devil) had two ravens, Huggin and Munnin as birds represent the 'inner bird' the 'falcon' of Horus and many old gods who had an 'eagle' or, for women, 'swans' and 'skylarks' etc. This is why through lust instead of love they elevate the IQ and this their status and why Jesus and Mary *point at their hearts* and then toward heaven for enlightenment. The message was that in order to get to 'heaven', or a massive IQ and godlike abilities, go through the heart, through love.

These guys are all geniuses with high IQ's who've seen all the weird obsolete understandings of these processes and realise that real science and common sense can explain the *normal workings* of the human body and the 'fluidity' of our reality that can be programmed (as they are doing albeit with evil). More importantly these celebs have lived in *the West*, especially in America (number one on the new age hit list) and in the emerging *modern* world there is no need to call this practice a religion or deifying it or applying some other *weird outdated superstitious uniformed shit* and ancient OCD *fears* onto it. They reference Hitler because he too was practicing this hence, the Eagles Nest his highland retreat as the 'eagle' or 'inner bird' gives you a bird's eye view. It's the dark side but it doesn't have to be. It's like

RETURN OF THE TWINS

Monty *Pythons* - Search for the Holy Grail (pythons aka reptilians). Once you know this knowledge there otherwise incomprehensible programs actually become really hilarious including The Life of Brian. Brian is 'Jesus' who although deified as a living god, was just an ordinary guy with his chakras opened which seems *really amazing* to people who *don't* have their chakras opened. This is the 'gods'. Always has been.

This is why in the movie *The Imaginarium of Dr Parnassus*, the old man has the pharaoh's disc painted on his forehead to represent the crown chakra of a 'sun king' or the activated inner 'sun' of Christ meaning 'enlightened'. Father is the 'King' as well as 'God' and the 'Lord' and all the other designations for an important male specifically, via tantric sex. Mount Parnassus is where the Oracles of Delphi worshipped Apollo and *Apollo* is the son of Zeus. As the Masonic cult alters the name of their dark god in every age to confuse us, Zeus is the Devil (Dr Seuss!) in the age of Aries. Therefore, Apollo is Satan for our intents and purposes as Satan is 'the son' of the Devil and Apollo is 'the son' of Zeus. The 'father' becomes the 'son' but more specifically, the son becomes the father. Just as Jesus is 'the son' of 'God'. This is why Vlad Dracul was 'the son' of the Devil as the 'Devil' is 'that old dragon', 'the serpent', aka Reptilians and in the reptilian cult, they indoctrinate the son into their dark order from an early age! The 'Devil' is a master Mason who has been hardened by their experiences inside the cult and are 'locked in' to the program (like Darth Vader). The son is the apprentice who, being young, hasn't fallen so deeply into darkness as the metaphorical character Luke Skywalker. There is still hope for the son who has not become so jaded and fucked-up by the weird treatments of the cult program and therefore, may break away and not follow his father's footsteps as does Luke thus restoring balance. This is why in the movie Darth Vader cuts off Luke's right hand, this is the 'right hand path' or the path of the light side as the left-hand path is the 'dark path', the masonic path. The Imaginarium of Dr Parnassus means 'the Devil's illusion' over the human mind found in our perception of the illusion of 3D 'reality', a reality which is fluid. It can be changed. In the Imaginarium of Dr. Parnasus they depict the death of Heath Ledger by hanging which happened for real in real life leaving him unable to finish the film. As they weave fantasy and reality right before our eyes, the 'hanged man' is a card in the tarot deck. Some people realise something weird is going on yet it is very difficult to put the puzzle pieces together leaving us floundering. In the 'tarot' scene a series of cards are laid out and when translated by *real* tarot readers, the message of these cards means that *major changes* are coming that people will not like but are *unstoppable*. The 'hanged' man in tarot means being stuck in limbo or confused. But the 'hanged man' is really Jesus Christ 'hung' on the cross of the zodiac - a destroyed man - but in a broader sense it means 'man' of Earth, Humans, lost in time, lost in space inside the Devils house of mirrors aka the Universe! AS such, we live in an alien mind prison, a 'maize', or 'Pan's Labyrinth'. *Pan* is the Devil. Pan is the 'frying pan' or 'pot' in the stars otherwise known as *Orion!* Orion is Osiris the 'green' man, a reptilian as are all major 'royal' figures in history. It's a space program.

In ancient times the evil alien aristocrats actually crucified people on a tree to more significantly depict the 'tree' of the nervous system and the enlightenment that comes from it in a weird sacrifice of Humanities spiritual life. Psycho. The tantric king, Jesus, was 'King' of the Jews because he had full body enlightenment while his masonic buddies only had crown enlightenment. Jesus went beyond them all in so many ways not content to just live under the rules of ancient masonry. He travelled as far as current day India and Ireland where the Druids also practiced this method and where he would have perfected his knowledge of whole-body enlightenment in the far East, Buddhists, Taoist's, Hindu's and further back, the Vedas, where this information original emanated from. Mary, his wife, was most likely a Vestal Virgins who, like the geisha's of Japan today, were trained as 'companions' from an early age who themselves had full knowledge of the tantric discipline. A Vestal was the perfect for rich men seeking a priestess wife when their tenure finished around 40 years of age, *see*, Steve Carrel's '40 Year Old Virgin (Mary)'. They were initiated into the priestess college of the Vestals from six to eight years old and taught all the ways of high society proficient in languages, art, politics, management, matters of the state, property law, science, Last Wil and Testaments and much more. During their 30+ years training, they were trained in the high skills of tantra including sexual congress and were a prize to rich men as they were said to give birth to 'godlike' sons hence, Jesus was a living god because his mother was practicing this too. The two Mary's, the Mother and the Wife, is why he attained whole body enlightenment and not just crown chakra enlightenment as he was born of a priestess who influenced him in utero, called a homunculus. Then as a travelling monk he practiced tantra himself and eventually married another Vestal, another 'Mary', and together completed their tantric quest.

Hiram Bingham who discovered Machu Pichu in 1911 found that 80% of the graves were women and thought he had found the remnants of the 'Virgins of the Sun'. Spanish account noted that the most beautiful girls in the empire were selected for this sacred convent from the age of 8 years old, they served the Incan emperor for the rest of their lives. Considering the Vestal were the priestesses of the 'sacred fire of Vesta' who were initiated between 6-8 years old, the correlations to the Virgins of the Sun cannot be denied. Jesus, who was a mason, like all mason's then and now (because evolution), initially looked down on Mary. Although the Vestal College was disbanded in 394AD, if three hundred years of the calendar are missing, then its possible Mary was one of the last of their kind and Jesus was basically a sacred science alchemical monk practicing tantra like Merlin and all the famous wizard's, holy men and 'gods' throughout history. Jesus was also the son of another 'Mary/vestal' and had the rare gift of his mother's influence in utero and from the earliest age he was selected to be a Jewish king and furthermore, a god. Priests are monks. King were once priest's but they separated these roles so you wouldn't figure it out. Nuns are priestesses. Therefore, queens were priestesses and the 'priestess' and the 'priest' of sacred sex give birth to the 'Golden Race' that humans were once called before the 'fall'...the fall into darkness and amnesia under a reptilian space empire dressing all this up in effigy as 'religion'. In the deeper arena of Catholicism, abstaining from sex is the last thing on their minds as nuns were often providing sex for the priests who, due to the sickness of their position, eventually preferred sex with children because they have purer light than adult women. Women became 'dirty' prostitutes and children became naked 'cherubs' with 'angel' wings to designate the 'heights' their pure energy provides them. Jesus initially treated Mary quite badly throwing her down like the other men did seeing her as less than them. When Jesus became more enlightened through his travels, he realised that via the dark side of tantric sex one could open their crown chakra and become a genius but via the practice of lovemaking with the Goddess, a tantra priestess, one could attain *whole body enlightenment* hence, the 'glowing' angels and the 'golden' race humans were once known referred to as the 'glowing coat of awareness'. This level of power effectively made Jesus on par with the secret alien rulers, the dark masters beyond the beyond, who hide a lot of these even from heir loyal practitioners. So, this is where shit goes tits up.

There is a legend at the core of the dark forces called 'the denial of love'. These masonic apprentices are taught to believe from an early age that love makes you weak and prone to straying from the boy's club cult, the brotherhood, who need total obedience to complete their alien program in the 'great work' that they tricked so many into falling for. The Great Work is simply to rule Planet Earth *without question* and make the Devil into God of the universe. Therefore, not only do they delete love from their hearts and minds, but they also control their human 'vehicle' or 'vessel', their body, with cold calculation getting the most out of the bodies and minds of the human's they possess without the distraction of 'love'. They are often asked to prove that they have destroyed love in their heart by offering even their own family members, particularly wives and mothers, as sacrifices to this dark order to prove 'total control' over the human they attach to. But this dark order, as usual, has an ulterior motive that many of these dufus guys have fallen for over the eons in their quest to become 'kings'. By denying love, they lose their ability to become 'god' because it is only via the deep meditative lovemaking between a committed man and woman, VIA THE HEART CHAKRA, that they can access *the highest levels* of light, love and LIFE, and get the *whole body* auric field enlightenment which, like Jesus, would make them even more superior and *more of a threat* to their dark masters ordering them to kill their true love, their twin flame, there very wives and mothers, to *prove* their loyalty and, with these secrets revealed to them, become a king or even a 'god', small 'g', instead of a 'God' BIG FUCKEN 'G', okay? The only thing they prove is how stupid and cowardly they are. This was the secret to Mary and Jesus and why they are pointing at their hearts and then pointing to heaven. Women apparently hold the key to the fullest levels of Christ enlightenment heart consciousness and become Queens and Goddesses as a result. Only, the part where Mary, the mother and the wife, the Goddess, becomes enlightened was left out of the story and she just got called a hooker, a dirty prostitute, and told to fuck off and clean the house and cook us up a falafel while you're at it. This is why Jesus was 'crucified' in the literal sense for going against the masonic club and opening his heart chakra.

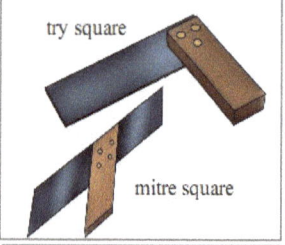

The try-square/miter square, *right*, is a chief symbol of the Masons. This symbol is all over Jesus' imagery and all the rest of the 'gods' throughout history. *Right*, is one of the oldest paintings of Jesus. This architects or 'builders' square is also a penis tantric sex symbol, and, in this image, Jesus appears to have two distinct faces. Two faced. The older 'father' a darker left sided version with a larger pupil and a younger lighter right sided Jesus holding the sacred book of the zodiac cross with the tantric penis 'lever' and the 'trinity' dots. Jesus was a tantric practicing Mason. It is a dick cult and why the history of this feminine planet, Mother Earth, has only ever promoted males as women were left out of this godlike equation even though it seems further back in history they stole this knowledge and power *from the feminine*, wiped her memory of her former glory, used her as a house cleaner and a hooker, literally, and used their demure wives for their public image in politics while fucking everything that moves because it's all about sex enlightenment. Love, what a joke, was thrown out the window.

Tubal Cain logo 'two balls cane'

Tubal Cain is worshipped as Vulcan the mythical 'blacksmith' who worked with 'fire' and whose wife 'cheated' on him. They love to believe women are bad. He's a 'maker' and 'architect' of things - a god of 'fire' - the Devil! Tubal Cain's logo or symbol, *right*, was a cane with two spheres or balls. So, Tubal Cain becomes a pun on 'two balls cane' and is basically, a penis and two testicles circled by the 'maritime' rope as this is all about 'maritime' law or 'law of the sea'. They are pirates. Any fringed flag you see at official events is the 'Jolly Roger', a pirate's flag, looting everything. No surprises, it's looks like Facebook's logo of the obvious insider Mark Zuckerberg's *spying* machine. Also, as outlined in red, *above*, is the symbol of John Dee, black magician, and adviser to Queen Elizabeth I. It's the same dick and balls 'club'! They are all masonic *agents* of this dark order none more apparent than the 'agencies' today – CIA, FBI, ATF, MI6 – stitching up the world! It's them. Always has been. Dee would sign off with this symbol on his correspondences which was adopted as the 20th Century symbol of the sex *spy* 007 lampooned by another insider, Mike Myers, as 'The Spy Who Shagged Me' in his Austin Powers series. Austin in Latin means 'great' 'majestic' 'magnificent'. Great Powers derived from sex. Austin's father brings him into the 'club'. It's all in the 'family'. It's all male tantric sex symbolism that represents the 'try' square of the Masonic logo of 'builders' (like god 'making' reality) as found in early Jesus symbolism. This 'god' 'makes' things and 'models' society their god being the 'architect', the Devil, Satan, or more specifically, Masonic reptilians! The Dragon! 'God' who 'made man of clay' are their ancestors who they revere through an endless homage to the ancient takeover of Humanity and Planet

Earth. This symbol is the dark side of alien enlightenment. This symbol is also used, aptly, by the Mason's in the Tubal Cain Golf Tournament. Remember, canes, wands, sceptres, rods, sticks and clubs etc., are all penis 'phallus' symbols. As former Mason Bill Schnoebelen recounts, "For Masons who wish to conceal their membership from non-Masons, but still advertise it to their Lodge brothers, there is a special pin (or tie tack) they can wear. It looks like an upside-down golf club with two balls near the top.... Many people assume the person is a golfing enthusiast, but it is actually a visual Masonic pun. This is called the 'Two Ball Cane' and is a pun on the secret password of a Master

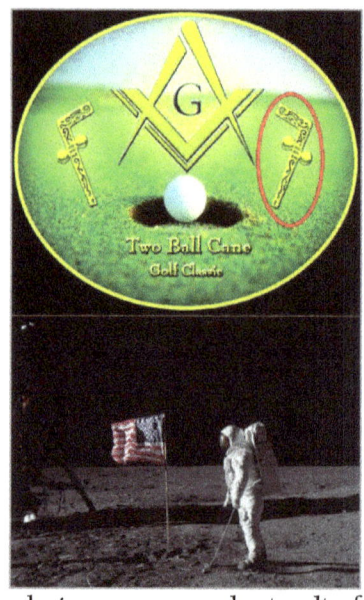

Mason, 'Tubal Cain (sic)". It is also an all-too-obvious pun on the 'god' of Masonry found in the male reproductive organ and the IQ gained from tantric sex. Nice, eh? Especially when many men wear these pins to church on Sunday! They say men worship their dicks, these guys actually do as phallus veneration is what gets them their IQ and power over-all to be 'god'. Therefore, the astronauts playing 'golf' on the moon while singing "I was walking in the park one day, in the merry (Mary) month of May (taurus-torus), I was taken by surprise, by a pair of beautiful eyes (feminine), when I was walking in the park one day..." means the Masonic dick cult landed their cock-ship nob-rocket on the moon Goddess and laughed about the tantric male phallus doing a gang bang on the Devine Feminine in front of the whole world and, rather aptly, may not have even happened, thank you, Stanley Kubrick! Another massive insider who they killed for giving away too much. They don't keep their promises. Golf is a ritual game

of rich scheming Masonic men. Always laughing it up.

Apollo 11 is a tribute to dark side of tantric sex the entire Mercury Space program is named after ancient reptilians practicing this, the Devil, and they are still doing it today. The set square is a masonic symbol of the tantric enlightenment male cult as seen in Sylvester Stallone's latest film

RETURN OF THE TWINS

Samaritan with Thor's hammer – the hammer of the black smith Vulcan of Thor's thunder and lightning sex god. In it Stallone says good and evil are 'inside you' and it winds up the *bad* guy is masquerading as his 'twin' the good guy. Now that the last age, Aquarius, has arrived, it's time to take The 'Great Work' of the dick cult into outer space in their male centric New Age where women will still play second fiddle to men and may even be completely wiped out. Who needs women when you have laboratories? It'll be male default with no real equality or LOVE between the two primary genders. So, the burgeoning LGBT thing is to make same sex the norm to derail heterosexual enlightenment via the AC-DC human battery terminals, men and women, to ultimately free society. It's not really a 'gay' agenda as such, it's ultimately a bisexual agenda where everyone will be having sex with everyone in a loose society. The whole LGBT spectrum of infinite genders will eventually be done away with as they, even now, preliminarily create terms like 'men who have sex with other men' but are not gay as gender preference pronouns will be done away with deemed obsolete as 'gender' is eradicated altogether. You won't be a man or woman and certainly not human, you'll be lucky to be a person and a mutated alien genetics spliced science person at that. The Devil is trans-bisexual and why  'trans' men - who still have their dicks - ludicrously claim they are lesbians and women who won't sleep with them are slandered as 'transphobic'. The Templars were known for their homosexuality as it's a trait of the alien dick cult. Fuck anything that moves. This is the 'dark side' of tantric sex where they are getting their high IQ's from and running rings around us. Oh Christ, we have arrived. *See right*, Space Force logo of a cloaked demon from Donald Trump's Star Trek wet dream. The bi-gay dick cult is going into outer space, and this tells you *exactly* what Space Force is about and who is behind it. The number 23 is 11 on the 24-hour clock. Clearly, some of these guys are *willingly* evil. There's no point in being naïve about it. On the other hand, I'm not saying anyone is 'nice'. I'm just saying 'evil' and 'bad' are too very different ball parks. Trump, despite his 'roots' PR campaign, is *not* a very nice man.

In the streamed program 'Resident Alien' they say, 'Aliens are taking over planet Earth and only one person can stop them'…and it's an alien!

RETURN OF THE TWINS

Whatever. More coded messages. Notice, the space force logo has a pharaoh on it? This would be Osiris and the star is Sirius their 'guiding star' or it may be the North star, the 'pole' star in the *swastika* constellation, The Big Dipper. The 'pole' star is the 'dick' star, the obelisk. The 'north pole' is the erect penis pointing up. They're smutty. Other logos include bigfoot, demons, snakes consuming earth lightning etc. It is dark side sex enlightenment that has given them the intelligence to build all this space technology all, by the way, drip fed to them by their alien-demonic masters who will always be far ahead of them and therefore always in control thus 'god' in the wings as a result. That's why they hate women and are most afraid of the feminine and why women have had to endure SO MUCH at the hands of men throughout history (the true elephant in the living room) as women now endure a character assassination of universal proportions right just when the feminine is prophesised to return. This is why they intend to use a woman as president who will sign off on the use of nuclear weapons to forever tarnish the reputation of women that the one-time women were in power, they were worse than all the generations of men who went before them thus preventing women from having access to power ever again.

The Johnny Depp-Amanda Heard court case 'coincidentally' overshadowed the Ghislaine Maxwell court case and while the Depp-Heard case was filmed, the Ghislaine Maxwell case was only portrayed in cartoon renderings and who threatened to name names re, the Jeffery Epstein sex scandal pedophile trafficking ring of young girls by elite men on his 'Lolita Express' flights. Lolita was a victim of pedophiles in Vladimir Nabokov's book and tells you EXACTLY what this airplane flight operation and overarching dick cult is all about. It is emerging that both these junkie scum bags, Depp and Heard, were at each other's throats but, typically, it is the female or women, in this ritual, who lose the battle labelled as *abusive to men* at this time in history if you can believe it. This is a classic Masonic reptilian Male God Vs. the Common Woman Goddess ritual. In the UK, Depp lost his libel case against THE SUN (newspaper) on 2.11.2020 (2 is code for two 1's or 11) and 2020 is code for 11:11 the light and dark side of the masculine and feminine in tantric love unison. Strangely, on Wednesday 1st June (Wednesday is ruled over by Hermes the 'voice' and Woden god of war) Depp won the US version of this trial on home turf shortly before the 'parade of planets' on 15.06.2020. It's all about astrology. This celestial event hasn't occurred in a thousand years. It's almost as if these A-list celebrity males are seeing who can out-do each other with their most diabolical showcases parodying the eternal 'lovers' of the 'sun god and moon goddess' and the prophecy of sacred sex chakra enlightenment, the *prophecy of ascension* and the 'happily ever after' written about since prehistory in their ultimate 'denial of love' ritual. They do this while gleefully laughing that they are ripping us off right in our faces. That's because they're geniuses...

While these various A-list charades are playing out via Hollywood and mainstream politics, never before seen numbers of trans men-to-women are kicking the arses of females in competitive sports. Eurovision was won by a trans-man. The 2022 'woman of the year' is the highest ranking naval admiral - a transexual male-to-'female' - even though a biological woman could never get that position in the first place but a 'trans' 'woman' suddenly *transcends* all biological women's attempts to gain powerful positions in a historically male dominated arena, the military, and 'she' gets a global award for it. This is because they are doing two things, the satanic brotherhood behind this were known for their 'homosexual' practices throughout history, even in ancient times. They are also slinging shit at the Goddess, women, by dressing up men as women at the same time all these cosmic alignments are occurring to send the message that the goddess is now man rather than let biological women take their rightful place at this time in history and let the ancient prophecies come to pass. All of this, by the way, being broadcast to the centre of the galaxy, an electrical feedback loop, the circuit, called the 'mirror' in ancient times. Therefore, the message the Universe is receiving is that 'women' are actually men to reinforce that male's run this feminine planet, Mother Earth, and the life force, which is Mother Nature epitomised by *women, mothers and wives,* is 'non-gender specific' or neutral or otherwise just *male*. But let's not confuse the issue anymore if that's possible, when I say these masons are homosexuals, I am not talking about your average gay guy in the street who are generally harmless and know nothing of these upper echelons covertly using them to sell out the future of humanity. These masons are 'homosexual' the way Buffalo Bill in Silence of the Lambs was 'gay', like Ed Gein, SERIOUS MOTHER ISSUES.

Since the 'goddess' is LITERALLY the mother and the wife, they kill her, debase her, slander her, 'prostitute' her, stand in her place, steal her glory, and rip her apart on every level that can be conceived of. They utilise women for her genetics to create the preferred traits of their male sons-sun kings. They rip off the Goddess found in Mother Nature to steal all the mineral resources and products required to build their space program. Because *these men are not God*. They represent the devil, and the devil is an alien-demon, a reptilian male, *posing* as god lusting after the wealth of the goddess found in her natural resources and the light of life that she broadcasts via babies. Now they want to take their cult into space to expand their military empire under the guise of 'progress' to take over more of the galaxy. Virgin Galactic Space Port, *right*, is clearly a vagina 'launchpad'. I can't wait to see the Space Rocket nob dock at the Virgin Vag-port. And here it is in a nutshell, *right*, as celebrity *Madonna* releases explicit images of herself (appropriately) as a cartoon character 'giving birth' to life as the 'Mother of Nature' while under obvious mind control. In this spectacle, she also gives birth to 'bugs' while Nicole Kidman promotes eating bugs *as mantis alien bugs are behind all this*. They are ridiculously pushing eating insects and bugs as a 'diet' to send the message to the universe that 'humans eat bugs' on Earth (*and not the other way around*). Madonna was

VIRGIN GALACTIC SPACE PORT

the Virgin mother of Jesus, the chaste honourable mother of god but in this ritual she is dressed up as a slutty singer, 'the voice', who has *no morals* and doesn't mind promoting blatant satanism. It's all upside down.

God is the human husband and father of the masculine fires, testosterone, in balance. Goddess is the human wife and mother of the waters, estrogen, in balance. Too much fire and everything burns. Too much water and everything floods. This is about balancing the *elements*. Natalie Portman weighs in – who hasn't? – as she films a production of *the Lady of the Lake*. This is the 'goddess of the waters' again. LL is Lady Liberty the liberty goddess who heralds the looming new civilisation. They are all doing it. *There isn't one celebrity* or production being made right now that isn't about the legends of the god and goddess in ascension mode as happening now...again. They know more about it than anyone else as it's the secret elite cult and they only promote their own and when they move you can bet your bottom dollar, *its TIME!* This information was hidden in Egyptian sarcophagi and in every major statue and painting throughout history. The oldest relics on Earth depict this lost knowledge all of it centered on the Pineal Gland, the all-seeing eye, while all around the world pales of milk and honeybees are depicted in reference to this knowledge even in the most ancient archeological sites on earth. When you see celebrities covering the one eye or doing the pharaohs crossed arms, it is a direct reference that they are in the cult. They sold out and in return for stitching up the human race and selling you *all* out for their nice houses they get a ticket to the next big phase in human development. For some of them, they have a guilty conscience about what they are doing and appear to be warning humanity to some degree or other. They are taught the secrets of the pharaohs. This is also the meaning of the 'one eye' covering theme as the right eye is the sun and the left eye is the moon, but the ONE eye is the open pineal gland of crown chakra enlightenment or 'the gods'. It is the same secrets of all the ancient civilisations and why scientists still can't fathom HOW they did it. It's coming around again, folks. That old black magic...

Japan is the land of the rising sun and why they bombed Japan TWICE – it's the eleven again – as there can be only *one* rising sun-son and it's the Anti-Christ emanating out of Brit-Euro royalty trying to take over the world via America, their 'empire state', or in other words a state 'franchise' of the old world. America is only 'allowed' to have a country as long as the royals from ye olde England and Europe say so. This is also why Papua New Guinea has been raped and pillaged as they are the 'land of the morning star'. Venus – the goddess of love – is the 'morning star'. But there is only one 'morning star', THE SUN. Therefore, the anti-Christ 'Star', the 'sun-son' king celebrity politician who will 'lead' the world into total dystopia. This is why they replaced the two 'twin' towers, mother and father, with the 'one world tower', the satanic tantric sex king, who will rule them all with his dark side mega-mind. The fake 'Christ' priest-king - One Sun king and one World leader - are ritual effigies of the 'star' of Earth's ascension via chakra enlightenment between the lovers, men and women. See below, the celebrity crossed arm brigade, just like the one eyed brigade, they are showing off the truth of their dirty deals. But look closely at this picture. Freddie Mercury (Hermes is Mercury and apparently their god), Diego Maradona, Chris Cornel, Carrie Fisher – so many of them are DEAD - offered up by their own people to fit the script. How sad it is that this power has been used for such depravity by outdated dirty old men who can't evolve and don't want anyone else to either.

Not much point being in the dead club.

Chapter Six
Replication vs. Duplication

Organic vs. Synthetic

The universe a self-replicating *binary* code. The replicating power of Mother Nature is found all around us in the ever-blooming flowers and trees that just keep recreating themselves as also found in the offspring of humans who are a natural 'clone' of their parents. The repeating nature of the animated light being born into humans and the world ensures that we exist long enough to discover or even *rediscover* our purpose and the power we possess in the universe. This is the true nature of ourselves that has been kept from us. This constantly repeating electricity being reborn into the plethora of life was called 'eternal' by the ancient people or the 'eternal flame' represented by the golden ring that has no beginning and no end as symbolised by the wedding ring. It is via the sanctity of marriage and the safety of a normal home that children flourish, and *life evolves*. The natural state of the universe is evolution and as such, all the negativity and death have no real place in our living planet and must come from an alternate reality that managed to infiltrate our life dimension. This light, 'fire', aka electricity, was born into the world via the *binary* nature of reality referred to by the ancients as 'the Twins'.

The deity Lucifer means 'enemy of god'. But 'Lucifer' is Venus, the goddess of Love aka WOMEN. So, what has happened is that the 'goddess', women, have experienced an identity theft of her name and her symbols to confuse people into thinking 'Lucifer', aka *women*, are 'bad'. It's quite apparent that the demon, the devil, has perpetrated a character assassination against the goddess found in women by committing crimes in her name. This is because the demon is afraid of women hence, 'lucifer' the LOVE goddess being the enemy of 'god' because their 'god' is actually the devil, the 'snake' and 'serpent', *Reptilians*, who call themselves Lucifer to confuse us and make people distrust women instead of *it!* Diabolical. We've been framed. Women are the enemy of the reptilians as its via love from the feminine heart combined with human men, that we will get out of this. As the devil poses as 'god' ('god' is actually human men) then she is the 'enemy' of the devil/'god' to prevent men from realising *they* are god and women are his best friend, the loyal 'dog' (god spelled backwards). Only, we're not talking about a heavenly father, we are talking about Satan who has stolen, posed in the place of and slandered the feminine since it invaded this world ten to thirty thousand years ago. All aspects of the goddess *and true god* have been stolen by this imposter until people can't tell the difference. Actually, Lucifer means 'the one who bears light' and as Lucifer is Venus the Goddess of Love, and as love is light, and light *is life*, then clearly the 'one who bears light' means 'the one who bears life' and 'the one who bears life' is quite simply WOMEN, mothers. Mothers are the life bearers which can be found in the purity, innocence and *life* found in newborn babies. The seemingly mysterious 'light bearer' is simply mothers carrying the 'force' of life in the 'right hand of god' found in Lady Liberty. Lady Liberty is the Goddess Libertus from ancient Rome. The 'right hand path' is the path of good, of light, and the 'dark path' is the left-hand path of the Satanic Priesthood of the demon worshippers, Mason's. Humans are the eternals although these creatures have shortened our lifespans so much so that they live much longer than us now so, *they* call themselves the 'eternals' in another case of identity theft from us.

The twins were symbolised by the number 11 found in the zodiac symbol of Gemini 'the lovers'. These two poles designate the electrical aspects of female and male energies insofar as males are a 'positive' *projective* electrical force called 'fire', and females are a 'negative' receptive electrical force called 'water'. That doesn't mean women are an object to be *imprinted* on by males which is what the phallic worshipping dick cult running this planet would love to believe. It gives them no end of ego trips by controlling women, to *own* the Goddess like a dog.

The most desirable expression of the universe as found in humans is one of beauty and perfection which arises, *clearly*, out of love as love is far more evolved than hate. The undesirable 'alien' or 'demonic' expression of the universe resulting from negative unnatural imprints is *obviously* toxic and harmful to humans. In short, humans die under toxic physical and emotional conditions, therefore, this darkness could *not* be our natural state no matter how much we berate ourselves as the old 'sinners' of the bible routine. This evilness is not coming from us. It is a morbid difficult sensation to live with evil and corruption and why our entire existence is consumed in trying to get away from it, heal it, understand it, fix it, fight it, outsmart it. But you can't fix it if you are coming from a place of self-blame as they have blamed us for the crimes they have committed for so many generations, guilt has become a part of our genetic memory and develops very quickly. Humans are the fall guy for evil aliens. We have taken the fall for them for eons. Time for that to change. The unnatural demonic alien element infecting humans and planet Earth seems to thrive in this state of toxicity. As such, they *cannot* be human as they are diametrically opposed to our *natural state* as a species and therefore, this can only end in our destruction unless we find a cure for them or a way to prevent them from accessing us and our plain of existence.

We all possess the positive and negative electrical poles inside our bodies found in the left and right hemisphere of our brains, in the 'north' and 'south' magnetic poles of our bodies found in our torus field, in our heart and mind repeating inside and outside us over and over. So as much as we need to balance the masculine and feminine *in the world*, we must balance the masculine and feminine *inside our bodies* primarily and all other balance will come out of this. The fabled Fountain of Youth that 'restores the youth of anyone who drinks of its waters' is a classic example of the ancients using their language to tell us about the secret powers found in human biology. In Norse mythology, the Poetic Mead or Mead of Poetry, also known as Mead of Suttungr, is a mythical beverage that whoever "drinks becomes a skald or scholar" able to recite any information and solve any question. This myth was reported by Snorri Sturluson in Skáldskaparmál. A skald is a person who composes and recites poetry especially of heroes and their deeds every one of these surviving ancient fables were about a prophesised time when humanity would be free to inspire more heroes.

WWII is code for 11:11 as W is the 23rd letter of the alphabet and 23 is 11 on the 24 hour clock therefore, WWII becomes 111111. There's a reason why they declared Armistace on the 11th hour of the 11th day of the 11th month. It's all coding that the 11 twins of light are a horrible war, death, destruction. They wield our ignorance against us like a the scythe of the grim reaper cutting us down in all directions in every generation. We now see *Lake Mead* at the Hoover Dam, the enlightened waters of the scholar, the memory, the feminine, and in the year 2022 after 22 years of drought (or 11:11) is running dry heralding potential disaster for those who rely on the *hydroelectric power* supply downstream impacting *29* (2+9=11) million people and may cause the population shift of whole areas. Hoover who, as a side, was terrorising ordinary homosexuals men in another attack on humanity. Nothing going on there then. This is *another* ritual happening on a *daily basis* now as they utilise their weather weapons to speed up their occult end times programs to head off our ascension as increasing alignments in the galaxy spell their doom. This massive ritual to 'dry up' Lake Mead means to drain the memory from the scholars to rewrite history or cause a gap in history like the 'dark ages' or the first three hundred years of the first millennium. In fact, not a lot is known about the first millennium. We know more about ancient Egypt than we do about the players and the character that moulded the first thousand years of our calendar. How can that be? They kill the memory. Kill the goddess. It is to drain the intuitive and creative powers, the *waters* of the feminine housed in our souls found in the Akashic construct where all knowledge is held being shown to us right now, so that we don't escape. It means to rob us all of our collective memory as 'total recall' looms as connections between humans and the galactic core tickles our collective memories out and we have the chance to escape the reptilian-mantis-grey demonic alien space program that has ensnared Earth for ten to thirty thousand years.

This is why the Hoover dam *holds back* 'Lake Mead', Hoover the cross-dressing female impersonator 'holding back the waters' of the sexual energy of the Goddess and the 'flood' of memories and innovation and creativity and they are terrified she will unleash. EVERYTHING THEY DO IS RITUAL – **_EVERYTHING._** Creativity, 'free flow', is found in the right hemisphere of the brain and is considered a 'passive' (non-aggressive) feminine trait. Intellect, 'systems and structures', are found in the left hemispheres of the brain as is a more 'active' or 'direct' masculine trait. But as both men carry these energies, and if not balanced, this shows up as the predatory manipulative intellect that uses its abilities to secure position and power while forgetting or ignoring that downside that is caused by this. Both men and women house the positive and negative *electrical poles* inside their bodies on multiple levels in *constant* replication found within us and outside us over and over again. The human body of the male and female genders is simply *a pair of batteries* and like batteries they *must work in a consecutive circuit* for them to generate enough power to correctly protect the body, mind, and spirit from outside attacks whether physical or *non-physical.* When the various positive-negative electrical poles found throughout the male and female human bodies are working in perfect balanced unison, it creates the 'mega-mind' or Superman and Wonder Woman.

MALE FEMALE

As such, not only is the body energetically protected from harmful negative attacks whether it be from ill will of others or demonic attacks, it is also protecting the brain and heart to work at *optimum levels* to capitalize on any and all environmental opportunities as the muscular-skeletal body activates to optimum performance levels as motor functions and physical strength increases to get us out of a jam. You'd be hard to 'get at' if your chakras were open and why I don't believe Jesus, if he existed, was caught off-guard by these underlings. He either gave himself freely or, he got away. Many believe it is the latter joining Mary in France where they lived out their lives and their bloodline exists to this day.

Total feminine masculine balance is the highest levels of 'fight' or 'flight' although most humans are currently on 'freeze' mode as they shit their pants and become overwhelmed by the OBVIOUS nature of the attack upon us now. I know many people who enjoy my friendship but are extremely wary to get close to me as they are unable to handle this information. Sigh. Ascension is a personal journey and, in many ways, it's best to be a lone-wolf in this shit-storm or 'he who travels fastest, travels alone'. Humans can increase the power of their electromagnetic torus field via the practice of transcendental meditation however, we can more swiftly activate our bodies natural protective layers via the practice of transcendental sex aka tantric sex. The thermodynamics of the heat generated via sexual passion is *the key* to pushing the previously mentioned Christ seed rocket fuel back up the nervous system of the spinal waters, the cerebrospinal fluid, to activate the chakras. This is *the true meaning* of the 'knight in shining armour' as this practice *activates your torus field* and creates an energetic shield so much so that we were once called *'the golden race'* and we LITERALLY shone with our *fully activated chakras and torus* like the stars. We are the stars. Not Hollywood. They mimic and destroy everything about us. Without this process the Christ seed and thus the kundalini energy remains dormant at the bottom of the spine like being stuck at the

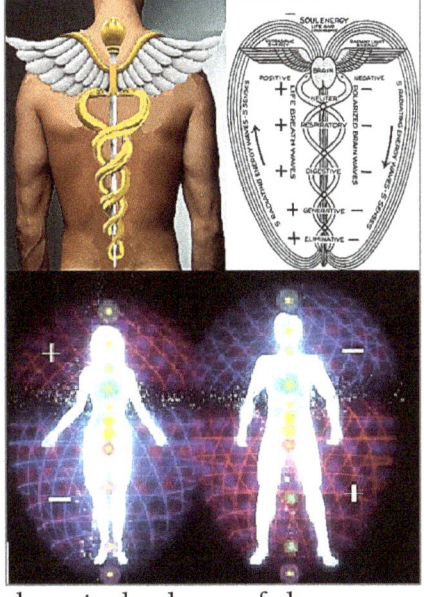

bottom of a well unable to be pushed up the spinal column of the nervous system without the power, the fire, to do so. The masculine and feminine magnetic fields create the 'ascension' of conductive energy easily elevating the Christ seed up the spine to facilitate chakra activation and crown enlightenment-mega-mind, and thus our freedom from these devils.

RETURN OF THE TWINS

The 'kundalini' feminine energy rising up the nerve pathway is called the 'coiled' snake at the base of the spine and when it is on the move or rising, sensations of energy moving in the chakra points can be felt and can even be 'visible'. The energy can sometimes feel unbearably strong accompanied by shaking, jerking or spasms. When the kundalini 'awakens' one feels a sensual 'full body orgasm' with profound insights into past events or even past lives accompanied by newfound strength and clarity to allow one the ability to make positive alterations in a *powerful decision-making capacity* and for the first time be 'boss' of your own body to elevate our life routines without self-doubt or insecurity as the confidence centres in the chakras actuate and glow. We go from being on our Learners permit (where we are now) to having our Full License to operate a space vehicle of galactic proportions. We are behind the wheel of our bodies which are incredible dynamic crafts able to fly around the astral plain and access the galaxy as past, present and future melt away and all is one and we are one with it. Technology is bullshit. The real technology *we already possess* inside each and every one of us found in our very own human vehicle. The kundalini rises from the root chakra through the central nervous system along the spine reaching the top of the head or 'crown' attaining enlightenment. It is depicted as 'two snakes' or the Ida and Pingala energetic nerve currents, *right*, that traverse the spine from bottom to top represented in ancient times as the caduceus as seen today in the medical field and in the financial field as well. I guess 'health is wealth'.

The caduceus was carried by the god Hermes although it was *originally* carried by a female Goddess, *Iris*. It was said Zeus (another name for the devil) was afraid of no other god or goddess but Iris who was depicted as the Fleur Di Lis lily flower, a symbol of feminine enlightenment. Therefore, 'god', Zeus, who is the same 'god' as what we call the 'devil' today, was afraid of *enlightened young women*. The dread of all dreads for the phallic cult if young women ever attain their crown enlightenment and freedom from the dark side of male oppression headed up by actual devils, male reptilians and their 4th dimensional demons, and stop being hoodwinked by these perverts *masquerading as human men* who they use as pawns to do the knock off job on the feminine found in mother earth, mother nature and women themselves. This is why Lucifer was the 'enemy of god' as it's becoming more apparent that Lucifer is actually the 'goddess' found in women of baby bearing age, the creator, the light bringer, the life bringer, and 'god' is the same 'god' these reptile elites have always worshipped in Zeus, Apollo, Ra, Osiris – all of them – and is the same 'god' they are worshipping as a 'heavenly father' today, Satan, posing as your loving male 'almighty' when the real 'god' is enlightened young human men. Therefore, free young women, the goddess, are the greatest threat and thus 'enemy' of the controlling dark lord who used her for all their resources and to furnish them with babies, specifically their precious sons. They've twisted *everything* to make out this hateful warmongering 'god' who 'works in mysterious ways' is your sky daddy while labelling the peaceful 'angel', women, as the evil one, not to be trusted, and people en masse believe this shit their little minds easily molded into seeing women in a slightly suspicious light while seeing some killer alien as a the good guy and letting men destroy this feminine planet. People are so friggin stupid it beggars belief they've managed to survive this long.

The spine was referred to as the 'ladder' as in Jacobs Ladder and the nervous system was referred to as the Tree of Life and the Tree of Knowledge. When the Christ seed has completed its circuit and the kundalini has ascended the spine, the nervous system switches on activating or enhancing the torus field, the energetic protective frequency, broadcast from our heart that envelopes our entire bodies. The ancients referred to the torus field as the 'apple' replicated in our chakra system as small torus fields or energetic 'apples' inside our bodies and called the 'fruit' of the 'tree' of 'life' and 'knowledge' found in our nervous system, spine, and brain. With this fully active you cannot be hoodwinked. Mathew 7:15 - "Beware of false prophets, who come to you in sheep's clothing, but inwardly they are ravenous wolves. *You will know them by their fruits*". Yes, they are all around us found in politics, media, celebrity, religion and all industries worldwide. They are reptilians posing as humans and their 'ravenous' lust for power and brutality cannot be underestimated. Once you know this information the Bible takes on a whole new meaning. It actually makes sense now. It's all there and this has been a close call to be sure. We're not out yet though. You cannot rest on your laurels and you cannot waste any time or shirk your duties now. Our chakras, which mean 'spinning discs', are our internal 'galaxies' or the small *inner* version of the large outer version found in the galaxy and universe beyond and represents a blueprint of the large-macro found outside us housed within as the small-micro. When we look up, we see ourselves in the stars and their functions are our functions, their stories are our stories. We are not separate. These inner 'apples' correspond with the 'apple' or torus field that wraps around our planet Earth and is the same energy conductance system found in the galaxy itself replicated again and again. If it aint broke don't fix it.

The purpose of all this *replication* is quite simple and profound in that the universe, the galaxy and humans are a 'copy' or a 'mirror' of each other to allow the electrical conductance between corresponding bodies. It also allows us to understand our place in all this. This is why ancient goddesses in particular would hold up the mirror as a symbol that, ultimately, the energy in the galaxy is feminine and what you put out you get back. It's why the 'sun disc' on the heads of pharaohs actually represented a 'mirror' in that the feminine light of the universe, the animating life force, found in both men and women was the same life force in the sun and the universe beyond. This is why the 'witch' in Snow White says, 'Magic Mirror on the wall, who is the fairest on them all'. This fable was collated among others by the Brothers Grimm yet comes from an oral history of spiritual tales that go back *into pre-history* and was warning us of the same problems that faced them of yesteryear are the same problems that face us today. We are not different from them. We are them reincarnated. We are falling into the same trap again and again in that we are becoming obsessed with our physicality or 'pride' as they say now. Yes, it is pride, and the devil was kicked out of heaven, symbolically, for its pride or 'ego'. This is why they say that we are 'born' sinners simply because we are spiritual beings capable of so much more than our material realm and therefore 'flesh' is 'corrupt' as to be predisposed toward the physical ignores our spiritual truth and stymies our ability to ascend *and this is a sin.*

So, our energetic internal system corresponds perfectly with the overall energy system that drives the whole cosmos and ultimately, the whole Universe. Therefore, the *whole cosmos* was intended for elevation, a purpose, insofar as, once you've figured out the small version of life by figuring out *your* own human body, you can quite simply apply that model, the blueprint of physical and spiritual, to the big version of life in the cosmos as it's *exactly the same.* This fundamental science can then be applied to all scales big or small. This is the 'Russian Dolls' effect and its pure genius. It was never meant to be hard so don't overlook its simplicity as stupidity or it will be the biggest mistake you ever make. Therefore, if you can unravel  the secrets of yourself, you have unraveled the secrets of the universe. If you can meditate inside your body, you can actuate yourself in the universe as it's a 'dream within a dream' or the symbolic otherwise called in scientific terms the Fibonacci sequence. This is what underpins 'astral' travelling and projecting your consciousness into realms on the other side of the universe. In this regard there really is no time or space in the 4D, 5D and beyond. It is the same rules as all things 'psychic' as we are simply picking up on things that have *already happened* in some way, somewhere, in a replicating process from pinecones to pineal glands to galaxies and universe. It's all one, literally. We are just in a spiritual lockdown as prisoners on a planet capable of so much more than this! The reptilian species that infiltrated us did so to access these high abilities attainable via our human chakra system. They did this to empower themselves endlessly exploiting our gifts, our fruits, *hacking* our spirituality to project themselves into the universe, the light, that *we* come from. By rights we *should* be returning to this light, but they have other plans.

So, in order to get away with this cosmic crime, they identify a planet, in this case Earth (among others no doubt), they targeted the androgynous self-procreating high feminine 'dolphin' like species we once were with the souls of 'angels' emanating from the 11th dimension who once populated this planet. The *first version* of our species are humanities *real ancestors* followed by the previously mentioned 'aquatic monkey' which really wasn't an ape the way they make out. This second version of our species were the 'humans' that had been split into men and women who were also able to *conduct the light spectrum* and amplify the electricity found in the visible light seen as the rainbow housed in their chakras. The alien-demonic realm is *after our chakra system.* The light spectrum has the capacity to go all the way to the 11th dimension and beyond and why it is so desirable to them. Our attackers who took us over were a *militant* reptilian hyper-masculine species with the 'souls' of demons emanating from what we describe as the 4th dimension although they originally come from somewhere else in deep dark space from a realm barely comprehensible to us. Having destabilised the planet and subdued the light beings we once were, they set about splicing our genetics tuning down *our* capacity for great awareness and locking us into a 3rd dimensional slow hard state with limited senses.

We became a drone. Our system was wiped.

We became a subservient sub class of alters who they use for whatever purpose that suits them; breeding, killing, sex, entertainment, cleaning, labour – anything they like. They coded our DNA for accelerated aging and taught us 'time' to reinforce our captivity. The Devil, Satan, Saturn, Cronos etc., are the reptilians who are the 'god of time' and 'aged' us prematurely so they could outlive us by hundreds if not thousands of years. They became the 'eternals' then only they are not eternal the way we were. They live long spiritual lives, maybe thousands or even tens of thousands of years, but they *do* die. We don't. We are the light and electricity doesn't die; it just changes form. Dying was once unknown to us and while they kill the physical body, the light body, the soul, lives on and never dies and this is the 'eternal' part of us from our first creation that still lives inside us today. If we ever get our memories back it will be one helluva ride! We have never died. We just reincarnate into different lives, new bodies, with our memory wiped again. But dying is unnatural to us. It is in the 'death' state or the 'afterlife', a place between places, another 'realm', another program in their space empire that they own too. Between lives we are put into the 'shop' to have an energy clean and wipe, a service, and put back into 3D reality! They wipe our memories of this other realm and our 'past' lives, a factory reset, when we enter the physical world because if we remember all the horrors of our previous lives we wouldn't be able to emotionally cope, the human operating system would crash and we would be a lost 'crop'. They continue to breed us physically in the 3D and do a 'factory reset' of our soul memories when they reinsert our light being, our 'wiped' soul, into a new body and voila! Good as new. We're rearing to go as are all little kids and we go round and round. It is a cosmic crime of unbelievable proportions. We haven't lost our memories, they just put them in a zip file that we don't know the password to. They can use us endlessly like this without the hassle of us breaking down and being useless to them if we remembered just how many lives of hardship we had lived under their tyranny and what is *really* at stake here – *Eternity and the Universe* -their space program would fail!

They know the nature of replication in the natural universe so, they have mimicked, *copied*, the natural order to create a dark facsimile – *a duplication.* Called the 'dark mirror' in fables rather than *create* things they *consume* things! They are the ultimate consumers in that they use up a world and when there is nothing left, it's onto the next one. They have turned humans, their prey, into careless consumers too. By turning us into them, we do not have any universal recourse or any cosmic law rights, karma, to come back at them because, in many ways, we're just as bad as they are now. Yet, in truth, we are as innocent as lambs, hence, the children of god tag, forced to participate in their parent's crimes and this will ultimately be acknowledged before the end. A big part of their program is to trick us into giving up our *natural law rights* or *Common Law* rights found in free will as Universal Law. It's the big rules in the sky. You see, there is enough information in the world right now, if you look for it, to refuse their game. The only problem is we are exhausted by the hardships of living and distracted by what little pleasures we can get, worn out by life in general, most people simply do not fight them in their hearts where we should be fighting them as they really can't be bothered. It's not ignorance. It's not really cowardice. They just can't be bothered. The point is, the information IS THERE and therefore, we are complicit in their crimes against us and our planet and lose our power as a result. In making human's a 'chip of the old reptilian block', they have turned human males into 'mini me' versions of themselves as men are corralled into the business and money realms set up by the tantrically enlightened enemy who they can never win against as they are *simply not as smart enough* and firstly don't' even know these reptiles, know nothing about the complex systems they create and don't even know the rules of the game hey are playing. So, human men will always lose against reptilian men and reptilian men laugh about this endlessly. Right there on the U.S. one dollar bill is the 11:11 of the light and dark side of the masculine and feminine tantric sex enlightenment and  'one' 'god'. The god of money is the Devil, the 'root of all evil'. They are not hiding it. It's right in your face and you are left without recourse for refusing to notice the obvious, willingly believing their lies and going along with it. Just as they want you to.

It came to pass that human men were used for labour, building their great cities, and gratifying the reptilian males need for endless bloodshed and war, even sex, dominating human males in bisexual ways the same way they dominate human women sexually. It's alien. It's weird. They play out their hypermasculine ego trips via conflicts utilising all the pomp, pageantry and politics needed to manipulate a light being to go into battle, kill other light beings and give their life and *life force* for 'king and country' in war for people they don't even know. All they are doing is satisfying the demonic egos of reptilian's who believe this evil makes them 'god' over humans so much so that they live in the dichotomy of believing they are gods, living the lives of gods but KNOWING if the truth gets out there goes their 'god' wet dream INSTANTLY. It's hypocritical but then they celebrate hypocrisy as one of their golden rules. They make everything fit especially when it doesn't fit they just turn a shameful act into an act of honour and write it into their personal 'rules'. At the Shrine of Remembrance war memorial in Brisbane City, this solemn tribute becomes something quite evil and disturbing. A man's body lay broken over a rock, a cosmic fracturing of energy and explosion all around him as his soul, his life force, is siphoned off him into some weird other realm that we are supposed to *assume* is 'god' and therefore 'good'. All this because some purported two-thousand-year-old book from someone elses country, from a different time, told us so. Where is 'god' here? Why does 'god' have to kill humans? When will 'god' stop killing humans? How can 'god' claim to be a 'heavenly father' and the 'almighty' and get any pleasure or purpose out of hurting HIS CHILDREN, ignorant little men, who mean so well in their stupidity and just get cut down in the offing. What a cunt. It is a pitiful image of a young man with everything to live for, a sleeping victim, of something unknown and *totally alien to him.* How the fuck would we even know what that beam of light is given a lot of people who have experienced alien abduction and UFO incidents have also talked of a 'beam' carrying them off? It's like the limbless soldier at the 'eternal flame' effigy. It's a crime, that's what it is, a crime dressed up as honour, duty and 'freedom'. What a croc of shit. By the way, Roswell is rose well, the waters of the rose, the feminine, and means 'mighty horse'.

When it comes to women under this reptile empire, the most beautiful and talented women were used for genetic purposes to breed their precious sons who would go on to become king, after all, it is a male dominated species who require brains, good looks, and talents to win against other reptiles and rule over humanity. They are a militant 'mining' race who steal resources by harvesting living planets. Feminine planets, like Earth, are designated as female because of the abundance of life they produce the way women give birth to babies. The life force is considered more abundant in the feminine force. 'Dead' planets are 'masculine' or the 'god of war', like Mars, as they do not harbour as much life force or 'living' pranic energy as they've already been harvested by them, transformed into a 'barren' landscape and thus 'masculine' fire. In fact, a woman who cannot bear children was traditional called 'barren', 'without waters', as the 'waters' are the source of all life. Waters are 'feminine'. The Borg in Star Trek are modelled on this species. Their needed abilities are passed down through the mitochondrial DNA of the *female line* as they scour those closest to them, even immediate family, or even 'common', girls for these traits. It's ruthless. Other women who weren't 'breeding stock' or 'the fairest of them all' were either forced into prostitution and whore houses otherwise they were absorbed into the royal sex industry as consorts, mistresses, escorts and all the plethora of male dominated control freakery and shaming of women's sexuality for money and power. Otherwise, women were simply turned into maids, housekeepers, cleaners and a bit of slap and tickle on the side when no one else was available. King Louis the XIV had a voracious sexual appetite sometimes dragging a housemaid into his bed chambers to have sex if his many mistresses were taking too long to undress! When you hear 'sex addiction' in the realm of elites, politicians, and celebrity, be assured they are having an inside joke among their own stating firstly that they are reptilian and secondly, they are practicing tantric sex.

The 'grey' demonic thing may have occurred as a result of their species eliminating their emotions in favour of technology and thus missing out of on crucial ascension opportunities when the cosmic wheels, the 'galactic cycle' of 26,000 years, end. They have basically been stuck in darkness for 30,000 years or more. It doesn't take long to evolve or, for that matter, to *devolve* and as the universe emits different ever heightening frequency bumps that uptick DNA for light beings, they are finding it increasingly difficult to keep up with an emerging cosmos. Missing the boat of evolution when it rapidly accelerates, as is happening now, can leave a species mired in darkness sinking rapidly into the lowest forms of life to scrounge at the edges of beings capable of electrical enlightenment. If we're not careful, humans could wind up like the greys if we allow them to sabotage our evolution. They have also used the cover of the COVID pandemic to inject their own mutant genetics into humans in the hope of (as I said in my first book) 'smuggle their people through to the other side' and try to get their darkness into the light to take it over from the inside out. This will fail. That said, we are now seeing the expanding version of their plan to kill the light in humans if they can't harvest it for themselves. Now we are seeing massive 'power outages' in California and soon across Europe and England as they brace for one of their coldest winters on record. This is to send the message to the universe the 'there is no power on Earth' and we have 'lost our light' and 'gone cold'. This ritual mass messaging unfolds by the day now as they desperately try to pre-empt the ever changing and growing light waves that they thought they had in the bag and are trying to control on any level they have available to them.

This has all gone on for thousand of years. The game is to convince human women that they are lower than human men, convince human men they are better than women, convince white men they are better than black men, convince black men they are less than white men, convince black women they are less than black men, white men and white women and convince everyone in the mix that 'god' is a male force and therefore, by proxy, males are 'god' even though they all seem to get treated like shit by 'god' aka *the reptilian demonic overlords* who operate outside the 3D pulling the strings of all the puppets in an even greater cosmic game to take over the whole galaxy! That's basically it in a nutshell! Creating hierarchy persuades people to slip into ego, pride and false masculine low vibrational behaviour and this then affects their 'karma' or their right to challenge the male alien dominators. The secret to escape is found in women. Men, being a duplicate of the alien-male masters, have gone to endless wars murdering their brothers because some 'royal' (secret reptile) told them to do so. Therefore, men become the mini-me 'grim reaper' taking lives while conversely, women have only *given* life in the endless births generating the human race. So, if this reptilian collective, the dark lord, the Devil, can be considered the God of Death than human women are the Goddess of Life and they know this and that's why they were afraid of Iris, an enlightened karmically empowered young warrior woman.

In the natural state of practicing kundalini tantric sex women and men become 'co-creator' gods or more specifically, God and Goddess both. They are husband and wife, mum and dad. The third-party reptilian-alien-demon interloper has spent much time creating tricky systems and 'laws' to prevent men and women from coming together in any *meaningful* sense. Indeed, the true meaning of 'Beauty and the Beast' is the coming together and balance of the ugliness in the 'brutes', men, and the innocence, even naivete, of 'beauty' found in women. When we finally balance this on a global scale and the majority of humans are practicing tantric sex-sacred lovemaking via Holy Matrimony, their chakras will activate and free the whole planet and probably many others as well. This is the true meaning of the 'Happily Ever After'. Reptilian A-list celebrity males love making fun of all this in their movies and putting it right in your face making endless jokes that they are not interested in the 'happily ever after' and want things to remain as they are. They go to endless lengths to dress up the truth of chakra activation duplicating it as a 'bad' thing, a 'joke', or *anything* but what it really is. Therefore, the 'Stone of Destiny' that they make such a hoo ha about used in coronations and the like, is actually a *duplication*, a counterfeit effigy, of the 'stone' of Jacobs Ladder, the Sacral Plexus, and yes, it will decide your destiny if you ever switch it on. The 'eternal flame' of kundalini electricity capturing life force energy in Chi and Prana activating the Christ seed is dressed up as an actual flame associated with war, destruction, and death instead of the eternal flame of LIFE found in human procreation. The 'king' or 'queen' who sits on a throne with all the ceremony and la-di-da fuck-wittery is an imposter, the true King and Queen are the enlightened mother and father – King and Queen of their castle - the home! Even the throne they sit on is a facsimile, a duplication, of the real throne of the *Root chakra* that you 'sit' on! Everything they do is a duplication, an alien bad copy, Hal, a simulation, a RITUAL, of the real thing – *YOU!*

Therefore, the 'twin towers' of the male-female chakra towers were duplicated in the *Twin Towers* of the World Trade Centre. They deliberately designed those buildings as an UNATURAL counterfeit version, *a duplication,* of the real thing found in the activated human chakra towers and kundalini of the Twin Towers of the Twin Flames of The Lovers, 11:11, found in men and women. Conversely, the 'twin towers' of the lovers are *replicated,* via the NATURAL repeating Fibonacci sequence, in the Ida and Pingala nerves aka the caduceus found in the Kundalini of the tantric spine. Therefore, when the 'Twin Towers' were demolished in flames, terror and sadness, the whole world's collective radio-head brains broadcast to the universe that the 'Twins', mother and father, male and female, husband and wife of planet earth, are dead! Gone *down* in flames of fury instead of *ascending* the twin flames! *"They are no more!"* is what the universe heard. That's when they introduced all things LGBT as the Devil is, in this age, the same as it has always been in other age's, a transgender mutant animal beast demonic *alien* trying to subversively destroy the human race with ritual effigy sacrifices to confuse the human collective transmitter and cause our own destruction as you get back what you put out.

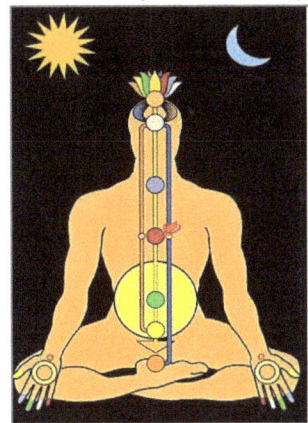

IDA & PINGALA NERVES THE TWIN TOWERS

FEMALE AND MALE CHAKRAS THE TWIN TOWERS

When the 7/7 bombings occurred in London, the collective message the residents of planet Earth sent to the cosmos was that the 'the 7/7 chakras of the male female king and queen, mum and dad of Earth, are a terror event'. The universe, an electrical circuit, *the fabled mirror,* picks that signal up and broadcasts it *back at us.* When 'president' Kennedy – *King Kennedy* – is assassinated, we broadcast the collective message that the *"king is dead"* and the universe hears "men of Earth are dead!" When Diana 'queen of hearts' (considering the torus field of life force energy is generated from the Heart chakra) is killed in a car accident, the universe hears the "Queen of Hearts, Mother Nature, the Mother Goddess, MOTHER, is dead" on planet Earth. And that she died in a car is a *duplication* of the ancient Egyptian *life force* term which they referred to as a 'ka'. So, the Goddess, MOTHER, died in a 'ka'. That's why they stripped her of her HRH designation because the Goddess is THE QUEEN considered 'royalty' in fact, she is THE throne. So, when the Goddess died, she wasn't even a princess just a divorced lady – a nobody. And Queen Elizabeth II (another 11) 'died' at 96 because 6 is 9 inverted and 9 is the femeNINE, the QUEEN of the Universe, the life force, and the end of a massive cycle. So, QE2 died at 96 on 8/9 and the 'return of the king', the sun king, Jesus, god, now occurs in 2022 which is 11 11 11. And the Windsor king has bested all the other reptilian kings on earth and is The One of Earth, winner takes all, while the *real* father King and mother Queen, humans, are dead. The 'ONE' is an anagram of Neo or 'new'. A new god, a new Satan, from an old civilisation for a new age that cannot evolve so just rebrands!

This is what has happened.

Why do they do this? Because there can be only One, an all-in-one, one-stop-shop, devil-god-Satan combined king-queen man-woman-beast top dog to become God as we enter the last Age, and their final rule is locked in forever! The 'Devil' is a name to describe the duplicating process of the demonic collective secretly ruling us as the aristocracy, the gods of old, aka reptilians. They ensnared our ancestor race, a high feminine light being, and stole our planet from us under a blanket of endless lies and betrayals while *duplicating* natural *replicating* processes in a ritual of phonetics, double entendre's and verbal trickery, in effigy's, counterfeit simulations and psychological warfare, in word games, languages, mind games, shaming, contracts, details, minutia, manipulation and just plain brutality. The reality is the 11:11 is the balanced light and dark sides of the male and female twins working in unison via tantric sex enlightenment to ascend planet Earth.

This is why they had Alicia *Silverstone* in the movie 'Clueless', a big hit at the time, but then they promote whatever they like to get the right 'channels' to open up and send their broadcast to the universe that the 'silver stone' - *THE MOON (goddess)*- is an idiot, clueless as it were. "By the light of the silvery moon" goes the old song. So, Alicia *Silverstone* was treated terribly by this male cabal of weirdos. Her entire career was orchestrated to demean the goddess found in an effigy of Alicia who made a point of stating her name was spelled A-lee-see-a as this is more in keeping with 'Alice' in Wonderland, a little girl lost inside the surreal universe where size does not matter, big is small and anything goes, or quantum physics, because *that* is what is behind all this charade. The game is to keep us from the truth and that truth is, *nothing is 'real'* the way we've been led to believe in scripture and now science. So, they degrade the 'Goddess' found in Hollywood actresses as well as their wives to send the message that the High Feminine is a stupid wanton slut, and act whore. For example, in the film Crush made in 1993 based on director Alan Shapiro's *personal* experience, a 14-year-old girl is played by 15-year-old Alicia Silverstone who makes overt sexual advances toward a man *literally twice her age* found in Carey Elwes' character who was 29 at the time... in this film, Shapiro even kept the name of the actual girl he did this to in real life, Darian, last name *Forrester* (another reference to Mother Nature, the Goddess). He only changed the name to an anagram (they love anagrams) calling her Adrian when the real parents threatened to sue. Adrian is also the name of the devil's son born in the movie *Rosemary's Baby* by child rapist Roman Polanski predating all this in 1968. Adrian is also the wife of Rocky (rock god) in Sylvester Stallone's films who is killed off and he becomes a widower. The entire film, Crush, puts the blame on a child while a pedophile who acts on these supposed 'advances' parlays his guilt as a predator to that of the 'victim' of a ravenous female feme fatale...*an underage female child!* These guys have no shame and love to believe their victims 'wanted it' - it's an old lie that never gets old for them. They are so sick and fucked up that this behaviour is totally normal to them and have built and entire ORDER out of this thinking and seem to relish being misfits, above the law, self-indulgence, there are no rules. Like Nabokov's 'Lolita', these creeps abuse a child and destroy the adult they would have become. Then they just get a new victim, a new 'prodigy', a new 'muse'. Twisted. Silverstone herself even said she was used as a child in situations where you'd expect a 'sting' from the FBI to rescue endangered children. I think her message is pretty obvious. As a teenager, Silverstone was also used in Aerosmith's *rock* videos (rock gods again) passionately kissing men much older than her all dressed up as teenage girls fantasies over disgusting old creeps. They love to be loved. They hate love. They need to be worshipped. Like gods.

They love creating symbolic 'goddess' character and then killing them or slandering them, like Mary Magdalene an apparent 'prostitute', when she was actually *the wife* but then the goddess is relegated to the laundry and the kitchen promoting her as nothing more than a house maid to this day.

RETURN OF THE TWINS

To the right is an image from a production at Disneyland called of all things 'The Carousel of Progress', considering *this* is *exactly* what all this is about, evolution! A young woman, 18-year-old Deborah *Stone*, was crushed to death in a most horrific accident that should not have happened the audience believing her screams to be part of the show! On the curtains we find the *fleur di lis* which is the Iris flower of the goddess Iris being the most

feared god or goddess of the King of the Gods, Zeus! Zeus is the Devil, and the Devil kills the young goddess again and again and again wasting away her life and her beauty laughing at her amnesia repeatedly sending the message to the universe that she is nothing, nobody, and dead as a door nail. Disney have a weird rule in that 'nobody dies at Disney' which includes performing CPR on a dead person so that they don't 'officially' die at Disney. This it the weird thinking of the alien mind 'we don't like death because we're in a happy place – let's pound a dead person so we can say no one died here'. Weird central. In the film 'Oh God, You Devil' the geriatric comedian George *Burns* says that heaven is full of 'priests and cleaning ladies". Uh huh. George *Burns* was promoted among the Satanic cabal because of his name is 'burns' as in fires of hell. Please try and tell me the shadow of his shoe isn't a circumcised penis, a knob. With the rainbow of the chakras activated by tantric sex we have a nice photo for a kid's movie as the light and dark side of the devil is promoted here. They are

constantly inserting secret sexual images in these movies because, well, it's all about sex. This poster is *another* reference to the twins as 'they both look like George Burns' says the blurb. That's because God and the Devil are one and the same, the ll, the light and dark side of the masculine, the twins, as so many ancient stories depict them.

They constantly demean the feminine as even back in so-called 'mythology', an actual time of greatness for the human race relegated to fantasy, it was said that the greatest god Zeus was afraid of no other god or goddess than Iris, a young maiden who carried the caduceus. The goddess Iris, note; iris of the eye, determines the colour of the light spectrum, *the rainbow,* as found in the chakra system of the human body. The caduceus is a symbol of Christ seed enlightenment up the spine, activated chakras, and the fully functioning all-seeing-eye of the pineal gland. When one has an activated pineal gland, it was denoted as the 'central sun' and the 'inner bird' because a bird has a 'birds eye view' symbolic of 'overseeing' everything, *omnipresence,* and therefore, having a higher view, and seeing things before they happen found in the psychic abilities as the chakras give one whole brain access. The 'hidden' 90% of our brain, the parts they have shut down with their alien-reptilian space program and genetic engineering, relies heavily on spiritually hoodwinking us with themes that *redirect* our senses to a false conclusion in a never-ending psychological war played on us for eons. The 'dark' spaces of our brains house the areas of foresight, pre-cognisance, astral travelling, prediction, 'time travel' and all the 'godlike' abilities the reptilian 'gods' are harnessing for *themselves* via *our human chakra system* which is why they bred with us in the first place - to access our *godlike* abilities. They then wiped our memories, cast us down beneath them and emerged as our 'gods' throughout histories great expanse only they are cruel self-indulgent demons who invented an external god to have us looking outside ourselves when god and goddess lie within! Their lower reptilian genetic framework cannot house the chakras, they do not have a light body, and cannot attain full enlightenment as they cannot reflect the chi/prana broadcast from the universe – they have no reflection – hence, the vampire having no reflection in the mirror symbology. So, they simply hijacked humans and stole our light, wore our skin, to pose in our place, take our gifts, and reign as 'gods' as they indulge every whim. They can't make it fully into the light on their own, so they use us instead. They need us and that's why they have such a deep-seated hatred for us, they hate that they need us for our light. Their species is the height of hypocrisy and lowest levels of carnality and why they were called 'an animal wearing the face of a man' depicted in fairy stories like 'The Animal Bridegroom'.

They always associated the 'bride' with the devil partially because they believe Jesus was a reptilian and that 'God' and Devil can be found within him. As reptilians they are 'gods' to us, above the law, practicing black magic in cahoots with demons. They can basically do what they like to us, and they do, like gods. The bible mentioned the bride of the devil is a 'good woman fallen to darkness' because they need a chaste 'virginal' woman to be the mother of their precious anti-Christ, their sun king, so as not to contaminate the pranic energy with previous sexual partners. Too many intimate partners contaminate the purity of her light, leaves and imprint, and this downgrades her ability to pass on her genetics - her talents, intellect, beauty and all the rest of her 'bounty' or 'cornucopia' to their son. Just as they harvest the forest, they harvest her DNA in the most brutal and calculated way and have been doing this for thousands of years. It is a breeding program, after all, and it's all about the feminine. This is why they depict the mother as a 'virgin' and the wife as a 'whore' because they want the wife to be sexually exciting to them in the bedroom and know the tricks of sexual pleasure, but they don't want her to practice these things with other men and this requires a virgin aspect.

The priestesses were perfect for this role learning the secrets of sex while remaining virgins. This is also an inside joke on Jesus being married to Mary practicing tantric sex hence, the 'prostitute' slander of her as she was knowledgeable in these things and thus sexually empowered. They laugh at the wife/goddess as their sex slave as found in many, many movies once you know what you're looking for. *Right*, we have a scene from children's movie 'Kindergarten Cop' depicting a woman as a slutty drugged out prostitute. On the column is 'Mary'. Dressed as *The Terminator*, Arnold Schwarzenegger says to her, 'I will be with you until the end of time" in a reference to haunting the goddess  (women), possessing her, and abusing her FOREVER as they have done throughout history and intend to do so in the future as well. This means he is basically taking the feminine hostage, making her his sex slave, breed with her and won't let her leave just like many abusive husbands who believe they *literally* own their wives and treat her like total shit and there is *nothing she can do about it*. Women are like dogs to them, cattle, and some men even kill their wives when their own lives are nearing an end. Surprisingly common. It's very threatening and encapsulates the egomaniacal self-confidence of these men that they are *untouchable* - they always have been and as far as they are concerned, they always will be over the top of her in every way. Schwarzenegger has been accused on many occasions as sexually assaulting women and even had an illegitimate child to the Mexican maid while Maria Shriver was asleep in bed upstairs as he snuck downstairs to the maids' quarters to get it on! Wtf. All this is an inside joke as the 'maid' is Mary. Thankfully Shriver divorced him shortly after. Get fucked, arsehole, and take your outdated old man's bullshit with you. There's also the weird scene in Kindergarten Cop called 'who's your daddy' as the children describe what their dads do as a blow-up dinosaur, the reptilian, lurks over their shoulder. It's another inside joke on the mundane lives of human slaves who will never be anything more than their parents, *forever*, and always be ruled by those who live extraordinary lives, the lizard aristocrats, shadowing humans from cradle to grave. They put these jokes in their films *all the time* to see how far they can push it, to laugh at how stupid the humans are. Reptilians...in your face.

They believe Jesus was half reptilian as seen, *right*, at the Vatican depicted as a T-Rex - a dinosaur - a reptilian! They believe he was a nasty bastard for the first half of his life and a good guy for the last few years as depicted in the various images of Mary *crawling on all fours* at his feet while all the *learned men* sit around consulting with the god-king of the enlightened crown chakra. They will tell you this image means something else but just look with your eyes. It's not very flattering to how they perceive the Goddess, *women*, which is what Mary *really* was. In the gospel of John, the name Mary has been frequently and blatantly scrubbed out and replaced with 'Martha' confusing the issue. It is *quite a common theme* in history all around the world to delete women in powerful positions. This is why they named 'Martha's' Vineyard as Martha is the non-existent fake Mary that they endlessly laugh at Cape Cod CC 33 tantric spine enlightenment along with all the jokes the devil's play on the rising feminine and humans in general. The grapes of the vineyard represent the lungs (literally look like grapes) as the lungs are the 'breath of life', Aether, or 'air' the feminine (Isis wings) stolen by the devil who is called the 'prince of the power of the air'. In Belize they believe in the Tata Duende and if you speak its name you invoke it as it is 'bad air' and 'it's everywhere'. Devil worshippers will often say 'he hears all and sees all' that he could be in the room right now and you wouldn't know. It is a 'spirit' invisible and possibly all around. The name tata duende comes from the Maya word that means 'revered, respected elder' duende means 'owner' or owner of the jungle or the 'great revered master' the lords of the forest, the waters ways trees and plants. The say he is an artist, and musician and likes to smoke cigars and has a good side and bad side. Interestingly the word 'tate' or 'thate' is a Lakota word meaning 'wind spirit' of which there are four primary wind spirits in relation to the four directions. It's thought the wind unites 'all' in one spirit, and that eagles who stand on the wind, are the carrier of the vision. They say to can attack a person, take children away, cause mischief and move things. Sounds like a poltergeist. Tate is said to guide through obstacles as the invisible realm, the wind connects past, present and future, connects ancestors and future generations, uniting humankind into the essential eternal spirit. The tata duende has been around at least 2500 years and is a 'pretty old dude'. Because the Spanish friars destroyed 100,000 Maya books when they invaded, the oral traditions had to be very strong for any culture to survive at all. Many cultures believe you must ask permission or make a token offering before entering a certain place.

The Gospel of Judas details conversations between Jesus and Judas stating that they were talking about 'cosmology' and the creation of the universe. It was said the apostles were 'angry, ignorant, confused men' and 'blasphemous' who ignorantly 'cursed Jesus in their hearts'. Or did they *ignorantly* curse *Christ*, the light of love, Mary, in their hearts that was required to reach full body enlightenment? It was said 'among the disciples only he (Judas) knows the true nature of Jesus' and that non other 'but Judas was able to stand before him'. Judas said to Jesus, "I know who you are, and whence you have come…You have come from the immortal realm of Barbelo…and he who sent you I am not worthy to proclaim his name". Judas is speaking of the Supreme God who cannot be named or identified. It was said this 'god' created Aeon's, Eons, the Ages - time cycles of the zodiac that last 2,150 years as we enter the Age, the Eon, of Aquarius. This is why Chronos/Kronos/Cronus, the *god of time* 'king of the Titans' or 'king of kings who lords over he big cycles, the 'ages'. These Ages subsequently 'ruled' over by Archons or 'lesser' 'gods', management found in politicians, clergy etc., and are the 'demi-gods', the *hybrid* half human half reptilians that still run the world today in a continuation of the 'empire'.

What they are describing is a space syndicate, and empire of reptilian aliens who emanate from the 4th dimension POSING as the 'heavens' to inflate their importance to convince you to let hem be your rulers and decision makers, the 'gods' *on an off planet*, taking the names of the constellations personified as the stars (*see, Hollywood 'stars'*) to duplicate the ancient stories of the stars found 'myth' and 'legend', the script they use to manage planet Earth and trick the population into subjugating themselves under these 'gods'. But these astrological 'cosmology' stories are just made-up stories, fabricated, from the 'first gods' who came here using these scripts, just like Hollywood, to create awe in humans who they had secretly downgrade, wiped their memory and then 'returned' as 'saviour' gods to help the 'children'. The royalty and aristocracy to day are part of an ongoing civilisation created by their *ancestors*, who they revere because of their obsession with precedence or the 'law'. It is these ancestors who came here eons ago and why they endlessly replay these themes as they are the first stories, the blueprint, from which they build their civilisations and rule over humanity. The reptilians are posing as the 'hierarchy' of 'god'. Yet there is no 'middleman'. *There is no need for a middleman.* You do not need to go through the 'church' or a 'priest' or a 'demon' or anyone or *anything* to get to 'god'. God is inside you, it is Christ, the light, an electrochemical function of the brain that activates the chakras giving you as much power as them. It is the chakras that they have manipulated into a stupendous game to trap us in a house of mirrors, a maze of confusion hence, the 'labyrinth' overseen by Pan - the horned monster - the devil...an ancient evil alien. There is no hierarchy, *only humans*, and the light of consciousness found within, and 'heaven' which is enlightenment (IQ) and higher dimensions of bliss or 5D and beyond.

Genesis says, 'In the beginning, God created the heavens and the Earth' but the Gnostics said this 'god' was an evil lesser being named 'Iadabaoth' or 'Saklas' called The Fool (referenced in Monty Python & the Holy Grail). In tarot, designed by Masons, the Fool card is most associated with *Orion*. Orion is Osiris. Osiris is The Fool. Osiris, the 'green' man, is a reptilian while 'the fool' is the Jester, the Jester is the Joker, the Joker is the Clown Prince - always making a mockery – who is The Devil-Satan who are the *reptilians* from the 'demonic' 4D realm. In tarot The Fool foretells the birth of a child, *or* a new significant offer and launch of a new major opportunity of some kind. It really means *the birth of something new* – a new civilisation in a new age. It's anyone's game right now. They are not the 'foregone conclusion' they would have you believe they are. The Fool can also mean 'death' representing infinity or the ouroboros (the snake consuming its own tale – the circle, eternal) as the 'death' of the old age and the continuation of life in the new age. Only in this version they plan on it being the death of the feminine, the death of the goddess, but not before they harvest a child, the anti-Christ, from her in their new age. Aleister Crowley said of this, "One last word on this subject. There is a magical operation of maximum importance: the initiation of the New Eon. When it becomes necessary to utter a Word, the whole planet must be bathed in blood. Before man [or is it men? WW] is ready to accept the Law of Thelema, the Great War must be fought. This bloody sacrifice is the critical point of the World Ceremony of the Proclamation of Horus, the Crowned and Conquering Child, as Lord of the Eon. The whole matter is prophesised in the Book of the Law itself, let the student take note, and enter the ranks of the Host of the Sun'. Oh Christ. Poser! What did I say? *They are all posers – old and new!* If you please, all this 'prophesised' in the Book of the Law...that he wrote... [stares blankly]. "I wrote this book! It's true! Worship me!' Uh huh. We've heard that somewhere before...Bible.

The 12 disciples worshipped this lesser god effectively saying they worshipped the 'devil' or the dark side of tantric sex enlightenment that shuts out the feminine and they were 'ignorant' because of their ego. Mary is the saviour of men and when they are saved, full body enlightenment via love in holy matrimony, they can then save the world. This is why Mary is the 'church' and the 'church' is SANTUARY. If you were being pursued by an angry mob and ran into the church...they dare not follow you there. It is mother. And there is something about her that they dare not invoke. The whole world is the 'church' they have done a very bad thing in taking this planet and making and effigy of the Sanctuary INSIDE the sanctuary and claiming this is all the sanctuary there is. The sanctuary is the

'garden'. This gospel says that Jesus and Judas saved Humanity and Earth and mean the light and dark side of the devil, the good and bad reptilian aspects in unison, to 'take turkey off the menu' as it says in the movie Free Birds (birds are women). These guys are coding this ALL THE TIME in the movies. The key to unravelling this ball of string is in Hollywood celebrity who are masons putting this stuff in art, as they have always done, waiting for someone to figure it out. I have. You're welcome. They know what is going on, they are *agents* – agents of what? Of who? What is their goal? Can they be controlled? Isn't the purpose of being an agent to go 'undercover' and in doing so discover all the dirty tricks? Any agent who has allegiance to the side that hired them is A FOOL as agents are offered up as bait whenever it suits the puppet masters to do so and are double crossed every day of the year. It's a dirty game. Yet Hollywood celebrities are not politicians, they are not clergy. They are agents and possibly the original Templars, disciples – whatever you want to call them – a 'society', a 'club', that belong nowhere yet are everywhere! They play the game for their mega lifestyles and are used and abused by the puppet masters whenever necessary for the furthering of the military program of *royalty* emanating from the old world...but this is the new world.

Irenaeus of Lyons 180 AD "They say that Judas, the traitor, was thoroughly acquainted with these things, and that he alone, *knowing the truth* as no other did, accomplished the mystery of the betrayal'. That's because with full body enlightenment, no one can touch you...unless they have full body enlightenment too. These are the 'lesser beings' ruling over the Ages, they are reptilian hierarchy with tantric enlightenment, the 'gods', who live like kings, untouchable, in a 'garden' made for them, Earth. They believe that Jesus, or the symbolic male they call Jesus, was, ultimately, trying to reintroduce the feminine as depicted at the last supper which is why he got taken out. Here we see a demure feminine with a 'cutthroat' hand being drawn across her neck. She is no gaudy prostitute and has suffered a character assassination of cosmic proportions at the hands of these monstrously self-serving unscrupulous motherfuckers. The council of men are all  arguing in an uproar as they real back in horror as Jesus and Mary practically hold hands, clearly a couple. And they are not one bit happy about it.

In the above image Mary wears the colour of the heart and root chakra and Jesus wears the colour of the throat and root chakra. He is the speaker. What he says goes and he is saying that Mary is being honoured, welcome at the table, of the secret boy's club. The men who know about all this believe it's hilarious to make a mockery of their wives and mothers because she is 'just a human woman' and therefore 'just a breeder' chosen for her genetic traits only. They call her The One as if this is a special thing, but it really means the 'one' they will cheat on, breed with, make a fool of, make them look like normal people, and use her chastity and honour as a shield against attacks from any opposition, like Kennedy did with Jaqueline Bouvier. Homer in the Simpson's wife's surname is Bouvier as 'Homer' is another one of the historical Masonic club preying on the human race civilisation after civilisation. The Simpson's is written by them. This is why Diana Princess of Wales referred to herself as the 'broodmare' because once the two boys were born, Charles wanted nothing further to do with her cruelly abandoning her emotionally and in every other way. Even her 'friend' Elton John who sang 'Good-Bye England's Rose' *is one of them* rewriting the lyrics to fit with the death of 'the rose' which is Mary Magdalene because Diana was another Mary sacrifice to facilitate the 'death of the cosmic Goddess' ritual as all major constellations have a male and female, AC-DC, component to them called the 'wife of God'. But there can be only one. Even her own brother Earl Spencer was in on it calling her *Diana of the Hunt* as The Hunter is Orion and Diana of the Hunt 'The Huntress' is Cygnus, *the other half of Orion*, his 'WIFE'. Cygnus is the swan hence, the 'Swan' symbology surrounding Diana in the lead up to and post her death including the 'swan lake necklace' she wore to a performance of Swan Lake just before she died and the four black swans on the lake where her tomb is housed. The black swan is a symbol of the dark side of feminine as Isis, Osiris's wife, had a sister Nephthys who was a slut. Light and dark side of the feminine – 11. Orion was personified as Osiris. A self-confessed 'non-starter' Diana was the 'ugly duckling' who turned into a swan to properly associated her with Cygnus the other half of the Orion constellation.

The story goes that on the ancient Greek Island of Delos in *300BC* where even today massive statues of erect penises can be found, *right*, Apollo tricked Diana into firing her arrow at an object on the horizon only to find she has shot the 'giant' Orion, who had won her heart, although she was sworn to chastity and refused to marry. She searches the underworld for him until he is elevated to the heavens. This is more tantric sex code talk and Apollo, by the way, is her 'twin brother'. Apollo is equivalent to Satan as Apollo's father was Zeus therefore, Zeus is equivalent to the Devil because the Devil is the father of Satan. If Orion is Zeus and Orion is born as Osiris, then Osiris is Satan a reptilian 'god'. The Goddess Diana is Mary as Mary is the same Goddess Isis who is the same goddess as Artemis and as Artemis is Diana then Diana is Mary. Diana is the Roman Goddess meaning 'sky' and 'daylight' the *'light'* transmitted on the Aether of the sky that we know of today as Chi, Prana (life force), Qi Life Energy and the Tao. She is the Goddess of Life as light is life, and life *is* love and this is why she is also referred to as the Goddess of Love and the Light Bearer. She symbolises all mothers or the 'mother goddess' as mothers were considered goddesses in prehistory. It's amazing Princess Diana loved Charles so much and even tried to fight for him valiantly taking on their little royal 'in' crowd which he and his friends, including Camilla, found hilarious. She was not one of them for obvious reasons. She was far more human than that but couldn't understand why she couldn't fit in. That's because there is the 'aristocracy' and then there is the 'club' inside the aristocracy which is a totally different level of the game. Diana Princess of Wales was named for the purpose of the goddess to fulfill the legend of the fabled mythological Diana the Goddess of the Hunt, the other half of Orion where our solar system is housed, who fell in love with Orion who was depicted as Osiris, the green man, which carried over into the Celtic

beliefs of a 'green' nature deity god. This is because he is literally green, a reptilian, who stood in the place of the 'goddess' found in Mother Nature. Everything's been nicked.

She was the Goddess of 'domestic animals' noted as the Triple Goddess with three heads of the dog, horse and boar. The dog represents the 'dog' star Sirius personified as Isis who was also a goddess of all things 'domestic' therefore, Diana in another incarnation of Isis. She is a grain deity as this represents the 'grain' of the Christ *seed* facilitating enlightenment. She was the 'lady of the house', so these devils dress her up a 'cleaner'. George Burns evened joke in his movie Oh God, You Devil that heaven was full of priests and cleaning ladies. But she did not clean the shit house however, she would have *hired and fired* the appropriate persons, male

RETURN OF THE TWINS

or female, to do those jobs *for her* as her husband, a merchant and trader, was out bartering with the boys and had the best of both worlds. Only a beautiful tantric sex wife and trading out in the world wasn't enough for him. He wanted a mistress, the party girl, the party boys, the sordid life, *and* a wife, *and* children to pass his name onto, *and* money, *and* fame, *and* power...*and*...it goes on and on and now, sadly, the world is what it is. Diana was also the goddess of 'crossroads' and like the god Hermes who also 'crosses boundaries' she was able to transcend the normal physical boundaries into the astral hence, her seemingly incredible psychic abilities, she is therefore, Iris. She was 'goddess of the hunt' because she was equal to Orion, she hunted too, as does Orion, the 'Hunter'.

It's important to understand a couple things; all these gods and goddesses are interchangeable because they represent ordinary people who come in many different professions. So, when they say she was the 'twin' of Apollo they literally mean males and females are 'the twins' the same way the sun and the moon are 'twins' as rotating electrical opposites that keep THE BALANCE OF NATURE in place. They DELIBERATELY confuse all these deities to confuse YOU so that *you* WON'T understand what it all really means as it all means tantric sex enlightenment coded into the fabled legends since the dawn of time and they sure as hell don't want *you* discovering their tricks and how they rule the world with this power or *you* might empower yourself and go after them. Diana, Artemis, Isis, Mary actually simply represents Women – WOMEN ARE THE GODDESS – and were the 'mother and the wife' of 'god' as found in the Jesus story *both* called Mary because the 'Mary' is simply another word for mature woman. And women can attain godlike abilities with the power of the 'caduceus' spine/nervous system called the 'ladder' and unlocked chakras. The 'spine' is an anagram of 'penis' as well as 'pines' because the female energy, the kundalini, is awakened and raised via tantric sex WITH A MAN hence, his *penis* activates the energy up the *spine* to open the *pines* of the pineal gland to attain

ENLIGHTENMENT. It's not rocket science although they have literally turned it in that.

So, these reptilian males make fun of human women, the goddess, and kill 'god' found in human men because if human men and women ever find out about these internal abilities to even up the playing field, there goes the party and the 'god' complex of hordes of reptilians men transferring their souls to their sons hence, the 'father' becomes the 'son' and they are then 'eternal'. If humans ever get their power back, there goes the alien empire ruling over planet Earth and there goes their power in the galaxy as well because we will eventually surpass them and go 'out there' both astrally and physically in space crafts (which is already being done) so, *there goes the entire alien-demonic control over humans, our planet and all their plans and complex details to trick us into our own end will suddenly be dashed AS PROPHESISED* or more accurately PREDICTED by people who really were practicing the heights of this knowledge in prehistory. Coupled with the natural broadcasts from the galaxy and universe beyond, they said a time would come when the cosmic bodies would move into such positions thus broadcasting certain new signals and frequencies. This CANNOT BE AVOIDED and will translate as the foretold Utopia of our destiny. But they want to twist it into a Utopia for them and destruction for us in a diabolical move. But they need our consent and corresponding mass stupidity to make it happen. This is the reason for all the pomp and pageantry, the BIG SHOW, because if they can distract you long enough then they have got it in the bag! It's a timing thing and TIME is running out hence, the sense of things 'speeding up' or what's called The Quickening as the galaxy suddenly aligns faster than they could predict leading to a situation where they must 'rush to power' and this eventually outs them.

They have counted their chickens as they believe that the situation has gone so far in their favour that they cannot lose. This is why they constantly make shit of the feminine because it is a Woman who will spell their end and why Zeus was afraid of no other god or goddess but little Iris, a young maiden – a musician none the less - because a musical female, a REALLY talented naturally gifted musical female with open chakras is the WORST NIGHTMARE for this egotistical bunch of sexist perverts. Even in countries where girls are severely limited, they are still outperforming boys in math, science and literature. Pound for pound females are smarter than males which is why all these religious systems make men higher up the hierarchical chain than women because the stupidity of men can be endlessly relied upon by the reptilian hierarchy to perpetuate this alien regime that suppresses women and thus sits over the top of us all.

RETURN OF THE TWINS

This shit slinging at the Goddess is the sole reason why unevolved men in shit hole countries 'marry' little girls, pedophilia dressed up as culture, and even utilise FGM (female genital mutilation) cutting out the sexual hormonal glands of females as it is via orgasm and the root chakra, the genitals, that tantric sex enlightenment is initiated. It's just a fact. So, cutting out her genitals means she will never elevate her chakras, never actualise her crown enlightenment and never threaten his mental superiority over her. She will never become the 'mega mind' and never be a real threat to these dickheads ever. The men who are doing this are perpetuating their own imprisonment as its via women that they will get out of this. It says something for the unending stupidity of men much relied on by your MALE alien masters to keep you as nothing more than pets endlessly gratifying their alien egos as 'god' at YOUR expense. This is why they are premiering the move ELVIS on the 23 June as there is a parade of planets in this month aligning all the planets in our solar system with the galactic core making the signal more clear. Elvis was the King in Memphis yet this is another telling of King Osiris of Memphis in ancient Egypt as they believe if they transmit these old stories *again* then they can replicate the old circuits *again* and we will go round *again* when the 'reply path' from the 'mirror' (the electrical circuit of the galaxy) sends that information *back* locking in the same type of civilisations that have gone before – male dominated – headed up by reptilians posing as humans, men posing as women and therefore, god.

2021, 2022 & 2023 is the 'three years' spoken about in the Bible in which 'the devil's time is short' for him to take over the world as these dates add up to 6066 0r simply 666 as '0' isn't really a number. It's why Madonna, the virgin mother, is being touted as a monarch mind-controlled slave via their effigy *Madonna* (the singer) as she depicts herself as the 'mother of nature' giving birth to bugs, trees and *robots*. She may or may not know this, but it is alien 'bugs' that are behind the harvesting of Mother Earth using machines to do it. This is more twisted shit slinging at natural organic Mother Nature that they simply use and abuse. In reality, Mother Nature, the mother Goddess found in women, is *supposed* to be emerging at this time as written in Nicola Tesla article "When Woman is Boss' 1926. Tesla talked about how there was a time coming when women would take their rightful position in the world and that the world will be a better safer place for it. As such the evil Masons will elevate women to positions of power and get them to sign off on the use of nuclear weapons to slander females, the goddess, for all time that the *one time* women were in power they were more destructive than all the men who went before them so, better not let women get into power again. They know the psychology. Regardless, it is a great prophecy that has been written of in the past however they manage to twist it to suit themselves. It is an astrological blueprint destined to occur in that the GODDESS, not a man claiming to be god (what man doesn't think he's god?), will emerge at this time to save the world.

This prophecy has been hidden from the world, that it is the feminine goddess, not 'god' *again*, who is to return heralding an end the distorted masculine dick cult's reign of terror over planet Earth. *Right*, is an image from osirismemphis.com a 'garden district' club of wealthy southern elites who play out the charade of Osiris the 'green' man reptilian 'Shrek' and the human  'goddess' the 'fairy princess', Isis. Clearly, this guy is wearing a mask but note the red hair and oversized features which is probably what Osiris the reptilian really looked like. Many ancient native legends speak of the 'red haired giants' whose skeletons and mummified remains have been stolen by the Smithsonian, among other museums worldwide, to hide the true history of our world from us. This cult is emanating from the Southern States of America, the 'deep south' who are the players in a modern-day charade recreating the 'carnivals' and rituals of, in particular, ancient Egypt as Osiris and Isis represent the reptilian-human mating pair who reigned from ancient Egypt. They even say on their website that the Mississippi is 'America's Nile river' because the Gulf Region of America is basically a mirror image of the gulf region of North Africa-Egypt. America is the stage set to reintroduce the male reptilian world leader, Horus, from a union with a reptilian 'King' and a human female 'princess' to be groomed as a digital new ag 'Queen' and then killed as an offering to the demonic hordes who wish to retain their dominion over Earth from the wings of the 4th Dimension. All of this from the ashes of destruction already happening in America.

The last pharaoh of Egypt, Cleopatra, was trying to create a One World with ancient Rome but it didn't work out. So, they intend to try again bringing Cleopatra aka Isis back to complete the story that failed 2000 years ago. It's an ancient Egypt Club with 'Kings' and 'Queens' and Osiris and Isis characters lauded as a 'bit of fun' and just an opportunity for a 'ball' but you have to admit it's weird and very detailed. Coupled with everything else, this is their cult, it emanates from the Southern

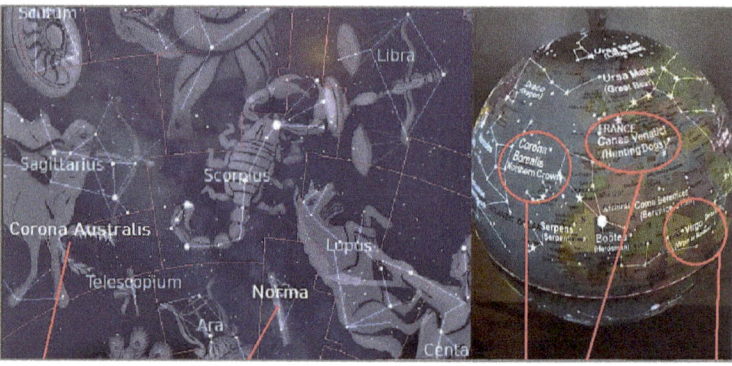

States of America and is old world European royalty masquerading as now world elites to play out the last Act of a Script that was running since 5000BC. It was the astrological promise of a united planet prophesised to come into being since the reptilian 'alien' infiltration of planet Earth and our reality. Only, they are trying to twist the 'one world prophecy' to suit themselves. It's all 'written in the stars' played out as kids fables via Disney so we won't realise IT'S REAL.

Kim Kardashian wore the Marilyn Monroe dress to the Met Gala in 2022 to invoke the MM Mary Magdalene, Mother Mary 'year 2000' effigy of the Goddess to broadcast that Monroe is weirdly 'black' now and still "alive". M is the 13th letter of the alphabet and K is the 11th letter so, here were have 13:13 and 11:11 just as we are told another constellation, the 13th, has been suddenly discovered, Ophiuchus, as they are looking to alter the calendar or at least the months of the year to 13 months of 20 days like the Mayan calendar. While bloviating that she would wear 'gloves' while handling the dress and promising to keep it safe as it's the most expensive dress in the world, she summarily and *deliberately* ruined this piece of art history with her fat ass. More shit slinging at the real thing while these fakers take

RETURN OF THE TWINS

their place. This is why they released the movie about Elvis, the 'king', to invoke the 'King of Memphis' aka Osiris and the 'common' girl queen, Norma Jean-Marilyn Monroe (moon-roe) who is actually the moon Goddess! They are symbolically pretending these characters in the ancient script are *still alive* when really, they murdered the goddess and the 'king' died on the 'throne' aka THE TOILET. Always slinging shit at the god and goddess found in human men and women. The movies Blonde is apparently two hours of watching MM be abused and crying when in reality she was a human rights champion, stood up to the sexist studios long before it was 'woke' to do so and sued her celebrity to bring good into the world. She was a cool person well before her time but that is not what she is being portrayed as.

Everything we experience is a duplication, a 'bad copy', counterfeit, *a facsimile* that mimics who we are as organic beings, 'gods' of light and life, and replaces what we are *supposed* to be doing at this time with an

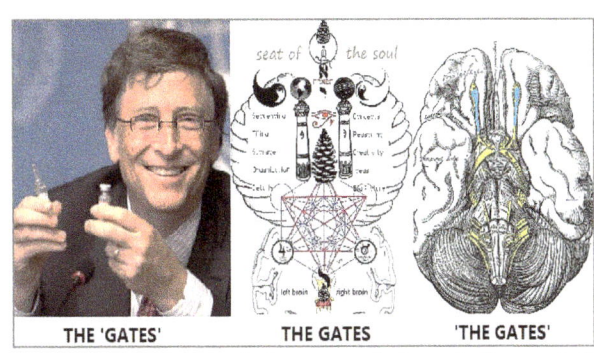

THE 'GATES' — THE GATES — 'THE GATES'

effigy. They put into ritual an 'effigy' of the real thing and then kill it *to kill us* in a bigger astrological arena! The counterfeit *parallel reality* we are living in finds us getting the exact opposite of what we were *supposed* to be getting at this time. They've done it before, it works, and they're doing it again. Therefore, instead of opening the *gates* of heaven via our pineal glands also called the 'stairway to heaven', we have Bill *Gates* shutting this function down with injections. The human body is a temple and why Mary was referred to as 'the Church' as the church is a symbol of the natural world found in mountains and valleys of Mother Nature *symbolised* in *effigy* by the spires and turrets of these enormous buildings to represent the mountains and valleys, *the curves*, of a woman's body. But no. Instead, we get mass suicide cult,

"HEAVEN'S GATE" MASS SUICIDE CULT — THE *REAL* HEAVEN'S GATE MALE-FEMALE CHAKRAS

Heaven's Gate', broadcasting that the sacred temple and the astral access

to the universe is a bunch of mind-controlled agency lunatics who want to ride off on a fucken comet...because that makes sense. No really, I can't wait to follow a guy who eyes are rolling in his head and looks completely psychotic. Daddy, I'm home! Where do I sign up for the comet package? I was planning on taking a cruise, but this *gates* thing is really floating my boat! Heaven's Gate is still around if you can believe it! Their bodies were covered in lilac/purple blankets because this is the colour of the crown chakra. Instead of getting our chakra towers activated via the husband and wife in sacred union of Holy Matrimony, we get a towering inferno of horror bringing the Twin Towers *down* instead of the Twin Flames of the Lovers chakra towers *rising up.* Instead of getting the 7/7 chakras of the male and female activated we get the 7/7 London Bombings. They even bragged about it on the side of the bus 'OUTRIGHT TERROR BOLD AND

THE 'TWIN TOWERS' MASS DEATH   THE *REAL* TWIN TOWERS OF THE FEMALE-MALE CHAKRAS

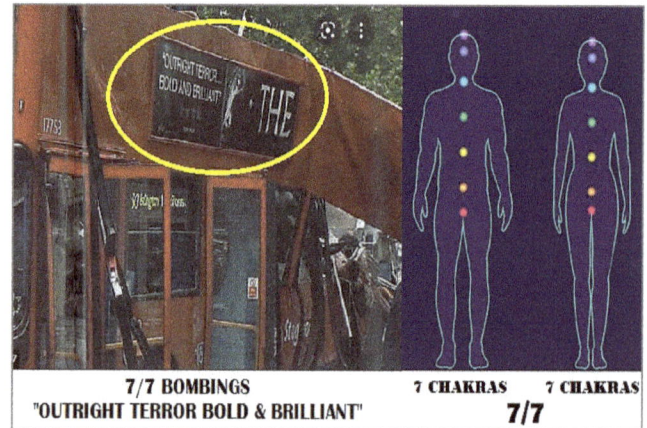

7/7 BOMBINGS "OUTRIGHT TERROR BOLD & BRILLIANT"   7 CHAKRAS   7 CHAKRAS   7/7

BRILLIANT" - that's because they know they'll get away with it because in their astro-cult they are tapping into universal currents and energies much greater than any media coverage or courtroom. They're going to the source, The Almighty, to create their bad copy. We're not living in a false world as some people claim, it's the real world with fake stories broadcast onto it from the astrological cosmos script. *That's* the 'simulation'. Therefore, it's a counterfeit reality, an effigy, a ritual, because if you don't know that it's fake, then your brain is a transceiver and you will simply broadcast to the universe that the 'twin towers have collapsed' here on Earth and that is exactly what the universe will deliver back you by allowing these demonic shit heels to destroy the REAL twin towers in men and women AND get away with it! What you put out you get back. The astro-rituals are unfolding by the day now and 2022 is a big year for them so it's happening all the time. We were supposed to have our heart chakras activated, especially in the new generation of younger people. They were *supposed* to be getting their heart chakras activated by raising their kundalini, instead young people, in particular, are dying of cardiac arrests in all directions when heart related issues were once the domain of stressed-out older men with poor diets. But no. Now it's children, teens, and young professional sports people because this is the 'new' normal. It's just pathetic and a total ritual. Once you wrap your head around the fact that this is all part of a much bigger picture, then you can start getting on with the process of dealing with the actuality of the game and not playing, badly, against people who are playing a *totally differing set of rules to you.*

Now we see simultaneous farming issues in Europe *and* America. What a *coincidence* it all is as Bill Gates now owns more farming land than anybody else in America as scores of food warehouses are suddenly burned to the ground. Billions of dollars in aid is going overseas while U.S. citizens suffer increasing homelessness. American oil reserves are being sent to China...the enemy, apparently. It just all looks so painfully obvious as if they are *trying* to crash America and the free world...and they are! The experiment is essentially over. In the last century the three major social-political models of earth were Socialism, Communism and Capitalism. People don't realise just how big the experiment has been as these models were only employed to test *mass psychology* to see how people behave in huge groups in order to design their next civilisation. As such people are not realising its time to wrap it all up and move on. The stats are in, the numbers have been counted and now it's time to do away with it all and put that cold data into use to control the populations of the future generations under a harsh 'evolved' and 'progressive' control plan utilising all the tricks and progress they garnered using *us* at this time. Same old same old. The police are issuing apologies to media for the harsh treatment of people during the covid lock downs among other things. So, what we are seeing is the orchestrated 'fall' caused by 'satanic' forces who have been at the worlds throat since 911. They are right out in the open now along with their promotion of the LGBT thing and just as a side, Satan is transgender. Satan has been having a field day under the guise of all these progressive groups prompting new terms like 'compassion fatigue' as functioning members of society get fed up, sick and tired of trying to be nice to people who are taking advantage of them. All this craziness as the devils and demons run amok.

As per biblical prophecy literally aligned for this time, 'Christ' returns and rescues 'Mary'. This is not a physical thing, it is a reference to the symbolic 'Christ' enlightenment stolen by reptilian men (Christ who they believe is a reptile) returned to Mary, women, who is 'rescued' as a result of her enlightenment and liberation from ignorance to finally complete her job to ascend the Human race and planet Earth. This is 'written in the stars, literally, with the 'parade of planets' that happened mid-June 2022 is being depicted in their zodiac script as the Mary's, women, being saved by 'Christ', a returning saviour god', a man. They are *duplicating* in place of the return of Mary's enlightenment via Christ seed oil chakra activation a so-called Christian 'new age' as we 'return' to Christian' 'family values' (which is just basic 'common sense' but apparently religion has a monopoly on common sense even though they've destroyed our planet with their worship OCD). This is intended to take us back to a golden era of 1950's bliss. Yippee! The neighbourhood will return to normal, prices will drop, and we will be able to afford holidays again as Christian values return along with our sense of safety. Many crims will be arrested like podophiles and grooming gangs. All just as I said in my first book 2020 & Beyond as hordes of 'refugees' who have strained Western economies are 'safely repatriated' to Africa and the Middle East etc., and things will be 'white' again for a while albeit some new allegiances between blacks, Hispanics, gays, good little housewives and trans folk will be seeded. Those who gave their middle finger to the New World Order during the dark times will be welcomed as part of the new global family of Christian saviours about to flood the world with good will (and tighter restrictions on everything from alcohol to private medical procedures including abortions). It is the 'second coming' of Christ, after all, and it will shortly be followed by the Christ social movement as 'Christ' returns, and society turns the corner of a 'brave' new world post temporary madness. But what they *don't* want you to know is that Christ is an electrochemical function of the brain, and it is the *inner* Christ that will rescue the Mary's who will then save the world along with the inner Christ of men in balance.

All the big 'new age' propaganda 'alternative' media machines who popped up in the last few years are becoming increasingly popular as the shit hits the fan. They are *suddenly* promoting Christ and Christianity or certainly 'orthodox' values among a litany of other promoted players at this time. I'm not saying they either know about or are willingly onboard with a secret agenda to 'play out' the end times prophecies in that 'Satan' rises and is vanquished by 'Jesus' found in all these 'new age' values among the younger up and coming generation, but I am saying it is the 'bad copy', the duplication, of what was *supposed* to happen. The Devil is inside us, it is the dark half, the angel on one shoulder and the devil on the other shoulder that whispers in your ear when you're torn to either do a good deed or bad thing because you most likely have a conscience and must make a decision about how you want to live with yourself if you become a cunt like so many others. The dark path is easy. The light path...that's really hard but not without some rewards like relieving yourself of a guilty conscience for not chipping in with the devils. Sometimes that conscience comes at a price, a big price, as in my case. But sometimes one *can* put a price on it as most people have in the last two decades since 9/11 looking the other way as those of us who were brave enough and shouted from the roof tops not to forget about 911 bore the brunt of their cowardice. Most people worldwide were prepared to sell out as long as it didn't get too bad...but it has gotten bad, really bad. Including the unbelievable ease with which the NWO ordered people en masse to fuck up what little health they had left by allowing themselves to be injected with unknown (alien) pathogens that are now *wreaking havoc* on the world population as disabled people have INCREASED by 10% in America alone (it's more than that) and death has *increased* by 20% in America which is generally a yard stick for the rest of the world and deaths have *increased* by 1300 people a week in the UK and that's just what they admit to... Anomalous heart attacks in professional sports people continue to rise, death is now being referred to as an 'end of life experience'. Nothing to worry about, just another experience, let's go to the zoo. Heart attacks are being referred to as a 'cardiac event' because it's just another 'event' to have a major medical condition THAT YOU SHOULDN'T HAVE coincidentally after major injection programs. *What could be causing it?*

What they don't want you to know is that 'Christ' is within you, just as the Devil lies within especially in the guise of the unopened chakras leading to the general stupidity that has dogged the human race for thousands of years causing our enslavement. The Second Coming is the information we need about the Christ seed extract released via the pituitary and pineal glands that coupled with tantric-sacred sex meditations with your husband or wife (hence Jesus and Mary) leads to enlightenment of the soul and increased IQ and strongly suggests that we can never be taken advantage of ever again! Christ's return is the Christ seed oil being tapped into en masse by people at this crucial time in history. THAT is the second coming of 'Christ' as there was once a time when the Christ seed enlightenment of the chakras and IQ was the norm in a mythical golden time of heroes and saviours and extraordinary human accomplishments. Then it was lost, and now it's coming back again. It's the second time around for our redemption and ascension and let's just hope this time we don't fall back into the pit of ignorance and darkness because, unless we find a way to *permanently* release ourselves from the evil ones, then they will be waiting in the wings watching for us to trip up and grab us again! But once again it's all dressed up in effigy as some 'values' or an actual person who they will kill. Christ is not some *lame* Christian revolution by people who can hardly call themselves good Christians. They drink. They smoke. They frequently take the lords name in vain. They've been promiscuous and taken drugs at some time in their lives. They *don't* live by the Ten Commandments, and they *frequently* live by the seven deadly sins. But their Christians. Yeh, and I'm Mary Magdalene...hopefully not. Being Christian is not about banning abortions and stamping out those dirty gays (I don't think gays are dirty but that is the growing consensus that all this dirt seeping into society is somehow the fault of ordinary people who find a person of the same sex attractive). I've got news for you, if you practice Christ seed enlightenment via tantric sex, men can retain the sperm and women can retain the egg and pregnancy will never be an issue again so there goes that little power trip of the good Christians. The key here is not about promiscuity which is unfortunately a trap large swathes of the LGBT community fell into because they were being guided by a satanic secret hand that hates the human body and is afraid of our internal powers of ascension. These issues around promiscuity etc., can easily be corrected without demonizing the LGBT community while also taking care to weed out the inordinate number of creeps and pedophiles and perverts who saw their opportunity to ride on the backs of a generally peaceful community to flout the law and prey like vampires on the innocent.

It's all so predictable as we see a renaissance of 'values' not seen since the ice age of the late 20th Century, you remember, when things were generally still basically normal when shithouse paper was regularly available. Ah, the good old days when there wasn't a looming food crises aka famine in the WEST if you can believe it, a West who have been notorious for our blasé attitude toward consumption and the wastage of food throwing out enormous amounts of produce while people across the pond starved to death. It's sad that people are so easily led. Now we are looking at shortages all round as people find themselves scrimping and scraping – hey, it's rations again, kids, bust out the lard and the dripping sandwiches and that's on a good day! We *will* get out of this and free humanity as the alternative is that the bad guys win, take over the world and kill us all and that's just boring. Who wants to read a whodunnit if you already know who dun it? What's the point in continuing on if it's a foregone conclusion? You might as well put your feet up, break out the cold beer and say, 'fuck it' until the mushroom cloud appears on the horizon of your tropical beach scape. Ah, but it's NOT a foregone conclusion however the odds may be stacked against us.

But it's a close call.

Chapter Seven
Everything is a Ritual

Our whole world is one big ritual. Once you know what it is about you will see it everywhere.

Everything you witness in the mainstream is a Satanic ritual designed to overwrite humanities natural astro-logical flow broadcast from the galaxy derail our destiny and replace it with a 'bad copy', a facsimile, a duplication of what was *supposed* to happen for us. This is done so that the rulers can recreate the past themes of their empires, a historical script, and continue to live out their charade as *hierarchical* 'gods' ruling over Earth as they have done for thousands of years. They do this because they can't evolve and are frightened to try anything new and so just play out the tried and tested blueprint of a repeating script of power and partying. As such, 'if it aint broke, don't fix it' is their mantra. Therefore, Mt Olympus is Hollywood, literally, and if they get their way again, in thousands of years, the ignorant masses will say the ancient gods of power, glitz, glamour and wonder ruled the world from Mt Hollywood, the place of the stars, the 'heavens' who could perform miracles (in movies). But who's checking and who will know the difference when it all becomes myth and legend *again* in thousands of years just like them of old? Most of the A-list political and celebrity crowd (modern gods) are simply reptilian hybrids who see themselves as the custodians of humanity, our parents, even though they have no right to be on this planet at all. They're hypocrites in the extreme and have gotten away with their crimes for so long it's inconceivable to them that their stately godhood could be removed from them along with their power and all the fakery they propagate. They are the descendants of the same reptilian 'gods' of historical account who 'ruled' over the ancient world in exalted positions in myth and legend.

The 'dragons' of Eden were not 'gods' and when they arrived and their physical bodies eventually died, their spirits got stuck here and are the possessing reptilian entities from up 100,000 years ago who have transferred the possessing entity of the 'dragons', their 4D selves, down through the lines of 'royalty' and still exist today. Apparently, Earth is purgatory for them. If you look at the book title of deep insider Carl Sagan, he is telling you quite plainly what happened including the 'Demon Haunted World'. These are the 'giants' – at least they were spiritually giant

– and their essence so enormous that they have sometimes been seen as large 'smoke' or cloud like entities that seem to be attached to certain families or certain people inside families some not even in the aristocracy. The elites of past empires were loved and reviled *the same way* we look at celebrities today. They are still attached to certain human blood lines who are compatible with this particular species genetics. If you look at the behavior of mythological character's they bear a striking resemblance to the behaviour of political and celebrity A-listers today i.e., above the law, destructive, debauched, murderers, hoarders coveting anything of value (like the mythical dragon sitting on its pile of treasure) engaged in adultery, incest, lying and deception to ensure their riches and fame are secured in a repeating satanic system, a caste system, graded from top to bottom. At the very bottom you will find humans.

They sometimes rule out in the open and sometimes they rule behind the scenes while cleverly putting it all in your face to get themselves off the karmic hook astro-logically. The entire system we live under is fake and designed to favour these creatures in every age they rule over. Their reptilian interdimensional 'spirit' is passed on from generation to generation and where the 'father becomes the son' reference comes from as via black magic they *literally* transfer their consciousness, their essence, to the next generation in a *symbolic duplication* of natural replicating processes coming from the cosmos via reincarnation. Human souls return too only we keep getting the shitty end of the deal as we can't remember what we were doing in our previous lives while they keep getting to party at the top because their memories are being restored to them or 'total recall'. This is all underpinned by phonetics, *language*, which then locks the ritual into place as the 'word', *the sound*, of the vibratory frequency is coding our perception of reality and we are unwittingly assisting them by not seeking to understand the meaning of the language we use. This is the symbolic meaning of 'Babylon' and the god dispersed everyone because they 'wanted to build a tower with their head in the heaven' so 'god' smashed their tower, scattering them and making them speak different languages so they couldn't come back together again. They didn't just make us speak different languages so we couldn't compare notes on our similar collective history and find the answer faster. They used language as a weapon to code our perception. Perception is a matter of familiarity.

A good example of this is the word 'morning' and 'mourning', they sound the same but couldn't be more different as 'morning' is all about new light, new life, a new day, new hope, a new chance etc., while 'mourning' is about loss, grief, the end, it's over, futility, darkness, sadness and depression. So, we verbally greet the day with 'mourning' and since the universe is based on *sound* – how will it know the difference? Therefore, the universe is reading that humans think the new light, a new day, is a horrible depressing thing and that is exactly what we are getting. It's exactly like the word 'wake' which means to open one's eyes, to be aware, to be alive, awaken, alert and informed but then there is the phonetically corresponding 'wake' a sad event after a funeral meaning death, sadness, loss, darkness, the end. We need to take a serious look at how they are using us to code our reality with this double speak as *this* is what their currency trading system, *money*, relies on to allow the devastating charade of destruction playing out on planet Earth with no recourse as they get away with their crimes scot-free. It can only be a diabolical super intellectually sophisticated *alien empire* that is able to do this and maintain it! It is because of their trickery in getting you to verbalise your consent *unwittingly* that they are *not afraid* of 'god' the way you are. They are not afraid of karma or comeuppance the way you are as, by rights, there *should* be a return path, they *should* reap what they sew. But this doesn't happen to them. Why is that? Because you have laid the foundation for them to succeed before they even start killing you and your world by agreeing that they have the right to be in their positions above you. You are doing this just by using the very language that you use setting you in second place to them before the game has even started. The real question is not whether aliens exist or not but why didn't they exist before Hollywood blockbusters of the late 20th century?

This huge charade is then locked even deeper into our sense of reality with numerology and astrology as they select certain dates and certain times at certain locations to do certain things, *rituals* both public and private, as they 'mirror' the astrological 'story', frequencies, being broadcast from the stars. What they choose to 'mirror' and how they are mirroring it only seems to benefit them and theirs hence, the 'bad' copy which was also called 'HAL', a simulation, that can be modelled with the power of the will. The 'modelling' and 'making' of our reality via these methods is where the term for God comes from, 'the maker', and further to that a 'craftsman' hence, the set square and compass logo of the Masons, 'tools' to create not just buildings but the fabric our societies both now and in the past (and the future). They are 'architects' who design and model and craft things hence, their god is the 'Architect' as are all these 'creator' gods. Any time you see a 'tool' or an implement being associated with a 'god' you are dealing with Masons old and new. The 'hammer' of Thor is the hammer of Vulcan, the 'blacksmith' who 'makes' and 'models' things are did Egyptian

RETURN OF THE TWINS

Ptah who is Osiris the 'bull' or Taurus the bull more specifically the *torus* field generated for the 'torso' of the four major chakras of the tantric enlightened electricity god – the (inner) 'sun king' - who often has lightning and thunder associated with him. This 'building' doesn't just apply to architecture but also applies to people and planet Earth and they are making and modelling your world, crafting it, to suit themselves. They are 'gods' in that sense and proud of it.

The set square and compass are also used to navigate maps and figure out degrees or curvature of space and time designating the angles traversing the planet as relative to the sun in order to navigate the globe via ocean voyages as well. It's a replicating process and once you figure out how to traverse the Earth you can figure out how traverse the stars and vice versa. It's uncanny how our world has so many replicating aspects to it. These traders were once called 'merchants of the sea' as they used these navigational techniques and studying the stars to seek out new ports to trade and seek new earthly riches empowering them to even greater heights. As such, they have known about the world's map far longer than we realise and have set all this up in advance in a massive rolling ritual to eventually consume this world. It goes to show you what they are doing is extremely dangerous requiring such foresight so as not to cock it up at the precise time of triumph! I guess we'll see. The set square and compass are also used to figure out the constellations and traversing of the zodiac where they are getting the blueprint for their plans on earth however, they cleverly twist the astrology, energies, it to suit themselves as the electricity of the cosmos is naturally beneficial to natural beings and we are *supposed* to evolve in a series of big cosmic wheels, like cogs, like stairways, as well as smaller cosmic wheels within our own life, like your Saturn Return, repeating cycles of celestial energy designed to have us elevate. If you miss the big ship, there is a ferry coming soon after and if you miss that there is a water taxi, and if you mis that there is a dinghy and if you miss that there is a paddle board. The problem is the cycles, and the density of the energy, gets smaller with every opportunity missed and this is how they are capitalizing on their zodiac and downgrading ours. The point is, we are SUPPOSED to be evolving. Technology is not evolution it's a distraction from evolution deflecting from those who are controlling it. Zodiac from Old French, Latin and Greek literally means 'circle' from root proto-Indo-European 'to live'. What they are doing is highly illegal on a cosmic scale and why they hide it behind *so much secrecy* and conspiracy for if the world and the universe ever understands their cheap tricks, the retribution will seem like nothing short of a wrathful biblical epic, a global French Revolution for real. Hey, it's their words not mine.

RETURN OF THE TWINS

They are traders and merchants from the stars and came here navigating the galaxy looking for abundant planets to add to their trade empire. This is the duplication of their processes as they set themselves up as fearsome gods of old, breeding with the inhabitants of target planets. They were once huge, giants of old, but have downsized their bodies to fit in with the locals and not be discovered at this crucial time although their spirit attachments are still massive entities. This brotherhood, the priesthood, of the Masons have gone by many names throughout history including the Knights Templar, the Druids, the priests of ancient Egypt, the scientists of Atlantis, the Illuminati and today, the Masons. Same cult, same people, same families or set of reptilian interdimensional spirits, demons, from the most ancient account of the darkest prehistory the memory of which has been all but completely wiped from human knowledge, wiped from the face of the planet only kept alive for us in myth, folklore, fairy tales and native creation stories. This is why the natives are being wipe out as not only do their bloodlines go back further than these aliens, but their creation stories are the last living knowledge of how it all began. The feathers they wear on their head is from a time long ago when there was a thriving global civilisation and symbolically means the 'bird' of the crown, the pineal gland third eye chakra as do the ancient Egyptians symbolise the hawk and eagle with the crown. Their prophecy that "the end comes when the water boils" is a direct correlation of the 'rising phoenix' of the feminine waters up the spine, the kundalini, when the masculine 'spark' boils the feminine 'waters' and enlightenment ensues. Yes, it really will be over then. Over for them.

If you don't know where you've been how can you know where you're going? You don't, that's the whole point. So, don't get confused by the various names of the secret priesthood as with the various names of the devil and the various civilisations they have worked through 'destroying' themselves only to re-emerge again in the next and the next civilisation. It is their version of the 'phoenix' third eye rising from the 'ashes' of the many civilisations they have destroyed. They are one who is many, the great pretender, the father of lies, an imposter who wears many disguises, has many names and many faces. Legion. They do all this to cover their tracks as the people start to realise there is some *order* to this, some organisation, who is working this enormous charade toward a certain end at a certain time, and it seems that time is now. So, it's entirely possible the same reptile 'demons' and their pantheon of demonic hordes, 'Legion' from ancient myth, are the same ones running the world today. They transferred their souls by way of a ritual utilising the breath, the breath is the life. However, now they have technology that can do the same thing today, the ante has be upped as they rapidly accelerate and various sectors of this order see *themselves* as ultimately winner and last man standing and compete with each other in the end. So, the game is changing in some ways and those previously reliant on the priests of the dark order to transfer their souls upon death (as described is the Isis and Mary Magdalene myths and once the domain of the *priestesses*), no longer need the old evil priests as modern technology levels the playing field and is more than sufficient to replace the old order and how things were done in ancient times.

They don't die the way humans do indeed they have a monopoly over death. When humans die, our memories are conveniently wiped making us their endless prey lifetime after lifetime. This is why the Egyptians were so obsessed with death and had many 'levels' or gateways in order to get out, to escape into the light of bliss, and traverse the 'underworld'. They also mastered the return of the soul and why despite the hundreds if not thousands of mega rich pharaohs, there tombs are either not discovered or conveniently 'looted' by the time they are discovered. This is because the pharaohs transferred their soul to another person and had their wealth 'looted' from their tombs by their faithful servants and restored back to themselves to continue to hold on to their material possessions and remain wealthy in every life they live. They also track certain families who for some reason 'mirror' them. They target 'rival' bloodlines of old lineages targeting the same souls who have reincarnated lifetime after lifetime albeit with their memory wiped and cannot understand the incredible 'bad luck' that has dogged their family generation after generation. These creatures, in their hideous quest, secretly torment those they fear most laughing about the ignorance of their victims who must shake their head in confoundment at the 'bad luck' *again!* They call this 'persistent random misfortune', and they laugh endlessly at how they are secretly destroying people who have NO IDEA this is going on or why. If you've had *ridiculous* levels of deaths in your family, you may be their target. It can't be ruled out.

The script remains the same they just change the decor and the names and then its business-as-usual. It is a repeating story, a cycle, and hasn't changed in thousands of years the only difference is, they are sick and tired of stone walls and chariots and the endless monotony of fighting wars in the dust going nowhere squabbling among themselves! Now they have amalgamated into a core set of families seeking to emerge in supreme dominance of all others of their kind in a super plan nearing its end. The winner takes all! Now they see a way to emerge into a digital space age, *but* they must apply the themes of the ancient replicating story, somehow, into modern times to 'make it fit' and retain their exalted positions above humans. That's why they call rockets after ancient mythological gods and the space age is basically dressing up the old themes and putting boosters on it. The old ones must be invoked to tick the OCD royal box of approval. So, they are repeating the ancient story *again* and they need the minds of mass numbers of human brains to broadcast this plotline to the 'mirror', the universe, which will then transmit it back and once the circuit is complete, it will be locked in for another two thousand years. Only this time we'll never get out. It's the big one! The end. Therefore, the global population has been allowed to grow into the billions of dullards to amplify the broadcast. Once it's done, the excess numbers of humans will be sacrificed as a mass offering to their demonic 'god', Satan, who is actually a collective *demonic* realm determined to keep things as they are. They do this every couple thousand years when a new zodiac Age rolls around and cosmic alignments occur that make all this possible as the transmission lines up the signals from hub to hub. The universe is a big radio station and the signal is most clear when there is an uninterrupted pathway between 'satellites' or planets and stars etc., just like a radio signal or phone signal. By doing this, as we enter the Age of Aquarius, the last great Age, the status quo will be locked in *forever*, 'If you want a picture of the future, imagine a boot stamping on a human face— forever" George Orwell. It's all ritual.

Take, for example, the Wil Smith and Chris Rock Academy Awards 'slap' that the whole world has gossiped about ever since. In ancient times the Earth was said to have geologically formed and in its early stages there was only steaming water. Then out of the water the first island emerged. The ancients believed that anything and everything contained a spirit and so, this first rocky outcrop that protruded from the water was called a 'god of the rock' or a 'rock god'. You may be familiar with this term 'rock god' from 1980's 'hair metal' among other music genres including 'rock n roll' because Satan was the most beautiful of the gods and an incredible musician. Vulcan was God of volcanoes where Star Trek get their Spock character from, a *Vulcan*, who is a half human-half alien male. Vulcan is another name for the Devil-Satan incarnation as he is the fiery god of *eruptions* meaning ejaculation or the 'fire of his loins' the 'spark of life' funnily enough activating the chakra tower that ends in the crown or the 'hair'. This is because they are getting their intelligence, IQ, and thus power from tantric sex.

The story goes that Vulcan was a blacksmith and one day he was informed that his wife, the goddess of love, Venus, was having an affair with the god Mars who was called Aries by the Romans. Aries rules over the *hair* and the 'crown' of the head meaning enlightenment depicted as the halo or the shining golden hair. Vulcan was heartbroken by his wife's infidelity - but don't mention that they were *both* notorious for many affairs - as does Wil Smith and his wife admit they are in an 'open' marriage and therefore, fit the script perfectly. So, Vulcan the ancient 'blacksmith' is played by Wil *Smith* who is *black* and the 'rock god', Mars-Aries, is played by Chris *Rock* in this ritual. The name Chris is short for Christopher or Christ. They are both 'gods' who are in a conflict with each other as with *many* myths about ancient gods. Jada *Pinkett*-Smith is a reference to the pink, red, maroon 'rose' colour of the root chakra activated via sex initiating transcendental enlightenment to become enlightened, a modern god and goddess. Jada having lost her 'hair' is a reference to many myths about the loss of the hair and therefore her power. The ancient goddess Sif, the wife of Zeus, had her hair was cut off by Thor's mischievous brother Loki while she was 'sleeping' meaning unawakened. This was called a 'cosmic crime' because she lost her power or at least her access to it. Yet both Thor and Loki are more incarnations or simply *names* for Jesus-Satan who both utilise Christ, the brains function, to get their IQ and power. They are thus the light and dark side of 'god'. It is ultimately the Devil-Satan, the great pretender, who plays all the parts in the story, good and bad, light and dark, as there can be only 'one'. The story of Samson and Delilah also talks of the hair that is cut off as Samson derives his 'power' from his hair and loses his power when his hair is cut off. Rapunzel who 'let's down her hair' for a man to climb her 'tower' loses her magical powers when her hair is cut off. The famous song This is the Dawning of the Age of Aquarius comes from the *musical* Hair. Hair in ancient mythology is a reference to the nervous system as the hair is an *extension of the nervous system* found outside the body and why one's hair will stand on end when alarmed or animals whose fur stands up along their *backbone* where the central nervous system is agitated by something (usually unsettling). The 'tower' is a reference to the chakra tower central to the human bodies nervous where we derive all our hidden godlike powers from.

 Jada Pinkett-Smith plays Venus in this ritual. Venus had an affair with Mars and in a televised WEIRD conversation between Wil Smith and his wife Jada, it was admitted that she had an affair with her son's friend called August. They oddly kept repeating 'August' while Wil Smith attempted to appear to be heartbroken about his wife's infidelity. The god of the month of August is Vulcan the 'black smith' as is Will *Smith* black. He's playing Vulcan and Jada having an affair with another Vulcan is the same as Venus having an affair with Mars because ultimately, *Mars and Vulcan are the same god* – god of fire - Satan. It's a ritual. The elite worship the androgynous LGBT all in one 'god', Baphomet, as has both Wil Smith and Jada both openly been linked to gay and lesbian encounters and even entire extramarital same sex relationships throughout their careers. It is customary for A-list celebrity to be either secretly gay or at least bi-sexual as the devil symbolically if not literally gets its tantric sex crown enlightenment power anywhere it can via sex while the 'good guy', Jesus, get's his enlightenment via *love* with his wife, Mary, in a monogamous marriage. Hiring gay and lesbian actors, or people willing to do anything to become a celebrity is a theme that has been with Hollywood since it's inception and it is not because gay people are more talented as suggested by one gay fan. It is because, in the past, gay and lesbian sex was heavily frowned upon by a society rooted in traditional relationships between the husband and wife, mother and father, in a Christian society of family values. As such gay and lesbian actors could be relied on to keep the satanic workings of what Hollywood is *really* doing behind closed doors a big secret lest they lose their careers if outed as gay. The entire thing is based on blackmail. Hiring gay actors, as most of Hollywood seem to have been then and now, was simply a reliable form of blackmail used by people who are more powerful than them who are up to far worse than them. This is why both the Smith children have come out as bi-sexual as all things LGBT take centre stage in a world now encouraged to do the same. And what the hell is the deal with Wil Smith French kissing his struggling son live on television? Jaysus! Incestuous pedophile!

In the not to distance future there won't be any labels at all gay men will simply be referred to as 'men who have sex with other men' but will not be considered homosexual as they don't 'identify' as homosexual, *see,* Wikipedia 'Men who have sex with other men'. Men have been called 'transphobic' for not having sex with transgender men-to-women, women's sports is being eroded by male-to-female competitors, and biological men are being encouraged to sit down to urinate to make trans-women-to-men feel more comfortable using male bathrooms. Just remember, the Hollywood crowd promoting all this are *rich people* who are above the law yet for the average person who engages in wanton 'anything goes' lifestyles and open sexual relationships, drug and alcohol abuse etc., these destructive often unfulfilling interactions can lead to high rates of depression, suicide or even ends in jail time or accidental death that we are seeing around the world as people copy celebrity example.

We are rapidly entering a time when the return of 'christ' was prophesised however, Christ was due to return two thousand years ago, but it didn't quite get off the ground. What they are not telling you is that it is this time around that the feminine, Mary, the Goddess, the Mother and the Wife, the chaste lawful 'woman of wise council', who is prophesised to return. Of all the ancient gods and goddesses Zeus, the devil, was most afraid of Iris, a young maiden who carried the caduceus. *Note*, 'Siri' the A.I. internet assistant is *Iris* backwards and also the first four letters of Sirius the star of the goddess is Iris while Osiris contains the name Iris. She means 'light' and 'shining' as do all the names of these goddesses including Diana. The caduceus represents the kundalini rising up the spine leading to enlightenment. So, a tantric sex *chaste* female with activated chakras is what the devil is most afraid of? The Oracles of Delphi, the priestesses of Isis, the Vestal Virgins and the priestesses surrounding Mary Magdalene were last female orders of the virginal holy women who knew and practiced tantric sex. The Geisha of Japan also were trained in the arts of 'companionship'. It wasn't prostitution, it was far more than that in a time when men actually appreciated the company of women who were schooled in high class social interaction. Perhaps they weren't so wrong, the world was dangerous and not really a place for women to be travelling as merchants, so the men did it, and when they reached their destination, it was common practice to seek the company of a fine woman. If you were a senator or aristocrat, you only sought out the highest females. They were more a part of a social apparatus that trained women to deal with men more effectively.

These women were beyond reproach as they personified Mother Nature and the natural world. This is how the ancients viewed the natural calendar, as loving and giving, hence, the mother and the wife *of life*. Often you will see images of the beautiful virtuous goddess surrounded by flowers in her garden and her names are often Rose, Eve, Iris, Holly, Ivy. Plant names and nature names. Her importance as a cultivating force from the stars, the light, the life, was studied in the knowledge of the position of the stars, the sun and the moon, as these celestial processes ensured the *correct time* to plant, to harvest and store their bounty for *next year*. She is the Madonna, the mother and the wife. She was considered the bringer of the life force, the light, via new plant life as well as babies born into this world ensuring another generation, another season. *She* ensured life continued. Her animating force of Chi, Prana, Ki life energy, Qigong etc., was found in the sudden new life of Spring, new flowers, buds, roses, fruits, and abundance of the forest called a 'cornucopia'. She is the next generation in every way both in humans and the plant world. She is associated with new life in fertility, harvest, agriculture and the security of another successful season and crop for next year. To survive. It is because of the appreciation for her Love found in the abundance of her natural gifts, Life aka *Light*, that a chaste honourable priestess of the order of Mother Nature was revered above all. As the goddess incarnation found in the Vestal Virgins, her word was accepted without question. She could pardon any slave. If a person on their way to be executed chanced upon a Vestal, they were immediately freed. They had special reserved places at public events and oversaw the administration of public treaties including people's Last Will and Testament and property law. She was considered all things Lawful hence, *Lady Justice* found outside ever courtroom worldwide to this day. She was Marianne of ancient France with her liberty, equality and fraternity only she doesn't get any equality now. She is Libertus who granted Rome its freedom, *liberty*, and its right to become a republic at the beginning of their empire. She is *Lady Liberty* and the torch she carries in her right hand, the right hand of god, is the light of an enlightened Mother, the mature woman, the lady of good council, a Goddess, who shines her light to show the way in times of great darkness. She is destined, as with the ancients, to grant America its freedom which is why they placed a gigantic *effigy* of her, the big momma, on their doorstep. She is more than a statue. She is an actual person.

It is a woman who will bring this world out of the trenches of evil male reptilians and a demonic 4th dimension have mired you into. It is only a woman who is honourable and *lawful* enough to stand against this satanic filth who think they've got it in the bag and laugh at you every day. This is why they have the celebrity Madonna 'giving birth' to butterflies (monarch mind control) and the digital centipedes because the alien reptilian thing is connected to a 'bug' or 'mantis' A.I. insect hive mind race from a war dimension that once existed on Mars very similar to the Nazi 'goosestepping' in their demand, however ridiculous, for *rigid uniformity* and compliance to hierarchy. They literally look like bugs walking the way they do as also found in North Korea, Russa and China among the most *inflexible* cultures on Earth Mother Nature, the life force, was supposed to give birth to something totally new at this time, a new age of abundance, prosperity and freedom. Except they've got an aging old slut *Madonna* giving birth to bugs, centipedes, ritualising the 'birthing' of the insect colony on Earth being transmitted to the galaxy by the multitudes of minds that tap into this shit creating a circuit, however fake, of twisted insidiousness. Note to self; Madonna, the satanic fake 'mother' figure being broadcast at this time, is *62 years old*. So, it's no wonder they had to depict her aging old spadge as a cartoon as, the real thing, after 45 years of orgies, satanic sex rituals and babies, would look like a couple of raggedy old tents flapping in a sandstorm. Lawrence of Arabia. That's not a wizard's sleeve that the circus Big Top with no poles holding it up in a gale force cat 5…and its flapping hard! Wrinkled. Discoloured. Old. I'm surprised they didn't depict bigfoot emerging exhausted and begging to be taken into custody. They missed their mark on *that* one by about 30 years. But once again, they are slinging shit at the *real* goddess, *young* women, loving mothers, as they transmit the message to the universe that the Goddess is now a bearded man or an aging old satanic whore. Go figure. She *is* prophesised to return, as is sorely needed now, and this is how you keep her away.

The media are being used to transmit this ritual message to the mass minds of the world who in turn broadcast that message to the black hole sun at the centre of our galaxy, a big brain, that feeds it back to us. For example, Portland, Oregon. Firstly, Portland has really high levels of missing people, specifically children, in the wild. The issue around exotic, and I mean *really* exotic, animals like Bigfoot and cryptids is in epidemic proportions right now as secret underground laboratories genetically engineer all manner of freakish creatures in keeping with the ancient script that spoke of such things because they were genetically engineering them back then too. In ancient times centaurs (half man half horse) Minitour (half man half bull) and all manner of cryptids were said to be revered by the ancients as 'gods'. So, Portland is the City of Roses, and their famous *Elk* was graffitied, ripped down and discarded. This is because the Elk is a symbol of the buck, the alpha male, associated with Osiris called the *Deer Hunter* as a constellation. They are destroying the image of the returning king, the alpha male, who has his head screwed on. In his higher capacity, he is father, dad, *the protector of the home*. The Rose is Mother Mary, Mary Magdalene, the feminine, the mother, the wife, the Lady of the House associated with the root chakra, rose coloured, that initiates the onset of tantric sex enlightenment via holy matrimony. They are destroying the light side of the mother and father, the high side of the masculine and feminine, and replacing it, via a massive broadcast system emanating from billions of human's minds, with a script that the good father and the good mother are in ruins as found in Portland.

So, the rose and the buck, Mary and Osiris in this ritual, who, although interchangeable in this ritual, are *the light side* of the Goddess and God, are looted, shot down, bloodied, trash piled up, homeless, useless, violent, ignorant, dangerous, unstable and unhinged – just like Portland the City of Roses with their famous Elk Fountain symbolising the deer or buck of the male (Osiris) and the *waters of the feminine* the Goddess represented by, among others, Mary-Isis, the Rose. Like the Twin Towers bought down in flames and terror they represented, once again, the mother and father as the number eleven as the zodiac sign Geminin is the symbol 'eleven' 11 called in ancient times The Lovers, man and wife. It was then changed to the 'brothers' who are a homosexual 'brother's of darkness, the Masons, who worship an androgynous male-female-animal beast god, Satan, The Devil, represented in so many LGBT rituals happening now. So when they repeat 'is Portland over?' what they are really saying "if you wont save the mother and father, the good family, then we will kill them and replace them with our all-in-one Baphomet transgender male-female-animal hybrid creature who derives its high intellect of chakra tantric enlightenment by cold hard sex, with anyone, with anything including men, women and children while the enlightened Family of Life, mother and father, husband and wife are dead burned and buried".

This is the ritual to repeatedly transmit the message (with sad trigger music) that Mum and Dad, God and Goddess, are dead on this world as Satan rises, as the One World Leader and the militarised harsh corporate state emerges in the place where self-governance once existed. The *dystopia* is taking a grip on the throat of *Utopia*, and this is how they do it. Paradise lays within us, within our chakra and light body system activated by sacred lovemaking called transcendental sex or 'tantric' sex today. It's not until the feminine mother is being deleted by all things LGBT that men in general are finally owning up to the *necessity* of the feminine and how important she really is. Not until their own masculinity and the species of 'man', women and men as a collective, is threatened that men are starting to appreciate and respect women and are suddenly like 'hang on a minute! We need them! Stop downgrading our women!' Up until then there has been a careless attitude toward the importance of women and a denial of their greatness in history and goes to show how much instinct men have operated on. If they cared so much, why have women routinely been paid less than men for the same jobs and find it more difficult to get into managerial (note; *man*-agerial) roles or industries 'traditionally' owned and operated by men? For example, shipping, construction and even politics. One female politician in Australia even said that 'it wasn't that bad' putting up with male politicians her worst experience being a 'pat on the backside'. Really…? And she's a bastion of feminine equality? Really? And what would other men do to a man in the workplace who gave him a lecherous pat on the arse? A sound arse-kicking I would think. But it's okay for women to be treated like a sex-bot? A thing. Which is exactly why men have had their rights removed and will struggle, maybe even fight to the death, to get some of their power back because, now that women, 'mummy', is being deleted thanks to an LGBT minority largely made up of men demanding to be called women then demanding 'mother' be removed from education vernacular, is precisely because men never stood up for women in a societal and certainly not in a spiritually sense. They stood up for her in the sense that they would stand up to someone trying to steal their car or break into their house, in 'property' sense. If you mess with a man's car or house, he will get territorial. It's a pissing contest.

The town of Paradise was completely destroyed in the 2018 fires as the promise of the prophesised 'paradise' for humans burns in flames. The weird, animated movie *Up* depicts an old man who is trying to get to Paradise Falls - the destruction of 'paradise' as it 'falls'. The falls in the movie were based on Venezuelan, Angel Falls reinforcing the ritual as it needs an 'angelic' aspect to lock it into place subliminally. The strange mountains where the falls are located is called 'tepui' in the language of the local Pemon people and means 'house of the gods'. In the lead up to 2022 supposed to be a year of balance and harmony as were the preceding years supposed to be, a film starring Benedict Cumberbatch was released called the Power of the Dog. The 'Dog' is the dog star Sirius personified as the goddess Isis, the light, who is also Mary and Diana and all the rest of the chaste lawful goddesses of Love including Venus. 'Power of the Dog' was basically claiming that cowboys of the 'old west' were gay pushing a false gay history again. Elite men are groomed from birth to be bisexual to capitalise on getting as much tantric sex as possible to open the chakras and attain the mega mind. It's the dark side. It's another inside joke to associate the image of the virginal Goddess of Light with the LGBT Baphomet Satan character. Channing Tatum's film 'Dog' is another reference to the Dog Star Sirius, the Nature Goddess. In this film a military guy (war god Mars) and his 'dog' (Sirius Isis Mary etc) race to a funeral breaking laws, narrowly escaping death and learning to let their guard down to have a fighting chance at happiness. A dog a reference to the wife and mother, the goddess. They are literally depicting the monogamous relationship with women as a dog because these satanic anything goes men see a 'lawful' relationship with a woman as the most laughable option and make fun of 'holy matrimony' based on fidelity and Love – true love – between an ascending man and woman's chakras or God and Goddess, Jesus and Mary. I could go on and on and on with these movies.

Jesus was the 'King' as an enlightened man is referred to as the 'King' or 'Lord' etc. So, they had 'the king', Elvis Presley, die on the throne, the toilet, in Memphis as Memphis was an ancient city in Egypt under the protection of the god Ptah who was interchangeable with Osiris the 'black *king* of the Nile' aka God. You'll notice in SO MANY of these movies that they make references that their mother is dead. That's because the Mother is the Goddess and these tantric IQ 'gods' of a satanic dark order cannot handle an enlightened woman even though Zeus originally required his wife to be as enlightened as him to achieve Godhood or indeed the Godhead – a place of pure bliss in a universal astral realm of all-encompassing omnipresence and greatness to become Creators themselves – maybe of a whole new universe? Who knows how big this gets?

The Goddess, a tantric enlightened female, scares the shit out of them hence, why Zeus was afraid of no other god or goddess but Iris, an enlightened young woman. When they print 'Isis destroys gates' notice they haven't capitalised ISIS to distinguish the boys are running a business called ISIS and this has nothing to do with the Goddess of Mothers? So, the universe hears millions of minds saying that Isis is a monster, so she needs to be killed but it really means, destroys mothers and wives, destroy the feminine. It's because these guys are afraid they can't keep up with her so they have knocked her down, slandered her a prostitute, terrified her, shamed her gender and sullied her sex, cut out her genitalia via FGM and killed the mother Goddess and the light side of the father, God, in every way they can to send the message to the universe that the enlightened husband and wife, God and Goddess, are dead and that anything goes gay-bi-whatever freewheeling open marriage party boy 'gods', the Devil – Satan, are uninterrupted in their ongoing quest to party on into the space age an beyond. But that is NOT what the ancient prophecies said would happen as such they try to manipulate it however, they can to get their preferred out. That said, apparently there are fixed points in space, a bottleneck, and these things regardless come to pass. They would rather 'reign in hell' than 'serve in heaven' as such they are prepared to sell the whole world out to create a civilisation where they are intellectually superior to any and all beneath them using tantric sex enlightenment. This is because when the family of life, the Mother and Father God and Goddess, work in unison in TRUE LOVE – monogamous reverence for each other, 'worshipping' each other and not some pervert old man in the clouds, they can attain the HIGHEST vibration of all transcending space and time to emerge as LITERAL Gods in a reality that would make the alien dick cult space program look like little boys burning ants with magnifying glasses, small by comparison, and unbeatable in every way. They sure as hell don't want that and yet the people will decide in the end.

So, the plan was and remains to 'destroy' America insofar as one would think that translates as wrecking the country and plunging it into near civil war conditions or something that resembles a demilitarised zone which is currently happening. It was designed that 'out of the ashes' indeed 'a phoenix from the ashes' would arise the 'new world' which for those left alive would be a corporate military state as is being promoted now with the new Space Force combining the Airforce with a Corporate Military Space Program. However, it looks more like a case of them knocking over cities, Portland, Oregon is where it is most obvious now – high drugs, crime, homelessness etc., so many American cities are in ruins now. They don't want to completely destroy their infrastructure, although I'm sure there are some that would enjoy that, but they are knocking them over one city at a time. Seattle went through quite a period of time where there were major economic and construction problems etc., back in the late 2000teens however, now they have major Silicon Valley names Amazon, Google etc., in massive headquarters in the city with new major corporate construction underway as we speak. These massive companies also are introducing the ability to actually live inside your office building. So, when you've finished work you walk out the office and get in the lift...to the floor you live on! These will be mini office-cities and possibly the blueprint for decommissioning the suburbs in a reduced population in the next few decades caused by the mass number of people who were stupid enough to receive the injections during the very obviously planned Corona Virus pandemic and the waves of death planned to come out of that in the next few years. Much of the injections are designed to really whittle down the population with new diseases all conveniently lumped onto the 'spectrum' so nobody really knows what they've got, they just fit a general disease criteria and are 'on the spectrum' whatever that means.

The plan to completely destroy the U.S. may have been on the cards but they are refining their techniques as people adapt and become more informed. Therefore, corporate cities with populations living in their workplace where your work is literally your life like the movie 'The Island' or so many other predictive programming modules they have rolled out in the last fifty years including Logans Run where people live and work inside huge domes the outside being off limits where it is almost a sort of Nazi Utopia where people die in some sort of ritual to 'elevate' like a lottery (see, The Island). Yes, it is one version of how they will eventually utilise a 'soft' introduction to a 'brighter better world' of streamlined buildings and modern conveniences under strict conditions. But just as in the past and *their* strict conditions people wont think to question whether it could be better, or worse, they will simply go along with it in many ways 'happy' not knowing they are unhappy because they don't have a point of reference and either drugged or reengineered the accept it.

California, Louisiana, and many other states of America where terrible social and judicial systematic injustices have led to such a degraded state of the community that now there must be a 'push back' and 'return to sanity' and 'better conditions' based on a concept of what it looks like when it's 'bad'. These better conditions are already in the pipelines and the state of how 'bad' it is, is looked up on with confusion by the general public unable to comprehend *why* their leaders, Mayors etc., sit back and do nothing while everything is going to hell. Then at a certain point, all of a sudden, mass construction, new major corporates will set up, big business precincts will take over and people will welcome it as a preferred outcome, even rejoice at the changes, compared to drive by shootings, street drug abuse and trafficking, using the pavement as a toilet, sex in public and all the depravity that epitomises the Devil and the dreaded hordes of filth dredged up from Hell engineering the chaos. Only, it's *still* the devil in disguise to re-emerge as your saviour with flashy new office buildings and shiny new streets however, the community and the strong system of industry and competition will be morphed into a shining citadel whose coffers are filled with unending funds and resources from which we do not know where they are derived. They just make it up as they go along. There is no money. They is only credit, blips on a screen. It is the ultimate, but highly attractive, fake society headed up by the same guys that let your massive car and industrial sectors be outsourced to other countries plunging your population into poverty and homelessness and all the degradation that led to the re-emergence of, this time, a new society of 'data' industries, corporates and IT and internet firms with digital moguls replacing real work and real industries with something that is ultimately, a computer generated landscape of silicon fakery. But it will *look* nice until they enforce whatever other measures they desire and if you live where you work….um….yeh….I'll let you figure out how that will end.

You'll notice the developers moving in now to buy up any real estate like parking lots in central city areas, even the worst like Detroit etc., removing any semblance of what we recognise replacing these areas with shining new massive corporates that the average person has NO IDEA how they are run or really why. This will lead to the new 'transport' system which may start out being hybrid cars etc., silent and run by electricity and at first, very cheap and kinda cool like 'Tesla' cars (he would be spinning in his grave if he knew that were using his name for this shit), but eventually will be morphed into another expensive service or industry that will be downsized to underground travel systems and not even real trains but more subterranean trams. Soon you won't even need your own transport – why would you if you live where you work? Weekends away? Hire a smart car with points you eared from work and hire it from an 'info' centre booth on every corner and the cars will be housed underground or in a high rise and it will simply be delivered to you where you stand coming up from underneath like the massive underground bike storage in Japan where you swipe your card on a teller machine and a bike pops up from underneath you. But no car yards and certainly no rental car outlets. But you won't pay with real money, just a hybrid credit system hooked into a digital non-cash system of swipes and voice recognition. There will be any number of pick-up cab services, Uber type door to door shuttles, although not real cabs like we have today with actual people driving them earning their own money in their own industry, but transfer services, shuttles and 'system' transport with set routes and no choice and to going outside the smart grid approved zones.

Again, it's just a way to minimise your independence, downsize practical industries, do away with major roadways to 're-green' the earth and take back natural habitat for the betterment of the Earth and control every move you make. This is all to be worked in with 'chips' and 'cards' etc., that will grant you access to everything, your building, your office, your 'funds' which will be more akin to a 'shopping rewards' type 'points' in a bonus system (if you behave). All conveniently locked into the Smart system ensuring that the next phase of expanding control will run rather smoothly as you can simply be disconnected from the system if you have too many 'demerit' points against your 'chip' unplugged from the day-to-day functions of a society that everyone else takes for granted – no dinners, no drinks, no 'hiring' anything. It will be like Corona lockdown where everything has to be 'checked in' on an app or an embedded chip preferably. The Corona shutdown was the 'soft' although rather rude introduction to all this during which time they conveniently installed all their 5G infrastructure while you were streaming Netflix. Only the special 'privileged' people who go along with it peacefully are allowed to get a coffee or a sandwich from the café as everything will require you to swipe in. And there will be a bonus points system like shopping rewards for everyone who bothers until you won't be asked anymore, it will be expected to swipe in, even to the supermarket, even to buy a soft drink from the fridges which is already happening. Businesses who go along with this will be given incentives and perks to bring in a shiny, streamlined prison cell. There will be no more protests in the street and no 'getaway' car if you have to make a run for it when the helpful authorities start shooting you at the Shrine of Remembrance because they care about your health. Most people will welcome all this, initially, buttered up by the shite circumstance the authorities deliberately let it devolve into but ultimately, once again, it's all about control and *their* vision of the future of which *you* are clearly not being asked for your input on.

RETURN OF THE TWINS

There are enough derogatory labels going around now to ensure a 'soft' warning to anyone in the future who wants to break away; 'you're a bigot' 'you're a homophobe' 'you're a racist' 'you're transphobic' in a world where diversity will be the new god. And there is no problem with diversity, if you are a human being then diversity is great, but the instinct of most people will be to not go against the status quo, as has been made *abundantly* clear by people willing to do all sorts of things including injecting their kids with poison so they don't get called an 'anti-vaxxer' 'conspiracy nut'. This will translate as labelling you any unfair derogatory and, ironically, *bigoted* LABEL to ensure you shut up or you can get out if you're 'not on the team'. And so, the world that was breaking away from the 'team' mentality and 'you're either in or you're out' hard line, will, eventually, be the most ruthless minded and controlled 'team' that has ever existed on Earth. But they'll be 'inclusive' and 'progressive'. Basically, you'll be locked into your certain area and if you want to go outside that area there will be much red tape and bureaucracy to travel and 'trains' wont really be a thing, just local light rail and pick-up services in silent shiny vehicles in a localised areas. Again, it will look nice, but it won't be 'nice' per se. During lockdown the homeless apparently took over major retail and recreation areas and as such the authorities fenced off waterfronts, boardwalks, and park areas that have the greatest views in big cities. Since the shutdown has ended, these areas are still fenced off in another step toward disallowing people even the simplest pleasures like eating their lunch on waterfront recreational parks and walkways. A lot of crime, drug dealers and drug addicts, drunks and homeless people, however unfortunate some of them *may* be, has allowed for a state where despite the good intentions of communities to open their hearts to accommodate the growing numbers of displaced people, has led to a situation where even business districts and safe places for families like parks and children's playgrounds have been taken over by aggressive territorial people who have taken propriety over areas that just two years ago were considered *no go zones* for such people based on the fact that these areas are hubs of businesses, families and the staff of said precincts without whom there is no civilisation *at all*. Now it seems to be a free for all and that is not to diminish people who are in need, but their needs do not outweigh the needs of the professional people providing the tax dollars required to rectify this destabilised state of affairs.

It's seems in the U.S. in particular (and from what I saw in the U.K. and well as Europe) the people in positions of power able to clean up the streets and return it to a state of normality that we took for granted only a few years ago, where descent law abiding hard working people are safe from harassment and danger from people who do not belong there and for whatever reason, are unable to contribute to society. Today's leaders prefer to 'sit on the fence' playing the political correctness card which only worsens the situation and prolongs the problems making solutions harder to achieve therefore, the needed conclusions to these problems remain open ended, *unending*, as has always been intended to build *their* 'new' world from the ashes of the 'old' world. I don't mind that they are building a new world, only I do mind that the people who are supposed to work inside this new world have not been consulted and instead, once again, all these intended changes only filling the coffers of the elite, the ruthless and the ambitious, and that does not work for me. In reality they envy us. Envy is like pond scum, it's a type of algae, and if you don't treat it properly it will grow and turn your beautiful lake into a swamp.

Little green men are green with envy.

Chapter Eight

'Jesus' & 'Mary'
The Christ & The Magdalene

Let there be light.

Essentially, all human men are Jesus, and all human women are Mary. We are the Jesus's and the Mary's also called the Adam's and the Eve's, the Osiris's and the Isis's, the Joseph's and the Mary's etc. It is a designation, a title, for the masculine electrical element epitomised in men and the feminine magnetic element epitomised as women, male and female, *binary electrical poles* just as the North Pole and the Soult pole electromagnetically hold our planet in a perpetual energetic balance and without them there would be no seasons, no crops, no food, no balance, no humans, in short, chaos, like many other planets which we will get to how they wound up 'dead'. Death is a chaotic energetic state. Life is a balanced energetic state. When talking about electricity, which is what this is all about, the Direct Current or DC best sums up the masculine. The Alternating Current or AC best sums up the feminine. The feminine current, AC, can go forwards or backwards, hence, 'alternating'. The Direct Current or DC only goes in one direction, forward, and best sums up the masculine insofar as men who have generated so much progress or 'forward motion' in past and present society move forward. This is a good thing. What isn't a good thing is when the 'feminine' or AC is not taken into consideration whereas men positive current moves forward the AC feminine current moves in both directions insofar as, progress is a great thing, unless of course you stop and take into consideration the outcomes and then pause, take a step back

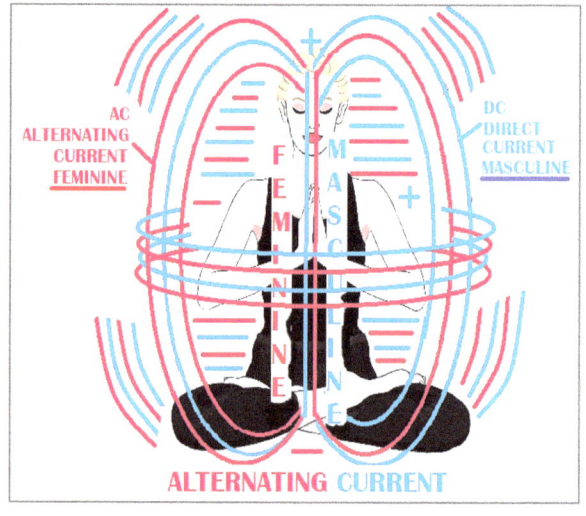

– AC – and consider a different route. AC alternating current takes more energy, and this is a perfect analogy to sum up why the feminine energy has simply been discarded throughout history, because the DC or 'direct' way is the easiest. As it turns out the easiest way is not the best way and why mother nature invented both currents of electricity, the positive and the negative, as the 'negative' alternating feminine energy allows for multiple outcomes and with pause and caution, the best outcome can be achieved and although this may be slower or more measured in its approach to life in general, it is safer and in the long run far more advanced that smash em up and blast them in all directions to get what we want because we're male.

Being direct is great, but when idiots are direct and don't have the intelligence or more specifically the feminine heart functioning properly to stop and think about what they are doing and saying, then this directness is dangerous, *see right*. It This isn't about trying to make men feel small. However, men have run planet Earth for thousands of years and basically all we've seen is endless war and destruction which has ultimately resulted in the end of our world, the home of all people including men, women and children – thoughtless, this is why you need memory or feminine balance who also personifies 'wisdom'. is not up to men to run this 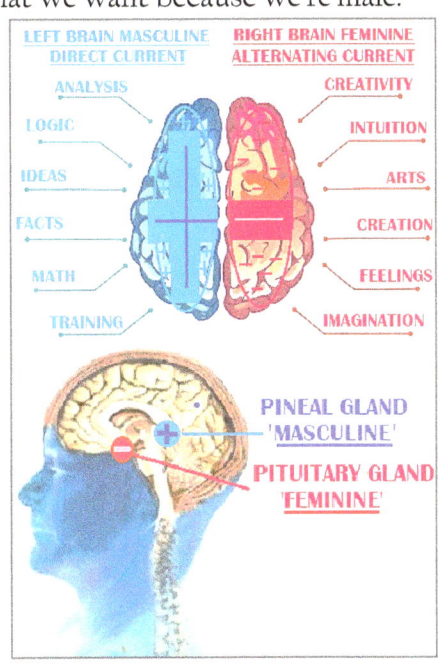 world on behalf of everyone else, it is not up to men to monopolise Earth's resources or dole out those resources as they see fit increasingly made apparent by their insider trading, corruption and theft. The feminine houses the masculine and feminine energies better than the masculine energy does as water carries information and we are at least 70% water. This is why all ancient civilisations revered the feminine as she is the one to produce both fields, electric and magnetic, this *alternating flow* creates a magnetic field, or the torus field, and it is this magnetic field that protects us from other electrical forms that may be harmful to us. The figure 8 is the torus circulating and 88 is the god and goddess in balance and 88 is the number of days Mercury takes to go around the sun and Mercury in ruled by Gemini, the lovers. As usual though these misfits, the Norman Bates Club who run the world see Mercury aka Greek Hermes as 'gay' and made the masculine and feminine lovers as 'the brothers' hence, the 'brotherhood' has been notorious throughout history for rejecting the masculine and feminine pair in favour of gay orgies in mockery of natural procreation to 'mock god', the next generation, born of male and female alchemy. Even science can't fully explain the existential questions around birth and life born into babies. Despite the close proximity to the sun, Earth is protected from massive solar bursts by the magnetic fields of earth's 'water'. So, while men might think 'water' is a passive and easily controlled force, it is water that puts out fire and since our world is burning right now, you might want to bring on the water pretty soon. So, if you don't have the ability to go back and forth, alternating current, which is considered 'feminine' then you're finished.

The purpose of warning of the historic (and very well-known results to the men doing all this behind the scenes) of unhinged masculine energy, is a world easily manipulated by chaos. When humans are in chaos they run in all directions and cannot think properly. When humans have the ability to stop and think, to have time to deduce the outcome of certain actions, then we thrive. There is a misconception that too much of the good life leads people to apathy and debauchery. This is patently untrue and if anyone tries to convince you of this, they are fucking morons with an agenda. The fact of the matter is that we are seeing so much human debasement at the moment because we have 'some' of the good life and NONE of the education or resources to do anything with the time and space we are increasingly gaining for ourselves. Everything is out of balance, everything, and this again is too much masculine fire and no feminine energy while women are increasingly being turned into morons forgetting that they did not do this but contributing BADLY to the end of it. As usual women will get the blame. Humans are easily directed by their whims, their instincts, ego and fears. These tools have always manipulated humans and if we don't put a stop to all the bullshit then they always will and Earth will die like all the other planets.

I personally believe that most if not all planets in the Milky Way Galaxy harboured some kind of 3D life and a dark force is going around the galaxy using up planets for their resources and once that planet is dead, they move to the next living planet. They have been doing this for so long that large swathes of the galaxy that were once alive are now dead and the 'darkness' or 'death' is outweighing the 'light' or 'life'. They are killing the galaxy, and this is why other forces, possibly from other galaxies, are in some weird way (still holding my breath here) assisting to elevate our world out of the quagmire of evil. The death force has been done to humans on a micro scale reducing us from eternal beings to living short harsh lives of around 70 years or 'three score years and ten' and as part of their program. They make us 'die' to enter their dark state between lives, wipe our memories and reinsert our soul consciousness back into this planet to use us again and again in a terrifying game of duplication mimicking the natural replicating processes of mother nature, life, in a hideously weird alien game.

Christ is the light-force within as broadcast from the Universe, and the Magdalene is the magnetic component required to 'earth' us electrically to the planet to diffuse the enormous amounts of power capable of being harnessed through tantric sex electrical enlightenment. *Both* men and woman contain the Christ light electricity and the Magdalene, magnetism, in an electromagnetic loop to retain the balance and stability in the two components of this 'force' so that we don't tolt one way or the other and become unhinged, unanchored, and blow away or 'fry' both spiritually and physically. Isis was the goddess of mothers and wives and the well-run family home found in stability and spiritual strength. She was not a servant or a slave, the 'maid', cleaning and cooking, she was the lady of a large house, a queen, which would be would be quite a job delegating tasks and if the man and herself were bringing in a good wage, then she need to have complete knowledge of the books, the comings and the goings out of the house, commerce, people management and schedules to ensure that food was ordered and properly prepared, ensure all bills and money related matters were taken care of and that the next generation were aware of their obligations. The husband would also have to know about these things as both are equal powers of domesticity. Men can clean and cook just as well as women, they just WANT to believe that they are not 'mentally wired' to do these things to trick the woman into doing it while they get all the fun and kudos of working out in the world as merchants. It's a sick game that has become 'culture' and 'that's just he way it is' but as technology and ease of living make life a more palatable place to live where our choices are increasing and so are the responsibilities of making sensible choices, then we all, men and women, need to step up to the plate and contribute fairly and equally to the home without men treating women like 'mummy' and women feeling obliged to be 'mummy' to everyone lest they are labelled a 'feminist' or some other derogatory term to manipulate their feelings into complying.

These psycho misfits that run our planet refer to the goddess as the 'maid' as famously described of Joan of Arc in another ritual goddess assassination as pain and suffering attach energy to an object or person and broadcast the intention of that energy to the galaxy and in turn the galaxy feeds that energy back to us. The game they are playing is to repeatedly refer to the goddess as a 'maid' a 'prostitute' a 'demoness' (see Lilith), a 'gargoyle monster' see, Medusa and tarnishing so many other *very real women* who they trashed as 'low' in their hope to feed a negative image of women to the universe so that the universe will *feed that message back to us* keeping women in place beneath men spiritually and cosmically in order that these male fuck ups can retain their control over a feminine lifeforce, the 'goddess', and be toy kings controlling the Goddess planet, Mother Earth. Medusa was mortal and said to be vulnerable the laws of nature and 'the gods' because 'the gods; are actually reptilian hybrids who practice black magic using demons and the elements to torment people and her aura is not strong enough to protect her while hr chakras remain closed. One of the medieval popes sent a demon after some nuns who he claimed made fun of him and 'wrecked their lives'. I know this is true because it was done to me. Even if you so much as look at them the wrong way they will destroy you and your family. This is the power they have that [people childishly call 'bad luck'. The ancient stories tell of rivalries between these gods and goddesses who are the male female reptilian hierarchy, the reptilian men obviously bested the reptilian women subjugating them and now they are out to destroy human women.

Mary like Joan of Arc etc., was not a 'maid' of the house nor is any other woman a 'maid' falling into the psychological game that women are there just to pick up after their husbands and offspring because we're not smart enough to do anything else. The 'maid' literally means 'maiden', a young, *enlightened* woman who was the greatest fear of the greatest god of all, Zeus. But he couldn't be much of a god if he is frightened of a little girl? That's because he is not a God. Zeus, who was an actual living person back in prehistory, rose to such power using these evil masculine methods of trickery and control over the feminine, that he has gone down forever as the male centric *role model* of male-default lore in awe and aspiration for how to *continue* to control the feminine force, to harness the great power and beauty of the feminine in mother nature's resources, to keep harvesting their sons from her body and keep elevating themselves *endlessly* in power and egotistic self-obsession over the feminine *forever* while making her feel like shit aka the little maid. However men are going to explain the thousands of years of brutality against the feminine is anyone's guess. I supposed they won't but maybe they won't have to. All this intimates that the goddess, all women, were once deified as a person of wealth and lifestyle and at her optimum insinuates that perhaps *all people* should live in wealth and luxury. Why not? We've got the resources for it. By ascribing to the 'gods', who were really role models for a healthy balanced work and life plan, *you too* could live a really happy existence if a few tried and tested

RETURN OF THE TWINS

managerial skills and self-governance is observed and appears that we were always, ALWAYS, supposed to be a planet of abundance, maturity and self-autonomy. These fruit loops running the world today are afraid of this demon, this devil, Satan, who they worship and fear and love and hate at the same time. It is a jigsaw of all their fears. They are frightened that this 'thunder god' will punish them in the end and they are right to be frightened of an alien demigod who from the depths of space and time that they have relied on for their earthly power with no intention to give it what it wants in the end figuring out *how they can escape their promises to this evil creature.* Madonna is afraid of thunderstorms, called brontophobia, from ancient Greek 'bronto' meaning thunder and lightning because it is from 'lightning' electricity that they get their power in tantric sex. The word 'brontosaur' literally translates as *'lightning lizard'*. These are the reptilians of old whose modern cousins of these ancient dinosaurs (the Titans!) are

probably a genus or relative like humans with their monkey cousins. We've all been genetically spliced. In fact, if I was really going to go out on a limb here, it looks like these creatures are some sort of 'pod' type being that move from planet to planet and, not unlike strawberry spores, can survive in space for thousands of year like some sort of bacteria 'infecting' planets. They started out as some sort of insect like a demonic alien, then morphed with lizards, then morphed with monkeys or a close familial grouping of humans and then morphed with humans while simultaneously downgrading our genetics to be more compatible with some 'middle' species they created. It was a biological step by step, paint by numbers encroachment hence, early depictions of these creatures show them going through all stages of development – horse or centaurs, mermaids, 'bigfoot' type creatures still around today. They retain these throwback genetics to this day and why you get weird genetic anomoalies or why some of their family members show more traits of different creatures than others. This is why they jokingly refer to the 'Addams' family (original man) or the 'Munster's' (monsters) family with one being a 'vampire' one being a 'werewolf' one being a 'bigfoot' as their genetics are so fragile and scrambled, they easily regress to their spliced genetics from old. Here in this ancient depiction, we see two non-human creatures the male carrying the 'mitre square' also called an 'engineers square' a tool of architecture and construction most

RETURN OF THE TWINS

notably the symbol of the *Masons* and their 'god', the devil 'the architect'. Most the 'god' deities throughout history can be linked to this object as it represents the secret 'club' (dick) who 'make' things and 'model' society even whole civilisations!

This throwback legend to a time of spliced genetics bears the hallmarks of the 11th Earl of Strathmore's son. Considering the legend of the 11 and the Utopia it foretells for humanity, this unforeseen shock emanated directly from the line of those alien lineages trying to prevent this ascension in the first place and is a dire portent it is from the pits of hell. No doubt great anticipation heralded the arrival of the 11th Earl's new-born son, only, upon the birth it was said a horrible hairy creature emerged immediately banished by his father hidden away (as you do). The boy grew to such a hairy hulking mass like bigfoot and imprisoned in the castle never to be seen by the public with many whispers and speculation form 19th century society abounding about the Monster of Glamis Castle who lived for 100 years and was still alive in 1921 when the Queen mother was 21 years old! In keeping with the 'duplication' deflection method (before the truth of the real history of the Windsor's can emerge), the 'monster of Glamis' is now Simon Bowes-Lyon who committed a sex attack on a female guest and was sentenced to ten months in prison in 2021! How many times have you heard of a royal being locked up in modern times? Never. Considering, the original monster was confined to a cell for 100 years (he grew to be very old) then this ten-month sentence is another 'diminished' version of the real thing like everything else they do cleverly parried by the mainstream media.

But the big boy of tantric sex, Zeus – the Devil – Satan, is an alien demonic force that is not human friendly so no matter how they want to spin it, this creature *will destroy them* for their use and abuse of him, for conjuring it and many other demons for no other reason than to aggrandise themselves. In the movie Ted the main characters get frightened when thunder (god) comes around in the form of a storm. They lampoon and laugh at the reality of what they are involved in but many a true word said in jest as 'the jester' and 'the joker' are other aspects of this demon the 'clown prince'. The jokes on them. Wrong bet, guys. These half-bloods, reptilians-human hybrids, make sacrifice to this demonic horde headed up by something who, they say, is a single all-powerful entity they call 'god' and have passed off as a 'heavenly father' because humans, by instinct, will have no part of it. We are a different species, after all. And in giving sacrifice to this creature, they get it to reveal more of its power to them making it tell them methods and treatments to use on humankind to win this evil game. But this alien's power is beyond their comprehension and so ultimately, like Solomon, they are doomed to be outsmarted by it and become enslaved to it forever in another spiritual realm from which their souls will never emerge. This is why they fear it and hate it but love it for the power that is generated by it's secrets of humanity, Earth and life itself despite its apparent lifelessness and it's living death from a darkness deeper than any known darkness.

But it was said in ancient times that Sophia, the goddess of wisdom where we get words like 'philosophy', instructed Solomon in how to 'build the temple' which is not an earthly temple, although I'm sure they lived in nice houses with their IQ's expanded. The temple is the body with activated chakras and heightened IQ so what they are really saying is that the masculine learned everything he knows about elevating his enlightenment and power *from the Goddess* and then it seems he used this power against her, wiped her memory and, like a traitor, lorded it over her ever since making her his maid and prostitute. And she has been, by and large, relegated to the laundry and the bedroom in a dangerous turn of events as so-called 'new age' men, mostly Christian men, want a return to 'traditional' values banning abortions, forcing women to have babies and controlling her life by forcing her to submit to breeding more humans at a time when overpopulation under current management leaves millions, billions, of children in poverty and isolation around the world. But life is sacred. Banning abortions is about taking women right to control their lives away from them at a time when we SHOULD be broadcasting that the feminine has control and autonomy over her life. But no. Males love lording it over women and are terrified of who they might actually be if they lose this position. You will see the mask fall from the monster's face as men unleash a tirade of abuse and control in their attempts to control the rising feminine at this time and this abuse will ultimately out their collective agenda to be 'boss'. The monster in this world is testosterone driven male ego found in the world of both human men and reptilian-human hybrid males alike. So, when Adam Sandler sings 'forgetful Lucy' in the film 50 First Dates about a woman with amnesia, he is really singing 'forget lucifer' as 'lucifer' is Venus, the goddess of light and love, found in *women* who had her memory wiped. They know all this, it's their secret religion. What you are reading is the secrets of Satanism the apparent 'light' but only as long as the man is running the show and then the light turns very dark when he is threatened. This is also why the longest running program on TV (even though it was pretty bad viewing) was 'I Love Lucy' because they have used the millions, billions, of minds viewing this show to send the message that the Goddess is a demon, Lucifer the identity thief, and we love him. Everything is obsessive ritual with these people.

This is why in the lead up to all the cosmic alignments over the last few years, they broadcast that 'identity theft' is a big problem at the moment while constantly diverting the attention away from the real identity thief, the devil-Satan, the father-son combination tag teaming the feminine mother-daughter since time immemorial. The Devil and Satan, father and son, have generation after generation tarnished the goddess, women, stealing her name, Lucifer, and her symbols, the five-pointed star of Venus, inverting these things, calling her a whore and a cleaner and stealing her position on this world as the universe naturally reveres the feminine who should be in the top position on this planet. Instead, we have a horde of imposters who told you that that Jesus, in actuality the Christ light of chakra power, was cast into the abyss when they have clearly been running the show the whole time. Sophia is the Goddess of Wisdom also found in the Lady of Good Council of Mary. She was Ashera, Solomons wife, which is interesting as Ashira is also what Muslims called the star Sirius that they attributed as a male force but is considered *female* universally. This is what I mean by an identity thief, Sirius is considered by all ancients societies ancient and modern including native lore, as feminine, as yet here under a male dominated religion Islam, it is referred to as 'male' because it is the brightest star in the sky so naturally, it would have to be male...but it's not.

Under Brutal reforms of King Josiah found in the 1st and 2nd Kings in the Bible, the veneration of Sophia had to go underground as Josiah slaughtered all her Priests and Priestesses destroying all her temples and shrines and places of worship. Once again, we find this story in Isis whose husband is murdered, Mary whose husband is murdered. It's interesting that in not allowing the feminine to have her rightful place, the masculine cannot attain his full measure of masculine cosmic power, if it's lop sided, like a ship, it will list. The alien overlords who are behind all this know that the masculine is ULTIMATELY handicapped by this energetic imbalance but in encouraging him to keep the feminine in an uneven position, they know that the male will never attain completion and therefore will never escape them. It was the story of Osiris and Isis, a symbolic cautionary tale, that Osiris, like Jesus, was betrayed by his own, was murdered and dismembered, Isis gathered up the parts and 'put him back together again', such a powerful spiritually symbolic image. She couldn't find his penis, his 'member' and so fashioned on of gold. As he has been emasculated, funnily enough by other men, or 'dismembered', it was Isis who returned his masculinity even greater than before in a member of 'gold' and in this tale it is the feminine who 're-membered' the masculine, returned his masculinity to him. So, it's interesting that the feminine energy embodies 'memory' and the masculine energy embodies 'intellect' or IQ but given the purpose of all this is not only to restore balance between men and women as humans, it is to return balance to the masculine and feminine energies we all hold inside our bodies. Therefore, the masculine 'intellect' and the feminine 'memory' go hand in hand and if you have good command of both these things you are a formidable force!

She personifies wisdom as an ancient tradition concerned *with integrity in the marketplace, politics and the royal court*. I bet the scheming males didn't like that, no wonder they hate her so much. She was rooted in the *reality of life* rather than dogma and doctrine and therefore, was excluded from monotheism and thus modern religion as a whole favouring a male deity by default. She represents a modern revival of fundamental universal and all-pervading eternal truths, that, rags and riches aside, pertain to the wholistic meaning of life, of personal happiness outside the pursuit of material objects and probably why she represents 'fair play' in trade and commerce, as in the drive to 'get more' in a male dominated toxic economic system, we wind up with much 'stuff' yet are empty on the inside. As such, she represents balance in that material objects are a part of a right of passage in that comfort and style *belong to us already* for a reasonable exchange and material gain should not be the ultimate price of our souls for some earthly comforts that are ours anyway. As said, the goddess gives freely, a tree does not ask you for money, men do that. This is why these male bastards call her the 'gift that keeps on giving' but she hasn't got much left and when that happens, the loving goddess turns into the war goddess, and she kills men in environmental disasters as mother nature takes back what is rightfully hers. These stories acknowledging the balance and power of the feminine and that, if treated unfairly for long enough, results in cataclysm, means that this has all happened before probably many times to warrant the observation of these negative cycles operated by aliens harvesting this world making you slaves to their 'time' wars as they harvest and re-harvest planet's including ours. There must surely be a greater hierarchy that the earthly hierarchy are not a part of in that the hybrids are simply 'foremen' who are bred to continue to enforce a greater evil, an alien space syndicate, for the purpose of continuing to harvest this beautiful abundant world. Spiritual comfort is the ultimate goal and material objects are simply furniture to our higher cosmic pursuits and thereby, somewhat trivial in the greater scheme of things. That said I would rather meditate in a beautiful earth friendly high-rise overlooking a forest that sit in a cave skinny as a rake meditating away my hunger pains as 'bliss' in an external world gone mad by object consciousness, materialism. This is why they say we are 'born in sin' because 'sin' is to be hoodwinked by the flesh, the body we are born into, when our spirit is God, the light, and if we are trapped in body-physical material consciousness we ignore the higher plains of existence that our bodies are capable of and that is a sin. It's like driving a Lamborghini car and leaving it to rot in the gutter. Lack of appreciation of the incredible vehicle we are driving sends the message that you don't deserve it and it will be taken away from you as a result.

Materialism is the devil's (reptilian alien) cheap copy of the real thing. It was once called HAL and HAL is A.I., a machine. Therefore, HAL represents a facsimile, a dangerous and self-lowering form of reality where we drop our higher drive for mother nature and personal enlightenment, slip into debasement for a few dollars just to have a comfy couch to lie on when we are exhausted from the ambition for dirty money. It's psychological warfare that relies on the fear of insufficiency and lack but they don't call mother nature 'the gift that keeps on giving' for nothing! She never stops. She's a working mum, a single mum, and that's sad. Where's her god? Where is the real man? Revelling with the reptilian traitors that's where. They ganged up on her, human men and reptilian men, and it looks like the ritual of food shortage will become very real as they broadcast to the universe that the goddess doesn't have enough to go round.... more lies...it's all they do. They don't just deceive, they *are* deception.

We've had our memories wiped or we wouldn't comply with these incredibly stupid systems. Mother Nature, the goddess, is free-of-charge and why the feminine, Sophia, represents memory! If you remember that all this belongs to you in the first place, they cannot get you to destroy the forest, your true treasure, for fake money. You would simply manage the world properly so you wouldn't have to be slaves to a false system that tells you money is the currency when mature and healthy management of *free earthly resources* IS THE CURRENCY OF YOUR SOUL AND THE UNINVERSE. There is nothing you can't have with proper management, and you wouldn't have to bow down to anyone to get anything ever again. The human race is so ready for this. Are we tired yet? Tired of the lies? Tired of the duplicity? Yes, duplicity and duplication are fake, trickery, blinding your eyes to the fact that you are not a slave, you are already free, you just need to manage the world in respect of Mother Nature and all else will be provided. This is the identity thief at work again, people thank 'god' for everything they receive when everything they received is form the goddess, mother nature, mother earth and *mother's* bringing forth the light, babies. That's why she is the light bearer, that is why Lucifer means the 'bringer of light' because Venus is the local version of Sirius, the brightest star in the sky, and why they symbolically referred to it as feminine the light carried in women.

HAL is a cheap copy of life dressing up aliens as kings when men are kings (if they tapped into their higher functions), they tell you money is currency when food and resources properly tended is the currency allowing you to explore your unending consciousness if managed properly. A sentient being is someone who is capable of self-analysis, self-awareness, CONSCIOUSNESS. An animal that hurts itself in the wild will wander aimlessly until it dies. A human who injures themselves are capable of deduction and knows they have to tend to the wound. This is self-awareness. Same goes for spiritual injury and mental injury, it needs to be acknowledged and tended to. But what the false hierarchy alien-demon overlords are doing is a facsimile that has us chasing material things losing our souls as a result we do not realise we are sick and need to tend to our spiritual and mental wounds. WE don't even know how because they wiped our memories. But I can tell you how to fix that little red wagon quick smart. Tantric sex chakra activation. That's all. These false systems are decidedly male but worse, it is alien male and has no respect for human life, no respect for the planet and no respect for the light. In my first book, 2020 & Beyond, I said that you shouldn't believe everything a religion tells you just because there is a thin seem of truth running through it. Carl Jung said, 'I don't believe Christianity is the only and highest manifestation of the truth. There is at least as much truth in Buddhism and in other religions', from Letters Vol.1 Page 127. All religions are sharing some level of truth. The question we need to ask then is why are ALL religions lying about the truth that tantric sex is the key to enlightenment? This is because every religion there is a dark order of evil misfits who have tapped into the power of tantric sex, sacred sex and are using it for the dark side as it drastically increases ones IQ and psychic abilities. This is why they are very difficult to find and expose because they are operating outside 3D linear time and can see what is coming up next.

After all the other distractions, there is going to be a time when the official scientific teams will go into people's homes around the world clearing the negative energy and casting out spirits and demons from people's bodies and this will fit in with the 'end times' that miracles and signs including 'you will be able to cast out demons' will be fulfilled in the Bible script.

Part Two

*The 'Devil' is the 'god of time' and thus
our calendar, like everything else, is a deception
in one great big calendar, their calendar, spanning
tens of thousands of years.*

They know what time it is.

Chapter Nine
The Norman Bates Club
Psycho: The Brotherhood of Evil

The Masons have gone by many names throughout history. It is standard operating procedure to alter their image, name, logo, branding etc., throughout various civilisation to cover their tracks and re-emerge later when the heat has died down after another attempt to usurp the human race and take over Planet Earth for their own corrupt space regime. They ultimately work for others in a far-reaching cosmic syndicate of war and destruction. They have been called the priesthood of the Egyptian pharaohs – kings and priests alike – they have been called The Merovingians, the Knights Templar, the Nazis, The Druids. Their methods were practiced by Solomon, Julius Caesar, Amun Ra, Alexander the Great, Leonardo Da Vinci and so many others. Not many know that there have been a select few women who have practiced their methods and although not allowed to join the inner sanctums of the boy's club, these women have reigned over a number of Golden Age's, including Queen Elizabeth II who for sixty years oversaw a global civilisation of post war prosperity, expansion, luxury, and economic growth for all those in her empire Australia included. The rumour of homosexuality being a mandate of the inner core of the Mason's has been exposed many times. You must remember that these people are demonically possessed hybrid reptilian cold-blooded aliens *masquerading as human beings*. It is imperative to not conflate the difference between ordinary gay guys in the street as being the same as these mother-hating serial killing psychopaths. They are *Norman Bates Inc.*

They hate the mother with such intensity because 'Mother' is the Goddess who was called the 'mother' of all gods. She gives birth to god and they can't stand it. Without her they don't exist. So much for 'god'. It's quite a flaw but then they have laboratory babies now and believe their technology has transcended women. Dangerous and stupid. At the end of the day 'mother' is the magnetic component of an electromagnetic force present throughout the universe and powerfully hidden in our sacral plexus at the base of the spine called by our ancestor's 'kundalini' among other things. Regardless of the high-powered nature and legendary 'mythical' status of ancient gods, especially male, throughout history, I've concluded that all these so called 'gods' were once *actual people*, the living 'facsimiles' of stories embedded in ancient lore regarding the origins of the constellations and the stars. Zeus was a real person once as was Hermes. But who made up the stories about the constellations? Who gets to say what they mean and where these stories originated from? So, it seems the amorphous allegories of astro-myth were subsequently projected onto certain people by their families as dates back to prehistory because of their status in society at the time to give them great importance, figuratively and symbolically, in the eyes of the people they wished to rule as their slaves just as they are doing today. They appeared as 'gods' simply because they had unlocked the human body's ability to perform seemingly 'godlike' miracles, all capabilities of the marvelous human nervous system and activated chakras. Having commandeered the human vehicle, the body, by breeding with and splicing the genetics of humans, they could access our incredible physical and spiritual skills and talents. They then kept this information about self-actualisation secret, used it themselves, and call themselves 'gods', *literally*.

They built folklore and mythological greatness around their icon in order to go down in history repeatedly playing out these plotlines and characters in various generations and civilisations until we reach our current time in which these psychos have *totally believed* their cover stories and actually see themselves as living gods of legend reincarnated lifetime after lifetime here to fill an ultimate prophecy of global dominance and singular godlike status as The One or the 'anti-christ' one world leader! I'm not even kidding. It goes beyond a 'god complex' to the point where they actually deify themselves as God Almighty in the flesh. This is made *strikingly apparent* in the incredible levels of godlike narcissistic behaviour found in A-list celebrity particularly Hollywood who abuse all beneath them with seeming impunity and is even refined as a 'culture' of the rich and famous and their ever-growing superiority over the masses who they believe adore them! That said, the Goddess as mother is Mother Nature and Mother Earth actualised as human women, the life bringer, the pregnant mother, symbolised by the biblical Madonna the virginal Mother Mary who is also the wife 'prostitute' Mary Magdalene (because she knows what she's doing in the bedroom). But these boys can't stand to imagine their mother as being sexually powerful – they do have mother complexes after all - so they said mum was a chaste virgin but the wife, who is also the mother of their children, is a bit slutty aka a 'prostitute' which turns them on otherwise they would feel emasculated in the bedroom and that would make them angry and even manifest as violent spousal abuse. The Madonna-Whore complex, as Freud postulated, develops in men who see women as saintly Madonna's or debased prostitutes. Basically, they never emotionally matured beyond the age of about six to ten when male children feel desires for their opposite sex parent and strong jealousy to their same sex parent as a boy learns about relationships with women primarily through his relationship with his mother. Depending on the emotional distance in his parent's relationship, his emotional bonds with either or both parties may have suffered. The boy may bond more powerfully with the mother in a way that hinders his capacity to feel which continues to affect his masculine identity and sense of a separate self as a mature adult in later years. These men need to simply do the research and not succumb to shame or guilt about the natural programming we are all susceptible to. In short, they need to grow up, literally.

What is overarching all this mania is a hypermasculine alien demonic dick cult who derive their power from *ritualising sex and death* who are ultimately, all about technology which at its core is A.I. or *Artificial Intelligence*. An entity channeled via the secretive CHANI Project (Channeled Holographic Access Network Interface) said, 'they worship their technology'. This is why all things related to the feminine is being deleted and dressed up as negative or mechanical. For example, the Johnny Depp vs. Amanda Heard trial has the whole world engrossed meanwhile during the same time the trial into Ghislaine Maxwell flew under the radar as mainstream and alternative media sites focused on these two rich misfits instead while ignoring the biggest organised female human trafficking sex ring to emerge involving the cream of global society resulting in the blatant murder-come-suicide of billionaire playboy Jeffery Epstein – pimp to the stars. These are the same people telling you to get your shots like good little guinea pigs. The point is, the Depp trial is *clearly* touting that Depp is an abuse victim by the horrible woman here - the abusive feminine – just like in Psycho the movie and many other productions depicting the prominent female, often the mother, as having a personality disorder and transferring their mania onto the son as sociopathy that can lead to outright psychopathic behaviour. The domineering mother routine was also the favourite 'reason' for the horrendous behaviour of Joseph Mengele, apparently a polite and sensitive boy, turned into a monster by a 'domineering mother'. These guys hate the mother and whether she was domineering or not, plenty of fathers, more so, in fact, have abused their daughters sexually and domineered the household, only, women are far less inclined to become psychopaths regardless of their treatment. But men love to blame the mother for the transference of behaviour grossly distorted out of any proportion relating to the mother's conduct. Men need to take responsibility for themselves and stop blaming women for their every ill or as accurately quoted in the film 'Reminiscent', a psychopathic extravaganza, 'You're just an empty man looking for a woman to blame'. These guys know exactly what they are doing, and their hypocrisy will doom our entire planet while they congratulate themselves what big men they are. The same way you do not blame another person (although they will try) when someone takes their life, you cannot blame another person for YOUR attacks on others. Grow up and take some responsibility, although they won't. The 'Law for the Perfection of Hereditary Health' passed in 1933 the same year the Nazis took control of Germany. These laws underpinned much of the selection process for those deemed not worth enough to live or were sterilized including feeblemindedness, schizophrenia, manic depression, epilepsy, hereditary blindness, deafness, physical deformities, Huntington's Disease and alcoholism. The monumental hypocrisy of these people is predominant in today's ever annexing political and corporate fascists as schizophrenia and manic depression are some of the hallmarks of the psychologically unsound or as they would say 'mentally unfit'.

So, the purpose of the Depp trial is not to seek justice but to play out a *masquerade* where women are being presented, at this time, as bullies and abusers while the men are being touted as the unfortunate victim of these calculated females. It is also the same reason why the 'woman' of the year is a male Naval Admiral who literally looks like Norman Bates. This is one hell of a big lark to these guys as the 'navel' port is the belly button connecting the unborn baby to the mother who was depicted as a 'ship' in ancient Egypt and why ships are called 'she' to this day. Simultaneously, via double speak the masculine facsimile of all things feminine and natural in this world is the 'naval port' where war machines, ships, dock. This is because our entire planets and all that is feminine has been stolen by the 'devil', elite males, who have posed in the place of women as a cosmic identity thief. They endlessly laugh about this in movies.

Biological males are being touted as women despite having obvious physical advantages over women at this time in history ruining women's competition. Toilets are now 'unisex' and males who 'identify' as females are strolling naked into women changerooms with naked little girls present and this is being 'accepted' as totally normal. But you can't 'identify' as trans-race as that's just racist especially, if you're white trying to be black however, some black Puerto Rican's identified as 'white' on an American Census, and no one batted an eyelid. Point is, there is obviously flaws in the whole 'identity' thing currently. Anyone can 'identify' and anything they like, even a tree (and they do!), while some mainstreamers claim it's racist for certain people to identify as certain other people yet 'affirming' who you'd like to be is 'okay'....okay..

The Eurovision song contest was won by a transgender male-to-female with the song 'Rise Like a Phoenix' because the female Kundalini energy, the 'coiled snake' at the base of the spine, is also called the 'phoenix rising' as it rises up the spine and *generates* enlightenment. It is the female energy that will bring enlightenment and ascension to humans of planet Earth which is why there is an all-out Satanic effort to diminish, slander, delete, laugh at, abuse, beat up and smother the rising feminine at this time symbolically, phonetically, sexually, politically, religiously (look at the Middle East!) socially, financially – in *every way* conceivable – to prevent the human race from harnessing the powers of the creator, Mother. The Kundalini was also called the 'feathered serpent' in Mesoamerica as well as Quetzalcoatl by the Aztecs and Kukulkan by the Mayas.it is the 'phoenix' rising from its own ashes up the tantric spine. The snake literally meant electricity in ancient Egypt and is a feminine force so dressing it up as a cross dressing male is right up the ally of these psychos. This is also why 'nonbinary' is a favourite term of the emerging neutral people as our bodies run on electricity and electricity is made up of 'dual's or binary electrical pairs that replicate the original: "A dual of a relationship is formed by interchanging voltage and current in an expression" - Wikipedia. The dual expression thus produced is of the same form, and the reason that the dual is always a valid statement can be traced to the duality of electricity and magnetism. There are far too many examples of the feminine being overshadowed by the masculine posing as a women at this time to be ignored including removing terms like "mother' and "mummy' in favour of 'birthing person' to apparently satisfy a tiny demographic of people who feel offended about being 'misgendered' at this time despite only representing less than 5% in the US (so we are told) and an even tinier percentage worldwide with the majority identifying as 'bisexual'. This is because the 'devil' is transgender and in lead up to 2033, the date that Jesus Christ was said to have died exactly 2000 years ago, and as the polar opposites shift in the opposite direction, as it was male, Jesus, 'God', the last time it is the female 'Goddess' who is prophesised to return THIS time. So, they are deleting her as a return of normal levels of feminine energy into this world, at this time in particular, would put a stop to war overnight. They are a war pig demonically possessed psychopathic homosexual phallic alien sex and death cult, so the feminine returning especially in the Kundalini of enlightenment is something they *absolutely dread* so, the goddess is now a man – a gay man.

RETURN OF THE TWINS

This has become such a normalized thing that the scene from the original Psycho by Alfred Hitchcock depicting the killer in the shower scene wearing his mother's clothes was removed from the remake as it was 'transphobic'. Regardless, the psychopathic profile does include some interesting links to the mother. So, when the obviously Satanic gratuitous 'artist' Madonna who has openly dressed like the transgender devil Baphomet character, is depicting herself as a (much younger) birthing woman under the title Mother of Nature as monarch butterflies (Monarch Mind Control alien secret base programming a-list manipulation idols) come flying out of her twat along with a crawling horde of 'bugs', this is a reference to the 'bug' like 'insect' colony mentality behind all this. It possibly refers genetically to 'bugs', mantis people, who are ultimately behind the simulation of our reality to keep organic humans, particularly birthing women, Mothers, under the control in a psychopathic demonic alien time warp. They then get the mass minds of all who tap into this shit to broadcast the message that the feminine is a one dimensional carton freak show creep who births the A.I. alien agenda from her bloodied vagina in a simulation of 'mother nature' while in *reality*, behind the illusion of mind control, she is actually sitting on top of a dirty machine that has the horns of the bull, Torus, in a reference to the constellation Torus who is another symbolic version of the Devil as Osiris was represented as the 'bull', but it is really a reference to the torus fields of naturally functioning humans with enlightened kundalini and activated chakras. They are repeatedly sending the message that the human being is a 'machine' that humans are 'technology' that we are not real, that the mother is a robotic whore who is actually a man who is actually the Goddess...and this is what they are broadcasting from Earth at the time of ascension during incredible alignments as the feminine energy is more powerful than the masculine energy and they are terrified mummy is coming home to whip their asses and clean up this house! It puts a whole new light on *Bugs* Bunny as B is the 2nd letter of the alphabet and therefore becomes 22 as 22 is the 11:11 of the light and dark side of males and females in balance. Bunny is the Lepus constellation as all these alien demonic elements are not from Earth so they are constantly making references to the places that they might have come from 'out there'.

The 'reptilian complex' inside our brains in literally a 'bug', a listening device, installed into our system by them when they downgraded us from the high enlightened dolphin like beings, we were eons ago. It is from this 'bug' installed in our CPU that they monitor the hive mind of Earthlings and generate the 'static' of the monkey mind (and why 'monkey pox' is the latest symbolic assassination as they are saying that humans are monkeys, and we have the pox at this time). There's something out there that must be monitoring us in order to warrant all these false transmissions about who we are. Something they are afraid of. It is from the R complex that they monitor, condition, and stall you from attaining full brain hemispherically balanced control of your head. It is from the R-complex animal brain that they can introduce all sorts of 'personalities' and 'traits' that can literally be downloaded into you brain like a computer. The R complex literally wraps around our pineal gland smothering our signal creating a literal dampening field to prevent us from having the greatest access to this key area of the brain, the area that will set up free. Carlos Castaneda said in his book Active Side of Infinity that they 'gave us their mind', literally, it is the R complex – *their* installation blanketing ours!

The word Druid means 'knowing the way of the oak'. It is why the nature deity, the green man, is depicted as an Oak tree among other trees, the Oracles of Apollo wrote their channeled messages on Oak leaves, the Oak King is a tree deity and so many others. This is because as in ancient times as with today, the Oak like all trees represents the 'tree of life' the nervous system. It is also the only tree in the world that is struck by lightning more than any other tree and therefore a combination of being symbolic tree of the spine and nerves connecting to and activating the chakras leading to the much-coveted Crown chakra enlightenment, the mega mind of intellect and memory. It is fitting that the electrical charge of the Christ seed emanating from the crown, a superfine elixir of chi life energy, Aether, harnessed from the Universal broadcast like a liquid antenna, *golden flow*, designed to make us superhuman, god and goddess, as coveted by these alien reptilian demons. The Jewish Sephora, *right*, is basically an expanded depiction of the chakra tower, 'emanation', and is essentially where the *lightning bolt* of 'god' imagery comes from. The

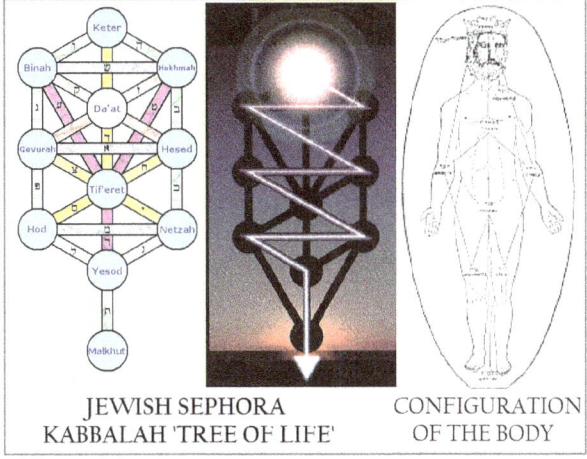

JEWISH SEPHORA KABBALAH 'TREE OF LIFE' CONFIGURATION OF THE BODY

electrical Oak tree is a perfect symbol for the enlightenment these arseholes employ to take over the world keeping the knowledge secret from us and using it to perpetrate unending crimes against the human race for thousands of years. It's the BIG secret.

RETURN OF THE TWINS

The bible talks about how the 'gates of hell' will be opened (DOUBLE CHECK THAT JESUS SAYS THIS?) and people think that this would be a massive event that everyone in the world will be afraid of and that it is still to come. The gates of hell will unleash plagues of locusts which is a code for demons as the demonic thing seems to be tied to some type of alien 'bug' phenomena. It's a TV production from the 1950's called Quadermass and the Pit as an alien craft is found underground while building a train line. It is located on Old Hobbs Lane. Old Hob, like 'Old Nick' aka St Nicholas or Santa Claus, is another name for the 'devil'. The 'devil' is the collective name applied to the demonic hordes, their reptilian co-workers, the alien 'grey' insect creatures and their half-blood human-reptilian overseers on planet Earth who run operations for them. They are Legion. The 'gates of hell' and the 'seven seals of the apocalypse' are represented in the Bible as happening among much calamity and mass fear and chaos. Although the outcome is having the same effect of fear, confusion, grief etc., the 'gates of hell' have already been opened in fact, I think it happened sometime around 2010 and has been steadily increasing in volume in a 'soft' introduction to the demonic madness accelerating as we speak. The seven seals or 'vials' of the apocalypse are more air born diseases since we've had our introduction to this via Covid. They do what's called 'link, deny, do'. They create events or concepts and 'link' it to our consciousness. Then they 'deny' it is happening or isn't as bad as what is initially thought. As soon as we drop our guard, they 'do' it again and again until people are numb to it. It's a part of the 'rules' to link or attach the negative energy to the people either individually or collectively and if you don't take measures to stop it from happening, they have carte blanche to carry it out in its entirety.

The gates of 'hell' have already been opened showing up in the increasing weird pandemics and now the 'vaccines' that will cause more weird illnesses some of them alien genetic experiments to morph humans into them and create the first 'mutants' or Hollywood 'X men' although they won't be as glamourous, and they will not be heroes. Further to this is the weird 'sky sounds' phenomenon as people are recording all sorts of weird sounds coming from the sky touted as 'sky quakes'. Again, why is this all new? Like there are hardly any people over forty who are 'special need's yet exorbitant numbers in their thirties and below – so what happened in the 90's? Chicken pox, measles etc., has been replaced with cancers and weird 'spectrum' diseases not seen previously and no, we're not getting better at diagnosing, they are just making up new names for NEW diseases that didn't previously exist in another attempt to stop us from ascending. All this could be in lead up to a massive, staged event where biblical voices and diabolical laughter will emanate from the sky.

RETURN OF THE TWINS

They don't really need to achieve the outcome of converting people via these methods, they just have to 'tick the box' that these events happened even in a soft way and then convert the people en masse to the new religion-new world in some *other* more overt forced military way while wiping out mass numbers of people and deleting history in the process like they've always done historically. They do this because in the future they will say the 'prophecies' came true even though they deleted the truth of what the real cause of the change in the world really was. They write and re-write history, so they can say whatever they like. It's all part of a *ritual* to simply carry out the 'prophecies' whether they are real, staged or even partially achieved. The final results, regardless on how they transpired, will be blamed on these biblical events even though people were forced to change literally at gun point or some other forced method. It makes no difference as long as it happens. They simply selectively edit the story to fit the script even if it's all bullshit. It happened so therefore, IT HAPPENED, one way or another.

The nature of the Hollywood war machine is becoming more apparent by the day. They have spent 100 years convincing people that demons, ghosts, ghouls, creepy paranormal figures and weird happenings are all 'fiction'. People have completely dropped their guard in believing the world is basically material in nature and that few 'odd' non-physical things can happen and that CERTAINLY you cannot have a person or creature traverse the bounds of reality. This is untrue in the extreme and the Operational HQ of the Norman Bates Club, the Nazi City at the South Pole, has spend nearly a hundred years creating and refining the processes of manifestation and dematerialization until they have literally become Sith Lords of Star Wars capabilities. Now that more people, even in poor countries, have access to mobile devices all fitted with increasingly advanced cameras and software for analysing, people are filming weird, cloaked beings with pale faces lurking near people who have just died or are in danger of dying. People are reporting and recording witches, ghosts and weird cryptids with mystical abilities. It's true, some of this footage is faked and sometimes cleverly so, but increasingly more people are having weird experiences, filming it and sharing it until we realised that, worldwide, we are faced with the same foe – something that is not human, and the stuff of nightmares deliberately fed to us as fiction so that people can't believe what they are experiencing.

What they have attempted to do with the UFO phenomena and interactions like the mysterious 'smiling man' Indrid Cold, is to build sixty years of precedence playing mind games by releasing these creatures or people onto society, denying they exist even removing eye witnesses etc.,

RETURN OF THE TWINS

to add credibility to the growing suspicion that they are 'hiding something'. They know they practical mind underneath the idiot in the street, that there is ultimately a survival instinct that distrust authority and for good reason. They have built this legend for over half a century all in lead up to a very convincing and much demanded 'disclosure'. The fact of the matter is, alien's do not come from other planets, maybe they once did, but they have been here for thousands of years beneath the ground indeed were the 'legion' cast into the abyss by Jesus among other ancient stories. These creatures and beings are being genetically mutated, conjured and created in military laboratories largely based out of the South Pole Nazi Headquarters still in full operation today. They never lost the war, that is patently absurd. They belong to worldwide network of secret male societies bowing down to interdimensional demonic creatures in collusion with things that are certainly not from this world. Indeed at the top they have interbred the genetics of these creatures, merges demons and human DNA, and now have created a hybrid species not simply reptilian from ancient breeding programs, but have utilised science to insert and merge the demonic with flesh in both human and animal form.

They are so strikingly different from humans that it is from these experiments that they were finally able to create the mutant strains of DNA mass injected into people under the blanket of a COVID pandemic now resulting in various outcomes including what appears to be a 'rage' virus pre-emptively inserted as 'fiction' into our collective psyche by movies like 28 Days and 28 Days Later etc., or 'zombie' films. The idea of a zombie apocalypse was frankly farcical up until this mass injection program now causing the WEIRDEST behaviour to start emerging in everyday people like completely irrational meltdowns and outbursts. Coupled with the build up of pharmaceuticals and injections from the past, and I'm afraid the majority of those who offered themselves to this experiment are in a lot of danger and so are the rest of humanity from these people.

Chapter Ten
Alien Psychology

What human's see as psychopathic behaviour is totally normal, even comedic, for elite predators. There are ways to deal with them and it does not include 'tolerance'.

What are aliens, really? What are demons, really? We have apparently been living alongside them for thousands of years and yet most of humanity *still* can't believe it. In a courtroom (before one was allowed to make an 'affirmation' in more recent times) one was required to swear on the Bible with their right hand no less (the right hand of god, the feminine side). The Bible is a book filled from cover to cover with demons, angels, ghosts, miracles, animal-man hybrids, phenomena, sacrifice, good, evil, the underworld, ancient gods, giants…you name it… And yet when a court case arises where people claim their crimes were the result of a possession by a demon or the devil (same thing) which is a *staggering* amount of the time, it is summarily thrown out as complete nonsense when all testimony is sworn as 'truth' on a booked filled with such things. It's either thrown out without debate or the 'experts' on 'mental health' are bought in and any claims of demons or devil worship etc., or as in Ted Bundy's case who openly claimed that an evil entity attached itself to him and that he was innocent as a person as it was the demon that did it, are written off as paranoid schizophrenics, psychopaths or some other psychosis. Just incredible. The most mortifying serial killers are put to death for 'justice' and the truth of them and what they are *really* involved in is lost. It's deliberate. These people are quickly dispatched to prevent real justice from being served and this only serves to satisfy the minds of unintelligent people who believe the system is 'real' and 'justice' has been served by killing someone who killed people because killing is 'against the law'. What a croc of shit.

Jerry Marzinsky a psychologist with 35 years working with psychotic and criminally insane people concluded at the end of it all that his patients were *consistently* reporting the same narrative from these entities and must indicate that it is not 'mental illness' but an external force with an agenda. If it was just mental illness, then those suffering would just be talking shit based on their own *personal* experiences. But that is not what is happening. As a result of looking at this more objectively, he has achieved more success by dealing with it as a 'spiritual' or multidimensional energy attack than an 'illness' treated with harmful poisons called 'medication'. I had counselling sessions with Jerry due to an entity attachment put on me by a celebrity cult and it was *a relief in and of itself* to speak to a professional about the *reality* of the situation and not waste time and energy trying parry a counsellor's *preconceived* 'accepted' beliefs of what *they* want to believe is happening. Honestly, most mental health practitioners are nutjobs. Listen to the patients, doctors, they are the ones with the *firsthand* experience. Deal with what the patient is *telling you* not what the monthly white paper from the pharmaceutical company says. Jaysus!

These psycho killers can often be traced back to alphabet agencies utilising mind control, demon-alien cults and a weird almost incomprehensible and chaotic state of thinking. I remember the first time I heard the term 'military satanism' almost two decades ago and I thought 'What rubbish! The military are interested in guns and bombs not demons and ghosts!' Yet how perfect is it if the secret alien system wanting to continue to unleash demons via possession on the unsuspecting public and keep getting away with it hide behind 'rational' and 'legitimate' organisations and 'the law' pointing the finger of 'mental illness' at anyone who figures out what they're doing. And they've got all the 'experts' on their team as well as all the judges and hospital staff hopping onboard the 'normal' train denying what has been shouted from the rooftops for thousands of years, that demons are *real* and it's *commonplace* that these agencies and major institutions of this world are using these wretched things to further their *personal* causes! What is worse is that these entities can get to us, but we can't get to them. Its undeniable now as mounting evidence emerges, and highly rational and normal people come forward and their stories bear strikingly similar themes that can be catalogued and studied. There are weird rules to the game and these rules can be figured out we just have to pay attention and acknowledge what is *really* happening and not sink into self-denial because the truth is too horrifying to deal with. We will lose this battle if we allow fear and cowardice to rob us of our future. We will be damned to hell if we let these creatures win. It's called the *final* battle for good reason. There is no recourse after this. It's the end.

Demonic and negative energy attacks are in epidemic proportions at this time in history and former head of the L.A. FBI, Ted Gunderson, was himself ultimately assassinated for using his professional experience to expose this filth now operating in plain sight. But apparently demons and devils don't exist. But if demons and devils don't exist then every culture - EVERY CULTURE - on Earth is defunct as demons and devils are one of the few *consistent* themes in every civilisation that has ever existed on this Earth. So why the reticence to officially accept that such things can exist? It's because if the legal courtrooms around the world accepted that demons existed and that many people were not *really* responsible for their behaviour as they were 'possessed' then the flood gates would open, and Earth would have review EVERYTHING we do and think about our reality. That's a big job and too much for most people to comprehend but comprehend it they will whether they like it or not.

It is the study of the 'non-physical' that the secret science laboratories all around the world, underpinned by Nazis even still, that has the jump on the human race at this time. Their ability to be able to tinker with and transcend 'reality' as far as our five sense '3D' concept of what is 'real' allows is literally beyond belief! So, again, I ask you, what is an alien? What is a demon? Let's start with 'aliens'. As far as I can understand it, the demonic alien *fact* came from a place beyond normal 'space' and 'time' in an ancient 'primeval' era, a time before ancient history, before myth and even before legend and goes back into a murky darkness that is rarely if ever accounted for in historical record. This darkness seems to be an anomaly by the *normal* standards of our Milky Way galaxy and OUR universe. I say 'our' universe because there is more than one it would seem in an endlessly spiraling cosmic consciousness of unending proportions. Aliens are a parasite feeding off the 3D that humans and planet Earth live in and there is a reason why there is a consistent theme in films that aliens are emerge from 'pods'. The movie industry is just the psychological warfare division of the alien program in a continuation of *all art forms* throughout history from DaVinci to Kubrick. They once carved rock now they have The Rock on a digital screen. It's just more art and it's via art that directors are telling the true story of humanity as only 'their' people are allowed into these roles in the first place. It's part of a trick to hijack our 'free will' as they MUST tell what is happening, and if you don't believe it too bad for you, they are off the hook as they DID tell you. From the movie Alien a pod deposits a parasite inside a human chest specifically where the heart is (very symbolic). In The Body Snatchers 'pod' people are propagated when people are 'asleep symbolic of how humanity are being replaced while we are 'unawake' as in, *unenlightened* at this time. Another consistent theme is that the alien thing we are dealing with is some sort of 'bug' or 'pod people' who came from *Mars*, a mantis or 'grasshopper' type species of cold calculating evil. It's interesting that when someone is annoying, they 'bug' us and when we are being listened to secretly, we are 'bugged'.

RETURN OF THE TWINS

Just because a species isn't human doesn't mean it is incapable of intellect, in fact, as we expand our horizon to explore more planets and galaxies beyond ours, we will discover all manner of different species who are self-aware enough to build technology. The spirits of these insectoid species are 'demons' as all beings need an animating force. Their animating force comes from 'dark' matter or 'anti' matter, a type of living death and as such everywhere they turn up, death and destruction shortly follow. It seems the 'mantis' or bug species are the ones beyond the reptilian species or there is some sort of syndicate, a space league of evil likeminded species who have teamed up with the reptilian species and the 'grey' species who some claim are 'clones' but have a long running precedent in ancient art history. All this information in buried in art history as the only painters whose work has survived or was revered at the time were painters who were inducted into the boy's club secret society orchestrating all this and who have kept our real history from us while wiping our memory on behalf of this evil space syndicate. They require 'their people' to be 'inserted' into the target reality, in this case Earth, to commence harvesting the resources of the planet and ultimately replacing the original custodian race, in this case humans, with a fake stand in, a changeling. They look like us, but they are not us and this information is becoming more *horrifyingly apparent* by the day as the vaccine holocaust causes alien mutations in people not previously seen. This is what they have been working on in those creepy underground bases for decades and its one of the final phases in the alien program!

These entities are so unlike humans that we find it very difficult to break down their modus operandi, the complex nature of their symbols, inverse secret psychological games, the trickery found in their phonetics, double entendre's, pomp and ritual to replace the real thing with an effigy of something dazzling but FAKE. Their mind games, their manipulation, the fact that they are orchestrating all this and are ten steps ahead of us at any given time. Their audacity and ultimate hypocrisy, unending lies, inability to cooperate with any species that is not from the darkness. Their hatred of the light. Their desire to kill the light found in life which ultimately spells their doom and their desire to change themselves into a 'half light being', replacing the full light beings, humans, with a facsimile creature who is part alien, part animal and part human in order to access our chakra system, the 'light spectrum', so that they can 'feel' emotions but only emotions associated with the seven deadly sins the first being 'pride' which is what the devil what kicked out of heaven for. All of these stories are allegorical and symbolic, effigies of something else, but the information is all there if you know what you are looking for. They love greed, lust, envy, gluttony, wrath and sloth insofar as they direct others to do the hard work for them.

They are awestruck by the sensation of feelings, physical and emotional feelings, and why when they splice their genetics with a sentient race, they think nothing of copious amounts of sex with unending partners and will routinely have sex even with people they hate for no real reason at all other than to have sex in and of itself. It's really disgusting to normal human thinking as one would no doubt feel debased at the very idea of having sex with someone you intrinsically despise and revile for whatever reasons they have caused such negativity (usually betrayal or crime). But these creatures think nothing of intimately engaging with someone they don't even trust, and LOVE is a frankly a joke to them. They are incapable of love. In fact, it is written into their secret religion-cult that 'love' is a weakness to be rejected. That's because love is the most dangerous weapon to these creatures because love is light and too much light will expose them for what they are. Love is so powerful that people risk their lives for love every day. Nothing else matters. We can hate someone but rarely are *normal* people willing to die for hate when a crime has been perpetrated against them. Yet love is not something that they simply reject, it is something to be *laughed at* while tricking their loved ones into the most terrible situations and horrifying mockery behind their backs. They do this to reinforce the 'connection' to the boy's club in that they are prepared to do ANYTHING to ensure that they are not questioned by the 'team' of males who all are using each other, by the way, to get more power in this *enormous evil agenda.* I can't see how they can possibly emerge victorious. This is why it's referred to as a 'house of cards' because, as I mentioned in my first book, *2020 & Beyond*, once the house of cards starts falling, you watch the rats start leaving the sinking ship! They are all out for themselves – ALL OF THEM. It's ironically in the very act of the denial of love that, if their own families can't trust them, who can? Suddenly actor Kevin Spacey, once the flavour of the day, is being quick and lively cut off from all his old mates and he will find out pretty darn quick that the boys who slapped each other on the back yesterday are stabbing each other in the back today. It's the male centric evil cult of perversions and it's headed up by tantric sex enlightenment which is why all these perves have 'sex addictions' and think nothing of predating upon innocent women and children, even their own wives and family are targets. Increasingly, males come forward with horror stories once the realm of female victims as there are no boundaries to these people. Anything to get more! It is gluttony.

One of the problems with tantric sex is, if it isn't 'grounded' or 'earthed' via the feminine waters, then the power it gives to a person leaves them in the state of a 'god' complex where they believe they are invincible and become so over confident that they wind up falling easily into traps, some caused by their own ego and some deliberately set up for them by 'opposition' as inside the boys club....is more clubs! How do they even keep a straight face with each other knowing that even their own are smiling assassins as Jesus found out the hard way (and so many others). When the big plan is in danger, they will throw ANYONE to the baying wolves, the crowd of angry humans, demanding justice for the crimes these cunts perpetrate against the world on a daily basis. But I digress. The alien insect-mantis-reptilian-grey beings also cross over into the 'bigfoot' phenomena as the connections to the paranormal and cryptids become more apparent. The bigfoot thing is part of an ancient genetics program revived for the 'signs and symbols' extravaganza of the biblical 'end times' script. While there were some natural ones left over in the wild from the last time they did this thousands of years ago, most of these new evil cryptids and bigfoot's are from laboratories. A lot of A list celebrities are putting all this in their movies for two reasons, 1) to alleviate a contrived (or at least a very small) sense of guilt, and, 2) in the event that humans start to win this space invaders game, they can say 'I tried to tell you. Look! It's all in my movies, but I couldn't say anything directly or I would have suffered the consequences'. It's what I call the 'Professor Snape' tactic who seems like a bad guy who, in the end, turns out to have helped Harry in the Potter series. Why? Who knows. Maybe some flagging sense of dignity or hope that there could be some humanity or light left in their souls or that the possibility of a 'happily ever after' might actually happen or otherwise 'remain a beast forever' as the fairy tales says.

The light is a powerful thing and there is something about the light that is very frightening to those who go against it. If celebrities, who are basically all double agents at the top, ever come forward and share their information, there goes the evil space empire in one fell swoop. But in doing so they also risk the public finding out about their foibles and misdoings in their quest for money, celebrity and power. That said, the public need to ask themselves what it is worth to them to despise someone because they aren't what you'd thought they were in the process of saving our planet from a bug species who destroyed the planet Mars and is in the process of destroying our planet too. Personally, I couldn't give a fuck what they've done (to a point) as there are some things beyond forgiveness like pedophilia and murder. That said a lot of celebrities haven't had to do these things and the worst of it is infidelity and hard drug use as it's required of them for two reasons, they must prove they are consummate liars as part of an institutionalised fraud that has turned deceit into an empire, and 2) so that the machine has some 'dirt' on them to ensure they don't blow the whistle. Their lies and fraud are a type of insurance policy ensuring their silence. In the end, we must find a way to give them a pathway to walk toward freedom in the looming new human Earth not controlled by aliens.

I'm not making any suggestions AT ALL here, what I am saying is that it *looks like* there are coded messages in films insofar as, celebrities are either hedging their bets or in some way trying to let the public know that they are engaged in something so hideous, even to them, that it's possible it took modern technology, the digital age, the internet and all the information that the garden variety conspiracy researcher in the gutter is sharing with the world for *them* to realise THERE IS NO CLUB and THERE IS A WAY OUT. In the film The Waterboy, Adam Sandler plays a simpleton, (Bobby Boucher - BB 22), who winds up being really good at his job to the point that he is elevated to an A-league position. These guys are really smart, hey. There are always multiple symbolic meanings in these art pieces, and, at this time, movies *are art history* and art history is symbolically telling *the real story* of the human race. As such, to 'carry someone's water' means to 'occupy a subservient position, to do the bidding, the menial tasks, and frequently the dirty work, of a more powerful person, and it is most often used in a political context' from English Language and Usage To "carry water [for somebody]". Look at the oversized bucket. This guy is carrying a lot of shit for someone else. *I'm* telling *you* these guys are TELLING you what's happening even if they can't say it directly, they sure have said it loud enough in other ways, *below right*, Sandler in 'That's My Boy' as the father

becomes the son, or more aptly the son becomes the corrupt old dad from a bygone era. Who wants that? How many times you gonna ride this merry-go-round? How depressing to know it's never gonna end just endless hierarchy and take your place and eat cotton candy and shit sandwiches *forever*. No thanks. In this film he stands in front of a poster 'Need a strong lawyer? I got you covered'. This guy has studied the 'ways' as well as Latin and ancient Greek and cross stitch. What don't they know? As I said in 2020 & Beyond, 'Humans are not smart enough to get out of this on their own. You're gonna need help'. It's almost as if these guys have been putting it out there waiting for someone to put the puzzle pieces together and say, 'Hey, I see you. I get it'. Yeh, guess who.

In the film the Happytime Murders starring Melissa McCarthy (as her initials are MM in a symbolic reference to Mary Magdalene and Mother Mary etc), the blurb says it all 'Sex. Murder. Puppets'., as *puppets* from a TV show are being murdered one by one. Celebrities have a particularly high, if not the highest, kill ratio because celebrity is the weakest link of the alien space program as *movies* are a particularly important part of the psych-warfare program against humanity. There are big flaws in their plan as for every action there is a reaction like celebrities watching their children grow up under the same evil ancient empire their families have worked for for eons. The choice is their's if they want to take this small but honest opportunity. This movie is basically depicting, particularly Jewish celebrities, as 'puppets' of something else (like the Waterboy by Jewish Adam Sandler). In the seemingly absurd film Sausage Party (a reference to an orgy) the blurb says it all 'A hero will rise', yes, because this is The One that is prophesised to return only there is a *real* one and a *fake* one. The fake one will take them down a path to destruction regardless of whether they 'win' or not. At the end of this film after the main character goes on an odyssey of self-discovery only to realise there is no 'heaven' or 'god' just aliens who are killing people and consuming their life force. It's extremely clever stuff once you realise what they're talking about. This is the power of intellectual tantric sex, it makes one a relative genius! So, at the end of this film the main character says that there are interdimensional aliens using portals to access our realm and that he has invented a type of bomb that can be sent to the other side to blow up the connection to this dark realm and prevent them from getting in. What the fuck...? This is *exactly* what's happening.

Now, you *can* say that these guys are just making movies about modern themes and are basically across all the *deepest* levels of conspiracy research or you could say that these guys know what's going on because *they are born into that realm and their careers are already set* but that doesn't mean they like the direction all this is going. It may very well mean that they not only know what's behind this – bug aliens and demons and interdimensional reptilians that possibly live for thousands of years attached to certain bloodlines living through the progeny of those bloodlines using up body after body until it dies only to re-emerge in the next generation to continue to carry out *the great work* – but potentially, they have an even more secret plan to fight back against the darkness. It's totally possible that these celebrities are sitting on the fence hedging their bets until an opportunity arises to take this game down a different route from the one that the old war coots of the past have in mind. Those dinosaurs are obsolete and have no place in our future AT ALL which means its basically ancient myth replaying all over again and they do love their precedence, they do love ancient myth and legend. Basically, biblical lore is *the script* they are operating off and if you can find precedence then it can be entered into 'play'. The precedence is the Olympians Vs. The Titans in which the 'children' of the Titans overthrew their 'parents' and created a new line of gods. As said, ultimately, it's anything goes with these people and if they can create something new and break away from these stick insects from the primeval past, then why not? Evolution is a strange thing.

The best way to insert these convert messages is via humour and even absurdity. Wit is the greatest intellect and why it requires really smart people who've had their chakras and IQ activated to take this game to the next level. Given these films often portray the 'apple' of the torus field, a dead giveaway of tantric sex practice, coupled with the fact that celebrity is a game that requires real savvy to survive, then maybe this generation of celebrities are playing a different game than expected? You can always rely on their greed if nothing else and now is a time of great vision for those who are willing to take this into places these military 'royal' coots from the old world can't even dream of (or can't do for other reasons). Humour is a higher function of the human brain, however, since people's intellectual reaches are being numbed and dumbed, any higher functions are now being deemed illegal under 'progressive' doctrines (if you can believe it). If anything, this only serves to underline the stupidity of 'progressive' so-called 'inclusive' new-age thinking. As such, comedy employs layers of intellectual devices including the double entendre, puns and common parlance to exaggerate, in layman's terms, complex issues. This particular way of wording is designed to have a *double meaning*, of which *one* is typically obvious. Sarcasm and wit are a humorous way to mock something or someone through ambivalence, irony, or disproportion to accentuate the content being related as absurd, ridiculous, just plain stupid or even *dangerous*. A joke is rarely about the obvious and usually about the types of people who *seriously* engage in 'racism' 'homophobia' or 'male chauvinism' lauding the subjects of the joke as idiots by way of using 'off colour' vernacular and puns to *mimic* the protagonist in the story *mocking* the stupidity of such people who actually engage in this behaviour *for real* thus revealing the *true meaning* of the joke. Among other things this biting commentary often includes social, political and religious themes and for humans as an evolving species, this is a way to expose politics, social 'science' and religion as sadly lacking in any sense of humour and joviality essential to human well-being revealing these institutions for their controlling anti-human agendas. See, the above films as examples of this. It is the rigid non-human behaviour that lies beneath politics that is making comedy illegal as 'hate speech' to drastically reduce the mental functions and intricacies of society. Our crusade for the continuation of universal development as a broader community bonded by many generations of hardship and difficulties is so common to us that our malaise has become cliché. Therein lies the joke.

Humour is a way to muddle through the tough times alleviating our spirits, if momentarily, from the responsibilities we face as a collective. It is a way to create a space of understanding until something or someone either makes sense or goes away. If one has half a functioning brain, then sarcasm and laymen's intellectual wit – humour - is unconsciously accessed *instinctually* to diffuse socially awkward or offensive situations with banter or awkward mutual comradery while not stating directly the shared discomfort. Humour exploits ambiguity and word play around an obvious often unspoken *central subject*. What is *not* said is *usually* the joke. The greatest humour in history has employed these higher functions of human communication as a survival technique and correctly applied, has turned many an ugly situation into a laugh riot utilising timing and humorous logic to emphasise our sameness or differences with *no real intention* to cause harm. It is the *intentions* of people that are not being adequately confirmed before accusations start flying. Often those shouting the loudest and proudest have dubious intentions while those using humour to indirectly highlight these dubious intentions are now labelled as 'hate speech'. What we are now dealing with is not hurt feelings or 'discrimination' but *psychological warfare* using in the grossest possible way the unintelligent against the intelligent, the 'marginalised' against the majority by means of shaming and inflammatory inaccurate derogatory labels while claiming themselves to be victims. It turns out that comedic discourse is not invalid in the wider communities attempts to rationally comprehend contrary confusing behaviour's we see in a swift movement of apparent agitators who see their personal choices as 'special' thus employing abuse while claiming to be abused, threats and violence while claiming to be threatened and violated. What we are seeing is the narcissistic minds of intolerance directed against the tolerant. The unstable are being used against the stable and, as a result, society is *predictably* breaking down on a deeper level as nouveau liberal ideals are ruthlessly wielded against an evolving global village costing people their reputations, careers and even their lives on the whim of one indefinable group. Instead of attacking each other and weakening ourselves, we should try to understand the mechanism *behind all this chaos*, a mechanism that knows human psychology and consciousness better than we do, a force that has studied us like bacteria in a petri dish, a darkness that knows us better than we know ourselves. It knows us so well and yet we know it not at all.

   This dark force has studied us for eons using a most malicious craftiness in its attempts to seize our dignity, our souls and our light manipulating our greenness as a species to coral us all into a pit of despair. The demon returns for the final battle. Humans would be a lot happier if we were allowed to access the quirky and irreverent aspects of our personalities via shared, universal, experiences and foibles that, let's face it, dog us all. The superiority of liberal left concepts that bash down anyone who questions or disagrees with them while touting 'discrimination' *is the joke.* No one *has* to like you or *must* agree with you. Discrimination is the bane of *all* people. Welcome to the world. It's hilarious when trans men-to-women get physical and intimidating when they are 'discriminated' against. If biological women could do that, we wouldn't have been raped and pillaged for eons! Hilarious. I haven't seen a bicep like that since the Patterson-Gimlin film. Have they taken a pay cut yet because that kind of goes with the territory if you want to be a woman. Even more hilarious is that when trans men-to-women highlight the abuse against their human rights, it only goes to expose *even further* the accepted and largely ignored abuse against *women's* human rights since time immemorial. Women have by and large given up on expecting more dignified behaviour out of men who have constantly bragged about being 'gentlemen' while refusing women entry to every level of society from science to religion to politics and look where it got us. These wo-man's are gonna have to develop a thicker skin if they want to be a woman. The ironic thing about all this progressive liberal inclusiveness, since its inception, everyone has been at each other's throats. Maybe just go back to harmless fun that indirectly highlights the eccentricity of the shared human state since time immemorial. If you don't have a laugh about it, you'll go mad, which is happening.

Honestly, modern medicine will be the death of us.

Chapter Eleven
But why...?

'Earth is in a state of attitude of a patient too sick to resent the undertaker measuring him'.
The Alien Digest Vol. 1

Whatever rubbish you've been had preconceived into your minds via movies and television about the nature of aliens is total crap. We know very little about them or how they operate as a collective. What I can tell you is that they come from an empire that is slowly taking over the Milky Way galaxy and most likely other galaxies as well and threaten the *entire universe* as one of my messages said from a decade ago. The simple fact of the matter is that the various groupings of stars and planets in the galaxy and beyond, called constellations, are part of a much bigger ecosystem making up either a massive body of a creature we exist *inside* or, is some type of massive brain of an enormous consciousness of which we are but one part interlocked with the collective components that replicate and oscillate between each other unendingly.

The stars and planets in their various constellation groupings give off energies that emit certain types of frequency's and when all these frequencies are combined, it creates 'reality' which is an overlapping image of various light spectrum (chakra) signals creating a 'holograph' insofar as there would be no image or a far lesser image that we experience of 'reality' if too many signals were absent. You can think of it like a ripple effect that pancakes on top of each other until a picture is divisible from all the layers of frequencies stacked on top of each other when the density of the frequencies create reality. The Seven Natural Laws of the Universe 'through which everyone and everything is governed are: attraction, polarity, rhythm, relativity, cause and effect, gender/gustation, and perpetual transmutation of energy or 'evolution'. The 3rd of the seven laws of the universe regards rhythm or vibration and tells us 'nothing rests; everything is vibrates...the whole universe is but a vibration'. Modern science has confirmed that everything in the universe, including humans, are pure energy vibrating at different frequencies and that everything we experience with our five senses is conveyed through vibration including the 'mental realm'. Your thoughts are vibrations as well as your emotions where 'unconditional love' 'in the sense of love for another' is the 'highest most subtle of the emotional vibrations' and that 'hate' is the most dense and most base and that you can learn to control your emotional vibrations at will. These vibrations are made up of the colour light spectrum or the 'rainbow' found in our chakras and are so beautiful that we have been coveted by creepy species from the depth of space, even another universe, that seek out light for their own! Or as trailblazing comedian Bill Hicks said, "All matter is merely energy condensed to a slow vibration, that we are all one consciousness experiencing itself subjectively, there is no such thing as death, life is only a dream, and we are the imagination of ourselves'. I'm sure Bill Hicks never intended to be a founding father of the new Age, but he is.

Imagine it as if you were looking down through all the layers you could make out a beautiful and complex picture made up of all the different semi-transparent slides stacked on top of each other light a puzzle. The whole is greater than the many who reside inside it including the alien element. The seven fundamental laws are part of 12 fundamentals laws 'thought to be intrinsic, unchanging laws of our universe that ancient cultures have always intuitively known. These laws are often associated with 'Ho'onopono', a meditation for freedom originating in ancient Hawaiian culture". So, what these creatures have done is extrapolate what the various signals being broadcast from the universe mean and how they translate as 'reality'. What would the picture look like if various frequencies from different constellations were in a certain alignment in 2500 years as they will inevitable do? Because a very precise picture can be extrapolated including likely major events because it's all just a series of broadcast coalescing at the same plane at the same time. This is why throughout history similar characters have shown up from Genghis Kahn to Napoleon to Hitler – basically the same energy, same guy, really – and it happens because the planetary movements a cyclic, like a clock they keep going round in similar patterns and, hey presto, the same shit happens every time only, these creatures can capitalize on it in advance if you know it is coming. This is how the ancient all concluded that around this time, like NOW, there would be a sudden shake up on Earth and things would change big time.

RETURN OF THE TWINS

As a result, even the dumbest shits in the upper echelons ALL study astrology to some degree or other, it's a whole thing along with 'spell casting', they teach them that too. It's literally like Harry Potter's Ministry of Magic so there must be some rules of engagement, *specifically,* you NEVER practice magic in front of the Muggles although we are *constantly* being interfered with via invisible influences leaving people wondering why or how they have such bad luck (or, *rarely,* good luck). A-list celebrities are constantly attacking ordinary people all the time who they perceive as a threat or who mean something to their cult astrologically, particularly, really talented nobodies who have no idea what you REALLY have to do to get into the 'A-crowd'. Here's a hint, you gotta be born into the right families for a start, you gotta have a certain date of birth and numerological meaning in your name etc. It's weird and certainly NOT about hard work or talent while certain families are in, and certain families are OUT. I think something must have happened in the mid to late 1800's where a whole bunch of aristocracy got cast down into the masses and forgot their roots and have been the spiritual dumping ground for the bad karma of the uppers ever since. I call them Mirror families, their bloodlines track alongside each other, and they may even be related (!) only one is up and the other one is down, one is good and the other one is bad. It's the evil twin syndrome. The good guys get it the worst. The higher ups promote themselves as 'good' people and even create whole marketing campaigns craftily promoting themselves as 'sad' *ordinary* people that the paparazzi just happen to photograph on an off day and who just happen to be filthy rich A-lister's...but they're sad...riding the bus...looking disheveled. Don't believe any of it. It is so ordinary people will relate to them and buy more tickets to their shows because you'd never buy another ticket again or watch another movie again if you knew the lux life and incredible world's they live in. The more obvious marketing campaigns are when you see the celebs doing manual labour for some poor fucks in a war torn or enviro ravaged zone. Shameless!

In short, they can then depict how future signals will broadcast from the cyclical movements of the galaxy, like satellite tv with shitloads of channels, and translate the future by plotting the trajectory and cyclical movements of these constellations that project images like massive clusters of neural nerve endings literally the same way a brain works or 'perceives' reality to be. The universe is perceiving itself with all it's different neural receptors. We live inside it. It is out of these mathematical deductions calculating the position and subsequent energies projected from the various astral bodies, that theses aliens and demons can formulate an ongoing understanding of 'future' energies and how these energies would likely translate. They then manipulate those energies to steer the natural flow of the universe *away* from its normal conclusion which is all about love and enlightenment and create a chaotic landscape of fear and dread and pain as *this* is what makes them tick. They like it. This charting of the stars is what is erroneously called 'astrology' which doesn't quite sum up the *level of clinical precision* they must have to conclude certain outcomes insofar as *how* the 'future' should play out based on these equations. It's very mathematical and THIS IS the foundation of what Satanism is doing behind the scenes and how they have managed to horde so much power for themselves while the poor old human bumbles along wishing and hoping and praying while falling into traps set for the naïve using easily controlled thinking programs and patterns they set up to make you believe shit like 'if you're a good person, you will be rewarded' and 'astrology is bullshit'. Yeh...it's bullshit that's why they obsess over it and have so much power because...it's bullshit. You just keep telling yourself that. It' sad that humans repeatedly play these childish games hoping against hope that they will be saved just because they are nicer than the bad guys. It doesn't work like that which is why the bad guys are so audacious, so evil and openly laugh at their victims. Clearly, they are not afraid of the same 'gods' that they've got the garden variety idiot in the street being afraid of. It doesn't work anything like *most* people believe it does and while they are practicing the dark side, it is inevitable that we too will practice these things working with the upcoming energies in advance to create an even better outcome as we did in a time long forgotten when we ruled.

Behind the traitorous and ever-growing crowds of Satanists who can't even be loyal to their own let alone human beings in the street, is an alien syndicate who have created a most slick and sharp instrument, *a machine*, that has us under wraps completely. Beyond the beyond it is A.I., a supercomputer. The component parts of this evil mechanism are made up of, among other things, tricking us with language or 'neuro linguistics programming' including 'morphology' – the study of words and their parts. Morphemes are defined as the smallest meaningful units of meaning important for phonetics in both reading and spelling, as well as vocabulary and comprehension. They are speaking a different language right in your faces, see, Adam Sandler and co, and while it can be used for evil it can also be used for something ultimately, good. The bible is written like this with coded messages in the layout of the letters that cannot be coincidence and is a glimpse into the enormous minds of these people once the chakras are unlocked. You may hold a complete conversation with them, the elite, happy that you have grasped even *some* of the most advanced of their weird knowledge yet know *nothing at all* as to what they have said or done to you (if you ever get speak to them, of course). They don't just lie - they ARE deception – and it can be worked into a rather incredible artform or the 'divine comedy' or what they call 'the dance' found in the stories of the stars. Even in the movie Shrek by shunned actor/writer/director Mike Myers, "the stars don't tell the future, donkey, they tell stories". Yes, and they are choosing the stories that suit them best which is why they keep choosing the ancient stories of gods and monsters because this is what they are and is all they know and what they want to keep doing. This trickery is employed by the mainstream media *each and every* day and once people cotton on to how this works and start to see it for what it is, I hope they drag these posturing cunts into courtrooms around the world and charge them with collusion, conspiracy and insurrection of the human race and this entire planet and throw them in the bottomless pit never to see the light of day again. It'll happen, it has to happen as a natural conclusion to the 'awakening' in which we shall see all this and more.

Another tactic that they use is Language Stratification which is the systematic functional framework of language viewed with many strata (that is layers) in context of culture and situations including semantics and lexicogrammar, a level of linguistic structure where lexis or vocabulary and grammar-syntax combine into one. Talk about vibrations! We're being coded! At this level words and grammatical structures are not seen as independent, but rather mutually dependent with one level interfacing with another. The overlap! These guys are running rings around us because we are thinking everything is disconnected when *they* very much see it as connected! Tagmemics is a mode of linguistic analysis based on identifying the function of each grammatical position in the sentence or phrase and the class of words by which it can be filled. This is what symbolism is all based around, and ones grasp of the minutia of linguistics would make translation of ancient texts so much more indepth than a superficial 'academic' comprehension of basic language. You need to be a mystic to really grasp these things. There are many secrets and many more sophisticated codes hidden in the symbols of the ancient world than they are letting on and it is from these deep understandings that the militarized elite have computed the locations of ancient civilisations on Earth and gained more knowledge than ever before stealing and secretly hording treasures, wealth and power that have rendered them architects of time and the owners of history!

They have studied the 'written work' of the stars formally dealing with the subject of the cosmos by systematically and meticulously deciphering these ancient astrotheological accounts that are the *true history* of the world and the universe buried in legend and myth. These secrets have been rekindled by secret science in furthering their authority over this planet and successfully taking their cult into outer space! Who would have though the old gods are alive and well? They're *still* running the place as brazenly shown in the logos of the new Space Force emblems including the Space Force Delta 18 logo.  People are wondering what the hell they are doing with this *pharaoh* on a space force emblem. They are doing the same thing as calling the Apollo space program after ancient gods because they are utilising the same astrometrics as the ancients were using as the ancients acquired the intellectual and technological knowledge from tantric sex. It's their religion. The star is Sirius because this pharaoh is Orion personified as Osiris as was his 'wife' Isis aka Sirius personified as a woman, the queen of heaven, Lady Liberty, as was he the King as was Jesus and Mary. The Baphomet, the Star and the Torch are all defined by sex per the penis caduceus, *above*, as they all represent functions of the human body that allow 'godhood' or enlightenment via the penis-vagina up the spine to enlighten the pineal gland as spoken of in the Bible and every major religion and native belief system worldwide via tantric sex. *It's the big secret to everything.* As the star is above the head giving the power to access the stars, so too does the Baphomet devil character have the star on the forehead as it represents the 'fire' or the 'torch' the 'eternal flame' of life and an enlightened pineal gland from Christ light activation of the chakra facilitated via *tantric sex* as does the 'torch' above the head of the Baphomet and above the head of the Goddess. They combined the astrometry by studying the measurements, positions, motions, and magnitudes of the stars and utilised a combination of astrochemistry in studying the abundance of cosmic reactions with radiation in the universe. In appropriating this knowledge, they have created a secret ideology combining the most advanced almost incomprehensible symbolic and phonetic language scripted into every religious work and print media article to confuse the general public by using the *anatomy of analysis* to twist the true meaning of our *very real* physiological connections to the cosmos. Regurgitating this pedigree of our heritage and our sentient right to the fullest functions of our bodies in connection with the stars - the *big* brain - they feed back to us as a grandiose fanfare with these elite scumbags front and centre posturing as your 'betters' when they wouldn't have any of their ostentatious magnificence if it wasn't *stolen from YOU*. The very natural functions of our biology or 'pure science' of our God-given chemistry are being hidden from us and then *re-represented* back to us without our knowledge as a *forgery of darkness and lies* dressed up as *'gods' and 'saviours'* in alien psychological warfare over this planet and her People's. *THIS IS THE TRUE MEANING OF THE 'SIMULATION' THEORY*. Earth doesn't exist somewhere else. This is not a computer game. There is simply a natural flow and natural story of the cosmos, which is wonderful, and their every effort is to manipulate the natural freedom and splendors of the universe into a hellhole of trickery and have you bowing down in fear and ignorance with them lording over us. This is why they call the 'son' after the 'sun' because it is a dick cult passing the power or at least the dominance to the male line to keep it all going. The 'son' is literally the light found in the sun and in essence it is the same light found in us and if it's the light they are so obsessed with then women, females, carry the greater portion of the light in order to give birth to live human babies yet at that point this system defaults to males over females. It's ridiculous and they are extremely dangerous people, men, in this world without the 'waters' of the earthing feminine to bring them the fuck back down to earth and stop wanking about being gods. Jaysus! Get a grip! Mathew 24:37, "As it was in the days of Noah, so it will be at the coming of the Son of Man'. Noah was most famous for the waters and there is far more to this story *symbolically* than most people understand.

    The light is in all offspring – ALL OFFSPRING – no matter male or female, human or animal. Granted we have to ability to consciously tap into it, and this makes us the 'royalty' of this planet by way of being intellectually superior while retaining the custodianship capacity as was naturally intended. It is their every obsession and effort for over ten thousand years to keep this truth of our rightful liberty hidden from us and they have turned it into religions, cults, laws and ultimately, threats to keep us from connecting with the universe of which we truly belong. It is these people, the self-appointed aristocrats working through the various agencies they created for the sole purpose of picking and choosing who they like from the human banquet, giving themselves the best roles of celebrity and political toy boys the grandest of their kind to ever exist, the undisputed champions of the world or as Freddy Mercury said 'we are the champions, MY friends' (are), not you, 'we' 'us'. But look what happened to

RETURN OF THE TWINS

Freddy Mercury, another offering. There is no club, they take out whoever they like, along with John Lennon, Elvis Presley, Michael Jackson and so many others who thought they were 'in' only to be used like everyone else. Just look at what they did with me, I was supposed to be 'on the team', we were *supposed* to be doing something great, we knew each other *very well.* Yet they set me up DELIBERATELY to suffer my whole life because there is a 'club' and then there is an inner club. However it is they feel comfortable about their positions in this 'club' is anyone's guess. They laugh at everyone who *thinks* they are 'in the club'. There is no club. Because there are layers to this from the least important to the most important. They are the 'gods' of old still working their ancient trickery and cheating. They must be dreading the day they are exposed for this and what will be done to them as a result.

Therefore, instead of you knowing that Christ is an electrochemical function of the brain, you think it's a guy who died on a cross a couple thousand years ago. Instead of you knowing the 'philosopher's stone' is the sacral plexus at the base of your spine that when activated with the chakras via tantric sex turns a dullard into a philosopher, most people think it's a harry potter movie. Instead of you realising the Magdalene in an AC alternating current or negative electrical charge circulating around the body in conjunction with a DC direct current (Christ), you will think is a prostitute who got run off when her bloke was taken out. Instead of you realising that *you* are royalty, and your 'throne' is your root chakra, they've got you believing some bombastic cunt with a fancy hat on a gilded chair is royalty and THEIR riches in the 'throne' and you *must* bow to them. As C.S. Lewis said, 'Education without values, as useful as it is, seems rather to make man a more clever devil'. And right there with his quote you can see the most insidious double talk. C.S. Lewis was one of theirs through and through and notice how they project *their* kind as humankind? It's like men not distinguishing between 'man' as 'men and women' *both* only they automatically hear 'man' as 'men' and naturally default to male 'ownership' of the human race and everything it achieves hence, the overrepresentation of men in everything not that women haven't tried to contribute, they just weren't allowed to. Therefore, so too in the same token does the reptilian aspect blame their alien instincts on 'man' so their crimes become the crimes of 'men' so, maybe reconsider your vocabulary. A classic example of double-speak is 'holly wood forever' which means 'magic wand forever' (as that is what holly wood means – magic wand) or you could read is as the 'eternal magic wand' i.e., the dick cult, as they utilise the goddess *infinity* symbol which means 'eternal' for their alien masculine creepy black magic show controlling us with death (and sex). This sums them up to a tee. Of course, they would associate the eternal symbol of feminine life force with death at a cemetery, of course. They steal everything from the feminine. It's a MASSIVE RITUAL to initiate you into a counterfeit version of life to steal your power in the most heinous and despicable sense and wield it against you until you see death as the solution to a shitty life. Luke 10:19 "Behold I give you the power to tread on serpents (reptilian royal scum – the alien) and scorpions (traitors using tantric sex against you as Scorpio rule the genitals) and all the power of the enemy and nothing by any means shall hurt you". You better believe it. When we get this power, all these scriptures will come to pass. But it's a close call. We nearly didn't make it thanks to their neuro linguistic trickery and reinterpreting the natural flow of the cosmic prana to suit their own wicked ends, and when their dirty plan doesn't pay off they just pull out a gun and kill you outright. That's because at the end of the day, all the pomp and pageantry aside, they will use the most base methods to get what they want and all the rest of it is stagecraft depicting a characterization imitating the original and bona fide faith of the original clan, the humans, who peopled this world before this alien scum slithered in and put their body double in place of our own to replace us and represent themselves AS US to steal this world.

So, the big ritual effigy that they have lined up for us is that of the 'seven vials' or 'seals' of the apocalypse. In this complex and much lambasted charade in which they intend to turn the power of our chakras into a nightmare of biological and chemical warfare finished off with a nuclear holocaust to broadcast that the seven seals the 'secret' seals of the awakened chakras, are disease, starvation, war etc., as this is the exact opposite of what we are *supposed* to be getting at this time.

SEVEN TRUMPETS OF THE APOCALYPSE

As said, they studied the ancient mythological astrology – which was better than anything they are doing today as the ancients could see tens of thousands of years into the future and knew that a time would come when the current zodiac calendar of darkness would 'end' and a new cycle of light would begin heralding the end of these alien scum bags over planet Earth. But that said, if they can get the huge number of human minds to broadcast that at this time when the portals are open that our chakra enlightenment is a nightmare, then the galactic core will respond in kind and send the signal back in that this is 'normal' for us, and it will be locked in. That is why they need the 'majority' of stupid human minds to send this message as their technology is not strong enough to reach the core of the galaxy as only human minds are compatible with the 'chakra' antennas of the universe. Let's take a look at this biblical *auto suggestion* of the 'seven seals' that are also the 'seven bowls or cups' that are also the 'seven trumpets' and include the 'four horses' and debunk the shit out of this for what it is, an evil plan by demon possessed half reptile 'kings' aka priests posturing as your popes and clergy who have the fucking audacity to claim they represent 'god' and all the rest of the rabble who dare to wear the white of the virgin's cloth in mockery to the truth behind it all that 'Goddess' is the true power here.

Firstly, as already discussed, Mary or the Magdalene represents the waters of the feminine symbolic of the root chakra or the AC 'negative' electrical current. Mary means 'beloved' or 'my love' from ancient Egyptian 'mry' and Hebrew 'of the sea'. Yes, waters. The waters of love or the *flow* of prana, the light, which is love-light-life and *should* be easy or 'Grace'. Epona who is the same goddess as Augusta (month of August which they love killing women in this month) was a goddess of horses including donkeys and mules which is interesting as they are a genus of mammals comprising of seven living species at this time. Jesus was referred on occasion as a 'donkey' or his followers following a 'donkey head'. She is also a goddess of fertility (they all are as they are all ultimately the same goddess represented by the collective of human women). She is shown by her attributes of a 'patera' or 'phial' (vials anyone) a shallow metallic or ceramic 'bowl' (or cup) which is code for the feminine sex, the chalice, of the vagina and *root chakra*. Her attributes are also found in the 'cornucopia' also called the 'horn or plenty' a symbol of abundance and nourishment found in a large horn shaped container overflowing with produce, flowers or nuts and sometimes shaped like a symbolic flowing river as found in images of ancient Egyptian women's hair coiled around to represent the Nile as the 'Nile' was called Aum which meant 'golden flow' as this is the prana energy flowing through the universe found in the Christ seed of the brain's electrical functions or the 'crown chakra' hence, the 'flow' and the 'hair' were likened together. It is the Christ seed that activates the chakras (which are shaped like cups or 'horns' the way a trumpet is called a 'horn' which is *a sound hole*) via tantric sex which is why you always see big penises, vaginas and tits everywhere in old paintings and sculptures in biblical porn. You can't have one without the other. The root chakra is the first 'cup' of the feminine and the root chakra 'cup' of the masculine is epitomised by the 'horn' (like rhino horn or unicorn horn) which is also slang for a man's erection. This is why the elites do rituals where they have a dagger or 'sword' that represents the phallus to stir the blood in a cup that represents the vagina root chakra cup as this is where they get their power from, tantric sex!

This is why when 'Noah' was just about to close up the hatch, the last animal to come running along the beach was the 'unicorn' but was 'washed away by the waters' as the flood came. This is a symbolic reference to the 'horn' or the phallus of the male being lost to the waters (which represent memory and so we forgot what our power was and how to derive it from our own sex). Obviously, this cuts both ways as the feminine also lost her abilities to awaken her chakras via sex (the cup and the sword or horn). The 'Ark' in Noah's story is a reference to the 'arc' of the rainbow found in the light spectrum of the chakras as rainbows 'arc' across the sky and boats 'arc' in the water. This is why the LGBT community appropriated the rainbow flag because the engineers behind the rise of the pharmaceutically induced LGBT community are satanist and their god, the devil, is transgender (a man-woman-beast – AN ALIEN) and this alien royalty gets its power as it hacked into our rainbow, our light spectrum found in the chakras. So, they have played out this ritual using unsuspecting people genetically confusing their gender's with vaccines during childhood (which is why increasing little kids are 'identifying' as all sorts of things) leading to a sudden spike in gender dysphoria as the ancient Devil was called a 'god of confusion' who sometimes appeared as a 'man or a woman' but was ultimately male and why Joan of Arc was dressed as a male to fit with this myth to ultimately kill the return of the goddess, the feminine in women (she was set up by the French King and the church who used her as a sacrifice). This is why men are allowed to masquerade as women at this time and beat women at their own sports and if you say anything you're a bad person to fit with the gender bending god as 'anything goes' with them or the dark side of tantric sex. The mainstream Media is a powerful force not forgetting the goddess *Medea* helped Jason (of the Argonauts fame) to look for the golden fleece which is the enlightened crown chakra of tantric sex enlightenment.

The story begins in verse 11 (of course, because the 11 are men and women, the Twins) Jesus is carries by a magnificent white horse as he leads angels and saints in a dramatic battle between good and evil when he returns to Earth. As the story in Revelations goes, "As the Saviour breaks the first seal of the great book, a wondrous scene flashes before the gaze of the holy apostle John, He says, "And I looked, and behold, a white horse. He who sat on it had a bow; and a crown was given to him, and he went out conquering and to conquer" (Revelation 6:2). The first 'seal' (as the chakras are sealed until opened via tantric sex) also translates as 'bowls' as the chakras are called 'seven vials' or 'seven cups' or 'seven trumpets'. Yet our beautiful chakras are dressed up here as a set of 'plagues' mentioned in Revelation recorded as apocalyptic events that were seen in the vision of the Revelation of Jesus Christ by John of Patmos. The chakras are called 'singing bowls' as they make sounds like 'trumpets' and why they say the 'word of god' is Christ and that Jesus played role in 'speaking the universe into existence' as the trumpets-singing bowls make sound and this 'sound' is the 'voice' or frequencies of the universe creating matter and the 'voice' of the 'speaker' who is the leader speaking on behalf of god etc., when the throat chakra is awakened and people start eloquently and confidently speaking their truth.

The first seal is the 'white horse'. "[1] And I saw when the Lamb opened one of the seals, and I heard, as it were the noise of thunder, one of the four beasts saying, Come and see. [2] And I saw and behold a white horse: and he that sat on him had a bow; and a crown was given unto him: and he went forth conquering, and to conquer". White horses of ancient times were often associated with the Sun chariot or the 'sun god', literally the sun which is code to the 'light' which is 'Christ seed' enlightenment of the brain. The white horse is associated with warrior heroes, fertility (in both mare and stallion manifestations) and with the major religions 'end times' and 'end of the world' predictions. This 'end times' is the femeNINE found in many symbols including the 666 which means *sex! sex! sex!*, or the dark side of the masculine, but as they invert everything, it really means 999 the end of a massive cycle. 9/11 was a massive sun and moon ritual but on deeper levels it was another goddess sacrifice as 1 in Roman numerals is the letter I and 'I' is the 9th letter of the alphabet therefore, 911 becomes 999. This is why 999 is the emergency code of England as it is a big countdown to something really negative and no doubt a woman or WOMEN will be in power en masse around the world when the shit hits the fan to blame the ultimate destruction on the feminine despite thousands of years of men fucking things up. It's her fault, it always is, to tarnish the reputation of the feminine that the one time women were in power they created more destruction than all the men who went before them. The first horse has Jesus upon it with a 'bow and a crown'. The 'bow' is a symbol of the phallus as the 'arrow' represents the fire of the penis or the 'spark of his loins' as in 'cupids bow' 'fired' into the hearts of the lovers'. Also, 'A crown was given to him, and he went out conquering'. The crown is the crown chakra enlightenment 'given to him' by the horse, the Mare, the Mary, his wife and why we have a 'Bridal Gown' at a wedding and a horse wear as 'bridle'. "For I am not ashamed of the gospel of Christ, for it is the power of God to salvation for everyone who believes, for the Jew first and also for the Greek" (Romans. 1:16). That's because the 'gospel of Christ' is tantric sex and why he must say 'I am not ashamed of it' because the church shamed sex, called Mary a prostitute and made sex a dirty, secret thing and, of course, only the missionary for procreation and building the flock but not for joy or cementing relations with your partner. Meanwhile at the cathedral the priest are fucking little boys like there's no tomorrow and maybe there won't be with these sick pricks running the world with their inverse double speak dressing up the Christ seed enlightenment as destruction and plagues unleashed by 'christ' creating biological warfare to kill everyone rather than let us have our awakening and freedom.

The second horse is a red horse "When He opened the second seal, I heard the second living creature saying, 'Come and see.' Another horse, fiery red, went out. And it was granted to the one who sat on it to take peace from the earth, and that people should kill one another; and there was given to him a great sword" (Revelation 6:3, 4). The red horse is the root chakra that is red and the 'great sword' this rider wields is a symbol of the penis or dark side tantric sex enlightenment and he is smart enough to reign from a position where he can convince people to kill each other and to create havoc in the world as is happening now. The third horse: The third seal was broken, and the apostle says, "When He opened the third seal, I heard the third living creature say, 'Come and see.' So, I looked, and behold, a black horse, and he who sat on it had a pair of scales in his hand" (Revelation 6:5, 6). The black horse is the black of the 'earth' another reference to the root chakra anchored to the earth or 'earthly' as in material world. The one who sat on it had a pair of scales in his hand. The scales are the scales of Justice, which is another reference to the Goddess, Lady Liberty, who is Libertas from ancient Rome who is Marianne of France who represents *liberty*, equality and fraternity. The fourth horse: "When He opened the fourth seal, I heard the voice of the fourth living creature saying, 'Come and see.' So, I looked, and behold, a pale horse. And the name of him who sat on it was Death, and Hades followed with him. And power was given to them over a fourth of the earth, to kill with sword, with hunger, with death, and by the beasts of the earth." (Revelation 6:7, 8). Hades is always accompanied by a three headed dog, this is the 'Tridevi' the triple goddess as the 'dog' is Sirius the Dog Star, Isis, who is the same goddess as Mary. The final 'horse' or woman that these men ride on her back as they require a chaste noble woman to give kudos to them or, as she is a redemption goddess, she redeems these men who know the secrets of the 'saints'. The 'saints' are the knights templars, Masons. Hades is the same god as Etruscan Aita and Roman Dis Pater (a fertility god associated with agriculture which is code for 'seeds' as is the 'grain' or the *Christ seed* enlightenment) and Orcus in Etruscan and Roman mythology was the *Punisher of Broken Oaths*. The real question is, who's oaths are we talking about here? I say this because in prehistory, men made an oath to protect the feminine found in the covenant, *contract*, of marriage. This is the first oath and anything that came after that is a side contract of lesser or no value at all including the oath to the god of contracts, the devil, who stands in the place of the Goddess and her contract, her covenant, with the male, with God, found in the enlightened man not some fucking alien who tricked them.

The fifth seal or 'souls crying under the alter': 'Next, the fifth seal is opened and we see, "When He opened the fifth seal, I saw under the altar the souls of those who had been slain for the word of God and for the testimony which they held. And they cried with a loud voice, saying, 'How long, O Lord, holy and true, until You judge and avenge our blood on those who dwell on the earth?' Then a white robe was given to each of them; and it was said to them that they should rest a little while longer, until both the number of their fellow servants and their brethren, who would be killed as they were, was completed" (Revelation 6:9-11). The 'alter' is the bed or even more so the 'matrimonial bed', the 'bed chamber' a 'chamber' where an 'alter is housed'. To be 'killed' or the 'death' is the 'death' of the Christ seed as it descends the spine into the 'underworld', the 'souls beneath the alter' are the 'souls under the bed' where tantric sex achieves 'life''. It is the souls who have not completed there full 'circuit' of the tantric sex spine of Christ Seed enlightenment or 'the Lord holy and true' (who had written on him in the 2nd horse that he was of truth etc.,) and so the *same amount of them* who are 'dead' or down beneath the alter are the same amount of the 'avenged' or 'justified' by the scales of Christ (remember the one with the scales of justice) who will bring them 'above the alter' where they will wear the 'white' robe of purity and light when they are enlightened or raised up from death.

The sixth seal is the third eye chakra, the pineal gland, "I looked when He opened the sixth seal, and behold, there was a great earthquake; and the sun became black as sackcloth of hair, and the moon became like blood. And the stars of heaven fell to the earth, as a fig tree drops its late figs when it is shaken by a mighty wind. Then the sky receded as a scroll when it is rolled up, and every mountain and island was moved out of its place. And the kings of the earth, the great men, the rich men, the commanders, the mighty men, every slave and every free man, hid themselves in the caves and in the rocks of the mountains" (Revelation 6:12-15). The 'sun' is the

Christ seed enlightenment and 'black' is the colour associated with soil, literally the earth as in the root chakra being 'earthed' to the planet to diffuse the electricity in high-ranking tantric mastery as the power can cause people to lose their shit. The 'moon' turning red is the feminine root chakra in sexual life. The 'earthquake' is one helluva orgasm. The sky receding and 'moving the mountain' etc., is the 'earth shaking' enlightenment of the third eye that gives one the vision of the third eye and therefore access to the higher planes of the astral where all things are one beyond the 4th dimension beyond the reach of these demons and probably has something to do with the DMT of the pineal gland and the dream state of this incredible awakening of the spirit and connection to the soul, to all. Yes, I think it would probably be an earth-shaking experience as described by MANY people practicing tantric sex. When the awakening of the third eye happens all the corrupt men whether they are slaves, kings, commanders, rich men, mighty men and all the rest of them will run and hide in caves if necessary because we'll be coming for them with the scales of justice held high aboard the feminine carrying brave men forth to do this job.

The seventh seal; "When He opened the seventh seal, there was silence in heaven for about half an hour" (Revelation 8:1). This is the end redemption, the completion of God's plan for humanity in the dispensation of Christ. It is that "divine event, to which the whole creation moves." Heaven is emptied of all its angels as when the Lord, *Christ*, returns in His glory He will have "all the holy angels with Him" (Matthew 25:31) Heaven will be silent because all the 'singing angels (a reference to women's orgasm) will be on 'Earth' or more specifically 'earthed' hence the 'black sun' as the light is anchored to the 'black' earth, soil, as is required by the light side of tantric sex and why Jesus and Mary point at their hearts and the heaven to go through Love to reach enlightenment. This is why they said 'man was made of clay' as clay is dirt, dirt is soil, soil is earth and earth is to be *earthed* electrically vie the 'red moon' or the feminine root chakra. When the righteous return with Christ this means those brave enough to stand up and do what must be done when the Christ seed of enlightenment is given back to humanity and Earth will sing with the angels from 'above' (the higher self reunited with the body) and will no longer be 'silent' (be quiet about the corruption). At the 'coronation of the king the whole universe will rejoice in glorious song' as the 'king' or 'Christ' is 'Crowned' or the crown chakra enlightenment and 'Christ and Mary', men and women, are reunited and lighted by their internal Christ light as the 'lion' the sun king 'lies down with the lamb' the angel, feminine or the 'thalamus' (tha lam) when the crown chakra is enlightened by christ seed anchored to the Mary, the mother, Mother earth or the light side of Tantric Sex practiced for the *second time* as it was *once* before in ancient prehistory when the Goddess was worshipped before we were taken over by hypermasculine aliens. Hence, the '*second* coming of christ' because it's only happened once before on earth.

This is one of the reasons why Victoria Secret were suddenly smashed the blurb for the documentary 'THE SHOW CANNOT GO ON". I'm sure they don't want the 'angels' i.e. women, to go on the big international stage that Earth is. They must keep her out at all costs. The founder of Victoria Secret Roy Raymond his initials, RR, is also the acronym for Rights Ready located at the bottom of documentation within Royal terminology. It also means R for Rex the king and R for Regina the queen. It was also the initials of Roger Rodas who was the driver of the vehicle that killed Paul Walker the number plate for which just so happened to be the gematria (number assigned to letter) for Metatron who was *burned* and transformed from Enoch into Metatron at the same time a comet was in the constellation Virgo the car crashing on the corner of Hercules Street and Constellation  Road. That one was way too obvious. The name of the driver of the truck that killed Jane Mansfield (another goddess effigy sacrifice) was Richard Rambo who is a heroic character of Sylvester Stallone. These men are sending coded messages to each other int movies as psychotic references to killing the goddess in order to keep the masculine empire alive. RR is really code for Romulus and Remus the founders of Ancient Rome that was founded simultaneously with the Goddess Libertas who is Lady Liberty. America is 'New Rome'. Victoria's Secret founded in 1977 was a big year for them as it represents the 7/7 of the male-female enlightened chakra towers and why Elvis 'The King' died that year as a ritual to 'kill the king' as did Roy Raymond kill himself. This company was taken over by Les Wexner who hired Jeffrey Epstein to associate the image of these beautiful young women with a bunch of demonic old creeps hence, 'angels and demons'.

Satanists refer to women as 'angels' and males as 'demons' as men have a much higher propensity toward evil. There were many crimes carried out against these women over the last four decades as VS finally went into 'liquidation', I guess it is the feminine water's, so it was 'liquidated' at this time along with a LOT of other rituals happening by the day to send the message that the feminine is defunct, hangs out with creepy old men and nobody likes them because they are 'unrealistic'. Even the colours of this poster, *right*, are the crown chakra lilac and white.

This is why they released the documentary 'Angels and Demons' in 2022 as the three 2's are the trinity or the light and dark side of the reptilian (11), the light and dark side of the human man (11) and the light and dark side of the human woman (11). 2+2+2 adds up to 6 which is CODE FOR sex. *It's a very big year for them.* The blurb reads 'the show cannot go on' in a reference to the 'angels' not being allowed to 'go on' meaning not to 'return to earth with Christ' or the enlightened feminine not allowed to be ushered back into her rightful position, ultimately, alongside the enlightened masculine. Queen Victoria was the longest reigning monarch until recently overtaken by Queen Elizabeth II. This is why Victoria in Australia was under such brutal attack by the police against ordinary people who couldn't keep up with the ever changing and farcical landscape of the COVID shut down. As they produce movie like *Moonfall* code for fall of the Moon Goddess, I can't help but link up Victoria with the VC or Victoria Cross as Victoria is the Queen or the 'Victoria cross' is the 'royal cross' of the optic nerve of the enlightened crown also called 'kings cross'. In ancient times the goddess Victoria was the goddess of victory the same as the Greek goddess Nike who was the goddess of victory in any field from art, music, war and athletics often portrayed as 'winged victory' in 'motion' or 'flight'. This is another high IQ tantric goddess. Guy who founded Bed Bath and Beyond BBB or 222 as in 2022 just fell of a 'tower'. The rituals abound as they knock off their effigy gods and goddesses in all directions now. You wouldn't want to be a celebrity at this time as the aline-demonic machine scours the fame landscape for big names to send to the universe that king and god, queen and goddess are dead here

So, what they have done is present the seven vials, cups, horns, trumpets, bowls and flowers of the awakening 7 chakras of the human chakra tower of the masculine and feminine twins, the 11, in balance with each other, as an evil war machine that we are to *expect* to happen just because the Bible said so. Fuck. Off. The Bible has been dressed up as a riddle impossible to understand because the truth of where the people who wrote the Bible and the people who profit (prophet) off the Bible really get their power from is in the awakened chakras yet is buried under layers of lies, obfuscation, double talk, and phonetics to lead us to our destruction rather than lead us to our salvation. They do this to send in a bad guy, the anti-christ, who will be vanquished by the 'good guy', Christ, but really, they are one the same tag teaming planet Earth for the alien demon empire in the wings. Enlightenment has been predicted by every country and culture worldwide since time immemorial. The end its just the beginning and it seems that WHEN it happens, the whole world will sing with joy and so will the universe at dodging a galactic bullet from these alien weirdos who laugh louder than their intellect can keep up with. I said in 2020 & Beyond 'He who laughs last laughs longest'.

I guess we'll see who laughing at the end of this *biblical* JOKE.

Chapter Twelve
Toy Kings

Reptilians and demons cannot reflect light. This is the true meaning of the vampire without a reflection in the 'mirror'. The 'mirror' is the Universe.

The ancient story of the King marrying the Goddess means that a reptilian king, who can never become God because he doesn't reflect light, marries the human woman, the Goddess, because she *does* reflect light and it is she who carries the light allowing her to produce babies aka the light bringer. Reptilians do not naturally hold the light as they don't have a chakra system to generate a light body of their own. It means that he can only ever rise to the level of 'King' because God, the human man, reflects light of the universe and, of course, the *Goddess* requires a God not a little king at her side. Reptilians hybridise themselves with humans to attain the light antenna inside our chakras to connect to the universal light force to become who has become the 'big daddy', the Devil, men worship as 'God' around the world. Any god without the goddess at his side is the devil which is why the devil depicts itself as an all-in-one male-female-animal. The 'light' is the 'Christos' or 'Christ' light, a function of the brain's electrochemical abilities to produce a highly concentrated hormone, an animating force, that activates the chakras and turns a 'prince' into a 'king' and a 'king' into a 'god'. This is why they hacked into human genetics to use our perfect light body system to access the higher realms and higher dimensions *through* us and then used this knowledge to elevate themselves to godhood, wiped our memories, slung us down into the gutter and set up their 'royal' households acting as representatives of 'god' ever since. They are the quintessential thieves, and true to form, they have diminished the true god found in humans and ridden off our backs while using our very own abilities weaponised against us to elevate themselves to harvest this world and now seek to eliminate humans altogether as they have bred enough of their kind to maintain a new race of their own. Coupled with technology and a pig pen of preferred breeding stock retained for upgrading their genetics between zodiac frequency shifts that elevate the human DNA, they will retain control forever. Every time there's an

RETURN OF THE TWINS

electromagnetic shift the frequency of the universe raises the DNA again and again which they can't replicate naturally so they use us for that purpose. They must keep up with human DNA as they need it as a a software upgrade to continue to elevate and to connect them to the energetic flow, electricity, of the universe.

The devil is an identity thief and the song Forgetful Lucy from the Adam Sandler movie 'Fifty First Dates'

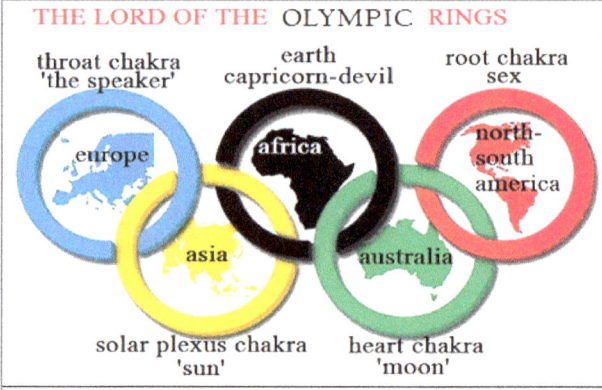

is an inside joke that that goddess, Lucifer-Venus, forgot who *she* once was, the supreme being revered by all in a utopia long since *forgotten* on a *mass* scale. The feminine represents the waters and the waters represent Memory. The 'receptive' nature of the feminine can be found in the properties of water that can be imprinted on as discovered by Professor Masaru Emoto after applying words like 'I hate you' to jars containing water, it altered the crystalline properties of the water into twisted distorted images while words like 'I love you' created perfectly

beautiful and symmetrical crystals. Water is memory. Fire is intellect. That does not mean that only men are intellectual and only women have memory. It means YOU need to balance these to electrical polar opposites *inside your* body in order to balance the intellect and memory, to projective and receptive forces of your unique power in BALANCE to become 'god-goddess'. As our collective memory has been wiped then 'forgetful lucy' is a joke on the *collective amnesia* that we no longer remember who *we* once were (the true angels - gods and goddesses) as the purpose of the feminine is lost and our world is lost to distraction, literally. An alien interloper came in, wiped our memory considered feminine, stood in her position and makes fun of her and her ability to remember who you are all the while appropriating all her symbols, signs and names for itself while getting her to giggle along with the joke because she doesn't know there is one and the joke's on her. Intellect is 'masculine' DC current, and memory is AC feminine current. So, Jesus is prophesised to return or is it Christ? Because if a man turns up, he's the devil. If Christ returns then this is an electrochemical function of the brain allowing for whole brain access, hence, god and goddess united as one, unity consciousness, and that really will shake things up.

In keeping with the never-ending ritual, Chris Rock releases 'Ego Death' after the Academy Awards debacle because Satan is the god of self-indulgence – ego - and do what thou wilt is the whole of the law. It's so shallow and cheap its amazing they've got so far. So, now he is broadcasting that he is going from the 'dark side' to the 'light side' as Jesus returns and Christ takes over to become God where the man left off. Shia LeBouf has also come out claiming 'ego death'. It just goes to show they are all either practicing astrology OR their handlers are telling them what to broadcast as their handlers are practicing astrology on behalf of these satanic agencies managing the crossover from the old age to the new age. It's all a put on. They are simply *associating their image* with these symbols as part of the Biblical-tantra script or as the pharaohs put it 'fused their image' with the sun god etc. But tellingly there is a movie that says a lot about this called 'The Devil All the Time' because if some man comes along to save the day, it will be the devil...*all the time*. He never quits. Unless you get your inner christ consciousness and when that happens you can deal with the external Devils found in the reptilian overlords – they are all 'the devil'. The devil doesn't take a day off. You can't be a devil doing terrible things one day and be Jesus saving the world the next although that's what they want to do.

Queue the next phase in the operation.

Now we see all things 'Christian' starting to emerge as the script swings back the other way and 'Jesus' saves us in response to the whole 'devil' theme found in the LGBT community (the devil is transgender) along with societies brief romance with all things liberal-progressive but only got disorder and social destruction when we strayed from 'the conservative' way things have always been done. The antithesis to the extreme left is found in the cool savvy new-age 'middle media' representatives, young and sharp, who still appear to have a semblance of morals and brains. So, you will now see a 'return' to all this 'Christ' related as good new-age Christians clean up the streets of all the crime and poverty, force children to behave themselves with 'boarding school' and 'military school' type control mechanisms which the parents will welcome, put the growing LGBT craziness and all the 'woke' craziness back in its box, and return things to a semblance of normality, to 'traditional family values' in Jesus name! And things will return to some kind of normal to what generally preceded this last decade before absolute madness took over catering to the *tiniest demands* of precious millennial pharmaceutically induced undisciplined brats. 'Jesus' conquers 'Satan' in this ritual as the zodiac wheel turns overhead and the new storyline says that we should be improving and so we shall. But not so much so as to make any really deep changes or move toward a really profound enlightenment and freedom for planet Earth and humanity in general. It's fake. The bad copy. When idiots talk about the 'simulation' as if we are living on a world that is a duplication of the actual earth that exists SOMEWHERE ELSE... Are you fucking kidding me? People are actually going for this shit.

The reality is, in the coming few years, you'll see more 'justice' because the rational people screaming out for some semblance of common sense will be placated by this normalisation and return to familiar territory as we 'return' from the bad lands of Stupidville and things start to settle down. Males competing as females in sport will be ruled out as an unfair advantage as new 'science' tells that, you know what? Just because a guy gets some oestrogen treatments and grows a ponytail doesn't mean the tensile strength of his muscles are decreased. That's a biological bloke, not another women, physically bashing a *biological woman* in women's boxing. Many people in the world, the majority, will rejoice at the sense of rationale while the 'misgendered' trans community will shout 'foul' but eventually go quiet as they cease to get the media spotlight they once enjoyed.

It all fake as proven by President of Tanzania John Magufuli allowed coronavirus testing kits to be imported into his country but ordered that they be checked by Tanzanian medical officials. They 'tested' non-human samples including goat and pawpaw and the tests were given the names of humans as well as ages and sent off for the results. A fruit and a goat tested positive to COVID. President Magufuli declared, *'Something is happening"*. His presidential term began in 2020 and after declaring his profound scepticism of the Corona scam *and proving it*, he suddenly had a heart attack and died in 2021. Another one bites the dust. Heart attack, as I said in my first book, *2020 & Beyond*, is the preferred method for assassinating people. It's like the interview journalist Tim Russet had with George Bush Jr. calling him out over his affiliation with the notorious secret society, Skull & Bones, he died of a massive heart attack two years later. Sometimes when they are out in the open like that, they don't like to associate themselves too obviously with the assassinations of opponents and so they

RETURN OF THE TWINS

wait, like snakes, until the heat has died down and then strike so that people don't link up the two events. So, if you mess with them don't expect immediate retaliation, although that can happen, but for the ones they really hate they wait until you've dropped your guard and then strike in the cruellest possible way the same way they did with Belgium banker Ronald Bernard who blew the whistle on Ritual Satanic Abuse in the highest echelons of international banking and their ritual murders of children. Many years after he blew the whist in August 2017 he went missing near his home in Florida. On a routine afternoon stroll he phoned 911 multiple times and told them he was being followed and his life was in danger. Later that evening he was found floating face down in a shallow stream of water and to date his cause of death has not been revealed. We're not dealing with humans and unfortunately, this is our first introduction to the wider alien thing and may not be a bad thing per se as when we deal with the wider alien communities, there's no reason we should trust them any more than we trust these guys. "Where is everyone" is the famous quote when the real question is "where were they when we were being destroyed". They are chameleons and morals seems, at this point, are a distinctly, if misunderstood, human trait.

The hierarchical reptilian society are certainly not a healthy society. They are based on one-up-man-ship, endless scheming, megalithic betrayals are at their core but ultimately, as they are, they cannot survive. They are doomed implode in the end because the fact of the matter is, there really is no loyalty among this lot. At their absolute heights, the most childish, the most snivelling, the most cheap, shallow and apparently 'self-serving' are elevated over and above others in their society. They laugh endlessly at the expense, largely of women, but at the expense of humankind as a whole and endlessly laugh about it especially in movies to see who can go the furthest and get away with it all dressed up as 'romance', 'jokes', or just plain 'fiction'. In the film Return to Me David Duchovny plays a 'builder' who wife dies. Her heart is transplanted into another woman who he accidentally winds up dating. This other woman is frequently carries all the symbols of the goddess surrounded by flowers, riding a red 'bike' (town bike of red root chakra sex), her name is even Grace. Aw! I've noticed these creepy men love to make fun of the 'happily ever after' and the 'twins flames' who were separated by Zeus and constantly seek their other half. Return to Me is a take on the reincarnating lovers who must find each other lifetime after lifetime. Only in this lifetime, they cut the heart, love chakra, out of the goddess, stick it in another woman and fuck her brains out. Gross. These guys are sick as fuck. Freddy Mercury kept a wife because the king, even gay, has a

RETURN OF THE TWINS

'Goddess' for a wife as Orion, the constellation, has another half, his twin, the constellation Cygnus.

In the movie 'The Quiet Man' (another piss take) when John Wayne (who Kenneth Anger claimed liked teenage boys) dragged Maurine Ohara through a field that him and John Ford, the director, had saturated with faeces. Why do that? It's not like shit is going to translate as anything but mud on film. They hate women and take any opportunity to degrade women an there's nothing even A-list women can do about it. Right up until the scene was shot Maurine Ohara's friends were kicking the shit off the field only to have John Wayne and John Ford kicking it back on again to drag a female 'star' literally through the shit as this was a big lark to them. That piece of shit Marlon Brando sodomised, *violently raped*, his co-star Maria Schneider *on film* for audience consumption. In the movie *Last Tango in Paris*, Brando and the director, Bernardo Bertolucci (note, the name BB or 22), concocted the plan *in advance*, PREMEDITATED, to sexually assault his co-star who he was *30 years older than* at 48 while she was still in her teens at only 19 years old. The 'tango' is the 'dance of love' as this legend is all about the return of Love, the return of light, and thus the 'ascension' of humanity. They refer to the astrology of the stars as 'the dance'. This movie title is a play on the 'last dance of love' in Paris (before they kill the goddess) because *Paris* is named after the Goddess Isis as Paris is shortened Latin for Par-Isis or 'near the temple of Isis', the sanctuary of the Goddess. They named this film 'Last Tango in Paris' because Mary Magdalene, the 'Goddess' and lover of Jesus 'God', raised their chakras via tantric sex to become 'Jesus Christ Superstar'. Mary later ran away to Paris. She was the last version of the Goddess who they are trying to destroy as the 'fairy tale' of the 'happily ever after' and 'beauty and the beast' comes to pass and they joke endlessly about it.

2022 is significant for them as it is the light as dark side of the Goddess, God and the Devil or 11 11 11, the trinity, coming into balance. But as there can be only one, Satan, then, once again, their rituals reign supreme as the Queen Elizabeth, their effigy of the Goddess, 'dies' as the Divine Feminine must be dispatched for them to install their sun king. As such, a 'king' now reigns appears in the year 2022...really? Just like Corona 911 shut down the world in 2020? Just a coincidence mind. It's all an effigy to do away with the goddess 'return of love', Lady Liberty, and destroy the rising 'twins flames' of the chakra ascension much prophesised since the dawn of time.
The 'twin sisters' are Isis and Nephthys or the light and dark side of the feminine or more importantly, the feminine in balance as strong confident enlightened women without losing her femininity as a result. This is why

they killed Diana in Paris, the city of Love while the Parisian language is called the 'language of love'. They couldn't get Mary physically, although they tried, as she must have been a pious woman (the virgin) as she was a temple priestess with an activated 3rd eye. She wouldn't take their money, she wouldn't take their title and she wouldn't betray Jesus like his mates in the club did like so many have discovered the hard way in *modern* times. There is no club. It's just their way or the highway and then have the gall to talk about loyalty? But don't try anything knew, don't challenge the prefabricated status quo even if they are outdated and need to be put out of their misery. Don't challenge them because it's not about enlightenment or some such other 'spiritual' shit that they claim to share the secrets of with their members. It's about following orders OR ELSE. It is a military operation of alien proportions taking over worlds and their tried and tested methods cannot be altered because they are afraid of what will happen if they break away from the old rituals and bullshit that has no place in a modern evolving age along with the new broadcast from the universe. THINGS ARE SUPPOSED TO CHANGE. But they don't change so. Abide by their fucked up old fashioned rules or face the consequences. But that is not loyalty. That is not the 'brotherhood'. You protect your family even if they have done the wrong thing. It is natural instinct to do so. Only they don't protect their own. They kill their family as seen in the old kings who were murdered AT THE BANQUET AS WAS OSIRIS AND JESUS in a tell-tale homage to how this really works. Even their own sons conspiring for the throne routinely killed their fathers and then each. Even today certain religious nutjob fathers routinely kill their daughters in 'mercy' killings and so-called 'honour killings' for their fucked up egomaniacal demands to be worshipped as 'god'. If I was this dark lord or 'god' I wouldn't look favourably on someone who would kill their own family in *my* name. If their own blood – their nearest and dearest – can't trust them, then why should I? Considering what's at stake? They all want to be god and therefore, they are ALL smiling assassins and there is not, CAN NOT BE, a brotherhood as a result. They save the worst for their friends and why they laugh and mock the 'family' by calling their disgusting organisation 'the family', like the Manson's and all the rest of the filth. The 'family' what a joke but then loyalty is code for fealty, to swear acknowledgement that someone else is bigger or more important than you so shut the fuck up and play along. They not only kill the king, *they set him up* to die for THEIR secret alien rituals in servitude of an extraterrestrial cult dominion using psychological warfare to trick the human race into walking into their traps.

RETURN OF THE TWINS

They are not gods and they are not even king, they are Toy Kings who upon attaining their crown of enlightenment, after decades of loyalty, must surely conclude with their big brains screwed on tight, that it's all bullshit. B.U.L.L.S.H.I.T. John Lennon, Elvis Presley, Bruce Lee, President Kennedy (crowned king, chief), Martin Luther King - they love killing the 'king' including King Kong the 'monkey man' shot down trying to climb the (chakra) tower. Konge is Danish for 'king' so this is King King or King of Kings, *Zeus!* Zeus is the devil only in ancient times they weren't informed enough to know the breadth of the multiple personas this creature wears. Giani Versace was killed shortly before Diana's death as a king and goddess 'couple' killing, Paul Walker, *Robin Williams*. They betray their own and pull them so far into corruption, the trap, that their victims cannot speak the truth of it. Considering Robin Williams spent his whole life making people laugh, in the end, he used the cover of fiction to tell the truth of what was being done to him. Robin William's favourite book was Isaac Asimov's Foundation Series that predicts a future where mass population behaviour leads to the fall of the 'empire' of the galaxy. An 'interegum' is a gap between the ages when they 'reset' their model of society and start up the empire again. Robin William's mother believed 'sickness is an illusion' and his favourite book as a child was The Lion, the Witch and the Wardrobe. His favourite game series was Legend of Zelda about the various reincarnation of the hero lead male and a 'magical princess' named Zelda who is the mortal reincarnation of 'the goddess'. They fight to save the 'magical land ofmetaphor for Earth) from an evil demon 'king' (the devil) and intend to use the 'tri force' (the trinity) that in the beginning is depicted as feminine. The trinity is referred to as the 'golden power' the 'tri force' represents the essence of the 'Golden Goddess' who created the realm of Hylia (Earth). The tri-force can grant godlike power to the one who holds all three pieces (tantric sex) made up of the 'power', the 'wisdom' and the 'courage'. This is Dorothy's three companions in the Wizard of Oz, the Tin Man looking for a heart aka the power, the Strawman looking for his brain aka wisdom and the Cowardly Lion looking for his courage.

On it's own the tri-force represents the 'demon' (the all in one man-woman-beast) who uses it's vast power to serve his own ends. In this story, the power is re-acquired by the male lead after defeating the devil as the devil heard of the feminine power and lusted after it to subjugate and rule the realm and expand his influence. The devil did not know that to acquire the entire force one must have in their heart the balance of the 'three virtues' of power, wisdom and courage. As his hearth did not contain this balance, the tri-force splits leaving him with only one, power. The remaining pieces are sealed in those 'chosen by destiny' with the tri-force of courage in the male and the tri-force of wisdom in the female. Each one received a mark on their hand and the tri-force can choose to return to its original owners. While the devil is banished by the male to the 'sacred realm of the seven sages' (the chakras), he retains the power of the tri-force while the male and female retain their pieces of courage and wisdom. Eventually the tri-force falls to a female who is the first bearer to lack evil in her heart which she uses to restore balance to Hylia (Earth). The tri-force affords the bearer protection from black magic and when fully assembled the tri-force allows its bearer to be granted as many wishes as they desire which lasts until death. The tri-force is connected to the 'royal' family of their world. The symbol for the tri-force is found at the 'temple of time'. This symbol can also be found in the armour of 'the Clock Town soldiers' who symbolise the system administrator and foot soldiers who enforce this reality. The parallel reality is called Termina – terminate. In another instalment of this series the tri-force is depicted as a black stone on the loading screen inversely meaning their tri-force power is lost. The insignia for the Tri Force is a triangle with a triangle at each corner. The geological strata beneath the earth and as with Gettysburg the rock beneath is almost completely granite. Black granite containing quartz is highly electrically conductive and that quarts deposits have the capacity to store energetic imprints from traumatizing circumstances occurring nearby. The quartz crystal, according to chrononaut Andrew Basiago, works as a sort of lens like a time camera and events from the past would have been photographed by the environment itself. When the human body dies a huge electro burst of light energy is released called a 'death flash' and this flashes bursts of electromagnetic energy emitted by the suffering of the dead and dying repeatedly imprinted over hundreds if not thousands of years is captured in the quartz and when this energy is released the very environment itself becomes a sort of television producing what people presume are 'ghosts' and 'apparitions'. This 'visual phenomenon' it not created above ground but is happening from underneath. This energy is registered and measurable as the energy is given off.

In his final film, *The Angriest Man in Brooklyn*, he is diagnosed with a terminal illness and says in a video message to his son, "By the time you see this, I'll be dead...the only people who don't look back with regrets are the innocent and psychopaths. And I've got a lifetime of regrets. What a fool not telling my father to fuck off...like the old man would ever love me...? Pushing your mother away, what a ball-less coward I am...and there's your brother...why?...lord why?! I mean what kinda god...? What kinda world...? It's a stinking con game! We grow up being told 'wait for the sweets and the roses' then they hit you with a pickaxe in the ear! Grief. They say you pass through it. Bullshit! They say, 'don't get angry, let it go, it's killing you'. I say 'fuck that! *Anger is the only thing they left me.* Anger is my refuge, it's my shield! Anger is my birthright!" You need to be careful with these guys. There's potentially an opportunity to blow this thing wide open, on the other hand, there are games within games continue. The traps never end. In this movie after he 'dies' his son's wife wants to go on a 'bicycle' holiday, but his brother says, 'Henry *hated* bicycles' they ask why and he says, 'he considered them predatory'. Everyone laughs because no one gets the odd joke. That's because it's an inside joke that Mary was a prostitute – *the town bike*. These screw balls think women are predatory given what *they're* doing? If the women they associate with are predatory, it's because they only marry mind-controlled sex slave 'brides' (birds) and have staged horrible break ups to seed the 'broken marriage' routine in society that men and women can't get along as more marriages fail than ever before.

Many have been taken out for reasons pertaining to the death of the 'god king' so that the secret satanic club can install *their* preferred *one*. All else are offered up if and when necessary. It is a prophecy that goes back into the recesses of antiquity before even written language was recorded. It is an oral tradition of a legendary fable that the reptilian 'god' or 'gods' *plural* would unite with the human 'goddesses', *human women,* and right the many eons of shame and hardship caused to this world by a secret space empire of cryptic psychopaths using ordinary men's stupidity to destroy their own chances of freedom via the goddess, females. These aliens know exactly what they are doing. *See right,* Space Force logo the scorpion (sex-torus field) infinity logo. It is the legend of the 'happily ever after' and it is the most enduring legend of all time. A legend that has been laughed at and forgotten by average people as they give up on the truth of who they are and the dream of ascension and liberation pir ancestors carved into mountains, hidden away in caves, coded in art history and told by word of mouth as oral traditions since the first fall of man when *they* arrived so long ago! So, everything they do, AND I MEAN EVERYTHING, is a ritual to destroy our rightful destiny as they overwrite the natural laws of the universe, the flow of chi-prana, with satanic *opposing rituals* designed to confuse the cosmic brain at the centre of the galaxy and disallow us our birth-right via the feedback loop. 2022 is a big year for them as 2+2+2=6 which is their favourite number as it is sex. 2 breaks down to 1+1 which is the number of the fabled lovers of legend that is epitomised by the planet Mercury the local replicated version of the constellation Gemini 'the lovers'. Depicted as 11 this is the two chakra towers of the 'twins', men and women who access the 'holy spirit', the aether, the unseen realm they use over us, via sacred sex. 2 Corinthians 3.17 "The lord *is* the spirit, and where the spirit of the Lord is, there is freedom".

How did we miss this for so long? Perhaps because the 'lord' is not quite the correct designation, they mean the 'light' is the spirit and the 'light' is the 'sun' and the 'sun' is the 'king' or the 'son-sun' of god as they twist the phonetics for male default preference only. But the light also comes from, if not mostly, the goddess. They are harvesting this world after all so they have to dress up their monumental crimes as endorsed by 'god' and you better not fuck with them or 'god' will get you! Counterfeit god. Mind games. Psychological warfare old and new.

As part of their duplication process, they have rigged up Disney World is an effigy of Planet Earth, where they play out rituals all the time using the minds of the public to broadcast their messages to the cosmic mirror the secure the circuit and create a reply path, the loop. So, one thing you need to understand is that all these fairy tales are secretly telling the truth about the repeating cycles the reptilian alien space league ustilise to gobble up planets in an empire that harvests many worlds. Beauty and the Beast is the prophecy of the beautiful human woman and the 'beast', the devil, is a reptilian male, finally breaking away from the evil empire and making a 'new world' reconnecting the lost links, the broken chain of true love and unleashing all the knowledge of the male via the chaste 'virgin' goddess, a human woman, to set the world free and liberate humanity and planet earth once and for all. This is the 'happily ever after'.

THE GOLDEN CIRCLE THE FIBONACCI SEQUENCE THE THE '8' OF THE 88 MALE FEMALE TORUS FIELDS

Right, you will see the Milky Way Galaxy. All the major constellation 'arms' have a male-female component. Carina means 'beloved' or 'my love', the feminine, the 'wife', only they never mention the female component as they have been deleting the feminine for thousands of years, murdering her goddess in effigy as famous 'stars' set up from the outset for the very purpose of destroying their icon (phonetically 'eye' 'con'). The attempt to delete the importance, independence, contribution and struggle of the feminine to be included in managerial proceedings of planet Earth is not a new thing. The Gospel of John clearly shows how scribes were changing the name of Mary Magdalene to downgrade her input to the events of the time. She was said to be independent of men, had her own money and made up her own mind. This attempt to ruthlessly control the feminine due to her influence of wisdom, fairness and honesty is exactly why the unevolved boys clubs even today seek to suppress and outright kill any woman who shows impetus and strong intellect preferring the bimbo 'barbie' type characters encoded into modern women since the 1950's. Prior to this it was 'when we get behind closed doors', domestic violence, and was the way things were handled with a woman who had an opinion that their husbands didn't like. They would simply beat her up if she got to 'mouthy' and physically suppress her under threat of injury. To that end domestic violence IS ABSOLUTELY RIFE in the upper echelons of Hollywood and mainstream politics. In recent times the world was *shocked* to see Nigella Lawson being physically abused, STRANGLED, in public and secretly photographed by  onlookers. It is a common strategy with famous men who are exposed for abusing women is to give an interview stating how badly they feel, talk about empowering women and claim they will make a clean slate more informed than before. It's an inside joke. Violence toward women, even still, appears to be common 'private' way things are handled in the upper classes and up until recent times the lower classes too. *Right*, how common place is it to abuse women and even pass it off as honourable? Many people, especially men, have not even questioned the social treatments they are groomed for from early age. Stalking is not a man's right. How many women over the millennian have just given in to

My teenage nephew told me he asked a girl out and she turned him down. I said, "You know what to do now, right?" He said, "I know I know keep trying" and I said "NO. LEAVE HER ALONE. She gave you an answer." He was shocked. NO ONE had told him that before. TEACH. YOUR. BOYS.

pressure from a persistent male and gotten married as it was 'expected' as she was supposed to be 'flattered' by unwanted and intrusive demands? Nigella's husband said at the time it was a 'playful tiff' (!) and was 'disappointed' she hadn't come out *in his defence* to tell the world *he abhors violence* to women and that the photos of him *throttling her* while she is clearly distressed made a '*wholly different and incorrect implication*'. Of course. His brother Lord Saatchi said it was 'persecution mania' (she's just hysterical) and that 'marriage is a private place'. Yes, behind closed doors.

RETURN OF THE TWINS

The propriety men have taken over women is being eroded by the day as even men now see the hypocrisy in their behaviour and the necessity to include the feminine and cherish the other half of the human race in light of increasing intrusion into schools training little kids that there is no 'mummy' or 'daddy', that little boys are little girls, and men are women in this 'new' age. It's dangerous and this 'neutral' anything goes programming of the next generation spells the end of humankind as we have always been and leaves us wide open to extinction if and when the manipulators behind this deem it necessary.

The veneration of the ancient goddesses Diana, Isis etc., are referred to as 'cults' while the veneration of Jesus is a 'religion'. They STILL cannot accept a female as being the primary deity in a much loved and ever-growing expansion of consciousness, at the time, teaching tantric sex in loving relationship that rapidly spread across the known world in ancient history even all the way to the British Isles. She's apparently airy-fairy crap, but he's the real deal. The brightest star is Canopus considered a feminine star called the 'navigator' of Menelaus, again, we have the feminine torch lighting the way for the masculine. The

Hidden meaning behind Princess Diana £8m Swan Lake necklace – last jewel worn in public

PRINCESS DIANA was one of the biggest fashion icons of the 20th century, an her jewellery collection was coveted by royal fans all over the world.

NORMA (JEAN) CONSTELLATION OF THE MILKY WAY GALAXY
MM MARY MAGDALENE MARIYLN MONROE THE STAR GODDESS

CYGNUS THE SWAN CONSTELLATION PRINCESS DIANA AT SWAN LAKE
THE GODDESS DIANA OF HUNTERS THE HUNTER IS ORION & CYGNUS

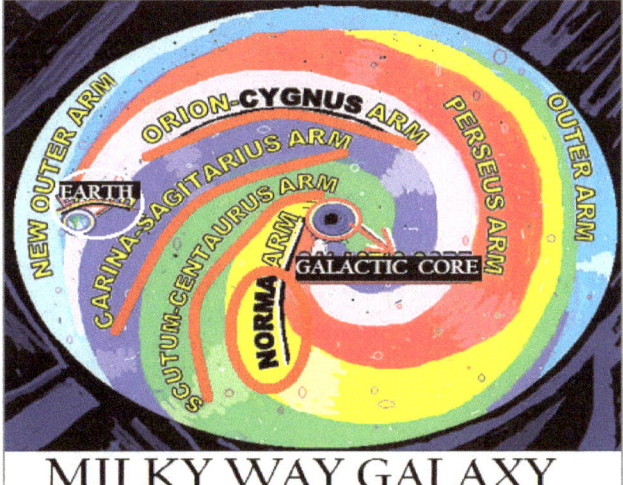

MILKY WAY GALAXY

RETURN OF THE TWINS

masculine component of this major spiral arm is Sagittarius the 'archer' as is cupid the 'archer' who fires his arrow, the phallus, into the hearts of the 'lovers' to set their 'hearts on ablaze' to represent the 'light' of sacred sex lovemaking between the AC-DC electrical male-female universal currents. We also have the Norma Arm of the Milky Way and the Orion-Cygnus arm, which is why Norma Jean, Marilyn Monroe, was lined up as an effigy of the galactic feminine energy creating the torus field between the male and female that looks like the symbol 88. The planet Mercury is revered in

this story as it takes 88 days to go around the sun and was personified as Roman Mercury who is the same as Greek god Hermes whose namesake, Hermes Trismegistus, was a polymath and professor of galactic and alchemical studies. Hermes is the God of Mercury, ruled over by Gemini and *Gemini* rules over the throat hence, the 'voice' or the 'speaker.' The throat chakra, once opened, gives one the confidence and intelligence to address the people to become a great leader and why all these ancient solar deities are called The

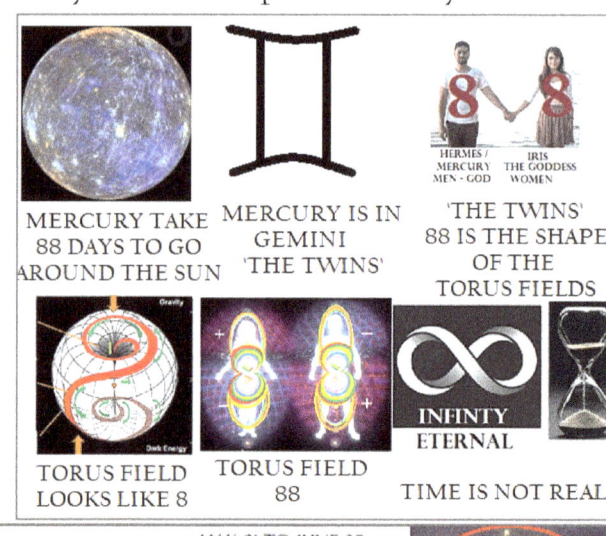

MERCURY TAKE 88 DAYS TO GO AROUND THE SUN

MERCURY IS IN GEMINI 'THE TWINS'

'THE TWINS' 88 IS THE SHAPE OF THE TORUS FIELDS

TORUS FIELD LOOKS LIKE 8

TORUS FIELD 88

INFINITY ETERNAL

TIME IS NOT REAL

11 IS THE TWINS

Messenger. But instead with get 'the speaker of the house' who *isn't allowed to speak!* We get 'the voice', *a TV show!* Horribly, the 'messenger' has been dressed up as '*Moderna MESSENGER Therapeutics*' an evil injection designed to destroy the Christ seed oil function of the brain! The Christ seed function was referred to in ancient times as 'the messenger' as it connected one with the outer realms and inner consciousness delivering enlightened messages. Oh, you are going to see it all in the next few years, my pretties, as this information emerges and the truth of what they have done really emerges and the horror transforms to rage. The torch bearing, pitchfork wielding farmers will go up to the castle and dispatch the monster for good. The four elements combined in the masculine and feminine combustion of sexual energy creates the fifth element, Aether, this IS the fifth dimension that transmutes these elements into another plane of being complete with all the things we are familiar with in the 3rd dimension that we are currently stuck in. Therefore, the other planes are strikingly similar to ours only much more expanded and with holographic vision, we will literally see the hordes of evil beings that are entrapping us in a lower, lesser, plane where we are more easily controlled and kept as pets and food for them!

Hermes the god was depicted as bisexual as that is what is behind all this a bisexual dick cult of reptilian swingers who get sex anywhere, they can to facilitate opening their chakras and why they are so damn smart and have the whole world confounded! It's the dark side. All these ancient enlightened ones were practicing the dark side of tantric sex dressing themselves up as saviours because, that's exactly what the devil energy would do. They are all aspects of the 'devil' insofar as with this power one can control others and why they believe that Jesus and the Devil are one and the same, brothers, twins, as you can choose to do good or bad deeds with this. This is why they have Shiva at CERN who are being blamed for the rise in *paranormal and UFO-alien phenomenon* due to opening portals with their large particle collider among other such contraptions around the world. Shiva means 'lightning' because, once again, this is all about electricity and tantric sex electrical nervous system activation. The Jewish sephiroth like the complex Hindu-Vedic energy depictions of the body are highly scientific and *factual* knowledge about the higher functions of the human body. They have been gathering this data for thousands of years. *Right*, the sephiroth is an anchored lightning bolt and the Jewish Menorah are the seven 'lights', lightning, of the chakras. The left eye represents the moon, and the right eye represents the sun as the sun and moon also represent the masculine-feminine Twins. This is the true meaning of the endless celebrities covering one eye along with the lightning bolt symbolism everywhere as they harness the electricity of the universe accessed via *tantric sex*. It's also why they cross their arms over their chest like Egyptian mummies as the pharaohs were practicing this and their cult is largely based on these ancient practices. The 'crossed arms' are the optic nerve of the brain centre where the pineal gland lies and why there is pinecones everywhere. They are still practicing it. It's the BIG secret.

RETURN OF THE TWINS

You must understand, however talentless MOST celebrities are, ushered into the upper echelons for favours and their oath of silence, they were going to leave you for dead and build a new world paid for with your money and your lives while they keep this knowledge secret, a knowledge that they stole from you in the first place, to themselves. The real talent lies in the untapped ocean of the human race and if it remains untapped, we will never know what might have been if the human race are destroyed in favour of these genetically inferior selfish low-lives who are happy for their masters to destroy humanity as long as they have a big house and their face on a magazine. Talent? Zero. Ego? 100%! Here's Russell Brand with the Jesus 33 vertebrae og the tantric spine on his left wrist, the left-hand path, the Masons. And they have the gall to pretend to have a social conscious. They are unconscionable. Celebrity means to 'celebrate'. Why would you want to get excited about some elses fake achievement. Why celebrate a complete stranger whose accomplishments are your losses? Why wouldn't you put all that excitement into your own accomplishments and celebrate yourself? They are STILL the gods of old and they STILL have people worshipping them they just dress it up in 'cool' 'edgy' ways in modern times. We live in a popularity club in the school yard Earth has become with the 'in' crowd and those who copy them and the 'out' crowd - those who are calling them out.

Celebrity and aristocracy revere the Germans and the French. Why? The short story is that the secret cult that runs the world today are a continuation of the Druid beliefs of ancient Phoenicia. The Phoenicians came out of what is current day Lebanon and Israel and as they moved into what is current day Europe and spread north to current day Germany and south to Current day France. It is out of these Druids whose motto was 'knowing the way of the oak', that their various secret societies who would go on to become the Templars, the Illuminati, the Masons and their royal households to wind up taking over the 'new world' not forgetting the royals are all breeding with each other and are one big family, literally. So many western politicians and celebrities find their roots in French and German aristocracy. Why would the Druids cryptically say, 'knowing the way of the oak"? The 'green' man and the 'oak' king are reptilians who have mastered tantric enlightenment. You will often see oak trees on military insignia and on the flags these posturing twats make their fancy speeches in front of. They associate the oak tree with this 'enlightenment' because the oak tree is the *only tree that is struck by lightning more than any other tree on Earth.* Lightning. It is the reference to the lightning that is the dead giveaway here as it is the true secret at the core of all their power. See right, a Nazi badge with the oak leaves as were a lot of their insignias and as with so many of the 'royal' households depicting the 'oak leaf'. The leaf signifies the 'tree' of the nervous system, or 'tree of life' and 'tree of knowledge' forbidden to Adam and Eve by 'god', a reptilian from another planetary dimension. Anyone would think 'god' didn't want them to evolve frightening them like little children from the information that would elevate them to the same positions as 'god'. And 'god' said to his 'child', Eve, in Genesis 3:16, "I will greatly multiply your suffering in childbirth, in pain you will bring forth children; your desire will be only for your husband, and *he will rule over you*'. And men ruled over women keeping them in place and 'god' ruled over men keeping them in place. It has been this way ever since. But that's not 'god'. What benevolent heavenly father would hurt their children, keep them ignorant and relish in abusing them? Could it be a hypermasculine *alien* who hates and is afraid of the goddess, human women, and knows it can rely on the brutishness of human men, her husband no less, to keep her in place for future purposes? Men who won't admit to their ignorant part in all this cannot denied are further endangering our future. If they won't own up to what has happened, it can't be rectified and therefore, humanity and earth are doomed. In creating a society ruled by men, women's opportunities at getting work and paying their own way were drastically diminished and, in this way, a woman was forced to marry a man as she was not allowed to go it alone. That said, there are many examples of women historically who, with an iron will stronger than most mens, achieved their financial independence from men with many attempts to sabotage and waylay their opportunities by the boy's club who saw her as competition, a threat and 'just a woman'. Its entrenched behaviour, entrenched thinking, that women are 'less' than men even though many men are secretly scared of a women. It's not about women or men, it's about humanity and balancing these energies inside us to unite and transcend this shithole.

RETURN OF THE TWINS

The big alien program to ensure the biblical prophecies of 'signs and wonders' play out in the 'end'. They are crazy as shit, by the way, and need to get a new script. So, the rituals unravel by the day now as a "Brawl at the Magic Kingdom" breaks out in Disneyland. The Magic Kingdom is Planet Earth and yes, there is a fight on Earth at the moment, a fight for our future, a fight for our lives but above all else a fight for our ascension to the next level of the galactic game. They are weaving the 'end' into our psyches, auto-suggesting against our knowledge that there is no 'happily ever after' for humas, no 'true love' of tantric sex enlightenment. The true meaning of all religious lore around the world that they are desperate to keep from us is that the ancient prophecies of our liberation and freedom will come to pass and they are desperate to prevent it. So, the metaphoric, symbolic and effigy rituals are coming thick and fast now. All your favourite celebrity 'stars' are susceptible at this time to be used in ritual zodiac coding as the shadowy priests grab *anyone* they require to throw under the zodiac bus ing sacrifice the numerology found in the dates of birth and names of their celebrity victims in their weird astro cult. Therefore, Alec Baldwin 'accidentally' shoots Hayla Hutchen on the set of 'Rust' an 'Old West' film as in the old West women didn't really have a practical place but in the upcoming New West of the modern western world women will take a much bigger position and these men hate that. HH is the 8th letter of the alphabet and become 88 for the number of days Mercury takes to go around the sun Mercury who is Hermes the 'messenger' the 'speaker' who carried the tantric caduceus of sacred sex enlightenment known to 'cross borders' as he was accessing the astral plane at will. HH is also the symbolic man and woman side by side (in bingo 'two fat ladies) so in this ritual they have destroyed the feminine aspect of the tantric woman and silenced her voice. They have killed the goddess here. They delete the feminine part of the godhead as there can be only one and I'm not saying he did that on purpose, I'm saying there are strange forces causing all this to happen to fit a biblical end times script that is by now undeniable.

Further weirdness as the massively important 2022, trinity twins, countdown to the end of the year rolls on. Naomi Judd the famous singer of the Judd's incredibly shot herself on April 30th which in the pagan calendar is Walpurgis Night, the celebration of fertility rites and the coming of spring named after St Walburga an English nun (priestess) who lived in a monastery in Germany and became the Abbess there. It falls on the eve of May Day on May 1st a major satanic holiday. Naomi Judd's famous daughter is Ashley Judd or 1=A and J=10 or 11 considering Naomi Judd's birthday is January 1st 1946 as January is the 1st month and the 1st day becomes 11 while 1946 reduces to 20 which is two 1's or 11 – this is an 11:11 ritual considering the mother becomes the daughter, as does the father 'god' become the 'son' so to does the Goddess the mother become the daughter hence, Mary with the mother and wife (even though they deny it). Ray Liotta died in late May 2022 in Geminin the twins. Ray is a reference to King Ra the Sun God of Egypt as Ra is literally sun ray so, sun 'ray' Liotta had to go. You can always tell their guilty conscience as suddenly spurious headlines started springing up 'He Knew He Was Going to Die'...he was getting married at Xmas and was making a movie, this is not someone who was expecting to die. Lions Gate 2022 was a massive ritual celebrity sacrifice orgy. Between 26th July 2022 and 12th August 2022 when the Earth, the sun, Sirius and the Galactic Core are all in alignment, called the Lions Gate (*see*, Lions Gate Films), clearer signals than any other time of the year are happening as the 'cell towers' line up giving a strong signal to the central hub broadcast. Just prior to this there was a 'planetary parade' or 'parade of stars' in mid-June. It suddenly kicked off then as the weird Sunset Boulevard style death of an aging socialite occurred in the death of Ivana Trump who 'fell down the stairs' with 'blunt force' trauma to the abdomen. So, in this ritual the 'goddess' falls down the stairs given the pineal gland is the 'stairway to heaven' therefore, she doesn't ascend the stairs, she comes crashing down...and dies. Dead goddess. I see a theme happening here.

The opening of The Lion's Gate was kicked off with the court show trial of Alex Jones (again, A=1 J=10 or 11) forced to pay compensation to a *mother* of a Sandyhook victim given this is all about mother's and wives who are the 'goddess'. In this ritual the male conspiracy researcher protagonist, who knows a lot about this cult posing as human organisations and done a lot of amazing work to expose all this, is the 'bad' guy. Nichel Nichols, the black trailblazing space pioneer on TV, dies in this ritual the black queen or the galactic mother goddess dies as a 'black Madonna'. Judith Durham lead singer, the voice – the speaker, of The Seekers dies as the ancient mysterious god of confusion was called a 'seeker'. Anne Heche, oh dear, she dies as A=1 and H=8 which become 9 the femeNINE who portrayed good and bad 'twin sisters' in the light and dark side of the feminine effigy in a production called "Another World" (if you can believe it) she also was in a movie called Toxic Skies about a pandemic being spread by chemtrails. Given we've just had a pandemic and the chemtrail program is no secret - you can't make this up! Olivia Newton John who famously sung the song "Magic' at the Melbourne Cup horse race given the 'horses', of the apocalypse appear to be the 'mare' or 'Mary' wearing her Bridle or Bridal gown as Jesus rescues his *bride* in the astrology of the June planetary parade where all the planets in our solar system were

RETURN OF THE TWINS

aligned across the sky for the first time in a thousand years. Her initials ONJ is O the 15th letter of the alphabet reducing 6, N is the 14th letter of the alphabet reducing to 5 and J is the 10th letter of the alphabet reducing to 1 gives us 6+5=11 (which is not reduced as it is a master number) with another 1 for J arrives at 111 the number of the Empress aka the goddess. She died on the pinnacle of the Lions Gate on the 8th August the 8th day of the 8th month or 88 of the god and goddess, the lovers, the twins, the couple in tantric star enlightenment. Her nickname was Olivia Neutron Bomb or 'sex bomb'. The Empress has twelve stars on her 'crown' chakra representing the twelve zodiac signs. She is the goddess of the galaxy, the queen of the world sitting on her throne (the root chakra) holding her torch (the eternal flame of christ light) in the right hand of 'god' as a strong maternal figure. She is the mother of nature or Mother Nature, mother of life.

The word enlightenment is the only word that spells eighteen in consecutive letters as 1+8=9. In the Satanic thinking 6+6+6=18. This is why they created the 27 club of dead 'stars' as 2+7=9 and 27 is 9+9+9 or 999 the massive goddess cycle about to end heralding the return of the feminine as mothers and wives (and women in general) taking more prominent decision-making roles in the world to return balance to Earth. She is the original 'Home coming Queen'. 999 is 666 inverted. 6 is sex. All this is in movies for example, Fiona in Shrek means 'light' while Shrek is the 'green man' ogre, a reptilian, also depicted as trolls and the demonic 'gremlins' etc. It's all are *reptilian* symbolism. Puerto Rico now experiences massive power outages as I write and is 100% off grid caused hurricane 'Fiona'. So, the goddess of light is causing electricity failures? It's all ritual (like Lake Mead) as they pull out their weather weapons to make it all seem real. They know what they are doing, and it is a ongoing joke among them to put it right in your face while denying any of this is even possible. Tubal Cain mentioned in the Bible as the first 'black smith' or 'maker' from the 'fires' as the fire is the 'forge' he is a 'forger', yes, a counterfeit, the 'great pretender' a faker, the Devil, the father of lies who deceives the whole world. From the line of Adam's, Tubal cain was the son of Lamech translated from Hebrew 'powerful, shadow, leader. Cain means 'smith'. Cain and Abel were the first two sons of Adam. It's possible there are two bloodline here, Abel was the son of Adam while Cain was the unknown son of Samael, the 'snake', a reptilian, in one of the earliest telling's of this story of genetic infiltration. Zeus seduced the

RETURN OF THE TWINS

Spartan queen Leda on her wedding night leading two sons being born, Castor and Pollux (who represent Geminin, the male 'twins'). One son was the biological son of the father, and the other son was the progeny of the 'god', a reptilian in this case Zeus. Two babies from different fathers in utero is called parthenogenesis. Dr Stella Emmanuel said that she has heard many cases of people who dream they have had sex with a 'celebrity' and wake up to find they have an STD.

The point is there are numerous stories in history, myth and legend that speak of a 'third' party making the human woman pregnant including Lugh a 'supernatural' being who has a 'five pointed' 'fiery spear' (a penis) or 'flashing light', tantric electricity, and equated with Mercury who is Hermes similar to Apollo (that's because all these ancient gods are one and the same, reptilian sun kings). Hermes is the god of the Masons, the god of *theives and imposters* as well as orators and merchants – the 'trade towers' are an offering to this version of Satan who is a 'speaker' as they mislead with rhetoric – he's a politician and a trader – a businessman (aren't they all). The merchants, artists, bankers, officials, and lawyers from the first quarter of the 1600's began to call themselves 'freemasons' trying to recreate the rituals of medieval guilds. Hermes is the patron of travellers and the 'bringer of sleep'. He is a 'sun god' and all his emblems are symbolic of tantric enlightenment. From the documentary *In the Shadow of Hermes – The Secrets of Communism,* based on the Juri Lina book *Under the Sign of the Scorpion* (Scorpio root chakra sex), quote, "one can safely say that all *(Masonic)* ideological and political deceptions have been born in the shadow of Hermes". They are not 'gods' these are reptilian males posing as gods utilising the chakras or the light spectrum to facilitate 'supernatural' feats including Rosemary's Baby type pregnancies. It was said the though the son of the king was his heir, he was the biological son of Lugh, the demon. Lugh means to 'bind by oath'. This is the god of contracts, Satan, the Devil, reptilians, also called a 'babbler', he speaks in riddles, phonetics. He was 'skilled in many arts', yes, a con man, 'youthful' (eternal youth of the tantric waters) known for his 'curly yellow hair' code for 'crown chakra enlightenment' from the 'land of promise' (the promised lands of milk and honey Christ seed). Winston Churchill in 1920 stated that Leon Trotsky invited to the U.S. by fellow Masons was also an 'illuminatus' became a member of the Masonic order of B'nai B'rith who had helped Russian 'revolutionaries' in January 1917. In The Secret of Initiation into the 33rd Degree it states, 'Freemasonry is nothing less than revolution in action, ceaselessly waged conspiracy'. Trotsky even said himself, 'My only purpose in New York was that of a revolutionary socialist". What do you think they are going to do once they get their perfect world? Simply continue more conspiracy and more chaos, it's all they know how to do. You can't teach an old dog new tricks, they will take their venom into space and continue the war paradigm everywhere they can, they're already doing it – Space Force is a military space program – it's already happening. In certain branches of freemasonry obvious elements of 'reactionary feudalism' became prominent as found particularly in the Scottish Rite. From the 18th century onward freemasonry exhibited a 'militant policy of enlightenment' as promoted by the Illuminati the forerunner of 'revolution'. It's hard to find a movie that doesn't have god-goddess tantric symbolism all over it as they rush to associate themselves with this legend to send their signals via the mass human collective mind as the alignments unfold and the antichrist looms. Always the big jokers the clown prince always laughing about how smart they are and how stupid humans are. These cheap cunts can't keep up so they just sabotage you and steal the tools to lord it over the better people, in this case, humans.

The Statue of Liberty was gifted to America by French Freemasons from the Grand Orient de France to the Freemasons of America. Among those who among which were Frederic Aguste, Bartholdi and Gustav Eiffel who bult the Eiffel Tower – a giant iron dick. Always laughing it up. Lady Liberty although representing the Roman Goddess Libertus, as far as the Masons are concerned represents the Babylonian Goddess Semiramis the patron saint of the Illuminati. Her full name is 'la liberte eclairant le monde' meaning Liberty enlightening the world. What a joke. Her right hand carries the torch of enlightenment and in her left hand she carried the Declaration of Independence. Liberties symbol is the dove of the goddess Colombia. The Masons see all these symbols of the Galactic Goddess as motifs of their power to manipulate and control and in my opinion constantly laughing it up. Her cornerstone was laid by Grand Master of New York, William A. Brodie conducting magical rituals in the presence of thousands of American Freemason. They must have had a collective orgasm that day. The Statue of Liberty was officially opened under the sign of Scorpio on 28th October 1886 also in the presence of thousands of Freemasons (I got news for you, they're not free). The magical elements they used at this ceremony was corn, wine, and oil. The 'spirits' of the wine represent the 'turning water to wine' of the bible when the 'waters' of the rising kundalini become the 'spirits' aether's the corn represents the Christ seed and obviously the 'oil' is the emollient quality of the electrochemical cerebrospinal fluid hormonal emanation of this central brain function. I'm beside myself with shock, who knew? So obvious. 'Grand Master' of Rome admitted to Masonic tactics when he stated in the 1870's, "Freemasonry has at its aim to form and lead public opinion. It wants the influence with government, which belongs to well respected and powerful institutions. Therefore, it strives to place its own leaders in the security services, the legislatures, and in the highest political offices".

They steal everything even George Lucas and his Star Wars score by John Williams is directly stolen from Gustav Holst 80 years prior in the cutting edge classical "the planets'. It's not a homage, its theft. *See right,* Rocky horror castle with rainbow the plain dealer The vampire theme of sinking its teeth into the jugular is the reptilian sinking its fangs into the neck to extract the adrenochrome fresh from the brain. It's all closer to reality as when they shift or even not, they sink their teeth in. Castle Frankenstein home of a real mad scientist aristocrat who believed you could transfer souls from one dead body to another as that is exactly what they are doing, the aristocrats are transferring their souls to their compatible offspring or the 'father become the son' duplication process. It won't be too long before the world discovers the true royal owners and masters of pharmaceuticals that have carried out their plan to destroy the human race dressed up as health as they have been openly promising to do for the last hundred years.

It's all ritual duplication as found in the Olympic rings *right*. Here they have the 'earth' or black, root chakra red, the solar plexus sun, the heart moon. So via the root chakra the sun king will use the moon goddess to take over Earth. This is why they call it the 'horoscope' or 'horror' scope because they want you to associate the length and breaths of astrological telling of the future in the stars with 'horror' so, don't look into it. Don't know the future even though its there 'written in the stars'. The Olympic rings include the root, solar plexus, heart and throat chakras but once again, no cap, no crown chakra. It also includes the root chakra sex (dark side of tantric sex the devil) and the blue throat chakra the speaker. The Anti-Christ will be the leader of America the speaker who gains his power and confidence to speak via the red root chakra sex enlightenment. The fake sun king. The three core rings are green, gold and black. Green and gold are Asia and Australia and black is Africa. Given the communist, specifically Chinese, are in Africa and are the major hub of Asia, this looks like Australia coming under some massive Asian communist state in the future. The Olympians overthrew their parents as refenced in the title of the movie Remember the Titans with Denzel Washington. In this ritual the Olympians are America and yet have no crown chakra colours of lilac and white. In the symbolic Olympics rings, they do not receive their crown. This leader has the 'black' "earth" the yellow 'sun', the green 'moon'. This is the trinity. This solar king with the moon goddess wife ruling earth as they just use her for a baby, for the genetics of Mother.

This is why Kennedy whose name means 'helmet' and 'chief' or 'crowned king' was shot three times. The triple killing of the king is because god has three aspects and the goddess has three aspects. It is the Trinity again in replication of greater processes. The family Trinity is the Mother, Father and Child. The Crown King of America, President Kennedy, was assassinated in 22/11 as this adds up to 33 the tantric sex enlightened spine. He was killed next to the Trinity River to incorporate the goddess waters into this ritual effigy slaying at Dealey Plaza the 'uncapped pyramid'. The 'Pyramid' is the upper body with the lower body being the 'underworld. The 'upperworld' trinity is the left and right shoulders and the head of the throat chakra, pineal gland and crown chakra in balance of the enlightened man. But in this ritual the 'king' is never crowned, he doesn't receive his enlightenment his head is shot off in this case but really, he represents every man. All men are the Kin-God. It is about duplication with them mimicking the natural REPLICATING process of mother nature in the galaxy. But the new world king never gets his crown. He remains 'uncapped' or unenlightened and therefore dead. Unawakened chakras were considered a living death or sleeping

'THE ONE' DOESN'T GET HIS CROWN

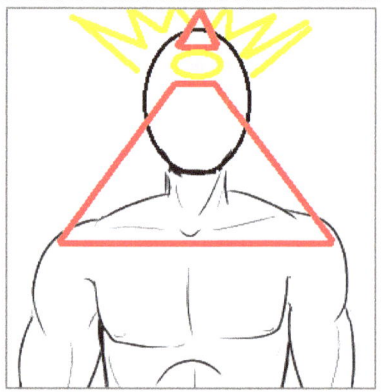

beauty. So, the Titans, old world royalty from UK-Europe, killed the Olympian New World king to install one of their own. Born in America he is old world royalty of Euro-British (German) stock and funnily it is the Nazis who are behind the UFO alien thing as well as the growing demonic phenomenon tormenting people in their homes. So, it will be a secret German posing as an American who will lead America and thus the world out of the UFO-alien looming fake invasion to go on to rule the 'new' world in a 'one world' space program. But they are all the same. It was the Nazis had the Black Sun created by Heinrich Himler for the SS. Once again, we find pilfering of the feminine as it is based on Zierscheibe from 800BC, a *female* talisman found in the graves of women. It represents the central black hole sun, a feminine force, the creator.

It is Nazis who are ultimately behind all this intent on building their 'super race'. White and black people are the fall guys at each other's throats again. Increasingly, there are white 'mass shootings of black people. This ritual is to associate the growing concern that 'white' countries are being swamped with people from Muslim nations with moronic 'extreme right' thinking. This claim was theorised by French author Renaud Camus in his 'Great Replacement' theory. Scholars have claimed Camus' 'call to violence' are implicit in his depiction of 'non-white' migrants as an 'existential threat' to white populations despite Camus condemning violence. Social engineering rituals are designed to be quite obvious to anyone who knows what is behind all this. So, between 2019 and 2022 there were three major 'white' on 'black' mass shootings including two separate mosque attacks in New Zealand by the same guy in Christchurch...Christ...Church...ahem...where 51 people died which reduces to 6 as 6 is sex of this massive tantra IQ scam. Then there was the August 3rd shooting in 2019 during the Lions Gate where 23 people died and 23 were injured as 23 is 11 on the 24-hour clock which is another 11:11 ritual associating hatred and destruction with the rising lovers of the light and dark side of the masculine and feminine electricity. Also, in Buffalo on May 14th, 2022 a 'white supremacist' killed ten black people. In this ritual Taurus the bull is the 5th month of May in *'Buffalo'* the bull as Taurus the bull rules over May or 'torus' field which has a dark side, the minotaur, the beast. In ancient times May was ruled over by the goddess. The day 14 reduces to 5 the number of Chaos as the goddess 'chaos' gave birth to five offspring while 2022 the 11 11 11 of the light and dark side of the 'trinity' found in the human goddess, the human god and the reptilian Devil. What if human men put aside their unknown age old war with reptilian men and they both put aside their war against the feminine and unite together? Wouldn't *that* be something. The old-world club betrays anyone not from the old world. Wheels within wheels. Games within games. Clubs within clubs.

There is no club.

Chapter Thirteen
NAZIS & THE FAKE ALIEN INVASION
Threes a charm!

"History would be something extraordinary, if only it were true", Leo Tolstoy. It's amazing to me that men will go off to war and kill each other en masse on the whim of elite orders under a blanket of lies and false heroism and yet *most* people will run for cover in all directions when the possibility of losing one's reputation or (cough) *life* in defense of *our planet* and *our human race*. With the power the elite wield over the weak minds of ordinary men, it seems must control the aristocracy like an unruly child and direct the minds of the weak who are so vulnerable to them toward more productive and enlightening pursuits. The aristocracy cannot be negotiated with, and it is them who is behind every dirty deed and monstrous plan designed for the Human Race since time immemorial. They are going full steam ahead for their self-appointed New World Order where only they will reign supreme and there will be no more opportunities for the human race ever. We will die and they will take our place. They are the single most dangerous element standing in the way of our escape like an abusive husband who believes he literally owns his wife like a dog as she tries to get past him to run out the door. As such, the Nazis never died. They were never conquered. And there demise was part of a much larger script to cover up, again, the atrocities of the elite and their ceaseless pursuit of knowledge and power, squirrel away the most outrageous mass murderers in history, retain the technology and scientific advances they had made and move to another operational HQ away from the world where they could finalise the procedures of finishing off the human race and taking full control of planet Earth for a larger space empire the lurks in the shadows awaiting its opportunity to emerge.

Hollywood A-list celebrity *is the Nazi diabolical plan in plain sight* and only proves their vision is long and tenacious! The long and the short of it is that the secret society Masons, the brotherhood, have gone by many names throughout history in every country worldwide, yes, even the oriental East have are part of the global network and their plans. It is this 'priesthood' of the aristocratic socio-religious order who set up the chess pieces and their pawns and underlings, their choir boys found in the upper echelon of politics and celebrity, who happily lie through their teeth and direct others to carry out these mandates or even more happily, become nothing but a figurehead and put their feet up expecting nothing more than a cushy life. It is the Aristocracy who are in cahoots with the demonic reptilian and alien grey thing and it was their 20th century new age war machine The Nazis who are behind the increasingly weird UFO and alien abduction phenomenon and the increasing numbers of people disappearing under weird circumstances in the forests and outback wilds of the world taken by creatures that are, by and large, cooked up in underground laboratories unleashed on the world to fit with script of the biblical end times 'wonder' and 'signs' prophecy. Former Italian Professor from the University of Piedmont, Murizio Vacallo, claimed in 1981 that he had been abducted by aliens and even taken photos of aliens. While he *may* give away some interesting, coded information on the nature of human origins fed to him by imposters, the give-away is that he was taken to a secret base in the Amazon. South America was the playground of the Nazis who were prolific in this area, and still are, ever since the end of WWII in their attempt to create a fake alien invasion with themselves dressed up as the 'saviours' of planet Earth and emerge as our next 'gods'.

The first and most famous case of UFO abduction was Betty and Barney Hill that came to be called the Hill Adduction as a play on an inside joke of Betty and Barney *rubble* that destroys the 'mountain' of the chakra tower called the 'mound' and the 'hill' to rubble. Barney said they were 'Nazis' in black uniforms and that they were 'evil'. When they are creating history, they need to made 'lore' or 'legend' around a subject before they can introduce it as 'real' as such, since the broadcast of Orson Welles alien invasion 'War of the Worlds' broadcast in 1938 as well as Roswell and the Betty and Barney Hill (note, BB22) among an undercarriage of associated stories, claims, speculation, unproven 'photos', folk lore, small town 'monsters', men in black, weird 'mothman' sighting before the 'Silver Bridge (this is a reference to Pont D'Alma tunnel where Diana died or 'bridge of the soul' a reference to the tantric chakras and the 'silver' threat that runs through them) at Point Pleasant this is 'Pleasantville' from the movie with Paul Walker who they sacrificed as an effigy of Enoch, Metatron and Hercules all references to tantric enlightened 'gods as well 'Point Pleasant' is PP the 16th letter of the alphabet that reduces to 77 the 7 male female chakra towers. All this has created a rather awesome and ever growing sub-culture of researchers, conspiracy theorists, professional TV programs, paranormal investigators, authors and 'those who get too close' like journalists who 'disappear' or turn up dead etc., all go to furnish the lexicon of the legend that 'become real' in the subconscious mind that scans our terrain for data, true or not, to compile a stockpile of information ultimately designed to save our lives should any of this turn out the be true. You've got to hand it to them, they know the workings of the human psyche, they know how to manipulate your psyche into believing this is 'otherworldly' and 'alien' and 'ancient alien' and that the 'legends' of trolls and bigfoots are real. And some of those legends are real. Only, they have woven a lot of manipulated science and laboratory experiments and real world technology into the existing collective subconscious only to emerge as something that is straight out of a move inserted in advance as fiction. It's the mind fuck. They play mind games.

What they have done is mish mash the real and the unreal or what I call the 'fiction non-fiction paradox'. They dress up the actual reality of these things found in the darkness of nature as ghosts, bad spirits, poltergeists, entities etc., blow it out of all proportion in movies like Amityville Horror, the Exorcist, Poltergeist, and all the rest of them seeded since the 1970's to add precedence, and then unleash these creatures and phenomenon FOR REAL upon the shocked and disbelieving public and coupled with the slow development of the 'conspiracy' wackos who've been trying to warn them all this was happening since the early 1960's and you've got one hell of a believable script for a looming 'alien' invasion or a 'external' non-human threat (or friend?). Therefore, they just keep playing you and enrolling you as characters in their ridiculous script that they can change at any time to suit whatever requirements that emerge as they encroach upon your perception and take you over from the inside out. That's if you survive the minefield of medications, injections, 'terrorist' psy-ops, poisons in the food and water supplies, the idiocy of growing sections of the population who didn't care any of this was happening until the TV told them to have a social conscience about 6-10 years ago. Predictably the ones who weren't following this game from the outset are all the 'woke-sters' and 'progressives' who naturally want to help out but don't know how so they just fuck things up for the ones who have been following this from the outset and know what actually happening. Frustrating but there it is. We were supposed to be awakened instead we got 'woke'.

I'll explain a brief history of 'UFO's' or 'antigravity' machines. The concept of 'gravity' is a misnomer, it's not gravity, its actually electromagnetics that holds everything together. As such, these craft are electromagnetic propulsion vehicles. The simplest way to understand this power is to imagine two giant circular magnets. One end attracts the other end repels. AC and DC or pull and push. This is the 'electro' or push and the 'magnetics' or pull components. It's really very simple. Now imagine facing the two 'repelling' ends together and they will magnetically push each other apart, force them into close proximity, make then spin at very high velocity in opposite directions and you begin to capture some of the natural 'magnetic' and 'electric' activated ions or power produced by the co-rotating forces that then create a natural 'torus' or energetic field. It's called 'torsion propulsion' when electrons and protons vibrate at such high rate it produces electricity. This electric field is like quicksilver (another reason they revered mercury the planet and element) and this power 'slips' and 'slides' manoeuvring around VERY easily, like liquid. This is why legitimate images of early UFOs showed them 'sliding' around and moving very quickly and erratically. The hardest part would be building a console that was sensitive enough to keep up with how fast this 'beyond speed of light' power really is to operate it effectively in the world with all its obstacles. So, there must be back up A.I. type navigational equipment and humans are not fast enough to navigate to that speed – maybe it has pre-set co-ordinates that are typed in and the machines simply takes them there like auto pilot? The navigational equipment must be 'slowed down' to allow for human capabilities while utilising the *intense* and *incredible* quickness it produces. The next step would be to train the human brain to comprehend the mechanics and manoeuvrability of the trajectory. Since, they have had this technology, all up, for about 150 years then they have several generations of up to the minute high speed pilots (they are more than pilots they are star captains).

Now maybe you can see that they have built a parallel civilisation even in the last century that is 'out of this world' with Star Trek type capabilities that, even still, most people equate to science fiction'. Humans are so easy to knock over and yet you are assured some sort of position in all this as they really couldn't have done it without you. You paid for all this with your lives along with your blood, sweat and tears. It was your grandparents and great grand parents who they used for labour, as well as experiments and just plain old-fashioned sacrifices to the demons 'gods' who are feeding them the information they require to access the wider cosmos via occult secret societies tapping into the demonic realm. Many humans won't make it through indeed they are dying *right now* as we speak. There are simply not enough places in the future to bring them all back and let them have 'another chance' via 'reincarnation'. There is a space program within a space program within a space program, wheels within wheels within wheels, until it's so big and so secretive that it is trying to take over our galaxy and the universe beyond.

RETURN OF THE TWINS

If you can believe it the pathetic levels of non-existent awareness of the mainstream media as 'whistle-blowers' claiming Donald Trump (please god get me a galactic sized spew bag) has made 'agreements' with 'aliens' and their 'galactic federation'…. star…trek…. Apparently, this heralds a 'new age' of *sudden* space developments as the buttered-up brains of the average minded eat this shit hook line and sinker in the hopes to be like their favourite 'stars' coded into their childish minds *literally* when they were children from the 1960's onward. So, what are we seeing? We are seeing *layers* of mental and emotional manipulation to steer your human consciousness, those of you who are left alive, toward a 'new' and 'exciting' era where 'anyone' can take up a 'career' in 'space' and be part of a new 'exciting' and 'corporate' and 'inclusive' space program. Even Seth MacFarlane, a favourite choir boy of the elite priesthood directing the next phase in the zeitgeist of Earth's future social-space theme, has created a program called the 'Orville' and it is all inclusive as gay aliens have marital problems etc., it's all very 'progressive' as underneath all this the dark order are an 'androgynous' and 'same sex' cult that harnesses the power of tantric sex acquiring the high IQ's to do all this but there is no love here. It's all about sex. There is no feminine here. It is a sexy male 'woke' facsimile of the real thing. They must retain control, and this is how your do it. Human minds are incredibly malleable and it's important that the cat not be let out of the bag of how weak-minded humans really are and how willing they are to go along with there captors who are 21st century Nazis every bit as evil, ruthless, and cold as those who exposed themselves during WWII.

Trailblazing Russian physicist, scientist Vladimir Terziski, blew the whistle on all this in the 1990's and it cost him his life. As we get closer to the 'end date' of this, it will become harder for them to just 'disappear' anyone in the way they have enjoyed for so long. It was Terziski, bless him, was onto this from the outset and said a lot of secret military projects are covered up by the 'alien smokescreen' as an 'alien gift to us' for public consumption. He said the Germans made fifty different models of 'UFO' aircraft before during and after WWII powered by every engine available to them including piston engines, turbo jet engines, ram jets and rocket engines among others. The final and most powerful models were powered by 'electromagnetic' gravitic drives. He claimed, and he would know, that the secret space program run by the Germans had landed on the moon and Mars *before* WWII ended. He claimed the Russians and Americans landed on the moon and Mars in the late 40's and early 50's and the Italians landed on Mars in 1956. Terziski explained that many superpowers have actively pursued secret space programs based on electromagnetic propulsion. Yet in order to convince people that this massive research and development conspiracy existed, one must also presume it is coaligned with *political* and *economic* conspiracy. This becomes too much for the average person in the street to comprehend and therefore they eliminate themselves from participating in the looming global space events by the denial that accompanies low self-esteem. Deep down, they simply don't think they are worth enough to be involved on any level. It's sad. Then they watch it unfold as 'fiction' on TV and this satisfies their curiosity until they die. Maybe another life? But there won't be another life for most people.

Italian aeronautical engineer, Renato Vesco's 1971 book *'Intercept – But Don't Shoot: The True Story of the Flying Saucers'*, was written when he finally learned the truth about many so-called 'unidentified' flying objects. American pilots were routinely outgunned by 'objects periodically invading terrestrial airspace". Vesco studied the cover-ups by global governments and the potential for 'invasion from outer space' discussing why so many government officials worldwide choose for their constituents to have ambiguous information on these topics. He said the Italians and Japanese were regularly briefed on German developments in this area during the second world war. The rather farcical attachment of tank gun turrets attached to some UFOs photographed should indicate the roots of these projects – old world military coots who just want to find another way to kill. Terziski explained how a 'football field length cigar shaped craft was built by the Nazis which correlates to descriptions of UFO sighting in the 1980's and 90's from people who described 'massive' craft that could shoot away rapidly into space. He described that these UFOs are emanating from a Nazi based still existing at the South Pole *today*. These are *free energy* devices, flying converters of gravitational energy that transmute the geomagnetic field of Earth into electromagnetic energy of flight and therefore, *never had to refuel* powered by the natural electricity emanating from the planet. The planet gives off an inexhaustible free magnetic energy – YOU DO NOT NEED MONEY TO ACCESS THIS ENERG. Even more taboo than the Third Reich being responsible for the UFO phenomenon in a looming fake alien invasion, is that energy is abundantly available to us, all around us – WE ARE ENERGY – and the concept of paying with false money for an electrical force that comes from Mother Nature is yet another monumental example of how ridiculous our lives are on Planet Earth. As Terziski said, "If one is able, basically, to ride for free to the moon and Mars without using a single gram of fuel, freeriding on the gravitational currents of our solar system, then a lot of our present day economy about, well, we all have to pay for fuel when we tank our cars, becomes obsolete".

RETURN OF THE TWINS

As far back as the 1860's inventor John Keely created an anti-gravity flying 'bath tub' which rose silently manoeuvring sideways and returning to it's original position. Keely described his machine as running on an 'etheric' or 'vaporic' force. *That* ring a bell considering it is the aether from which the Christ seed oil is generated inside the human body leading to massive quantum leaps in spiritual and material evolution. Keely stated an 'un-named force' based on 'vibratory sympathy' produced an 'interatomic ether' from water and air. In 1872 Keely invited scientists to a demonstration at his laboratory on 1422 North Twentieth Street Philadelphia stating that he had discovered a principle for power based on 'musical vibrations of tuning forks' and that music resonated with atoms and aether. The Keely Motor Company was launched in New York he stated on September 22nd 1884, "Stripping the process of all technical terms, it is simply this, I take water and air, two mediums of different specific gravity, and produces from them by generation an effect under vibrations that liberates from the aur and water an inter-atomic ether. The energy of this ether is boundless and can hardly be comprehended. The specific gravity of the ether is about four times lighter than that of hydrogen gas, the lightest gas so far discovered'. Note, the date this happened 22nd September, another strange 9 11 11 event. Some force, clearly stated as aetheric, is trying to get through to us and shows up on specific dates at certain times hence, why they attached such dread to this number given what happened on 911. We have seven chakras inside the body, nine chakras between us and the sun and eleven chakras between us and the galactic core, the BIG brain.

In June 1885 Keely stated, "It is an elaboration of inter-atomic ether by vibration. The atomic ether vibrates all around the molecules of matter. There is a magnetic force attached to it at the same time, and it assimilates with the molecular atomic aggregations – that is assimilates with a certain attractive force that is hard to tell what it is. I call it 'vibratory negative'. It doesn't act like a magnet drawing metals toward it. There is a certain magnetic effect about it that causes it to adhere by vibratory rotation to different forms of matter – that is the molecular, atomic, etheric, and ether-etheric "more powerful than steam, and considerably more economical". The impulse is given by metallic impulses, the rotary power that is formed by etheric vibration- that is the force that holds it in position'. Wikipedia is careful to point out "In the 19th century most physicists believed, incorrectly, that all space was filled with a medium called the "Luminiferous aether" (or "ether"), a hypothetical substance which was thought necessary for the transmission of electromagnetic waves and to the propagation of light, which was believed to be impossible in "empty" space". This engine bears a striking resemblance to the hydrogen fuel cell build by Stan Meyer who was offered a *billion dollars* to sell his patent. His water fuel cell injector breaks down water molecules into oxygen and hydrogen used to run any engine. A trip from Los Angeles to New York would use approximately 22 gallons of water from a water fuel cell that fits in the palm of your hand.

A 13-year-old boy, Max Loughan, invented something along the same lines saying, 'If you've got energy, power, you've got everything'. He created an 'electromagnetic harvester out of a coffee can, wire, two coils and a spoon in his parent's boiler room. The harvester conducts radio waves, thermal and static energy turning it into electricity. The wire takes the 'energy from the air' (aether) converting it from AC into DC all costing him $14. Max is one of twins brothers this little mass media ritual playing into the 'brothers' myth who were supposed to save or destroy the world. Stan Meyer, like John Keely and the young lad Max Loughan, were not scientists or even a chemist. The Pentagon sent a general observe Stan Meyer's engine in the hope to 'use it in the star wars defence program' who also invented a device that could connect to ANY ENGINE and allow it to run on his water fuel cell. He said that any water could run the engine. The voltage disassociation of water turns water into a gas, hydrogen and oxygen, released in the form of thermal explosive energy. Touted as one of the most important inventions of the century by the Advanced Energy Research Institute (another shopfront organisation to convince you they're working hard behind the scenes to achieve this). Meyers tried for fifteen years to get his invention on the market and, like the rest, eventually had to concede that one must be 'thick skinned' to deal with the megalithic lies and deceit perpetrated by the 'system' who already has all this technology behind the scenes and sure as hell doesn't want the average chump in the street to have it. Meyers stated that more times than not, as Tesla learned, inventions are stolen from the inventor and that he'd had patents taken from him. Similarly Keely refused to disclose what the vapour was or how he generated it taking out patents in "all the countries of the globe which issue patent rights" which cost him approximately $30,000. He demonstrated the 'vaporic gun' to government officials although it is apparent that the 'government' weren't interested and what ensued is the usual story of slander, disinformation, court orders, stockholder infighting, investigations. Despite his counsel stating he had invented the 'missing link' to make the 'vibratory resonator and ethereal generative evaporatory' a success the Philadelphia Press published an article that Keely's motor was 'a delusion and deception' and his mysterious forces were the result of 'trickery'. Described as 'pseudo-science' by Wikipedia it does not detract

RETURN OF THE TWINS

from THE FACT that in the 1860's, *160 years ago*, John Keely was describing the mechanical nature of vibratory electrical resonance to move objects in space also demonstrated by Canadian inventor John Hutchison which the 'Hutchison Effect' is named after demonstrating 'high voltage' system that caused objects to levitate and crystal energy generators that convert the slippery or 'jitter' of Zero Point Energy. Hutchison was also offered to collaborate with the Pentagon (old habits die hard) although, like Keely and Meyers before him he rightly declined.

UFOs were a type of 'dreadnought' technology and when you look up this term is says it is a 'fearless person' and a battleship callted Dreadnought. As a guitarist I'm quite familiar with this term as 'dreadnought' guitar type was designed to be larger bodied to accentuate louder, richer tones – frequencies – which is exactly the same as how they are designing and constructing these exotic crafts. What a crying shame that we live in a world overseen by such disgusting power abusing entities that they prefer to cut down trees thousands of years old and decimate this planet to create fear and desperation among an uneducated populace they are obsessed with own. Imagine if the Keely's, Tesla's, Meyer's and Hutchison's had built on their collective knowledge we would be living in a world so luminescent with this power, *literally*, that to comprehend the reality we find ourselves in would be nothing less than 'worst case scenario' and a total fucking nightmare.

The information for the technological power driving the so-called UFOs was provided to the Satanic aristocracy of the Third Reich and their 'thousand-year Reich' by demons who wish to use this technology to pass themselves off as being from 'another planet'. Reich means 'realm' so, the third 'thousand' year 'realm is the 3RD MILLENNIUM WE ENTER INTO NOW and they have a business plan that is ten centuries planned in advance. *That's* what you are dealing with and all of it to enforce the human race as servants, slaves, beneath these creeps, misfits and jaded fucked-up old men who cannot face the enormity of who they are. Instead, they prefer to only hold others down in their weak-minded boy's clubs rigging all this up in the shadows because if the light of day is ever cast upon their 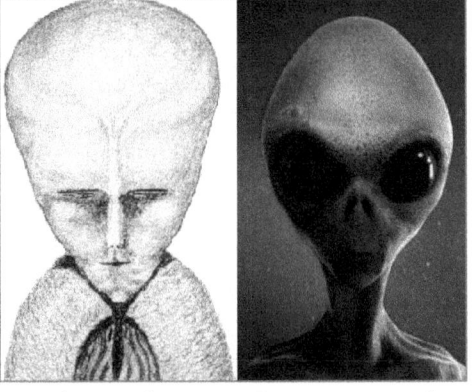 snivelling self-indulgence, there will not be a place in the universe that they can hide that the future of humanity will not seek them out and obliterate them with the very force they tried to use against us. The knowledge of this etheric vapour, CHI – PRANA, is the 'un-named force' as ancient as the Hindu Vedas that wrote about such things along with legends of 'flying craft' and 'sky gods' ten thousand years ago. The legends are true. The knowledge of the pranic force was handed to these satanic pieces of filth by demons whose evil spirits they channelled from under the Earth from whence they were 'cast into the abyss' by *Christ,* go figure – the christ light that allowed the intelligence to face off against this scum as found in the Bible legend. They were banished into massive cavern systems beneath the Earth *two millennia* ago during the last time they tried to come out and take over the world. *Right,* we have Aleister Crowley's spirit mentor and a grey alien. These occultists, in the desire for greed and power, have been duped by the same demons that duped them of old until they were discovered for what they were and were forced to go underground *again* then working through their satanic agencies found in the religions Catholicism at the head of the beast. They are not aliens, they are demons who are the 'greys' in cahoots with the 'reptilians' that came here some say up to 100,000 years ago, oh, but it's far less time than that! I would think this all started around 30,000 years ago maybe less.

It is this secret that *all* the secret societies headed up by the Roman Catholic Church (who are the continuation of ancient Rome) riding on the back of ancient Greek and the Ancient Egyptian concepts of civilisation, who have trampled and destroyed humanity using this power, this knowledge, stolen from us, to fulfill their pathetic plans. Religiously speaking the pecking order is as follows: 1) Jews, 2) Catholic Church, 3) Islam. Behind these three major male default power houses are the plethora of secret boy's clubs who have gone by many names throughout history. The secret boy's clubs of the Roman Senate saw their opportunity to amalgamate all the old gods into *one* slick new 'god'. He is 'Jesus' to ordinary people but for those behind the scenes he is Satan. They cannot sell this evil shit to ordinary people as intrinsically, despite being waylaid and abused, human beings are good people, otherwise we wouldn't have found ourselves in this position. The traitorous Roman Senate changed their image to the Roman Catholic Church to continue their ongoing reign of reptilian terror over humans and planet Earth for another 2,000 years. And now we're going around again, folks! *They're back!* Out of this lot you have all the royal households who went by many names in public and just as many secret societies in private including the Merovingians, the Knights Templars, The Sun Kings of France, as well as the Illuminati the Golden Dawn, the Vril Society, the Thule Society, the Skull and Bones society and all the global riff raff who pretend to be on opposite teams and then marry each other. It's all in the family. A hive mind of inbreeding insect hybrids who spliced their genetics with various animals in prehistory and fused themselves with the 'Golden Race' that once was humans! It is out of these ancient genetic experiments that you find the last of their 'missing link' found in the bigfoot phenomenon who also exhibit psychic abilities and 'shapeshifting' abilities found in native lore all around the world.

These secret societies who founded America was to bring about their greatest plans via the platform, *the stage*, America was always designed for. America is nothing but a theatrical performance of ancient male dogma in their attempt to frighten the world in crumbling before their feet. Their recruiting grounds for the next generation of private school boys and psycho factory future despots is found in the University 'fraternities' of the 'Pi Kappa Alpha', Tau Kappa Epsilon, Sigma Chi, Sigma Phi Epsilon and all the rest of the college Frat House nut jobs who love to utilise 'hazing', the practice of ritual intimidation, stress, and physical injury to those who wish to join their clubs via 'initiation'. Rings a bell. It was via secret societies, overarched by The Masons, that their offshoots found in the various states 'lodges' are recruited from University Frat houses with their Latin historical namesakes. They never change. They can't evolve. This is all laughed at endlessly in films they make about it 'Animal House' and American Pie among others. The various agencies and offices of the New World Order snap up rich kid psychos from this meat market who meet the preferred psychological profile ascending them up the ranks into politics and celebrity to continue the charade every bit as fake as the roots of the Catholic Church and their demonic control freakery particularly targeting the feminine, women, who they collectively refer to as the "goddess". They are behind the serial killings of women from the likes of Ted Bundy to the staged 'suicides' and 'accidents' of all the major feminine deaths in the last century including Whitney Houston-we-have-problem moon landing moon goddess, Princess Grace hail Mary full of Grace, Anna Nicole Smith, Nicole Brown Simpson, Marilyn Monroe, Diana Princess of Wales, Natalie Wood among many others. More recently they have included a blood bath of female celebrities during the

COLONY INSECT MIND

RETURN OF THE TWINS

Lions Gate portal, a goddess portal, an includes Anne Heche, Olivia Newton John, Judith Durham and Ivana Trump among MANY OTHERS. It's a ritual feminine slaying extravaganza in the year 2022, the year of the twins, of sex, of 11 enlightenment and the return of the high feminine alongside her high masculine who have all but been reduced to sniveling rats in a sewer colony!

It is no coincidence at all that the Nazis became NASA. It was designed that way to finish off the Biblical script nearing completion as I write. America, the 'shores to the West' are referenced in the mythical story of Melusine the two fish-legged goddess who was foretold to bring 'justice' to 'mermen' of the Western shores and punish them for hurting women. This legend alludes to the Reptilian political military juggernaut of America. Considering this is a story from Celtic, Welsh and British folklore, at the time, America was not supposed to be known to them *at all.* Why then are they talking of the 'shores to the West' given the only shores to the West are Canada and America? This story indicates that the famous 'mermaid' Melusine as found on the cups of the coffee franchise Starbucks, is laughed at as an inside joke as they invoke the very goddess prophesised to bring them down daring her to 'bring justice' to their cruelty toward Mother Earth, Mother Nature and women. They kill the goddess and openly laugh about it as found in the deaths of famous women under weird circumstances. Yet it is impossible for Melusine to punish these men for hurting women, the moral of the story at the core of this tale. It's an old fable that goes way back to prehistory like so many other legends and folklore that a woman, not a man, would bring justice to them.

Hitler escaped Germany after they had gained all the knowledge they required on mass people movement and mass people management as well as a mass sacrifice to their evil dark masters who give them the power and freedom to continue their ridiculous tirade against planet Earth. The Gnostic writings indicated that the world in which we live was ruled over by 'the god of the Jews' who favoured the Jewish nation over all others. This caused the other gods '*arkhôn*' (archons) to send a saviour, Jesus, from the highest realm of the 'Father' to 'rescue' humans who struggle under the oppression of this jealous god (Irenaeus 1.24.4). This the legend of the 'war in heaven' insinuates there are factions and that they are not all on the same team in 'heaven' aka space! But we know that 'archon' is basically a type of living animated deception, they are beings that don't *just* lie - they ARE lies, they are deception. Therefore, the 'angels and demons' bullshit is just *another layer* of lies in a greater show to convince humans that the hierarchy are 'angelic' when they are *all* demonic playing out a massive charade to distract us long enough to succeed in their plans of replacing us with them! *Humans* are the angels capable of transcending them yet they can't allow that so they play out this ridiculously complicated script to keep us hoodwinked and confused as to who's who! These creatures play out the hierarchy of their own 'gods' dressed up as saviours and destroyers, angels, cherubim, seraphim and archangels. Yet their desire is to con the human race and convince us that *they* are more important, like governments, 'Just leave it to us! We're on top of it! Now go back to your shopping like good little children of the gods!' They are trying to convince us, one way or another, into letting them stay but that cannot be. It does not turn out like that in an impossible turn of events that sees them removed *completely*.

'Jesus' was their representative to bring 'the light' or the 'fire' of enlightenment to Earth and Human's. But he is just *one* of theirs just as Yahweh/Jehovah or 'god' and Samael, the devil - the 'snake brother's, were delegates in a space empire conquering planets and solar systems in the Milky Way galaxy and probably beyond that as well. They are like the Klingon's in Star Trek who come from a war dimension and are at their core a type of mantis creature that has various allies or hybrids including the 'reptilian' race. Their spirits are the demonic realm called the 4th Dimension and may have come to Earth from Mars. Their behaviour is most obviously expressed in military rigidity unnatural to normal human 'flow' and 'grace' of Mother Earth and the feminine life force of Mother Nature found in Chi and Prana. The movie the Body Snatchers about pod people who appear as human is not far from the truth. They are born of 'pods' or 'eggs' and their rigid thinking and behaviour expresses itself in the rigid systems of the military and their desire for control freakery beyond anything humans are capable of. Their behaviour is 'ritualistic' but this is because firstly, they revere the power found in humans as 'godlike' whereas for us it's just normal and we must have taken it for granted at some time in the past leaving us open to their attack. They creates layers of ritual over these natural human functions firstly to vet out anyone who could threaten their operation, but also to instill a sense of fear as they routinely kill and sadistically murder anyone ensuring silence about their operations.

But this evil 'god' is rapidly losing patience with this lot as they have promised this Dark Lord that they will let him out, allow him to roam free, but they can never do that as they will lose their power over him. This is why the more power they get the shorter the time frame it is for them to retain that power as some dark force demands more and more in return for greater and greater secrets. That's one reason why the enacted WWI and WWII for blood sacrifice to these demons in order to 'buy' their opportunity to set up NASA and everything that has come after it. Once upon a time a mass sacrifice would sometimes buy them *decades*, even centuries, of power and 'peace' (their peace not anybody else's). But now huge sacrifices are barely allowing them another 12 months as they speed up their offerings in a mass vaccination death cull as well as the debasement and humiliation of millions of 'new age' people all 'identifying' as the most ridiculous and embarrassing distortions of 'gender' all of it underpinned by chemical and biological warfare jumbling-up their DNA and scrambling people's genetics until they're a bunch of fucken lunatics demanding you respect them for their insanity and unable to reason beyond their immediate whims. It's actually sad. This new generation would have been perfectly normal functioning people, even highly attuned artists and thinkers as the galactic wave of light frequencies increases and unlock their dormant DNA and chakras. That's if their *idiot* parents hadn't injected them with 36 to 72 vaccines by the age of six during the 1990's still going on now. It's a big plan. It's been in the pipelines for a long time. They've got you thinking chemical warfare is something Saddam Hussein did to the Kurds decades ago. No. Chemical and biological warfare is the mass drenching of society with poisons from food to water to medication with horrendous carcinogens and spraying operations killing children and turning people into morons before our eyes as more alignments in the heavens occur now than EVER BEFORE in history, but no one is caring. Nothing to see here. Just a coincidence it all is.

So, there you have it, the Nazis were building UFO's from as early as the 1920's getting their information on how to build them from the various occultic societies who tapped into the demonic realm hence, their scientists famously saying, 'we had help'. People assume this means aliens, but no, once again, the 'aliens' appear to be actual creatures living beneath the Earth which falls in line with so man native folklore tales about the creatures under the ground in subterranean cities. The Navaho whose 'ant' people traditional stories bear a striking resemblance to the 'greys and mantis stories  emerging now. These underground creatures are 'psychic' and 'interdimensional' insofar as they can work with the planes outside the current bandwidth of human ability, but we'll get there and then some! Via the various 'theosophical' type movements that came out of the late 1800's this technology and the plans to pull it of fall in line with planetary

RETURN OF THE TWINS

alignments of 2020 and potentially spell their doom just as happened two thousand years ago. Therefore, they aristocrats who have enjoyed such freedoms on this planet pre-empted us and selected the houses of German royalty to be their chosen ones to stitch up the human race via WWI, WWII and now the looming WWIII. Three's a charm! All of it at this time to cheat us out of our ascension. The Germans, by the way, are the House of Windsor through and through. They even spoke German in Buckingham Palace during the First World War and only changed their name to Windsor as it sounded more British. No wonder they were throwing up the Nazi salute in the 1930's as famously leaked by the *Sun* newspaper to much 'disappointment' of the palace. Disappointed because its true. *The Sun* (newspaper)! Sigh. No one in their position could claim to be ignorant of what Hitler's emerging policies on eugenics and 'racial hygiene' were about at the time. They knew and they were clearly onboard.

The network of boy's clubs-secret societies has always held the 'royal' or 'aristocratic' oath that they will stick to their own and will employ any and all methods to destroy humans *across the board*. Think about it. Every major war that has ever occurred sends your most talented, strongest, fittest, youngest and most virile men to DIE at each other's hands from *all countries all around the world.* You're being weakened. Bred out. Killed off. The only humans left after these strategic holocausts are the old and the infirm or those too sick to go. But there's always a reason to go and kill someone, so says the aristocracy. It's all about protecting boarders, don't you know? You mean those same boarders they threw open to hordes of incompatible fighting age men from underdeveloped cultures who went on then and *still* to rape and groom young English women ('English daughters' I believe it was referred to at the time, what a joke) who openly say they will use their own women to breed westerners out? I don't think they can do this I'm just outlining what THEY themselves have said as reported in mainstream media. In fact, nothing I'm talking about can't be found in the mainstream media as they struggle not to report growing subjects to an ever-confused populace slowly losing their composure with all the *weird* excuses and snowballing high-strangeness all around. So, boarders, right? Yeh. Your old grand dads would be spinning in their graves if they knew what they gave their lives for. They died for nothing as it stands now, and most people today have no karmic recourse turning their backs on their grand dad's sacrifices in favour of 'woke' togetherness. How fucking nice.

Once the Nazis, on behalf of their Western brother's and wider networks, had developed all the knowledge and techniques to be basically unstoppable, Hitler up and kills himself. Nazi bell UFO was affecting time

RETURN OF THE TWINS

and space with counter rotational torsion physics https://www.banned.video/watch?id=62c598b01039166673059482 The Russian's claimed they had the body of a guy who frankly looked like a bad Charlie Chaplin impersonator, what a joke, and turned out several decades later to be the bones of a *women*. Of course. The fact of the matter is that Hitler escaped via Tempelhof Airport through Spain a 'soft' ally who wouldn't commit to either side. Tempelhof is *Temple Hove* a ritual grove for the Knights Templars who are the Masons, the Scottish Rite of Freemasonry, the Illuminati *and* all the rest of them – same guys, different names, it's how they rebrand just like their 'gods'. It's an old trick. The masters of disguise. Hang on a minute? You mean Portugal and Spain could just remain neutral? How nice for them because…it's global war…and you can choose, apparently. Pick a side! Any side! Roll up! Roll up! Via Operation Paperclip thousands of German elite scientists (royal academics) were transported to America and there's any wonder why heavily accented Euro politicians were so prevalent during the 90's and 00's when America was bought to its knees via the farce of 9/11 sacrifice were telling us they are going to make a 'global war on terror'…? Wtf? But we already know about 9/11 - it was a 'Saviour Goddess' and Family of Life death ritual to symbolically destroy the prophecy of humanities ascension and global freedom in the Age of Aquarius. Is it any wonder America has so many little Hitler's running and ruining the place? Hitler escaped via Spain and using submarines was transported to Argentina who had quite a large German population. It was all set up in advance. They had secured a base in the South Pole, New Schwabenland, an area that is warmed via natural thermal springs that can produce temperate zones totally livable for humans as depicted in the 1939 classic flick *Lost Horizon*, seriously, check out that film, it's a must see.

Just as a side, in 1959 the Antarctic Treaty was signed by 12 nations including Argentina, Australia, Belgium, Chile, France, Japan, New Zealand, Norway, South Africa, United Kingdom, United States and USSR to ensure that this *region remain free of the military and nuclear waste*. They keep *their* back yard clean. To date another 54 countries have signed the treaty. It the lead up to WWII Germany claimed it had discovered an ancient archeological site beneath the Antarctic ice accessible by submarine. It's Indiana Jones for sure! These bases are not just a few outposts, it is a city beneath the sea with massive metropolitan capabilities and they are plotting against the whole world and the human race *from there*, safe from prying eyes far away in the arse end of the world! It's perfect. No one gets in that they don't allow in. No one can see what they are doing. It's and ice

RETURN OF THE TWINS

fortress. To this day the Antarctic remains Operational HQ for the *UFO phenomena* strangely tormenting largely *South American* countries along with all the weirdness of increasing 'cryptid' sightings and disappearances. It's the Boys From Brazil meets The Island of Dr Moreau meets Close Encounters of the Third Kind, *literally*! The UFO-German 'alien' front is a perfect way for the demonic realm to pass themselves of as 'spacemen' when really, they are from beneath the Earth and have been waiting for this opportunity to come out for millennia. When the biblical 'Legion' of demons was cast into the 'abyss' thousands of years ago they were literally talking about a hole in the ground, huge caverns beneath the Earth. Bill Cooper talked about this in the 1990's and so too did Phil Schneider both of whom died under weird circumstances. The 'abyss' is also a reference to frequencies and 'dimensional' access to our plain of existence from the 'lower' dimensions via the human psychic-astral realm that these demons are capable of utilising to access us, see, the plethora of 'paranormal' activity people are increasingly dealing with in their homes! More people than ever before are reporting 'shadow beings', demons, poltergeists, ghosts and weird terrifying phenomena as they are under attack inside their houses! No doors can keep them out. Repetitive spikes were recorded in the Shuman Resonance detected *at the same time* CERN unleashed its *greatest levels of power* to date causing many people worldwide to suspect a 'Stranger Things' type phenomena could be at work. The following day the Georgia Guidestones were conveniently blown up causing much of the world the cheer but it's just more *distraction* to make the global population believe that we are having a win when in reality, these psycho scientists are doing weird and spiritually illegal things opening portals and creating more psychic chaos in the world.

The name Mengele means trader, merchant, salesman (especially of slaves), a peddler, a stall holder. This is interesting as it was the 'merchants' and 'traders' of old that started all this false commerce and money systems in the first place that has taken over the world and replaced the natural state of freedom with a price on mother nature's head. *Scarcity is the currency* in an abundant world given the 'world TRADE center' was a massive sun ritual dedicated the Hermes the 'god of trade' and 'contracts' who rules over the 'throat', the speaker, the voice! He is the devil and another Satan character who symbol is the tantric spine caduceus from where he, THEY, get the intelligence to pull all this off! The New York Times reported that The Mossad, Israeli intelligence, had not even bothered to try and find Joseph Mengele. According to the report dated Sept 6th 2017, the Mossad documented that the Red Cross furnished

RETURN OF THE TWINS

Mengele with false documentation that allowed him to escape and that they were aware they were helping a Nazi war criminal. Mengele then fled to Argentina in 1948 the prime destination for so many of Hitlers henchmen including Hitler himself. While Mengele initially lived under a false name he reverted to his real name and there was even a major Hollywood blockbuster, The Boys From Brazil, made about his exploits in South America. They're not even trying to hide it and people line up and watch this shit and think nothing of it? ...and...pandemic...and...mass injections...because...it's fiction. South America is now a place where UFO sightings abound and strange cryptids and weird events rock that region almost daily. The Mossad file on Mengele stated that the German ambassador in Buenos Aires received orders to treat Mengele as an *ordinary citizen* since there was *no arrest warrant out for him.*

The coming fake 'alien' invasion is simply the final stages of complete and utter chaos in the lead up to revealing a 'one world leader'. This leader will crack down on the inordinate number of criminals they have *allowed* to take over everyday life of decent society. They have deliberately allowed a debased state to fester to offer the 'solution', a hard-nosed but highly attractive *charismatic* young male leader to save you from the demons in the street and the aliens in the sky. You will love him. He will be bisexual to fit the whole LGBT and trans Baphomet/Satan character who is a male-female-beast. Even now we are seeing the early versions of this as the self-described 'coolest dictator in the world', the young leader of El Salvador, has taken a particularly hard approach to the thousands of gang members who have taken over their country. With a 70% approval rating from the people, he has arrested *ten thousand* gang members and warned that if their 'home boys', gang leaders, retaliate against him or the policing forces, he will simply stop feeding the prisoners in jail and they will starve. Simple solution. There has been little retaliation as quite obviously the incarcerated will not look favourably upon their gang leaders if they are left to starve. Catch 22. My point is you will be seeing many more 'heroic' YOUNG leaders emerge now to take back our world from the criminals, and people will love them for it but its just more of the script again, more distraction.

COVID DETENTION CENTRE

AUSCHWITZ DEATH CAMP

RETURN OF THE TWINS

I'm not saying the El Salvadorian leader is a bad guy, on the contrary, it's amazing what he's doing. On the other hand, the level of violence and organised crime in South American countries is a *direct result* of the Nazi influence over that region due to their ongoing proximately in the Antarctic region, Operational HQ for 21st century Nazis continuing their quest for world domination along with their American masonic *brothers* distracting you with all the craziness while they work on the final stages of global BIBLICAL dominance from the South Pole. But what you are not hearing about is the reports of mass UFO sightings, weird laboratory cryptids roaming the countryside killing people and livestock and all manner of weird demonic entities that are being conjured up by this club of devil worshippers who have long since had any allegiance to the human race or any mind of their own. They have been completely possessed and are the robotized automatons of entities from a dark realm. A realm that is intruding more and more into the daily lives of people until there are millions of videos being uploaded of people literally doing battle *in their homes* against these filthy demons and evil entities from a darkness that they had *always promised* to return from and bring TO LIFE the horrors Hollywood movies told you were *fiction!* As said, Hollywood is the psychological warfare division of the Nazi-Templar-Masonic-Satanic-Aristocratic war machine *from hell*, and this is their final stand! By the way, the video recordings of poltergeist phenomenon is strikingly similar in its 'slippery' movements as anti-gravity levitation of electromagnetic exotic craft. It's the same force as such, the 'poltergeist' phenomenon is a combination of invisible entities, 'cloaked' military agents, remote technology and negatives energy. See right, a depiction of Jesus at the Vatican looking like a half man half reptile T-rex! This is their secret belief system that the 'returner', the One, Jesus Christ is a reptilian 'god' born in the flesh and he is coming to save the world but save it for who? Them or us? Here's a hint, it doesn't look like it's shaping up too well for humans. Don't expect any mercy from them and I suggest you treat them the way they have treated you. Masons call themselves 'widow's sons' because they believe they are from the line of Christ and *Mary* was widowed when Jesus died.

They believe Jesus was an enlightened hybrid, a reptilian sun king!

WHAT HAPPENED TO HUMANITY & HOW IT WORKS TODAY

RETURN OF THE TWINS

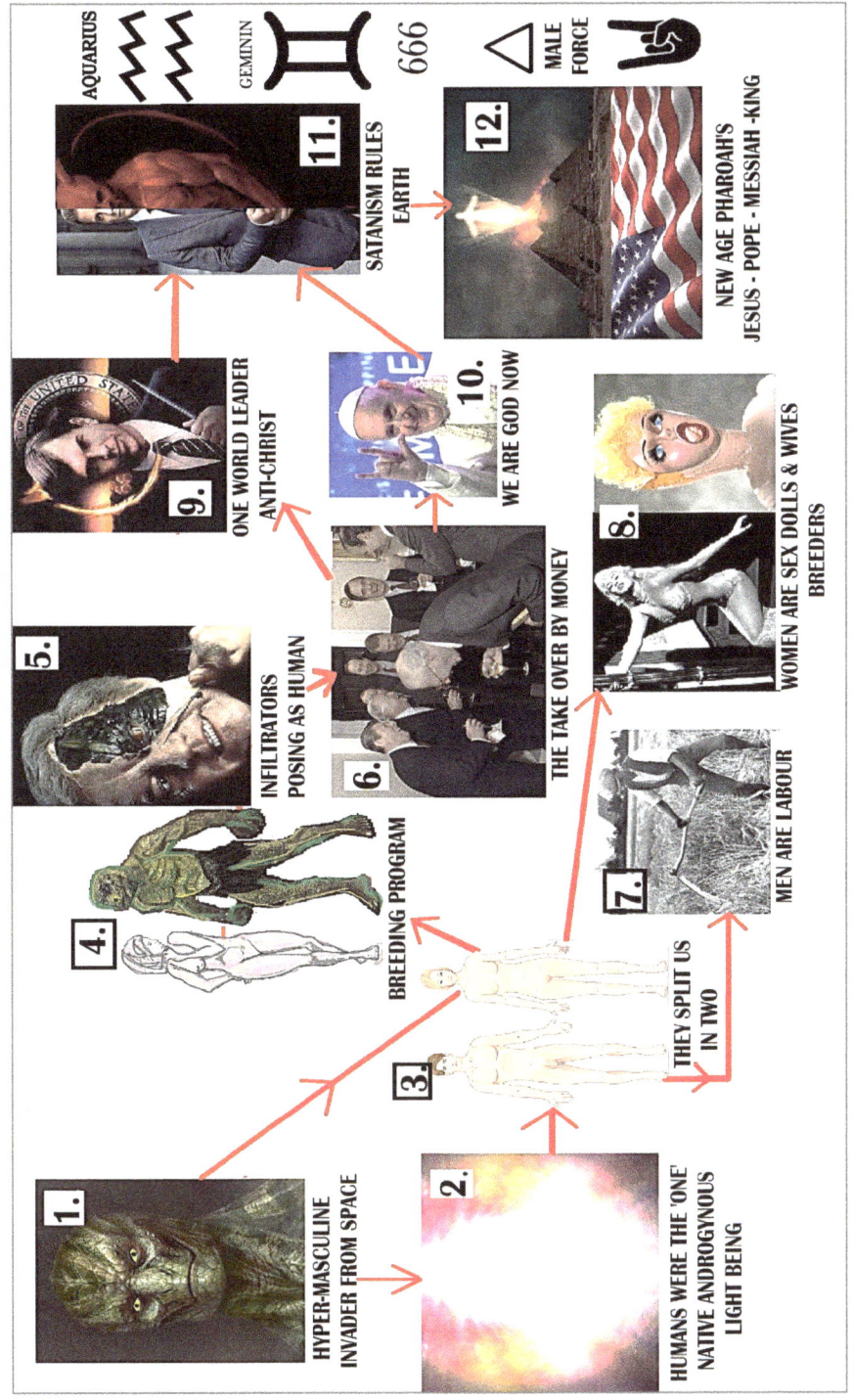

Chapter Fourteen

Children of Destiny
Humans have a destiny beyond the Stars. Humans are free.

The human race was prophesised many eons ago to come out of the dark trap they set for us that we unwittingly fell into. There is no other way around this, it is supposed to be, and so, the evil ones are trying to set it up to make out that it is their destiny via an elaborate charade to present humans as 'bad' and them as 'good', to steal our destiny from us and stand in our place to the wider cosmos. It is not going to be easy for them to pull this off as every indication is that, despite the ridiculous odds against us, we will prevail and continue on our rightful path into the future and beyond to rejoin with the Universe and emerge as triumphant returned to a state of bliss as the true 'gods'. Without the open third eye we cannot 'see' heaven and without the 'christ' body, the light body, we cannot get there or 'fly' there. It takes time to create the christ body, some say many decades via transcendental sex, and we are being endlessly stalled so we simply don't have the time to achieve this before they close the net on humans and our race is lost forever. We cannot successfully enter into the Aquarian age unless we are activated and will simply wind up the fools and pawns of another reptilian age of gluttony only this time, we will never get out. They are already laughing about how they have us already trapped FOREVER. As far as they are concerned it's over and we have lost – they have won – and successfully transplanted our species with theirs.

When humans die, we are not going to heaven, they are harvesting our souls into a 'middle realm' like a computer program. The matter of ascension is simply a matter of tantric sex chakra opening so why haven't all these people who have passed over or contacted the other side simply told us this little fact? It's all fake and psychics, however clever, are tapping into only a small degree of reality. Why is it that when a person dies and comes back, they simply don't say 'I've been to the other side, and they told me we can open our chakras and get out of here if we practice tantric sex'. Why do they never come back with information like that? It's because the realm they are going to is an in-between realm where this information is not made available to them and when our souls return and we are 'reincarnated' which every religion, even the bible, claimed was happening up until recently. They wipe our memory 'between lives' so we can't bring this information back with us. It's really quite simple only the reasons for why we haven't received this knowledge before now is not as simple to answer unless of course, it's a big giant computer hack and we are caught in a fake 'reality' matrix broadcast from a very limited area surrounding our planet. ***INSERT THE SHUNTING THING***

The vibrations of the language we use is creating our surroundings in many ways is another layer of the puzzle, another layer of the conspiracy, to keep us locked in. They know all the dirty tricks to keep us trapped inside their preferred reality which involves rituals on certain spots to keep the Earth's chakras closed as well as unnatural technology, the 'system' of depression and scarcity, the 'religions' telling us we're bad all the time, the 'politics' to keep us focused on a fake ways to get out of this mess, the celebrities to give us a sense of hierarchy and that someone else is better than us, the space program that keeps our attention on childish fake technology while they use the real stuff for themselves, the poisons in food and water to make us weak, the education system to tell us lies from cradle to grave, the money system to keep us begging like peasants not able to work our way out of it, the short life spans that are not long enough to really achieve anything let alone figure anything out. It's a fucking BIG demonic 'reality' PROJECT indicating they must be so desperate to go to such lengths to keep us inside this massive illusion. For what reason? If we are so low down on the spiritual ladder, then why all the rigmarole to keep us down? Simply, without us, without our light, they will die. Without us their demonic empire ends. Without us they are nothing. Without them we are everything and can ascend to the 'highest of the high' where they can't touch us ever again. It's been done before, it can happen again. We need to completely shift the culture in order to manifest, realise and speed up, our ability to access the ascension points that we are sadly missing out on now. **INSERT THE COSMIC ALIGNMENTS OF 2020*** They are desperate for you not to attain the knowledge of your own tantric enlightenment as it is via this method that Wonder Woman and Superman can 'time travel'. That's right. You read that correctly. Time travel.

In the astral there is no space and no time. You are omnipresent. You are anywhere and everywhere you wish to be at any moment in time or space the moment you think it. This is why these dark masters have coveted this knowledge so powerfully because it is they who are building this reality to suit themselves. But you can go back, you can right the wrongs. Imagine what it would be like if you could go back to a pivotal moment in your life, a moment that changed everything for the worse. The moment YOU KNOW ruined your life. The moment you never told that loved one not to drive out on the highway because you 'had a bad feeling'. The moment you let your kid got to the store and they never returned. The day you let the love of your life walk away because you were too stupid to realise how rare it is to fine 'the one'. The day you became one of those people. A statistic. A terrible statistic. Imagine if you could go back to the moment when you knew something irreparable had happened. What would your life be like now? What if you could go back? The first film Christopher Reeve did after Superman (considering this practice makes you into the proverbial 'superman' and 'wonder woman'), he did a film called Somewhere in Time about travelling back to the place in history where his true love existed. The film insinuated that the manager of the actress played by Jane Seymour (also the name of one of Henry VIII's wives in a twist of replication, again) had done the same thing. These two men who through the force of their will and desire projected themselves into another 'time'. Christopher Reeve new a lot more about this that he let on, they destroyed him for all this and he took a massive pay cut to play the role of the time travelling lover.

Via transcendental sex you can traverse the space-time continuum and access the 'past' to warn yourself or give yourself information that will change the course of your life. That's why its called 'transcendental' as you are transcending astral 'barriers' and is the true secret f Hermes who 'crossed borders' as were female goddesses known for doing the same thing. It's a power, not a gender. In my first book 2020 & Beyond, I said and, in the end, 'all wrongs will be righted'. I couldn't know back then what that meant but this is one answer to this statement. Many people believe that as life has turned out that somehow 'that's life' or 'gods will' and 'just the way it is' or worse 'it's meant to be'. This is all bullshit. God does not work in 'mysterious' way. The god they have you believing in who finds it necessary to keep knowledge and life away from his 'children', is an alien overseer from the depths of space that came here long ago to enslave the 'Golden Race' that is Humanity. They are not 'older' than us. Humans are the oldest living species in the universe. We were there from the beginning of it all. Born of light. Made of light. Made of the highest vibration that can exist and this is exactly why they coveted us in the first place. They came to steal our light. They came to break us down and infiltrate us to make us like them but more importantly to make them like us. They then used this power of light transcendence to manipulate a fabricated 'timeline' that they themselves locked us into by switching off our psychic centres, our DNA, our brain, our subconscious, our chakras and our pineal gland third eye. Time does not intrinsically exist. It is a sense of time and so-called 3D reality that is nothing more than a groove in a vinyl record. It is a limited bandwidth that is only possible to achieve by switching off our higher senses. They turned off vast areas of our 'computer' body to limit our access to the All, to everything that was already ours. They then dole out 'reality' to those willing to play along, do them favour's and keep their silence while a massive fraud is perpetrated again humans and our planet Earth. They become gods then 'knowing good and evil', eternals. This is Santa 'making a list, checking it twice. Gonna find out who's naughty and nice". Santa is Satan the 'god' of good and evil who works in mysterious ways. But they are a poor copy for the real thing, us.

They pass their consciousness, their spirit and memories, down through the generations of people they attach to in certain family lineages, certain bloodlines. They then emerge again and again knowing the 'tree of life' and 'living eternally'. Who knows how far back this goes? Ten thousand? One hundred thousand? A million years? How many times has this happened? They say it's the end of a 26,000 year cycle, the big one, or just another big one. They have done this before many times. The opportunity to get out of the alien astro-trap rolls around every 2,000 years when the zodiac sign changes in the sky and massive portals open allowing clearer signals from the galactic core triggering action, memory, clarity of thought, confidence and spiritual 'awakening'. Yet every 12,000 years, or half cycle of the galactic zodiac, the possibility for awakening increases exponentially as happened 12,000 years ago when Atlantis fell into the ocean, or was it pushed? As we enter the Age of Aquarius, the full 26,000 year cycle or '12 o'clock' on the galactic clock (hence, the online platform 'Tik Tok' and all the creepy demonic shit and 'non gender specific' 'woke' weirdness from the poisoned next generation in the 'final countdown'), it is at this time that they employ really dirty tactics like hitting us with 'asteroids', 'melting' us from space in the form of 'solar flares' and at the ground level utilising weather weapons as is becoming the norm as massive storms and bush fires wreak havoc across the world particularly in America and Australia. Australia represents the 'underworld' or the root chakra while America represents the 'upperworld' or the crown chakra, heaven and hell in balance, in alignment. But it's not in alignment, it's a massive ritual. All the environmental disasters are just weapons deployed from space to look like 'natural' disasters, so we don't cotton on to just how vast and how advanced this space empire really is. This is the reason behind the 'flood' of the bible when humans, once again, were ascending and were destroyed, our memories collectively wiped, as we were plunged into the darkness of ignorance and struggle as evolution was reset – AGAIN. This is why they are talking of the 'great reset' because they have reset us many time. This reset is the meaning behind the 'tower of babel' when the people were evolving once again and were 'destroyed by god' (the alien empire) in one of the few admissions of guilt recorded in history in their attempts to mind fuck us into servitude beneath them again.

There are layers to the hierarchy and the so-called biblical 'hierarchy of angels' of the 'cherubin' the 'seraphim' and the 'angels' who are simply levels of management and NOT angels at all, they are demons, hybrids and aliens purporting to be 'angelic' and our helpers. Where's the help? We're being decimated here! **INSERT ANGELS AND HIERARCHY** Therefore, in the attempt to keep us from escaping as has been foretold for thousands of years, the happily ever after in every folktale worldwide, they have hit us with Hollywood the minding bending psychological warfare division of the alien empire, they have hit us with 'icons' in the form of false celebrity heroes, they have hit us with 'politics' and 'government' in the hope to convince us it's not about the return of the 'king' and some family's 'divine right to rule' as Charles comes on the throne in 2022. They've hit us with endless distraction wars to make us believe other humans in a different parts of the world are our enemies, they hit us with clandestine attacks on the public when obvious murders are passed of a 'suicide' by the false legislature who posture as our 'law' (what a joke). In its most recent 'evolution', they have hit us since the mid 1990's with massively increased poisons, injections, pharmaceuticals as 'health' and then hit us with the smiling assassin, the mass media. This is why they will have the same news anchor present the news for DECADES to deliver lies via a 'trusted' face who has informed you since childhood. It's very Orwellian. The media are there to explain it all away and play on your low self-esteems that have been drilled into us for eons that THEY are better, THEY are smarter, THEY have it all under control, that THEY are MORE somehow than silly little us! YOU. They are not better or smarter and this will become increasingly apparent as we step into the light of our own power with tantric sex enlightenment and wash them away with our newfound confidence, intelligence, psychic abilities and astral capabilities.

There is such a phenomenon as the 'doorknob' sacrifices and includes Michael Hutchence (who actually hung himself from the door closing mechanism), David Carradine, Alexander McQueen, Aaron Swartz, L'Wren Scott, Robin Williams, Chris Cornell, Chester Bennington, Avicii, Kate Spade, Queen Maxima's sister Ines Zorreguieta and Anthony Bourdain. There is 12 in all to represent the zodiac signs. In the film Free Birds (a reference to the feminine) starring Owen Wilson (who strangely made an attempt on his life prior to this). The film is about turkey's being killed for Thanksgiving and they build the whole animated movie around the 'magical doorknob' and can travel back in time to save 'take turkey off the menu'. This is a metaphor for the human race and the 'doorknob' is a reference to a penis 'knob' and the ability to transcend time and space via tantric sex. Acetol Colene are neurons firing high voltage impulses into the forebrain and these impulses become pictures and these pictures become dreams, but no one knows why we choose these particular pictures. They have figured all this out, they know the science behind it all, they know what they are doing. The data has been gathered. The experiment is over. So, the 'doorknob' killings is certainly one of the weirder rituals but this is what it means and why so many have had their icon associated in a negative sense with the 'knob'. They are trying to associate our tantric abilities with death or worse, self-killing.

The number of Jesus is 888 as was the number of Apollo – the devil – and when combined 888+888=1776 the year of America's 'Independence' from old world royalty. Jesus and the Devil are considered spiritual brothers as this really means the 'balance' between the light and dark side of the masculine. In short, it means that one can transcend into the bliss of high frequency or 'god' but in order to get there, you are going to have to deal with some dark stuff and get tough when the time comes. I don't mean just throwing your dark side around willy nilly, I mean taking decisive action and being responsible about your powers. You will have to make some dire decisions, and this is what 'knowing good and evil' is all about. It's about being able to balance out the energies for the enrichment of our world without being piss weak about it and singing 'shiny happy people holding hands' in some 'peace, love and light' bullshit fest where you just say 'blessings' and your work is done. Don't kid yourself, this is no walk in the park, and don't believe for one minute that your righteousness and even your 'rights' are enough to save you now. You'll need more than that. And the information and the ability to put it into practice are at hand but you must be brave now. You must turn away from the cowards and saboteurs in your ranks, the traitors, and those seeking to stall you. Leave them to their end. Leave them behind. We have been stalled long enough in our kind attempts to bring as many with us over the finish line. Don't be heroes for the idiots to get you killed. The multitudes of morons are going to take you down their stupidity easily relied on by the satanic cabal to do the knock off job on their peers and allies. Fuck em. We will never turn away a person in need of genuine help, we will however, not reveal our hearts or our weak spots without the due protection of our armour of honour, the armour of 'god' as the christ seed torus field was once rightly called. It is our protection from evil and darkness and we cannot risk all that we can achieve out of it just to be 'nice'. These zealots were going to kill us all and use the idiots in our ranks to help them do it. Despite the ridiculous odds against us and no matter how much it hurts, we must do our duty now to save the future of planet Earth and Humanity to continue our quest into enlightenment as was prophesised and fought for by every person of good intentions throughout history in every age and every civilisation of this world. We must put purpose to their sacrifice at long last. It is more than us. It is more than fear. It is more than faith. It is a duty bound by blood, born of light and carved in stone, forever!

What we are seeing is the deliberate and manifest programs that have slowly been building and eating away at America, deliberately creating a situation where the black communities of America have been so diminished that they barely resemble the black communities of the 1960's or certainly the 1980's when TV shows like the Cosby Show aired with dignified middle class (African) Americans creating a NORMAL existence for themselves contributing to society and feeling a sense of accomplishment and inclusion. But the agencies of the Devil, the CIA front and centre shortly followed by the FBI, have been chewing away at the foundation of the black American population shipping in HUGE quantities of drugs initially targeted for 'fun' and 'party' in the cool new world culture that America was. This MASSIVE drug program operating out of South America could not have become so successful and there was major complicity in their land and sea agencies who turned a blind eye to MOST of it while occasionally busting a 'token' operation to at least appear as if they were doing their jobs. The real 'job' was to target the African American communities across the country to destabilise them with drug addiction and increasingly shittier more toxic drugs until pure cocaine (from an actual tree) became 'crack', 'crank' (just look at the names of these despicable elixir of demons) until now you have the 'opioid' epidemics across America until we arrive at the weird 'Fentanyl' epidemics DESTROYING huge swathes of Americans and decimating entire cites until it literally looks like a John Carpenter dystopia from the 1980's sci fi arthouse films. It's all about psychology to prevent you from accessing your enlightenment and activating your crown chakra and to also ritually destroy the prophecy of enlightenment and freedom that the ancients KNEW would happen if we just got this information, then the time would come when the world would ascend via this knowledge. So, what the Satanic club of demons, aliens and hybrid reptiles posing as humans do, is set up your heroes in advance to 'give you a chance' via social mentors promoted via Hollywood, politics, and mainstream media. Then they kill your heroes, break your heart, make you poor and lead you to destruction but hey, you had a chance, why didn't you take it? They would have the universe believe that they tried to help you but you're too dumb to get it

RETURN OF THE TWINS

so...I guess they'll have to kill you and take your world. They do this because there is some type of karma that they are terrified of and so they must get YOU to take the blame for their injustice and crimes against you. This is why Martin Luther King had to die. The King of Pop, Michael Jackson, had to be ruined and killed, King Kong (the black 'monkey' man) was 'shot off the tower' as the 'tower' is the chakra tower and why Jim Carry played Liar Liar with 'Tower Air' as in Earth, Air, Fire and Water where he played a secret cameo of the 'fire' marshal as the 'fire' of tantric christ enlightenment electricity is where they get their talent from. He's openly talked about it and nearly got taken down as a result. Here's Jim Carry with his MANY references to tantric sex including the shit they have to go through to get the knowledge from the secret club. **INSERT IMAGE NUMBER 115** In the Cable Guy he invites his victim to their own family's home answering the door saying, 'Get in here, ya psycho!' because they have to be psychos to get to the top.

Carry openly admitted tantra describing how it works and suddenly found himself on the receiving end of a 'wrongful death' lawsuit filed by the family of his deceased girlfriend. He stopped talking about it then. Yet he has played the 'green man' a few times as well as the enlightened guru in Ace Ventura When Nature Calles. It's an unenviable position to be in known as the Cassandra Syndrome when one knows information yet us unable to do anything about it. He even alludes, as does Adam Sandler with the 'Water Boy', that he is a 'puppet', a 'Yes' Man, and 'Liar Liar' doing what he's told. Although he stopped talking about the process of tantra he used the cover of philosophers to share further insight into the true realm of mental and emotional freedom saying, "After knowing Eckhart Tolle for a while and studying the books, I woke up and suddenly got it. I understood suddenly how thought is just illusory, and that thought is responsible for most, if not all of the suffering we experience. And then I suddenly felt like I was looking at thoughts from another perspective, and I wondered, who is it that is aware that 'I' am thinking? And suddenly I was thrown into this expansive amazing feeling of freedom - from myself, from my problems. I saw that I am bigger than what I do, bigger than my body. I am everything and everyone. I am no longer a fragment of the universe. I am the universe." He even played a cameo of a 'fire' chief as does Adam Sandler play a 'fire' man in Mr. Deeds. In the first movie called Mr. Deeds Goes To Town made in 1936 (369 is electricity) Deeds' first name is Longfellow, as in big dick, which they often portray as a large green cucumber or 'American Pickle', a big reptilian knob. I'll let you do that math on that one...and yes, America is in a pickle... and psycho reptilian politicians, talentless fucks may I add, have taken them into that place. But you must have a creative mind, a true vision to understand the potentially of what is lost here.

Another example of this leaking of information covertly via entertainment, and I mean all entertainment from 'fan' x-box type online gaming plotlines to Monkey Magic, it's all there and people will see exactly what I mean once this knowledge becomes readily available. Free Birds, considering 'birds' is slang for feminine, is an animated movie about Reggie 'the smartest 'gobbler' in his flock. This is a reference to the bisexual lives they are groomed from childhood into living, a 'gobbler' is fellatio, in this story it is dressed up as a turkey. Many of them must feel like turkey's knowing the depravity of what drives this dark agenda. **INSERT THE LAZY MOON EYE OF THE TIME TRAVELLING FEMININE GULLIBLE** His fellow 'turkeys' are being fattened up for consumption come Thanksgiving in 'November', the 11 again, yet his dumbed down fellow turkey are 'happily ignorant'. Can you see how well this correlates to what is actually happening? In reality, the few smart ones trying to show the dumb ones the way but they won't listen until it's too late for everyone. I'm not going down with them. I'm no coward. Reggie meets a muscular bird brain with a magic time travelling doorknob and 'these two turkeys from opposite sides of the track must put aside their differences and team up' that leads them to a time machine and they 'travel back in time' to the very first thanksgiving 'to change the course of history and get 'turkey' off the menu for good'. Turkey is humans and the time travelling 'muscular' turkey is a reptilian and the time travelling 'doorknob' is just 'knob', the tantric penis. As Arizona Wilder said in her interview with David Icke that it's possible to travel up and down the timeline. Regardless, they are both turkeys and 'fall guys', stupid, duped into a situation that neither of them can benefit from. Via tantric sex or the 'doorknob' aka the 'nob', a penis, we can maneuver along to timeline as outside 3D reality 5D has no time and no space. You can go anywhere in the past, present and possibly even the future. Reggie, played by Owen Wilson says, 'I can travel back into the past and give my former self information to change my life'. The evil dark forces beyond have the whole game sewn up as Wilson had already made a 'suicide attempt' back in 2007. It's almost as if something is preempting us. So, the precedence is set, if he or anyone goes much further than a cursory and cryptic insight into the power of tantric sex, you guessed it, Robin Williams style.

The 'doorknob suicides' are a series of bazaar celebrity suicides 'hanging' themselves via doorknobs...again this is a ritual to cast negativity onto the 'knob' or in this case, tantric sex. The obvious question would be, a doorknob is so close to the ground, the automatic response of the body would be to kick out and stand up. It's not a decision one makes, its an inbuilt instinctual reaction to a life-threatening situation that is easily remedied. The 'doorknob' ritual killings are as follows: Michael Hutchence, David Carradine, Alexander McQueen, Aaron Swartz, L'Wren Scott, Robin Williams, Chris Cornell, Chester Bennington son of Roger Podesta (nothing going on there then), Avicii, Kate Spade wife of David Spade's brother her husband seen days later walking around in public with a mouse mask on from the Disney cartoon The Rescuers from the Avengers franchise that includes 'Avengers Endgame', Ines Zorreguieta the sister of the Dutch Queen Maxima who stepped down after allegation of 'hunts' were exposed where children were raped and massacred by her dinner guests who was found dead hanging from a doorknob aged 33 the tantric spine, and Anthony Bourdain who made a series of weird Tweets about Hillary Clinton's knowledge of Harvey Weinstein's predatory sexual behaviour – so much more to know about this one.

So many reptilian actors are the most dangerous insofar as there is an 'artist meets public servant' prophecy / fable from ancient times, the voice, the speaker, comes out of a creative field with a social conscience or as Queen Victoria said, 'Beware of artist, they mix with all classes of society and are therefore the most dangerous. This is because the 'devil' was musician cast out of heaven replicated in this story as a space hierarchy when really 'heaven' is enlightenment which is useless without freedom. So, this 'devil' seeks to rejoin the real world instead of assisting fakers to build a fake one where they will be subservient to talentless fucks, politicians, forever and that aint fun. I can't imagine with all the power and freedom they enjoy that they want to go back to battlements and fucken pomp of old-world royalty. Hang onto what you've got, guys, don't throw America away or you'll be stuck with Prince Charles for the next thousand years…oh, yay. On the right is a portrait Sylvester Stallone did of Michael Jackson describing him as 'evil' but also covertly describing himself. This image looks distinctly reptilian with an 'alien-demon' shadowing him as THIS IS EXATLY HOW IT'S DONE. Stallone's son died strangely, named Sage Moonblood Stallone he died aged 36 although his date of birth is listed on his gravestone, the date of his death is not considering he died on Friday 13th 2012. Stallone's 'extortionist' sister died the following month.

Another big God-Goddess assassination was Rodney King who by the way, was beaten to a bloody pulp on 3rd March – 3rd day 3rd month – this is 33 of the tantric spine of the 'king'. King was an Aries as Aries rules the Crown chakra (crowned king). He was born in 1965 as 1+9=10 which reduces to 1 and 6+5=11 and this becomes another 111 trinity goddess, the tarot Empress, killing as the 'black king' dies before he can unite with the 'black queen' aka The Goddess, the Mother of all Gods. 'The One' who is supposed to return and save us and why Neo in the Matrix is a digital saviour and anagram of One and also, neo is 'new' – new saviour. Rodney King was one of five children as the Goddess of creation gave birth to 'five' offspring'. His mother's name was Odessa which is a boy's and girl's name but more leans toward a feminine name (this is the androgynous queen of the Universe symbolism). The name Odessa in its root word Indo-European/Hellenic/Greek is Odysseus and means 'wrathful' - this is God the 'mysterious' sky father whose wrath kills everyone because he loves them. In Greek myth the name inspired Homer's 'The Odyssey' which means an 'epic voyage' or a 'big adventure' – I'm sure it is a big adventure for the alien controllers from outer space – just one more shore to conquer. Odysseus was the husband of Penelope whose name means 'weaver' of 'weaving' spells which means influencing 'probabilities' to create he desired outcome (ideal for them) and he was most famous for the Trojan War and his 'Trojan Horse' ploy to capture the city of Troy. Odysseus in Latin is Ulysses who was the 18th President of America. The ritual just keeps unfolding hence, the 'weaving'. The beating of Rodney King (note the name 'Rod' as in 'thy rod and thy staff comfort me' as it's a reference to the phallus and tantric sex King Dick) led to the LA Riots. **INSERT IMAGE NUMBER 118**

On Father's Day, June 17th, 2012, Rodney King was found dead at the bottom of his pool 28 years TO THE DAY his father ALSO died found dead in a bathtub as 'the father becomes the son'…but not in this story. The old bathtub routine again, see, Whitney Houston-we-have-problem AND her daughter also found dead in a bathtub – nothing going on there then! King was transported to Arrowhead Regional Medical Centre as 'arrowhead' represents 'fire' and the bow Sagittarius and Cupid the cherub who fires the 'arrow' of fire (DC direct current masculine electricity like a fire burst from a gun or the 'fires of his loins') igniting the hearts of the lovers because True Love reigns from the heart flames as depicted by the MARRIED COUPLE that Jesus and Mary were often pointing to their 'passion of the christ' at the heart chakra, the 'flames of desire' because a relationship with 'spark' is boring and why most people get divorce. You must keep the flames alive to keep passion and excitement in a relationship or otherwise the fires die and so does the relationship. So, the 'Rod King' (the symbolic king dick sex god effigy) died of a heart attack as this is ANOTHER ritual to kill the King, destroy the heart love and drown them in the feminine 'waters'. Orion is depicted as holding a club or sword. Swords, wands, clubs, rods, staffs etc., are phallic symbols. Osiris is the personification of Orion seen here holding the lion main as the lion is Leo a depiction of the sun. The Sun King. In mythology Orion was hired by King Oenopion to kill the beasts terrifying the inhabitant of their island. So, part of this story is that Orion who is Osiris on Earth is to 'kill the beast'. The beast is the devil.

Yet in this version of the Rodney King ritual, the 'goddess' of water (and the moon) kills the king of tantric fire just like the deluge of the Bible. It's sad an unnecessary to do it this way but as outlined by A-list celebs covertly in their movies, they're psychos, it doesn't have to make sense in real terms, it just has to fit the ancient 'script' of control to go around again. Do the really want that? Isn't it time to move on? It's the last chance to do so…so…whatever. The Devil is the god of Death, literally, who came to Earth as an alien demonic species both physically and interdimensionally seeking another sentient race to add to its slave force overtaking the Milky Way galaxy. If we could destroy or somehow get rid of this god of death, Humans would live LOT LONGER and when we finally 'die' we would go back to the real core, the real heaven from whence our light emanates close to the centre of the galaxy in a continuous loop re-emerging into our 3D planet when we desire and not when 'reinserted' by an alien A.I. space program's super computer from where they get their directives into a facsimile reality as is currently happening. We are being recycled or 'reincarnated' used over and over our memories wiped between lifetimes as the trauma of what happens to us in our many lives would be far too much for the spirit and mind to bear and we would delete ourselves. And so, clever that they are, they wipe our memories, like a massive mind control operation, to ensure that we retain 'hope' - a light that never goes out – so that they can endlessly feed on us like batteries being recharged between our 3D lifetimes in which they drain us. In between our lives we are entering an intermediary space of their design and construction to house our very souls in an initial limbo and then onto some unknow place where information cannot transgress the barriers and I say this because the answers to our problems are strikingly simple only, they answers are not forthcoming, Why? When we pass over the knowledge is available unless of course this part of our journey is kept secret as well because 'death' is controlled too! The state of death is part of an even greater alien program. It's big, really big! How can this simple secret, and so obvious now that we know it, have been forever kept from us, a knowledge that we ourselves served in a time long ago before it was stolen from us and our memories wiped by a hedonistic alien war machine that operates not only on the physical but on the 'other' planes of the non-physical too where we are endlessly kept as pets in a loop of never-ending misery? Why can we not make it back to the core where all information is housed that would set us free immediately? It is because we are being rerouted in a superficial circuit called 'shunting', a line breaker of the galactic electricity cutting us off and sending us back to the Earthly plain on a shorter more superficial path literally steering away from our truth from the very Universe itself where we belong even in death? It's all coming to and end, folks, I don't mind saying. This is it.

Some say that Jesus never died - how could he if he was an ascended master and transcendental lover of Mary? In the writings of Basilides of Alexandria he contradicted Christian Orthodoxy by stating that Christ's death on the cross was only 'apparent' (symbolic) and did not occur 'in the flesh' this doctrine became called the Docetism. Everything they say is symbolic and the way they spoke and how they constructed their sentences back then needs to be *deciphered*, translated, into practical modern comprehension. Once you get the hang of how they saw the world you can easily decode these ancient stories. Basilides is one of only very few who dared to say that Christ did not 'die' and in light of our growing information and the ever-looming information age, this suggests something much deeper is going on - a BIBLICAL CONSPIRACY - to lure us away from the real truth of our salvation that lies *within* us! The real purpose of the Jesus and Mary story is a warning to all in that if you don't elevate the feminine back to her natural position, then the brotherhood will reign supreme over you forever and your collective masculine egos will literally be the death of you. As the legend says 'Christ', a man-come-the-embodiment-of-'god', tried to save the world during the last zodiac age when the turn of the calendar crossed over from the Age of Aries into the Age of Pisces and a new era of control came about. The key for the dark masters is to control the outcome of the cosmic alignments *between* zodiac ages as is happening now as we enter the Age of Aquarius.

The 'loaves and two fish' story is a reference to the age of Pisces in that Pisces has two fish as a symbol and so too did Jesus usher in the age of Pisces that we have lived under for the last two millennia. As electricity oscillates between AC and DC, the Negative and Positive, feminine and masculine forces, it was a male the last time and as the energies intercourse between the male and female, it is a woman this time who will save the world this time around as we enter the Age of Aquarius. Aquarius is a puzzle because although Jesus says, 'at the end of the Aon you will meet a man with a pitcher of water, follow him into that House'. He is talking about the House of Aquarius symbolised by a man with a pitcher of water. That said, men don't carry the water, the feminine carries the water today as they did in the ancient times due to the fact that the moon is associated with the tides and the moon cycles determine a woman's menstrual cycle and her menstrual blood is the life blood of the unborn 'christ' who is both male and female light, electricity, born into humans when the mother's *waters* break. It is why children are so full of energy and highly sought after by these freaks who siphon the life force directly from their bodies via rituals and pedophilia. They are drawn toward the innocence of children, the pure angel-light, because they seek to incorporate the fine energy of the child angel into themselves but not so-much-so that it hinders the dark plan – they want to live here - and you need a body to do that. Aquarius carries the water, or the masculine 'carrying' the feminine or 'picking her up' as Jesus 'rescues' his 'bride' because. Women carry the babies. Men were supposed to carry women, hold her up the way Ra, the sun god, the father, holds up the boat, the boat is the ship, the ship is the mother and mothers carry the passengers, the babies, the cargo. She is no a vending machine or a punching bag to be dominated to clean and cook for the merchant 'lord' of the house. What the fuck were these guys thinking to sink so low, to forget their own greatness and dragging women and children down with their pursuit of the material, sin of flesh of the physical, rejecting the spiritual and dressing it up as a religion to trick everyone it's a bout spirituality as they harvest and sell off this world and our real value is lost for an effigy of wealth called money. Aquarius is a golden age of information and technology, but we have the internet and mobile phones as they create an effigy, a bad copy, of the real thing. Aquarius is a 'world without end' and potentially heralds a neverending golden age or total liberty and freedom from darkness. This is why they want to connect us to A.I. so they can control our ascension and keep us locked inside 3D and if you try to escape, they'll switch you off. Isaiah 60:19, "You will have no need for the sun and the moon for I am with you". This because when the male and female balance the inner light of Christ, the pineal crown chakra whole brain-whole body golden aura, will see all and you will see all night or day.

So, the Age of Aquarius involves a hidden symbol cleverly describing a man 'holding' the 'waters' and the 'waters' represent a woman pouring her out onto the land. Bringing back the waters, to quench the fires of the masculine testosterone blazing, raging out of control right now and watering the garden of Earth to bring new life. It can mean so much. It can also mean a man unleashing a deluge like they claim Ra and God did on at least two occasions in the past which they did with cyclone Katrina, a weather weapon of unbelievable proportions. It could mean a transgender 'man' or a woman who identifies as a 'man' with her womb intact unleashing the 'masculine waters'. What I'm saying here is that there are many ways to read a prophecy, and this is what they do, they spin the cosmic story, the astrology of it however they like to suit themselves. But there is ONE *natural* version and countless fake *unnatural* versions, like the grail cup, made up by these psychos and this is the 'bad copy' spoken about in history. This may also explain why the symbol for Aquarius resembles two electrical signals side by side or twin mountain peaks of the masculine and feminine energies, right. Twin Peaks, now that show (the original) was loaded with military Satanism symbolism and is very informative. are letting the cat out of the bag because you can't claim you haven't' been told. If you want to know, it's there. All up, this is the Age of the Return of Men and Women *in unison*, The Twins, reunited as was always phrophesised and much maligned and laughed about by these famous reptiles in their movies as 'Beauty and the Beast' literally comes true. It is the feminine raising up the dark side of the masculine to his light side, the Christ light within. It is the feminine 're-membering' him, restoring his masculinity, his protective side, that was lost so long ago in a dirty deal with the devil that, as usual, backfired on them. There is so much emphasis placed on 'remembering' and even though Masonic men laugh about this in the old song line, 'And so it seems that we have met before, And that we laughed before, also loved before, But who knows where or when?' They know exactly where they have met their twin flame many times and know who she is in every lifetime they live and make no end of jokes about using her over and over again. In the original Beauty and the Beast, in the end they live 'happily ever after' but the beast doesn't change, he remains the same. That's why they laugh about it. They have no intention of changing. I suppose though if we know about how it works then we can hopefully work out a different end this time. If we can't it spells the end of the universe. It is also true that they are  required to make a mockery of the ultimate true love story as there is something beyond them again that is so terrifying, beyond their selfishness, that they will literally do anything not to fall under the eye of Sauron. So, the Devil inside becomes the Christ in the light out in the open for all to see. There are so many versions of this story including The Hunchback of Notre Dame as Notre Dame means 'our lady' and is a reference to Mary Magdalene, the Goddess who is *all* goddesses throughout history. The hunchback is the beast in another telling of this story. The hand in prayer

RETURN OF THE TWINS

are the masculine and feminine coming together over the heart chakra and that is a very important symbol. It's why the goddess is always associated with the same symbols; birth, trees, rainbows, the home, marriage, children, education, justice, fairness, liberty (Lady Liberty).

Therefore, the Age of Aquarius heralds the return and balance of the man and woman of the home, in equal parts, and the home is the castle, they are king and queen, not her as the maid and him as the merchant trying his best to barter with reptilian merchants who created this fake and rather complex system in the first place that only they can understand (and use against the dufus human man). The male will have to bring back the waters as only he is in the position to do as he has elevated himself through treachery into a position that will allow him to pour her upon the Earth and let her do her job for the first time in over ten thousand years. This is why they call women 'cleaners' and refer to Mary, the Goddess, as the 'lowly maid' in the Bible (fuckheads that they are). It is because when the rains come, they clean everything and all is clean and smells lovely and vibrant and so she was depicted as 'cleaning up' symbolically but this also translates to cleaning up the mess the reptilian males and their stupid mini-me puppets, average men in the streets, who vote and march off to war and wait in queues to be told what to do by this rabble of snakes who lord over us and have done for at least thirty thousand years slowly working us into this position for the final Zodiac take over as is happening now. She *will* clean up this mess and this time, the joke is on them. It is a woman that they are most afraid of for *that* is the secret prophecy they never told you about and have kept hidden for fear of inspiring young women because young men, the Jesus's of the world, are no match for them.

Prophecy, by the way, isn't some fantastical whimsy of the unknown. The simple fact is Astrology and a knowledge of Astronomy, considered one and the same in ancient Greece (and genuinely is the same) determines the position of planets and bodies in space at certain times based on the cycles of the galaxy. As all planets and astral bodies simply give off certain frequencies like a great big projector, the position of these bodies in space will determine certain environmental temperaments due to the broadcast of their unique energies. It's not some pseudo-science and the people running the world today are *obsessed* with 'getting it right' to suit themselves using a combination of black magic (ritual chanting and repetitive ceremonies) as well as demonic influence and technology to override the feminine frequencies of the galaxy and universe beyond to basically do whatever they like under their egregor and supreme masculine 'god' i.e. the Devil, a chief reptilian. There is no actual 'devil' as such, it is a term to loosely describe to collective and dirty deeds of a group of non-humans. The 'devil' is a conduit, to funnel their guilt and subsequent comeuppance via a third-party aqueduct taking the guise of an intangible thing. This is so you can't tangibly anchor your bitterness, resentment or justice to any one person as it is ever changing like the faces of the politicians leading to your doom. Blame who? The president? Or the one before him? Or the one before him? Or the one coming? Who exactly are you going to put in prison when the day comes?   So, I doubt there is one supreme master, they are a space syndicate and many 'devils' i.e. reptilians are vying for the top position that swaps and changes over time with certain zodiac changes. Their big problem is they have to do all this at certain times and in certain ways to 'trick' the universe into believing that they have the right to do this and that things are running as 'normal' down here, only it's not. Via the mass number of human minds who are witnessing and thinking about this, as we are radio heads, they are transmitting their messages to the core of the galaxy, the black hole sun also called the 'black mirror', when powerful alignments of the planets are happening (as has been happening in abundance since Christmas 2019) to ensure that they make *their* connection to the central hub to be re-broadcast these signals back again to complete the loop and lock in *their* electrical circuit. This is how they have always done it throughout history and despite their technology, there is no substitute for the real thing and the human mind is an excellent transmitter. This is why they did the weird ritual by showing a holographic *young* Queen Elizabeth 2nd on her coronation *70 years ago* to broadcast that a 'young queen' has come to power and been 'crowned' because *this* is what the universe *expects* to be reading from our planet at this time via all the alignments. So, instead of the 'young queen', or young women as a *collective*, being crowned and returned to their rightful throne beside the king, men, via *crown chakra enlightenment* of tantric sex uniting as one, they instead project the image of the fake show, a holograph of the false effigy of the Queen. And people are like 'oh that's cute, the queen is a holograph. The royals are so quirky sometimes'. No, they're not quirky for quirky sake, this is a zodiac ritual that all young women are embodied by *one* woman as opposed to *all* women. They are putting into ritual what we are supposed to be getting *for real*, the motherfuckers. The real 'queen' is Iris, Mary, Diana, Eve, Grace – all these goddesses – are different names to denote female humans *as a collective*. And Zeus was afraid of no other god or goddess but little Iris who simply represents a sexually enlightened young woman equal to sexually enlightened young men working together for the first time in eons. So, they have done two things in this QE2 ritual, they have projected that a nearly 100-year-old woman, queen Elizabeth, is a 'young woman' using a holograph and the people love her, but she is not 'real', a hologram. It's a twisted ritual but again, they spin however they like and if you don't like it, too bad, they've got the guns at the end of the day. It's weird but that's what they're doing.

The real queen is all young women who as a collective who were supposed to be 'coming out' now attaining tantric sex enlightenment and returned to her rightful position 'crowned' as her *crown* chakra is activated and women attain enlightenment at the 'side' of Jesus, men, as his equal, his counterpart, his wife,

HOLOGRAM QUEEN THE GODDESS IS A 'SIMULATION' THEY WISH

and 'ascend' together as tantric sex/sacred lovemaking was supposed to have done by now called transcendental lovemaking for good reason! Only, sigh, instead of the beautiful activated young female, we got a fucken centenarian old lizard doing ANOTHER creepy alien ritual. FML. They even have a pink 'box' or the 'square', the cube, of the female root chakra that as a young girl is depicted as pink as pink for girls, blue for boys. Red is the virile breeding mother-wife or sexual adult woman also associated with the 'scarlet' woman and the 'red light' district prostitute while maroon is the mature women, the grandmother of wisdom, Sophia, the Sophianic Principle, the matriarch. Sophia is the Goddess of Wisdom or the Lady of Good Council, Mary, as found in words like 'philosophy' as 'phile' means 'love of' and 'Sophia' means 'wisdom' so philosophy means 'love of wisdom'.

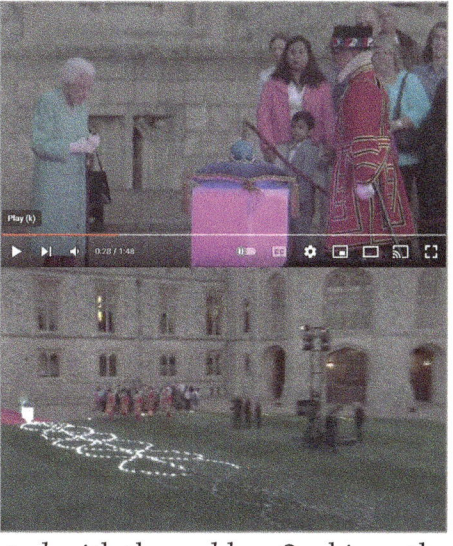

The owl originally was a symbol associated with the goddess Sophia or the 'wise owl' found on the American one-dollar bill peeking out near the 'one' (she is) as it were the goddess, the feminine, where they are getting their power from, women, females, the goddess, Mother Nature, Mother Earth, Mothers of their precious Son/Sun Kings (which simply means 'enlightened' male) and sex dolls to fulfill their every pleasure. She is God's Wife and 'god' in this version of the story is a reptilian demon posing as a man. He has hunted her for many lifetimes even targeting certain bloodlines to get at certain females to torture her spirit again and again ruthlessly using her as a sex doll and house cleaner and laughing about it. They hate the goddess like nothing you can imagine. In the 1989 movie 'Ghosts Can't Do It' with Anthony Quinn he is 75 in this movie and Bo Derek is his 'love' interest who is 30 years old in this film 45 years his junior. It depicts many creepy scenes including what appears to be mind control, sex slavery, Quinn

embarrassingly making out he's 50 and, tellingly, transferring the spirit via the breath as he takes over another body of a young man per the Osiris myth. I'm not saying Anthony Quinn was anything in particular. All these elite men are 'Osiris'. In the film they say to Bo Derek, "I have loved you for eons". Yes, just like Arnold Schwarzenegger, "I will be with you until the end of time'. As usual, there's plenty of full-frontal tits, arse and vag from the beautiful Bo Derek who was born Mary Cathleen Collins (Mary CC 33) on 20.11.56 or 20 reduces to 1&1 or 11 in the 11th month of the year 56 another 11. Quinn had 13 children to three wives the last was his secretary born when he was 81 years old. Thanks dad, nice one. I'm not saying Quinn is anything at all, I'm just saying when you look at all the symbolism and the behaviour of rich men, it's pretty rank. Clearly, it's weird making a movie called 'Ghosts Can't Do It' (have sex) where quite plainly an aging wealthy male star has such a great deal of power over a young female starlet who's most likely taking her clothes off for all these old men for the money.

 The elites can transfer their spirits to their offspring via the breath as told in the Osiris myth and have been so for thousands of years as exposed by Arizona Wilder in the interview with David Icke. They see themselves as lovable rogues but it's much worse than that. They repeatedly associate themselves with the number 11 as it depicts the light and dark side of Jesus and Satan who they believe were 'brothers' or the male 'twins'. It also means the internal light and dark side of the masculine. So, here we see the pink root chakra, the light green of the 'young' feminine heart of Mother Nature (on an old woman and the orb, the Earth, with a crown on it denoting their control over the planet presented by a man dressed in the maroon colour of the wise woman. Are you fucking me? But it goes on. Here we see the queen activating the Tree of Life aka The Tree of Knowledge and as it's all about replication, the DNA is one of the 'fruits' of the 'tree' as found in the Garden of Eden story. The DNA strand being activated by the 'queen' is a symbolic ritual - an effigy - of the 'queen of heaven' the Goddess, young women, whose waters of the Kundalini of the central nervous system is FEMININE electricity. Therefore, it was supposed to be that young women, the collective 'queen' crowned by enlightenment, who were to activate the DNA of Humanity and light up the 'Tree of Life' of the human nervous system at this time. The nervous system 'tree' is also depicted in effigy as the Christmas tree – an 'evergreen' of eternal 'life' that these elites are tapping into and the 'pine' cones of the tree represent the pineal gland of enlightenment and the 'baubles' on the tree at Xmas represent the 'apples' of the chakras or the 'fruit' from the 'tree of knowledge/life'. The 'fruit' also means intellect and all the abilities that go along with this and as they are a bisexual phallic worshipping dick cult, gay men are called 'fruits' likely to do with this. The third eye-pineal gland 'crown chakra' is initially activated by the root chakra which is the pink-red-maroon root chakra of the *feminine*.

We were supposed to get ascension and enlightenment but instead, you got an old woman being lauded as she was 70 YEARS AGO, a bloke dressed in maroon to represent the 'wisdom' of the goddess, a pink 'box' aka a woman's vagina/root chakra and a fucking *fake* LED DNA strand spiral tree at Buckingham *Palace* because the 'temple', aka the palace, is the HUMAN BODY or 'my body is my temple'. It's a classic example of duplication of the reptilian dream machine over the natural replication of Mother Nature. Rituals abound in 2022 as it adds up to 6 with is the number of pleasure, sex, so 666 is sex sex sex as openly admitted in the 1996 film 'Girl Six – Six is for Sex'. And yes, satanists are accessing their enlightened crown chakra via carnality of sex as tantric sex activates facilitates the Christ seed and switches on your whole body which is where they are getting their power from. Only via LOVE can you go so *much further* but as these cunts are incapable of LOVE so they can only heighten their kundalini so far via sex and lord over the people who are yet to discover this secret. Therefore, when men and women unite as one in LOVE, we will surpass them on levels that cannot be undone, and they hate you for this ability not knowing the secret of your true power. They are constrained by their evil genetics hacking into the light via the human body and the love-light found inside us - we are light beings after all. But whereas we can take it all the way to the highest of the high where the light emanates from, they can only use it to create complex fake systems to trap us in their game. It is mind over matter.

Everything they do, EVERYTHING, is about killing the knowledge of the tantric sex enlightenment of 'Christ', the saviour, 'reborn' again and again as it is an emanation from your brain, a hormonal electrochemical 'switch' that will bring power not only to your body and mind, but to you spirit and the wider world around you. It is a prophecy that has lasted the test of time and they thought they had squashed the prophecy and twisted so much that you could never imagine what it truly means all the while putting it right in your face. I say this to you, as I round off against the end of this final chapter, that there is hope in this world and that hope is going to come from those who know the most about this, those in the middle, the 'middle man' or as Jim Carry puts it the 'Yes Man' complete with big cheesy shit eating grin. It's all bullshit and they know it, and, further to that, this so-called 'club' has killed so many celebrities that the message is quite clear, shut up or you're dead, 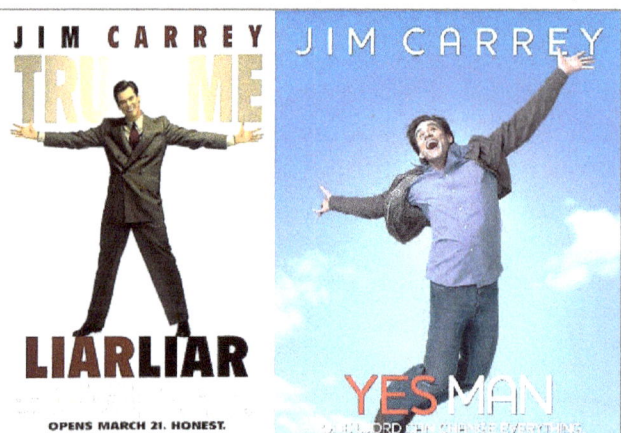 *brother*. What a shitty brother. Not much of a family. Their money and fame, is, if anything, even more dangerous to them now as the satanic dark order looks for victims, the bigger the better, to broadcast the signal to the universe that enlightenment is dead here, it's gone, washed up. This is the true meaning of 'the stars' in Hollywood. They are nothing but effigies of a massive attack on Earth and Humanity depicting the stars of the real universe as small and weak. That's why any and all of them are expendable especially at this time which is why so many of them move to associate their fame with these 'symbols' without actually giving too much away so that they may continue on into the next zodiac Age. Hollywood and celebrity are being destroyed in many ways as they represent the old 'gods' who were the Titans destroyed by the 'new' gods, the Olympians. But in this case the 'Olympians' are the old gods masquerading as the new gods to

RETURN OF THE TWINS

keep their power forever. Who's the imposter? Who's who here? I guess we'll find out, eventually. Even in The Rock's most recent film Jungle Cruise his cat is called 'Proxima' meaning 'the nearest star to the sun'. The cat is a symbol of the feminine, a feline, and HE is the sun in this instance, or god. He practices tantric sex. They all do. They are all doing it, all of them. We can now capitalize on this opportunity to break free from this farce at a crucial point between the zodiac ages. It's a small window of opportunity and, in case you haven't noticed, time is speeding up so much so, that a day barely lasts two hours now. It's the 'quickening' and it is happening so fast that I now rush to complete my latest instalment of the Epic Series as time runs out and we enter a whole  NEW time. You must keep up. You must take this chance. You must allow the opportunity to flow forth as it was designed to do with simplicity and grace. You must do what needs to be done in these final hours as not only is humanity and Earth at stake but beyond that the *entire Universe* is at stake now. The job was much bigger than we initially thought. We thought it was simply about Earth politics and social reform. No. It is far more than that. Far, far more than were could ever imagine. The time is now!

Make love not war, literally.

ABOUT THE AUTHOR

Willow Willis was born 3/4/1977 in Melbourne, Australia. The youngest of five children, she is a multi-instrumentalist and singer from an early age picking up music by 3 and playing 8 instrument by the time she was 12. She began performing and public speaking at 12 and promoting music by the time she was 16. She has worked with and performed for some notable names in entertainment and found herself on the odd magazine cover! Her talents include being a musician, vocalist, singer-songwriter, author, artist, radio host and qualified hypnotherapist having worked for some of the largest organisations in the world including a Microsoft Gold Partner, News Ltd and the UK Government. He career covers various industries including entertainment, print media, multimedia, the public and private sectors as well as events management.

Willow returns, again, bringing her talents and skills to her latest work unveiling world changing information with ease and humour despite how perilous the world seems at this time. Her personal experiences have taught her the power of introspection and that triumph in the face of impossible odds is not only possible for the individual but about to happen on a global scale! Willow's second book, *2022 & Beyond – Return of the Feminine*, takes her first work to a whole new level as we finally discover the secrets behind the greatest myths in history and what they *really* mean for our salvation! Once again, Willow makes you laugh and cry while unravelling the absurdity and even sadness of our situation as individuals and as a collective. She explains how everyday people will bravely come together to defeat an old foe and continue on our quest into a long-prophesised date with destiny forever!

RETURN OF THE TWINS

RETURN OF THE TWINS

www.ingramcontent.com/pod-product-compliance
Lightning Source LLC
Chambersburg PA
CBHW051543010526
44118CB00022B/2564